FERGUSON'S FAULT LINES

THE RACE QUAKE THAT ROCKED A NATION

Edited by
KIMBERLY JADE NORWOOD

Cover design by Elmarie Jara

Printed in the United States of America.

20 19 18 17 16   5 4 3 2 1

Cataloging-in-Publication Data is on file with the Library of Congress.

Names: Norwood, Kimberly Jade, editor.
Title: Ferguson's fault lines : the race quake that rocked a nation / edited by Kimberly Jade
    Norwood.
Description: First edition. | Chicago : American Bar Association, [2016]
Identifiers: LCCN 2016011068 | ISBN 9781634253727
Subjects: LCSH: Discrimination in criminal justice administration—Missouri—Ferguson. |
    Discrimination in criminal justice administration—United States. | Police misconduct—
    Missouri—Ferguson. | Police misconduct—United States. | Race discrimination—United
    States. | Racism—United States. | United States—Race relations.
Classification: LCC HV9956.F47 F47 2016 | DDC 363.2/308996073077865—dc23
LC record available at http://lccn.loc.gov/2016011068

www.ShopABA.org

Contents

Chapter 7: If Michael Brown Were Alive, Would He Be Employable? 121
Terry Smith

Chapter 8: The Geography of Inequality: A Public Health Context for Ferguson and the St. Louis Region 145
Jason Q. Purnell

Chapter 9: Media Framing in Black and White: The Construction of Black Male Identity 167
Candice Norwood

Preface

Kimberly Jade Norwood

In the months following the eruption in Ferguson, my youngest, then a sophomore in a predominately white public high school, found herself at the center of debates at school dealing with the fallout from the death of Michael Brown. The debates included: the framing of the issues by the media in black versus white, the policing of black and poor communities by law enforcement officers, poverty, looting, rioting and the color and face of crime as portrayed in the media, the identity of the black male narrative, and the relevance of black life, whether and how it matters. She was blindsided by the racial division, turmoil, hate, and anger displayed throughout the media and even in her environment. She did not know what to do, how to respond, what to feel. As part of an effort to begin a process of understanding and thus healing, she wrote a poem, subsequently published in our local newspaper. It is reproduced below.

This book expands upon the innocence raised in that poem in provoactive ways. The information conveyed in this work is designed to push readers to ask of themselves the very questions raised therein with a commitment to seeing the challenges our nation faces as revealed in the aftermath of Michael Brown's death and to committing to work towards the eradication of the barriers of injustice reflected herein. This book is full of hard questions we all must ask of ourselves and of others, soul searching we all must do, and brutal honesty we all must face. Race is still an issue and while uncomfortable to discuss, can no longer be ignored. We have to figure out what to do and what to say. The future of our society depends on it.

What Do You Say?

Veronica Jade Norwood

What do you say when you have so much shame for your country and so many emotions race through your mind that the words you search for are never found?

What do you say when your heart aches so much that you don't even know if you can make it through the night?

What do you say when you're trying to get people to listen to you and then realize they hear your words but they just don't care?

What do you say to your community to get them to see that instead of helping justice prevail they're destroying our homes and dreams instead?

What do you say to them to make them see the hypocritical actions of fighting for justice by destroying businesses to get that message through?

What do you say to a nation that allows hate crimes to still be an issue, while they say they will make changes but never do?

What do you say to your children when you have to explain to them whether a person was shot because of the color of his skin?

What do you say to someone who is not conscious enough, to make them see that racism does in fact still exist?

What do you say to someone who has been a victim of this hatred when the comforting words of "It will get better" surely feels like it never will?

What do you say to those who treat this stuff as a joke, or don't even acknowledge that this is an issue?

What do you say to someone who doesn't understand integrity or refuses to accept equality?

What do you say about those issues to the people in power, when they are the ones causing them?

What do you say when you don't even know how to feel safe in your own city, in your own country?

What do you say when you're ashamed of yourself, for not doing everything you possibly can to make this country a safer place for all man- and woman-kind?

What do you say to bring change?

What do you say?[1]

---

1. Veronica Norwood, *What Do You Say?*, St. Louis Post-Dispatch, Dec. 10, 2014, http://www.stltoday.com/news/opinion/what-do-you-say/article_1b502ccf-22f2-5a1f-871b-20763c2a5956.html.

Acknowledgments

The idea for this project began in the winter of 2014. A year later, the project was completed. The commitment and dedication of many people allowed this to happen. My husband, Ronald Alan Norwood, is owed a very special thank you. His editing, patience, support, insights, manifold reviews of this work were phenomenal.

My administrative assistants, Beverly Owens and Jane Box and several law school library staff members: Hyla Bondareff, Mark Kloempken, and Kathie Molyneaux were indispensable in helping me complete this work. A special thank you to them, as well.

Of course, I am deeply indebted to each contributor. This project was on a very tight time line and each stepped up to help bring this product to fruition.

Thank you also to Research Assistants Adam Dwyer, Robert Fields, Brian Hall, Nicholas Papadimitriou, and Jason Vu who, always on short notice, got the jobs needed done.

I must also extend a sincere thank you to Richard Paszkiet and Tamara Edmonds Askew. Tamara, a native of St. Louis, was the brainchild for this book. Tamara and Rick reached out to me in the weeks after the Brown killing. Together we made this project happen. A special thank you, too, to Shannon Bridger-Riley, who stepped up during the most difficult time in the production to make sure this project had everything it needed to be successful and complete.

It takes a village. I had one. I am indebted to you all.

Foreword

Paulette Brown, President of the
American Bar Association, 2015-2016

As I write this foreword, my hometown of Baltimore, Maryland, is experiencing its own version of Ferguson, Missouri. This timely book addresses the deeply rooted perception of inequality and injustices experienced in Ferguson, Missouri, with a keen focus on the legal and social reverberations following the death of Michael Brown. But, it is also about Freddie Gray and Baltimore; Eric Garner and Staten Island; Walter Scott and North Charleston; Tamir Rice and Cleveland; Sandra Bland and Waller County, Texas; Miriam Carey and Washington D.C.; Laquan McDonald, Quintonio LeGrier and Bettie Jones and Chicago; and it is about so many other people and communities for whom we are not even aware. It is about recognizing that this perception is not a new phenomenon. At the core of this book is the serious need to address, in very broad terms, the state of our justice system, not only in Ferguson, but in America as a whole. It is about confidence in the judicial system and maintaining the rule of law.

In almost every highly publicized case of police using deadly force and killing unarmed individuals, the person killed was an African American male. These incidents have caused dramatic erosion in public confidence in the justice system and America's promise of equal treatment under the law.[1] Following the investigation of the incidents in Ferguson, former U.S. Attorney General Eric Holder found numerous injustices that were "not merely unconstitutional, but abusive and dangerous."[2]

I believe in America's promise of liberty and justice for all. We are a nation bound by principles undergirded by the rule of law. Those of us who are a part of the legal community can do better. As lawyers we are viewed as leaders. As members of the communities we are charged to serve; people naturally look to us for solutions. As the first woman of color to lead the American Bar Association (ABA) as its president in its

137-year history, one of my goals is to review and analyze diversity and inclusion in the legal profession, the judicial system, and the ABA. I created a Diversity and Inclusion 360 Commission to formulate methods, policy, standards, and practices to best advance diversity and inclusion over the next ten years. The Commission's work includes training resources concerning how neuroscience can affect decision making (known in some circles as implicit bias training). We will explore, for example, the possible impact of implicit bias in the decision by a Baltimore judge to set bail for a teenager who committed a misdemeanor offense and who turned himself in to the police at twice the amount of that set for police officers charged with murder, an obvious felony offense. Solutions must be developed to sustain confidence in our judicial system.

Change is necessary and begins at many levels, but it starts from within. First, we must recognize our own biases. We all have them. No one is exempt. I encourage everyone to take an Implicit Association Test (IAT). The test measures the test-taker's associations between groups of people, such as African Americans, LGBT people, and women; evaluations such as good or bad; and qualities such as nurturing, clumsy, or mathematically gifted. These implicit biases are often subtle and unbeknownst to us. Many people are surprised after taking the test, but come to understand its importance particularly in how our biases can unwittingly cause us to engage in behaviors that are not productive.

The biggest challenge, however, is not to merely identify these biases. The struggle is to figure out what we do once we recognize them. For those working in the justice system, from police to prosecutors and judges, and yes, even public defenders, the consequences have broad, far-reaching, and sometimes even fatal consequences.

Arguably, implicit bias is at the heart of our nation's "School-to-Prison Pipeline." It is the antithesis of the dream we had for Brown v. Board of Education 60 years ago. This phrase has become shorthand for the continuing failures in the education system where students of color are disproportionately, incorrectly, or overcategorized in special education; disciplined more harshly; stigmatized by lower than average achievement levels; and funneled directly from schools into juvenile justice facilities and prisons. Youth in America are processed in the criminal justice system and imprisoned at much higher rates than in other nations, and youth of color are disproportionately overrepresented at all levels of the juvenile justice system. For nonviolent youth, interaction with the justice system often does more harm than good. A 2013 study, conducted by Brown University and the Massachusetts Institute of Technology, showed that young offenders who were incarcerated were a staggering 67 percent more likely to return to jail by the age of 25 than similar young offenders who did not go to prison. Moreover, youth who were incarcerated were more likely to commit "homicide, violent crime, property crime and drug crimes" than those who did not go to jail.[3] It is with this type of backdrop that we find ourselves in Ferguson and places that are similar to Ferguson where residents don't have the opportunity to experience access to justice.

There is no shortage of statistics to show us that implicit bias permeates our justice system. The disparities in police stops, charges filed by prosecutors, and sentencing decisions clearly show us that bias, race, and punishment are inextricably entwined. As legal professionals we have a role in ensuring that there are open and frank discussions so that we will not be contributors to the "fault lines."

To that end, we, as legal professionals, also must do better to educate ourselves, our clients, and our legislators about the collateral consequences of criminal conviction. Oftentimes the consequences of sentences punish people in ways that are unknown at the time of sentencing. These actions that are triggered as a consequence of conviction disqualify people with criminal records from so many activities, including jobs and licensing, education and housing, and voting, among others. There are more than 1,100 federal collateral consequences alone, to say nothing of local and state laws, that operate so often as an insurmountable barrier for persons with a criminal record to get a job and pursue a normal life. In short, these collateral consequences can result in never-ending punishments that disproportionately impact minority communities, especially African Americans, who are incarcerated at nearly six times the rate of Caucasians.

For the last decade, the ABA has focused its advocacy efforts on overincarceration and federal policies that contribute to it. We have long had the view that federal sentencing policies are the single most important factor in the skyrocketing build-up of our state and federal prison populations over the past 30 years. The enactment and operation of mandatory minimum sentences for nonviolent drug offenders are the most fundamental and critical areas to reform. The ABA has never supported mandatory minimums and believes they are unsound as guiding principles in sentencing. They have resulted in very large numbers of low-level offenders going to prison, disproportionately from African American and Hispanic communities, and today, an unsustainable fiscal and human burden.

Finally, implicit bias may play a deadly role in states where "Stand Your Ground" laws are in effect. The ABA's National Stand Your Ground Task Force embarked upon a comprehensive legal analysis of the impact of the Stand Your Ground statutes, which have dramatically expanded the bounds of self-defense law in over half of jurisdictions in the United States. The study analyzes the degree to which racial or ethnic bias impact the construction, application, and/or operation of Stand Your Ground laws. In particular, the role bias may play in influencing the perception of threat precipitating the use of deadly force as well as its effect on the likelihood of selective or prejudiced investigation, prosecution, and/or immunity determinations.

This book comes at a critical time in our nation. It comes at a time when there is bipartisan agreement on over incarceration, the inappropriate use of deadly force, and the lack of fairness in sentencing. Now is the time for lawyers to take their rightful leadership role, use the power of our law licenses to ensure fair, just access to justice for all. I thank the contributors to this book for sharing their insights on the intersections of race, inequality, and justice in Ferguson, because as we have seen in Ferguson, Baltimore, and elsewhere, Ferguson's fault lines not only are national, but have consequences for us all.

Notes

1. Cara Tabachnick, *Young People Have "Little Confidence" in Justice System*, CRIME REPORT, Apr. 29, 2015, http://www.thecrimereport.org/news/articles/2015-04-young-people-have-little-confidence-in -justice-system.

2. Rebecca Kaplan, *Eric Holder: "Implicit and Explicit Bias" in Ferguson Policing*, CBS, Mar. 4, 2015. http://www.cbsnews.com/news/ferguson-policing-eric-holder-implicit-explicit-racial-bias/.

3. Zack Beauchamp, *Study: Throwing Kids in Jail Makes Crime Worse, Ruins Lives*, THINK PROGRESS, June 17, 2013, http://thinkprogress.org/justice/2013/06/17/2166481/study-throwing-kids-in-jail-makes-crime -worse-ruins-lives/.

Introduction

Kimberly Jade Norwood

Where is Ferguson? This was the number one question asked of me by hundreds of people around the United States in the days immediately following August 9, 2014. Although I lived only 12 miles away, even I could not answer the question initially. Ferguson is a small city of about 21,000 people. I have driven near, around, and past Ferguson thousands of times during my 25 years in the St. Louis metropolitan area. But even I did not know Ferguson.

According to a Department of Justice (DOJ) investigation in the shooting death of Michael Brown,[1] on Saturday, August 9, 2014, at approximately 11:50 a.m., Michael Brown and his friend Dorian Johnson were walking eastbound down the middle of the street in the Canfield Green Apartments, located in Ferguson, Missouri. A convenience store video recording shows Michael Brown and his friend stealing a package of cigarillos and leaving the store a few minutes before. As captured on the store's surveillance video, when the store clerk tried to stop Brown, who towered over the clerk, Brown forcefully shoved him away. On-duty police officer Darren Wilson, who was driving westbound down Canfield around this same time, encountered Brown and Johnson a few minutes later walking down the middle of the street, a municipal ordinance violation known as "manner of walking." He ordered them out of the street. There are conflicting accounts of what happened. It is undisputed that Brown and Wilson exchanged words and that Wilson discharged his gun while still sitting in his car, injuring Brown's hand.

Brown then ran away from Wilson, heading eastbound on Canfield Drive. Wilson gave chase. Brown ran at least 180 feet away from Wilson, turned around, and took approximately 21 steps back in Wilson's direction. Wilson fired several shots at Brown. Within two minutes of their initial encounter, Michael Brown lied dead on the pavement. And lie he did. For over four hours, on a small residential street, a mere 24 feet wide, on hot summer day. Crowds gathered, pictures were taken, children cried, residents were shocked and angered. The "Ferguson" we know today was born.

Over the next few days, protesters gathered in the streets of Ferguson near the Canfield Green Apartments. Crowds swelled. Tension and anger were strong. People demanded the officer's name. Police were dispatched to the area in riot gear. Fully armed with shields, K-9 units, and rifles, police patrolled the area in military-grade armored vehicles. Loaded rifles were pointed at protesters. Rubber bullets and tear gas were used against protesters and news media alike. Some officers were recorded calling protesters animals. Vandalism of some businesses occurred; a QuikTrip convenience store was burned to the ground. Hundreds of people, including news reporters, were arrested. People from around the nation, and the world, descended on Ferguson. Even drones were spotted circling the area. This "revolution" was televised. And many watched their televisions asking: Is this America?

In the early days after the shooting, St. Louis County Prosecutor Robert McCulloch announced that he would present evidence to a grand jury for it to decide whether an indictment of Officer Wilson was warranted. This announcement caused tremendous consternation. The prosecutor came from a family of police officers; his father, also a police officer, was killed by a Black man. But for an amputation to his leg as a child, he would have become a police officer himself. He was not trusted by many in the Black community because of his unwillingness to pursue charges against police officers who had killed and seriously injured Black people.[2] Although stepping aside was an option, he refused to take that path. This fueled more resentment.

A week after Brown's killing, Darren Wilson was finally identified as the officer who shot Brown. That disclosure was released simultaneously as two images broadcast around the world: one of Officer Wilson receiving an award from the Ferguson City Council and the second of video surveillance from the convenience store showing Michael Brown "strong arming" the convenience store owner. Outrage was renewed.

Two years before Ferguson erupted, a scathing document on municipal court abuses in the St. Louis area was published.[3] The Arch City Defenders' Municipal Courts White Paper reported on dozens of the 90 municipalities in the St Louis area, some a square mile wide with only a few hundred residents, and many predominately black, predominately poor, that used their police officers to generate revenue. The

Washington Post did additional follow-up on this blockbuster report after Michael Brown's killing and the story of overly aggressive policing, known in the St. Louis community for years,[4] became a national story.[5]

All of the data in these reports was subsequently confirmed by another DOJ report, this one focused on the practices of the Ferguson Police Department (FPD). This report found excessive targeting of Black drivers (stopped for speeding, for failure to have special stickers, for nonfunctioning brake lights, for sitting in their parked cars looking suspicious, and more); once stopped their cars were disproportionately searched for contraband (unlike Whites, who, the report found, were neither stopped as often nor searched with the same regularity despite their much higher likelihood of possessing contraband); and then disproportionately arrested. People were even ticketed for baggy pants, "manner of walking," and other "quality of life" violations. There was a pattern of excessive fines and warrants issued. People who could not make bail or pay fines had their drivers' licenses taken and were fined or jailed for inability to pay their fines. Some courts operated out of what looked like homes, many operated once a month (a problem, then, for a person arrested who could not make bail in time to secure release before the next court date) and were open for 3–4 hours. Images of long lines of people, all Black, snaking outside the courthouses patiently waiting to enter in the heat, in the cold, in the rain, and in the snow were common. There was no court-provided day care, as other some other court districts have done, and children were not allowed in court. This created another burden when parents had to choose between missing hearings because they could not find babysitters or risking charges of neglect leveled against them if they came to court and left their child in the car while they went into the court to address the fines. The DOJ report on the FPD found a pattern of unconstitutional stops and arrests in violation of the Fourth Amendment, violations of the First Amendment, and a pattern of excessive force.[6]

The DOJ report also found "substantial evidence of racial bias among police and court staff in Ferguson. Police supervisors, including Darren Wilson's supervisor, and court staff circulated e-mails stereotyping racial minorities as criminals. One e-mail joked about an abortion by an African American woman as being a method of crime control."[7]

All of this occurred in a largely Black city that was politically dominated by a White power structure. At the time of the Brown killing,

Ferguson was approximately 70 percent Black. The mayor of Ferguson was White, five of its six City Council members were White, and 50 of its 54 police officers were White. The prosecutor, the municipal court judge, and virtually all of the court's administrative staff were White.

The mayor of Ferguson denied that there were any racial differences in his city.[8] He was wrong. There were in fact two Fergusons: one mostly Black with the highest percentage of Section 8 low-income renters in the state and the other White, affluent, and living in well-maintained homes.[9] And, as the DOJ reports revealed, these two populations lived completely different experiences.

Almost four months after Brown's killing, the grand jury reached its decision. At around 8:30 p.m. on November 24, 2014, the prosecutor announced the grand jury's decision not to indict Officer Wilson. As the decision reverberated throughout the area, violence erupted and looting broke out and spread. Despite the governor having declared a state of emergency, activating the National Guard in anticipation of the announcement, and famously vowing that "violence will not be tolerated,"[10] Ferguson burned. Neither police nor the National Guard protected the businesses or the people in Ferguson that night. By daybreak, smoke filled the area and property worth millions of dollars was destroyed.

From August 9 through November 24, 2014, people of all races, ethnicities, and walks of life, from all over the country, descended on Ferguson to join what had become a movement. I protested alongside young, old, White, Black, Asian, disabled, and many other people. I watched, in disbelief, as the media portrayed protesters as violent, thugs, criminals, and Black. This was inaccurate and unfair. A movement was taking place, and it was not just about Black people and it did not involve only Black people. On one level the protests were absolutely about Michael Brown's death, triggered by the simple act of jaywalking; but on a larger level, the protests were about much more. They were also about police use of force against Black people; they were about the excessive tickets for traffic, quality of life and housing code violations that preyed on the most vulnerable; they were about unemployment and underemployment; they were about inadequate health care and public health concerns; they were about inadequate housing; and they were about substandard schools.

For decades Black people have complained of these ills to no avail. They simply were not believed. It took a killing, it took outrage, it took property destruction, it took social media, to open the collective eyes of the world to see the "cancer" of injustice that had been spreading in the community for years. Throughout the nation (including New York, Los Angeles, Chicago, Detroit, and Washington, D.C.) and throughout the world (Britain, France, India, and Palestine, including Palestinians in the Gaza strip), people had heard of Ferguson, knew where it was, and understood what it represented. The word "Ferguson" became synonymous with the struggles for equal justice and equal treatment throughout the world. Yes, property was destroyed. Yet, but for the protests, the violence, and the destruction, we likely would not know the name Michael Brown today. And without that name, we would not know Ferguson. Property destruction cannot be excused but it should be put into perspective. Property can be replaced; lives and futures cannot.

Ferguson is a microcosm of thousands of communities throughout America. We often talk about urban areas: Cleveland, Detroit, Chicago, St. Louis, and Baltimore. Few Americans realized, until Eric Garner in Staten Island, New York; John Crawford III in Beavercreek, Ohio; Michael Brown in Ferguson, Missouri; and Sandra Bland in Waller County, Texas, that the issues of police brutality, the targeting of Blacks for driving while black and the many other structural forms of discrimination as reflected in housing, employment, wealth, health, and education, are not limited to major urban areas. They exist in suburbia as well.

This book examines the various laws, social conditions, and economic and political policies that disproportionately impact Black and Brown people in America, that contributed to the frustrations of many residents in Ferguson, Missouri, and that ultimately sparked a global movement. The movement started in Ferguson demanded acknowledgment that "Black Lives Matter," a phrase created after Trayvon Martin's death in Florida. And while that phrase was often rebuffed with the retort "All Lives Matter," this book demonstrates that there is a different treatment of people in our society based on the color of their skin and their socioeconomic status. There are two Fergusons as there are two Americas. We cannot change this reality unless we first acknowledge it.

This book has 13 chapters. Chapters 1 and 2 deal with the history of racial oppression against Black bodies in the United States and the psychology of that racial violence, including a careful look at the harm of stereotypes and implicit bias and how those poisonous schemas inform the way in which society sees Black people and Black men in particular. Chapters 3 and 4 examine the prosecution of Darren Wilson, the policing of Black communities, and the municipal court system in the St. Louis metropolitan area. Chapters 5 through 9 focus on larger systemic issues that also contributed to the sense of unfairness that resonated with communities worldwide: the history (and continued present) of segregated and unequal housing, segregated and unequal schools, unemployment and underemployment, inadequate health care, and the media complicity in the false narrative of who Black men are. Chapters 10 and 11 discuss the psychic trauma and distrust experience by residents of a community, including its children, when they feel betrayed by a system they thought would protect rather than violate their constitutional rights. The final two chapters look at the problems of how law enforcement polices Black communities. Chapters 12 and 13 specifically deal with policing: one analyzes the debate on the effectiveness of body cameras; the second examines potential police reforms and how policing can and should look in our future.

Seven months after the uprising in Ferguson, its mayor continued to denounce the evidence of racial disparities in his city.[11] On the one-year anniversary of Michael Brown's shooting, protests, highway shutdowns, and yes, some lootings and some arrests all occurred anew. The collective response of the media was why? Why are people still protesting?

The real question, of course, was what has changed since the death of Michael Brown for people in communities like Ferguson and in the Fergusons around the nation? Indeed, despite the passage of time, not much, in fact, very little, had changed. Poor schools, unemployment, inadequate housing and health care, and deadly police encounters continue to plague Ferguson and other American cities even as I type this introduction. Over the past few months my contributors have begged me to hurry and get this manuscript to press because they are constantly editing their chapters to add yet another name to the list of deadly police encounters or yet another story on racial confrontation and strife in America. We recently added Laquan McDonald, Quintonio LeGrier, and Bettie Jones to this seemingly never ending list. My contributors rightly and sadly wonder who will be added next.

We cannot learn the lessons of Ferguson if we bury our heads in the sand. But we must learn from Ferguson. If we do not, the fissures that divide this country by race, color, and class will only widen. And this means that they will not just *go away* with time. Exposure is the first step to consciousness. Consciousness is the first step to correction. Correction is the first step to justice. And justice is the first step toward healing. This book is an effort on the journey to correction, justice, and healing.

Notes

1. *See* Civil Rights Div., U.S. Dep't of Justice, Report Regarding The Criminal Investigation to the Shooting Death of Michael Brown By Ferguson, Missouri Police Officer Darren Wilson (2015), http://www.justice.gov /sites/default/files/opa/press-releases/attachments/2015/03/04/doj_report_on_shooting_of_michael_ brown_1.pdf.

2. Pema Levy, *Ferguson Prosecutor Robert P. McCulloch's Long History of Siding with the Police*, News-week (Aug. 29, 2014), http://www.newsweek.com/2014/09/12/ferguson-prosecutor-robert-p-mccullochs -long-history-siding-police-267357.html.

3. Koran Addo, *ArchCity Defenders Saw Problems with Municipal Courts before Ferguson Turmoil*, Apr. 15, 2015, http://www.stltoday.com/news/local/metro/archcity-defenders-saw-problems-with-municipal -courts-before-ferguson-turmoil/article_f1493907-7c8c-55af-a68b-6e36df0c2cae.html.

4. Julia Craven, Ryan J. Reilly & Mariah Stewart, *The Ferguson Protests Worked*, Huffington Post, Aug. 5, 2015, http://www.huffingtonpost.com/entry/ferguson-protests-municipal-court-reform_55a90e 4be4b0c5f0322d0cf1?kvcommref=mostpopular.

5. Radley Balko, *How Municipalities in St. Louis County, Mo., Profit from Poverty*, Wash. Post, Sept. 4, 2015, https://www.washingtonpost.com/news/the-watch/wp/2014/09/03/how-st-louis-county-missouri -profits-from-poverty/.

6. Civil Rights Div., U.S. Dep't of Justice, Investigation of the Ferguson Police Department (Mar. 4, 2015), http:// www.justice.gov/sites/default/files/opa/press-releases/attachments/2015/03/04/ferguson_police _department_report.pdf (finding, inter alia, that "Ferguson's approach to law enforcement both reflects and reinforces racial bias, including stereotyping[,]" . . . that this "disproportionately . . . [harms] African Americans, and [that] there is evidence that this is due in part to intentional discrimination on the basis of race," *id.* at 4).

7. *See id.* Evidence of this sort is certainly not limited to police and court personnel in Ferguson. *See, e.g.*, Willard Shepard et al., *Miami Beach Police Officers Exchanged Racist Emails: State Attorney*, NBC Miami (May 14, 2015), http://www.nbcmiami.com/news/local/Miami-Beach-Police-State -Attorney-Holding-News-Conference-303777561.html; *see also Florida, California Police Forces Scrutinized for Racist, Sexist Communications*, RT Network (May 15, 2015), http://www.rt.com/usa /259069-miami-sanfrancisco-police-racist/.

8. *Ferguson Mayor Addresses Racial Tensions, Number of Black Officers in City*, CBS St. Louis (Aug. 13, 2014), http://stlouis.cbslocal.com/2014/08/13/ferguson-mayor-the-african-american-community-has -something-against-law-enforcement-in-many-ways/ (Mayor James Knowles III stating "[t]his is not representative of our community."); *NewsNation with Tamron Hall*, MSNBC (Aug. 19, 2014), http:// www.msnbc.com/newsnation/watch/ferguson-mayor—theres-no-racial-divide-here-319506499946.

9. John Eligon, *An Indelible Black-and-White Line: A Year after Ferguson, Housing Segregation Defies Tools to Erase It*, N.Y. Times, Aug. 9, 2015, http://www.nytimes.com/2015/08/09/us/an-indelible -black-and-white-line.html?hp&action=click&pgtype=Homepage&module=first-column-region&region=top-news&WT.nav=top-news&_r=0.

10. Wesley Lowery et al., *Governor Activates Missouri National Guard in Advance of Ferguson Grand Jury Decision as FBI Issues Warning*, Wash. Post, Nov.17, 2014, http://www.washingtonpost.com/news /post-nation/wp/2014/11/17/gov-jay-nixon-activates-missouri-national-guard-in-advance-of-ferguson-grand-jury-decision/.

11. Carimah Townes, *Ferguson Mayor Rejects Department of Justice Report, Says There's "No Proof" City Has a Race Problem*, Think Progress (Mar. 7, 2015), http://thinkprogress.org/justice /2015/03/07/3631113/ferguson-mayor-refutes-doj-report/.

Chapter 1

Michael Brown, Dignity, and Déjà Vu: From Slavery to Ferguson and Beyond

Christopher Alan Bracey

There is a rhythm to the destruction of black lives by American law enforcement. Each death or episode of brutality strikes at the core of our humanity—a vicious and tragically familiar downbeat. Next is the incendiary cocktail of emotion—anger, sadness, outrage, guilt, and fantasies of retribution. The burst of emotion transitions into exhaustion amid a crescendo of cries for justice. These calls rarely elicit a meaningful response, but instead are routinely met with deflections, or an effort to blame the victim, or worse yet, a deafening silence—a long pause that yields to a familiar lamentation to systemic inaction, a begrudging, tacit acceptance of the status quo, and a swelling sense of racial resentment. Then the universe delivers another downbeat, and the cycle begins anew.

Situated within this rhythm of destruction is the killing of Michael Brown, an unarmed 18-year-old, by Ferguson police officer Darren Wilson and its aftermath—a tragic turn of events that is remarkable and, on a deeper level, entirely unremarkable. Nothing has proven more corrosive to American race relations than the manner in which African Americans are stopped, detained, arrested, defiled, killed, and incarcerated more than any other racial group. The killing of Trayvon Martin, Eric Garner, James Crawford III, Michael Brown, Tamir Rice, Rekia Boyd, Walter Scott, Freddie Gray, Sandra Bland, Samuel DuBose, Laquan McDonald and others and the institutional and popular responses represent only the most recent and publicized incidents through which this rhythm of destruction has played out.[1] It is important to remember that this cycle of brutality, outrage, and inaction is a

1

rhythm of racial oppression that has been pounded into our social conscience, week after week, generation after generation. For nearly half of a millennium, racial oppression has played out through the ritual destruction or defilement of black bodies by law enforcement officials.

The events in Ferguson cannot be dismissed as a social anomaly—a blip on an otherwise steady radar of the post-civil-rights era of racial equality. To the contrary, the shooting of Michael Brown is reflective of a much older and deeper pathology that lies at the core of our shared national identity. The U.S. Constitution declared Americans free from the confines of English aristocracy, and signaled a fundamental commitment to freedom, equality, justice, and prosperity for all.[2] Yet at the time of its ratification, Negro chattel slavery had existed in America for more than a century.[3] America, the world's beacon of light for freedom and equality, was also the home of one of the most devastating modes of racial oppression the world has ever witnessed—a most peculiar institution committed to the simultaneous valuation, devaluation, commodification, and destruction of black bodies.[4] In short, a core founding principle of this nation was the belief held by whites that blacks did not possess equal humanity and therefore did not deserve equal treatment—that they could be thoroughly objectified, exiled from civil society, and enslaved for benefit of whites.[5]

This widely accepted percept of American culture, rooted in the ritualistic denial of basic dignity and equal humanity, underlies a great deal of historical racial interactions in American life. It reveals itself in the killing of Michael Brown as well, which may explain in part why his death cut so deeply into the American cultural consciousness. For many of us, but especially perhaps for African Americans, these events are acutely tragic because they repeatedly strike us precisely where we have come to expect it—in that place where our serial racial wounds, from the minute to the magnificent, never seem to receive sufficient time to heal. Officer Wilson may not have committed an offense for which he can be prosecuted under federal civil rights laws. However, the cultural context in which he performed his law enforcement function that resulted in the death of a black child has been revealed as one powerfully shaped by racist attitudes and racially disparate treatment.

For this reason, Michael Brown's death becomes part of that familiar rhythm. Whether blacks lives are snuffed out by an officer's bullet, choked out by an officer's bare hands, or defiled by an officer's nightstick, the message delivered and received is the same now as it has been before: black lives are not worthy of equal dignity. Once again, African Americans find themselves in the absurd yet familiar position of having to plead their equal humanity—to proclaim that "Black Lives Matter."[6]

The connection between the Ferguson shooting and our racial past does not end there. Indeed, one cannot fully appreciate what happened in Ferguson without reference to the epic struggle for racial equality in American life. This chapter provides both the theoretical and historiographical grounding for a deepened discussion about the shooting of Michael Brown, the popular and institutional reaction, and the prospect of emancipation from the rhythmic destruction of black lives.

The Theoretical Lens: Racial Oppression as Dignity Expropriation

The fact that African Americans once again demand to be treated with basic human dignity—nearly 150 years after the ratification of the Thirteenth and Fourteenth Amendments to the Constitution, 50 years after the passage of the Civil Rights Act of 1964, and nearly a decade after the first African American President of the United States was inaugurated—is a sad but not unsurprising development when the struggle in Ferguson is understood as simply yet another redux of the never-ending struggle to overcome the legacy of attitudes, assumptions, and beliefs about the status of blacks in American life. Put differently, racial oppression, including racially discriminatory law enforcement, is at its core a dignity expropriation enterprise.

By dignity expropriation I mean that racial oppression, particularly when enabled or carried out by the state, is at its most fundamental level an effort to deny the basic dignity and equal humanity of others simply because they are of a different, socially disfavored race.[7] Like any other act of expropriation, racial oppression seeks to strip away or modify an element of central importance to the individual—basic human dignity—in service of some larger agenda. The means to accomplish this end can be individualized or structural, physical or sociocultural, transient or permanent. Importantly, the act of expropriation is understood, from the perspective of the taker, as entirely justifiable on political, social, or moral grounds. This notion of racial oppression as dignity expropriation is of transhistorical significance because it helps us understand and comprehend more fully all modes of racial oppression, from slavery to Jim Crow to racial profiling to the maintenance of the prison industrial complex.

Humans are communal in nature. As social beings, we define ourselves and often thrive in our relations to one another. Our individual existence often relies upon a larger mutual dependency with other people.[8] Our social and communal interactions are arguably the key features that designate and distinguish us as fully human.

This communal nature is an essential feature of American democracy. Consider the preamble to the U.S. Constitution, which declares emphatically that "We the People of the United States, in order to form a more perfect Union, establish Justice, insure domestic Tranquility, provide for the common defense, promote the general welfare, and secure the Blessings of Liberty to ourselves and our Posterity, do ordain and establish this Constitution of the United States."[9] The Constitution, which provides the very foundation of our American national identity, rests upon a deep sense of community and shared destiny.

The discourse of "community" may evoke the image of social and political sanctuary, but it is equally effective at conjuring and delineating boundaries. Communities typically have criteria of membership, and it is this feature of community—the power of inclusion and exclusion—that becomes powerfully relevant in the race context. At the time of the framing of the Constitution, when the American people came together to form a democratic nation of individuals vested with equal dignity and equal humanity, Negroes (slave and free) and other racial minorities were designated as social and political pariahs. How are we to reconcile these two competing phenomena?

The answer, at the time of the founding fathers, rested in the definition of "community." In American society, the default political community has always been defined largely by citizenship. Chief Justice Roger Taney would later explain in the infamous *Dred Scott* decision that the rights and protections of the Constitution extended only to members of the relevant political community, which categorically excluded Negro slaves. This was not his personal view, but that of the framers of the Constitution themselves who, "by common consent, had [excluded the Negro race] from civilized Governments and the family of nations, and doomed [Negroes] to slavery."[10]

The placement of Negro slaves outside the relevant political community was of particular consequence in America, where our national identity rests upon the twin premises of basic dignity and equal humanity. The question of citizenship, in Taney's view, was (and perhaps still is) at bottom a question of humanity. When we acknowledge citizenship or bestow it on an individual, we embrace that individual as a full member of our political family. We are, at the deepest levels, acknowledging and affirming that individual's essential humanity. We are telling that person that he or she is one of us—our political, social, and cultural equal.

The refusal to recognize Negroes as citizens, as members of the relevant political community, therefore represented far more than a simple status determination by the Court. Rather, it was a statement about the essential humanity of Negroes or perhaps more accurately, the Court's *perception* of whether or not Negroes deserved to be treated with equal dignity. Answering that question in the negative, Justice Taney explained:

> [Negroes] had for more than a century before been regarded as being an inferior order; and altogether unfit to associate with the white race . . . ; and so far inferior that they had no rights which the white man was bound to respect; and that a the Negro might justly and lawfully be reduced to slavery for [the white man's] his benefit.[11]

From this dignitary perspective, the *Dred Scott* decision is a particularly tragic moment both in American legal and cultural history because it represents such an emphatic rejection of the idea of black humanity. Dred, Harriet, Eliza, and Lizzie Scott, as well as most, if not all, other blacks, did not simply lack equivalent legal status as whites. In the eyes of the highest Court in the land, they were judged to possess a deeper, sociocultural failing. Blacks, according to the Supreme Court, were social and cultural pariahs, unworthy of basic human interaction and certainly not worthy of inclusion in the political community or family of nations. Put differently, the Court's legal determination that blacks were not worthy of citizenship was simultaneously a denial of their essential human dignity.

One should keep in mind that these dignitary implications are not purely symbolic, but also have distinctly materialist effects as well. That is, dignity expropriation through racial repression is both symbolically stigmatizing—marking someone as an outsider, an "other"—and economically debilitating. The lived experience of the Scotts and generations of black families before and after reveals that dignity expropriation through racial repression leads to inequality in educational and employment opportunities as well as a diminishment of the full range of wealth-generating and life-sustaining activities.

The *Dred Scott* decision is powerfully illustrative of the idea of racism as dignity expropriation, but it is important to remember that it did not represent a significant departure from what had come before it. As commonly known, the founding of the American Republic embodied a formal commitment to the liberal ideals of freedom, equality, and democracy for all. Yet this formal commitment took shape against the backdrop of devastating modes of racial oppression. Thus, American culture from the outset embodied both the triumph of liberal ideals and an unflinching commitment to the principles and practices of racial subordination, exploitation, pain, and death.[12]

Dignity expropriation lies as the heart of the institution of Negro chattel slavery, which was premised upon the notion that one could own property in man. It was an axiom of plantation society that a slave deserved a life of humiliation for having refused an honorable death.[13] It was the central animating feature of Indian removal,[14] and Eurocentric immigration and naturalization policy as well.[15] It also drives modern modes of racial oppression, such as employment discrimination, housing discrimination, discriminatory lending practices, and the like. And perhaps most tragically, dignity expropriation is implicated in discriminatory and deadly law enforcement practices like the ones at issue in Ferguson, Missouri.

Dignity Expropriation as Concept in the Modern Era

Basic dignity is (and always has been) a central area of concern in the struggle for racial justice. Early proponents of racial justice were well aware of this connection, although they perhaps did not describe it in precisely these terms. The Reconstruction Amendments, of course, directly repudiated Justice Taney's declaration in *Dred Scott* that blacks could not be citizens because they were widely regarded by whites as "being of an inferior order, and altogether unfit to associate with the white race."[16] Indeed, as others routinely point out, the repudiation of Justice Taney via the Fourteenth Amendment was done in a manner that would grant Congress, in the words of one commentator, substantial enforcement power "to enact certain laws designed to affirm that blacks were equal citizens, worthy of respect and dignity."[17]

The dignitary interests attended to by the Reconstruction Amendments were openly acknowledged and affirmed in the Court's first interpretation of those amendments in the *Slaughterhouse Cases*.[18] Justice Samuel Miller, writing for the majority, stated unequivocally that the Reconstruction Amendments should be interpreted in light of their overriding purpose: "the freedom of the slave race, the security and firm establishment of that freedom, and the protection of the newly made freeman and citizen from the oppressions of those who had formerly exercised unlimited dominion over him."[19] The Court reiterated this sentiment eight years later in *Strauder v. West Virginia*. Justice William Strong, in striking down a West Virginia statute that systematically excluded black jurors from participation in trials, addressed the twin dignitary concerns of self-worth and social value with surprising candor:

> The very fact that colored people are singled out and expressly denied by a statute all right to participate in the administration of the law, as jurors, because of their color, though they are citizens and may be in other respects fully qualified, is practically a brand upon them, affixed by law, an assertion of their inferiority, and a stimulant to the race prejudice which is an impediment to securing individuals of the race that equal justice which the law aims to secure to all others.[20]

Despite these episodic acknowledgments of the interests of dignity, the early 20th century would become infamous as a period of radical expansion of segregation and racial repression.[21] Although the latter half of the 20th century would provide an important resurgence of human dignity as a concept in American law and culture, dignity remains an underappreciated value within society.[22] The evasion of the interests of dignity today represents a crucial failing because it deprives us of a coherent and comprehensive moral vision or theory of racial justice. Law and culture that overlook the dignitary harm of racial oppression are fundamentally nonresponsive to the core feature of racial inequality. This may explain why contemporary race jurisprudence—civil rights and constitutional law cases dealing with race matters—remains fundamentally unsatisfying: whatever it is doing, it is not doing the work of cultural remediation, of replacing prevailing attitudes of complacency and indifference to racial disparities with a culture fundamentally committed to basic dignity and equal humanity.

Dignity Expropriation and Police Culture in Ferguson: The Department of Justice Reports

The events in Ferguson, Missouri, reveal a police culture trafficking in the ritual denial of equal dignity and equal humanity to African Americans.

Indeed, the pattern of disparate law enforcement in Ferguson uncovered by the postshooting Department of Justice (DOJ) investigation bears an eerie resemblance to disparate law enforcement of the late 19th century that was explicitly designed to oppress Negro slaves and newly emancipated blacks. A brief review of the DOJ's findings highlights how racially disparate law enforcement in the modern era—at least in Ferguson, Missouri—is part and parcel of the long-standing dignity expropriation exercise.

The DOJ completed its investigation of the shooting in March 2015, and issued a report in which it concluded that the evidence was insufficient to support the criminal prosecution of police officer Darren Wilson for the shooting of Michael Brown, an unarmed 18-year-old, the previous summer.[23] Officer Wilson had testified that he feared for his life after Brown first tried to grab his gun and then came toward him in a threatening manner.[24] The DOJ found that Wilson's account was corroborated by physical evidence and eyewitness testimony. Given Officer Wilson's perception of the threat posed by Brown, DOJ investigators determined that it would prove difficult to establish that Wilson "willfully"—that is, knowing that it was against the law to do so—used unreasonable force against Brown.[25] Thus, the DOJ investigators concluded that there was not a sufficient basis upon which to prosecute Officer Wilson for a specific civil rights violation in connection with the shooting.

However, the DOJ released a second, and far more unsettling, report on the overall police culture in Ferguson.[26] In this second report, investigators describe "a pattern or practice of unlawful conduct within the Ferguson Police Department that violates the First, Fourth, and Fourteenth Amendments to the United States Constitution, and federal statutory law."[27] At nearly every stage of law enforcement, there appear to be truly surprising racial disparities.

For instance, the percentage of African Americans among persons charged with petty offenses (95 percent of persons charged with "Manner of Walking on Roadway," 94 percent of persons charged with "Failure to Comply," and 92 percent of persons charged with "Peace Disturbance") is unusually high given that African Americans comprise 67 percent of Ferguson's total population.[28] A similar pattern was revealed in the context of vehicle stops and arrests: DOJ investigators found that African Americans represented 85 percent of people subjected to a vehicle stop, 90 percent of people who received a citation, and 93 percent of people arrested pursuant to a stop.[29] Interestingly, investigators found that African Americans are more than twice as likely as white drivers to be searched during vehicle stops, but are found in possession of contraband 26 percent less often than white drivers—a fact "suggesting officers are impermissibly considering race as a factor when determining whether to search."[30]

Racial bias and excessive harshness seem to permeate police culture in Ferguson. DOJ investigators found that African Americans were more likely to receive multiple citations based upon a single incident. During the same data collection period, the Ferguson Police Department issued four or more citations to African Americans on 73 occasions, but issued four or more citations to non-African Americans only twice.[31] Similarly, African Americans seem overly common targets for the use of unreasonable force. Eighty-eight percent of documented force used by Ferguson police officers was used against African Americans.[32] One hundred percent of the 14 canine-bite incidents during the data collection period happened to African Americans.[33]

Racist jokes e-mailed by Ferguson police officers to one another about the First Family and blacks more generally also provide a window into a police culture suffused with racism. A few of these e-mails trafficked in familiar outmoded racial stereotypes. For example, one e-mail noted that President Obama was unlikely to complete his term because "what black man holds a steady job for four years."[34] Others simply demonstrated a striking level of cultural insensitivity, such as one that included a photo of a bare-chested group of black women, seemingly dancing in Africa, with the caption, "Michelle Obama's High School Reunion."[35] Still others proved downright hateful and disrespectful of blacks as a class of people, whether ascribing minstrel dialect to blacks, or suggesting that the correlation between race and criminality is so strong that a black woman should receive a cash award from "Crimestoppers" for having aborted her black baby.[36] This is the cultural context in which Officer Darren Wilson performed his duties as a law enforcement official for the Town of Ferguson—a town in which the majority of residents are African American. Although these findings might not sustain a criminal prosecution, they are powerfully indicative of a culture that does not view African Americans as worthy of equal dignity.

Historical Antecedents: From Slavery to Ferguson

The sickness reflected in Ferguson's police culture has deep historical roots. To be sure, there has been substantial racial progress in this country. The fundamental ideals of freedom, justice, and equality that were denied to blacks well into the 20th century are now enjoyed as a matter of course by millions of African Americans. But it is also true, despite the radical expansion and transformation of these liberal ideals and significant progress in American race relations, that racism, racial inequality, and the corresponding denial of basic human dignity remain naturalized elements within the American cultural landscape. And it is often the case that these norms of racial oppression get instantiated in our criminal laws and law enforcement policies.

If one were to look back in an effort to identify historical antecedents to the racially disparate treatment by law enforcement officials at issue in Ferguson, one might very well begin with a review of slave codes. Slave codes, of course, were laws enacted by whites that applied specifically to Negro slaves. Although some provisions did apply to whites and free blacks,[37] the general thrust of these laws was to construct a parallel system of laws designed to manage interactions that slaves had with nonslaves and each other, and to generally reinforce the core values of the slavery regime—the monetary value of slaves as property, the security of the master class, and public tranquility for those concerned.[38]

In most jurisdictions, the slave codes contained specific criminal offenses, authorized punishments, and rules of criminal procedure that applied only to Negro slaves and free Negroes. For example, the first specific crime listed in the Virginia slave code was "rape of a white woman," which was punishable by death.[39] The second specific crime listed was murder of a white person, which was also punishable by death.[40] Further down the list, one discovers that slaves could be punished by stripes (i.e., public flogging) for "provoking language or menacing gestures to a white person."[41] None of these offenses or their corresponding punishments applied to whites.

Contrary to popular belief, many slave code provisions applied to free Negroes as well. In Virginia, free Negroes were required to register with the county in which they resided—not unlike modern-day sex offenders—because of the inherent danger they posed.[42] Furthermore, every white person in Virginia was empowered by law to make an arrest of a person accused of being a runaway, and could demand a reward,[43] which predictably made free blacks the target of increased harassment under the guise of law enforcement. At the same time, free blacks were constrained in their ability to defend themselves fully against whites or anyone else. Possession of a weapon, which would have been useful and perhaps necessary to fend off would-be slave catchers, was illegal under Virginia law and punishable by stripes.[44]

The DOJ investigators found that Ferguson town officials engaged in racially disparate assessment of fines and court fees against black Ferguson residents. These fines and fees imposed significant and, in some cases, severe, financial hardship against a population already disproportionately poor in order to secure funds to maintain the very institutions (the police and court system) engaging in the discrimination. This particular mode of oppression has its roots in the antebellum era as well. Particularly instructive on this point is the Fugitive Slave Act of 1850,[45] a federal law designed to facilitate the orderly return of runaway slaves to their masters. The practice of slave catching was a notoriously messy business, with unscrupulous slave catchers often attempting to claim free blacks as slaves that would then be subsequently sold at auctions. When citizens of northern states began to interfere with slave catchers, Congress stepped in to ensure that proper protocol was respected.

The Fugitive Slave Act established the creation of commissioners who would receive all claims on runaway slaves. A summary review process was required before any slave catcher would be allowed to remove a Negro from the jurisdiction. However, commissioners would be compensated differently, depending on how they ruled on the slave catcher's claim. Specifically, if the commissioner denied the slave catcher's request for a certification of removal, then the commissioner would receive a fee of $5.[46] If, however, the commissioner granted a slave catcher's certificate of removal (i.e., validated the claim), the commissioner would receive double that amount, or $10, as his fee. Thus, the slave catchers and commissioners, much like Ferguson law enforcement and court personnel, had a strong financial incentive to request and grant certificates of removal—perhaps even in circumstances where removal was not warranted.

The same was true after the Civil War and ratification of the Thirteenth Amendment, which abolished slavery. All southern black codes relied on vagrancy laws to pressure freedmen to sign labor contracts. South Carolina's Code, enacted a mere 12 days after ratification of the Thirteenth Amendment, did not limit these laws to unemployed persons, but included others such as peddlers and gamblers.[47] The Code provided that vagrants could be arrested and imprisoned for up to one year hard labor.[48] But the county sheriff could "hire out" black vagrants to a white employer to work off their punishment. The courts customarily waived such punishment for white vagrants, allowing them to take an oath of poverty instead. The custom of convict leasing in South Carolina and other southern states enabled those jurisdictions to generate substantial revenues on the backs of victims of discriminatory law enforcement—much like the assessment of racial disparate fines and court fees in Ferguson.[49]

The Familiar Call for Equal Dignity

#BlackLivesMatter[50] is a painful reminder that the call for equal dignity and equal humanity has, in certain segments of society, remained fundamentally unanswered. Whether it is Sojourner Truth's "Ain't I a Woman,"[51] Fredrick Douglass's emphatic claim that the Negro is "self-evidently a man, and therefore entitled to all the rights and privileges which belong to human nature,"[52] Malcolm X's insurgent demand for dignity,[53] Martin Luther King's dream for equality,[54] or Rodney King's nonrhetorical question "Can we all get along?,"[55] each generation has called for justice with the full knowledge that such cries routinely fall upon deaf ears.

For many of us, the sad truth is that we have been conditioned over the years to expect and, to some extent, accept the sorry state of affairs produced by decades of efforts to deprive blacks of their dignity—the reality of racial disparities reflected in virtually every index of socioeconomic well-being. The police culture in Ferguson is part and parcel of a larger and perhaps more insidious culture of racial inequality. How exactly does one go about eradicating the culture of racial inequality—this centuries-old enterprise of dignity expropriation that continues to confound us today? How are we to remedy a culture that for nearly half a millennium has worked the magic of blunting our collective sense of outrage over the profoundly uncivil and unequal treatment of racial minorities in America?

The most obvious response is to promote a culture of racial equality and racial inclusiveness. But how exactly does one do that? In my view, the key to accomplishing this may lie in placing greater emphasis on the issue of paramount importance to the Dred Scotts of the past, to black Americans of the present, and to the future Michael Browns: the acknowledgment and deep affirmation of equal dignity and equal humanity of all races, enforceable by law.

This requires us to historicize, contextualize, and deepen our public conversation about race in American society. One cannot acknowledge another's equal humanity without first interrogating the nature of that person's humanity, as well as one's own. This entails, among other things, a strong consideration of the lived experience of racial minorities as well as a thorough examination and appreciation of both the historical and present forms of oppression that provide content to the peculiar racial reality of subordinated racial groups. For African Americans, this may entail a deepened sense of appreciation of how the legacy of slavery, segregation, and stubborn beliefs in cultural inferiority continue to negatively impact their lives. For Latinos, this may entail a greater appreciation of the ritual degradation and ethnic discrimination experienced by immigrant, low-skilled workers as well as members of established Latino communities that is not altogether different from the African American experience. For Native Americans, this may entail a greater sensitivity regarding the extended history of governmental and nongovernmental oppression, alienation, and stereotyping that continue to constrain social and economic mobility of indigenous Americans. For Asian Americans, this may entail a greater appreciation of how the legacy of alienation and marginalization exemplified by racist naturalization policy, labor exploitation, and internment feed contemporary mythology of Asian Americans as "perpetual foreigners" that plagues and confounds second-, third-, and fourth-generation Asian American citizens.

At the same time, affirmance of equal dignity and equal humanity also demands that we take seriously the task of examining and dismantling existing barriers to social inclusion. If whites are to affirm the dignity and presumptive worthiness of inclusion of racial minorities, a necessary precondition is that whites examine critically and self-consciously not only the effects of racial subordination on minorities, but the myriad ways in which the culture of racial subordination has distorted and disfigured majority society in general and white identities in particular. That is, dignity demands that whites not only indulge the prospect of an ever-expanding circle of people deserving respect, but also reflexively examine the question of what allows some white Americans to see racial minorities as their presumptive inferiors and unworthy compatriots in the first place. This requires a level of reflection and introspection that few institutions and even fewer individuals are willing to voluntarily undertake. Such an admission not only opens one up to stigmatic injury (having been denoted a racist), but also to legitimate claims for significant racial redress.

Michael Brown's death is yet another vicious downbeat in the rhythmic assault on black humanity—a tradition of oppression that has been a part of the American cultural consciousness since the founding era. We know this absurdly tragic and familiar pattern all too well. We now assert our collective demand for equal dignity and humanity, as we have so many times before. History teaches us that for racial minorities, and blacks in particular, respect and equal humanity have proven notoriously difficult to secure. Consider the words of Brown University professor and race scholar Glenn Loury, who reminds us that "people do not freely give the presumption of equal humanity. Only philosophers do that. . . . [T]he rest of us tend to ration the extent to which we will presume an equal humanity of our fellows."[56] The criminal indictments of police officers involved in the deaths of Walter Scott in North Charleston, Freddie Gray in Baltimore, Samuel DuBose in Cincinnati, and Laquan McDonald in Chicago. give reason to be optimistic.[57] Perhaps things will be different this time. If not, we must nevertheless remain vigilant and press on in pursuit of equal dignity—either because we imagine some future victory for racial minorities in America, or because, in the final analysis, we really have no other choice.

Notes

1. Deborah E. Bloom & Jareen Imam, *New York Man Dies after Chokehold by Police*, CNN (Dec. 8, 2014, 5:31 AM), http://www.cnn.com/2014/07/20/justice/ny-chokehold-death/ (Eric Garner); Michael Pearson & Greg Botelho, *5 Things to Know about the George Zimmerman-Trayvon Martin Saga*, CNN (Feb. 26, 2012, 10:51 AM), http://www.cnn.com/2013/02/25/justice/florida-zimmerman-5-things/index .html? iid=article_sidebar (Trayvon Martin); Elahe Izadi & Peter Holley, *Video Shows Officer Shooting 12-Year-Old Tamir Rice within Seconds*, Wash. Post, Nov. 26, 2014, http://www.washingtonpost.com /news/post-nation/wp/2014/11/26/officials-release-video-names-in-fatal-police-shooting-of-12-year-old -cleveland-boy/ (Tamir Rice); Mark Berman, Wesley Lowery & Kimberly Kind, *South Carolina Police Officer Charged with Murder after Shooting Man during Traffic Stop*, Wash. Post, Apr. 7, 2015, http:// www.washingtonpost.com/news/post-nation/wp/2015/04/07/south-carolina-police-officer-will-be -charged-with-murder-after-shooting/ (Walter Scott); Sasha Goldstein, *Chicago Cop Charged with Killing Unarmed Young Woman during Off-Duty Confrontation*, NY Daily News, Nov. 25, 2013, http://www .nydailynews.com/news/crime/chicago-charged-killing-unarmed-young-woman-article-1.1529041 (Rekia Boyd); Evan Bleier, *How Did a 27-Year-Old Black Man Die of an Almost Severed Spine after He Was Arrested? Baltimore Investigates Mystery Death*, May 5, 2015, http://www.dailymail.co.uk/news /article-3045937/Baltimore-hospital-says-man-injured-police-encounter-dies.html#ixzz3Yi3tlqmx (Freddie Gray); Chicago Cop Indicted on 6 Murder Counts in Laquan McDonald Slaying, Chicago Tribune, Dec. 18, 2015, http://www.chicagotribune.com/news/local/breaking/ct-jason-van-dyke-indicted-laquan-mcdonald-met-20151216-story.html (Laquan McDonald).

2. U.S. Const. pmbl.

3. A. Leon Higginbotham, In the Matter of Color 26 (1982).

4. For an interesting discussion of the valuation, devaluation, and commodification of black lives, see Robert Evans, Jr., *The Economy of Negro Slavery*, in Aspects of Labor Economics 185–256 (1962).

5. Prigg v. Pennsylvania, 41 U.S. 539 (1842); Dred Scott v. Sandford, 60 U.S. 393 (1857).

6. The #BlackLivesMatter movement began as a hashtag after George Zimmerman's acquittal for the shooting death of Trayvon Martin in 2013, and gained momentum after the shooting of Michael Brown. For more information, visit http://www.blacklivesmatter.com (last visited June 24, 2015).

7. For more on the importance of dignity in the race relations context, see Christopher A. Bracey, *Dignity in Race Jurisprudence*, 7 U. Pa. J. Const. L. 669 (2005).

8. *See* Andrew Fagan, Human Rights: Confronting Myths and Misunderstandings 136 (2009) ("Human rights exist . . . because of the degree to which we are exposed to one another and, to some extent and in some respects, mutually dependent upon one another.").

9. U.S. Const. pmbl.

10. *Dred Scott*, 60 U.S. at 410.

11. *Id.* at 407.

12. *Compare* U.S. Const. pmbl. ("We the people of the United States, in order to . . . secure the blessings of liberty to ourselves and our posterity do ordain and establish this Constitution. . . ."), *with* U.S. Const. art. I, § 2, cl. 3 (counting Negro slaves as three-fifths of one person for political representation purposes), *repealed by* U.S. Const. amend. 14, *and* U.S. Const. art I, § 9, cl. 1 (allowing for the importation and federal taxing of slave labor until 1808), *repealed by* 9 Cong. ch. 22, Mar. 2, 1807, 2 Stat. 426, *and* U.S. Const. art. IV, § 2, cl. 3 (creating a constitutional right to the return of fugitive slaves), *and* U.S. Const. art. V (prohibiting amendment of the slave importation and taxation provision of the Constitution prior to 1808). As former president John Quincy Adams famously explained, "[C]ircumlocutions are the fig-leaves under which these parts of the body politic are decently concealed." John Quincy Adams, Argument of John Quincy Adams, Before the Supreme Court of the United States (1841), *in* The Case of the United States, Appellants, vs. Cinque, and Others, Africans, Captured in the Schooner Amistad 39 (1969). *See also* Kwame Ture (Stokely Carmichael) & Charles V. Hamilton, Black Power: The Politics of Liberation 29 (Vintage 1992) ("From the time black people were introduced into this country, their condition has fostered human indignity and the denial of respect. Born into this society today, black people begin to doubt themselves, their worth as human beings. Self-respect becomes almost impossible.").

13. Kenneth Greenberg, Honor & Slavery 109 (1996). It is important to remember that degradation, dishonor, and remarkable disparities in socioeconomic well-being were both the desired and *intended consequences* of slavery. *See* Orlando Patterson, Slavery and Social Death: A Comparative Study 182, 183 (1982).

14. *See* Worcester v. Georgia, 31 U.S. 515 (1832).

15. *See* Ping v. United States, 130 U.S. 581 (1889) (*Chinese Exclusion Case*)

16. *Dred Scott*, 60 U.S. at 407.

17. Akhil Reed Amar, *Foreword: The Document and the Doctrine*, 114 Harv. L. Rev. 105 (2000).

18. Slaughterhouse Cases, 83 U.S. 36 (1873).

19. *Id.* at 71.

20. Strauder v. West Virginia, 100 U.S. 303, 307 (1880).

21. For a discussion of the explosion in segregation laws across the country following the Court's decision in *Plessy v. Ferguson*, 163 U.S. 537 (1954) (upholding racial segregation state laws under the separate but equal doctrine), see The Origins of Segregation (Joel Williamson ed., 1968); C. Vann Woodward, The Strange Career of Jim Crow 97–109 (3d ed. 1974) (noting spread of Jim Crow laws both before and after *Plessy*, which had the effect of "constantly pushing the Negro farther down"); C. Vann Woodward, Origins of the New South 1877–1913, 211–12 (Wendell Holmes Stephenson & E. Merton Coulter eds., 1951) ("It took a lot of ritual and Jim Crow to bolster the creed of white supremacy in the bosom of a white man working for a black man's wages.").

22. In the late 20th century, dignity began to figure more prominently in Eighth Amendment jurisprudence. *See* Furman v. Georgia, 408 U.S. 238, 270 (1972) (Brennan, J., concurring) ("The primary principle [advanced by the Eighth Amendment's prohibition on cruel and unusual punishment] is that a punishment must not be so severe as to be degrading to the dignity of human beings."). More recently, the Court has championed human dignity in the sexual orientation context. *See* Obergefell v. Hodge, 576 U.S. ___ (2015) (declaring that all states must recognize gay marriages because "there is dignity in the bond between two men or two women who seek to marry and in their autonomy to make such profound choices."); Lawrence v. Texas, 539 U.S. 558 (2003) (invoking the concepts of respect and equal dignity in striking down Texas statutory ban on sodomy).

23. Dep't of Justice, Department of Justice Report Regarding the Criminal Investigation into the Shooting Death of Michael Brown by Ferguson, Missouri Police Officer Darren Wilson 78–85 (2015), http://www.justice.gov/sites/default/files/opa/press-releases/attachments/2015/03/04/doj_report_on_shooting_of_michael_brown_1.pdf.

24. *Id.* at 6.

25. *Id.* at 85–86.

26. Dep't of Justice, Investigation of the Ferguson Police Department (2015), http://www.justice.gov/sites/default/files/opa/press-releases/attachments/2015/03/04/ferguson_police_department_report.pdf.

27. *Id.* at 1.

28. *Id.* at 4.

29. *Id.*

30. *Id.*

31. *Id.* at 5.

32. *Id.*

33. *Id.*

34. *Id.* at 72.

35. *Id.*

36. *Id.* (quoting an e-mail stating "An African-American woman in New Orleans was admitted into the hospital for a pregnancy termination. Two weeks later she received a check for $5,000. She phoned the hospital to ask who it was from. The hospital said, 'Crimestoppers.'").

37. *See, e.g.*, Va. Code tit. 54, ch. 190, § 32 (1849) (denoting it a crime for a white person to "assemble with Negroes for the purpose of instructing them to read or write").

38. State v. Mann, 13 N.C. 263, 268 (1829) ("[I]t will be the imperative duty of the Judges to recognize the full dominion of the owner over the slave [as] this dominion is essential to the value of slaves as property, to the security of the master, and the public tranquility.").

39. Va. Code tit. 54, ch. 100, § 1 (1849).

40. *Id.* § 2.

41. *Id.* § 8.

42. *Id.* tit. 30, ch. 107, §§ 1–3, 6.

43. *Id.* tit. 30, ch. 105, § 4.

44. *Id.* § 8.

45. Act of Sept. 18, 1850, ch. 60, 9 Stat. 462.

46. *Id.* at § 8.

47. South Carolina Black Code, *reprinted in* Civil Rights and the American Negro: A Documentary History (Albert Blaustein & Robert Zangrando eds. 1968).

48. *Id.* at 224–25.

49. For more on convict leasing, see Matthew Mancini, One Dies, Get Another: Convict Leasing in the American South 1886–1928 (1996).

50. *See supra* text accompanying note 6.

51. The conventional narrative is that Sojourner Truth delivered this signature line in connection with a speech delivered in May 1851 at the Women's Convention in Akron, Ohio. That speech was subsequently published in *The History of Woman Suffrage*, which was edited by Elizabeth Cady Stanton, Susan B. Anthony, and Matilda Joslyn Gage. But according to at least one scholar, the phrase "Ain't I a Woman?" was never uttered by Sojourner Truth herself, but instead was introduced by the publisher as an embellishment to the original speech. See Maxine Leeds Craig, Ain't I a Beauty Queen: Black Women, Beauty, and the Politics of Race 7 (2002).

52. Frederick Douglass, *Prejudice against Color, in* The Life and Writings of Frederick Douglass 2:130 (Philip Foner ed., 1975).

53. Malcolm X, *The Ballot or the Bullet, in* Malcolm X Speaks: Selected Speeches and Statements 23 (George Breitman ed., 1988).

54. Martin Luther King, "I Have a Dream" Address (Wash., D.C., Aug. 28, 1963).

55. *Rodney King Speaks Out: "Can We All Get Along?"*, N.Y. Times, May 2, 1992, at A1, A6.

56. Glenn Loury, The Anatomy of Racial Inequality 87 (2002).

57. Optimism in Baltimore may be tempered somewhat as jurors were unable to reach an agreement on any of the charges against the first Baltimore police officer tried in connection with Freddie Gray's death. Justin Fenton and Kevin Rector, *Mistrial Declared in Trial of Officer William Porter in Death of Freddie Gray*, The Baltimore Sun, Dec. 16, 2015, http://www.baltimoresun.com/news/maryland/freddie-gray/bs-md-porter-trial-jury-wednesday-20151216-story.html.

Chapter 2

The Psychology
of Racial Violence

L. Song Richardson and Phillip Atiba Goff

The tragic killings of unarmed black men and boys at the hands of the police compel the United States, once again, to face its sordid history of racial violence. These cases include the well-known and highly controversial deaths of Laquan McDonald in Los Angeles, California and Michael Brown Jr. in Ferguson, Missouri,[1] as well as the deaths of 12-year-old Tamir Rice in Cleveland, Ohio;[2] Eric Garner in Staten Island, New York;[3] John Crawford III in Beavercreek, Ohio;[4] Ezell Ford in Los Angeles, California;[5] Dante Parker in San Bernardino County, California;[6] Vonderrit D. Myers Jr. in St. Louis, Missouri;[7] Walter Scott in North Charleston, South Carolina;[8] Rekia Boyd in Chicago, Illinois;[9] Freddie Gray in Baltimore, Maryland;[10] Sandra Bland in Waller County, Texas,[11] and Sam DuBose in Cincinnati, Ohio.[12] Recent reports suggest that black suspects die at the hands of the police at a rate five times greater than white suspects.[13]

Unsurprisingly, the conversation surrounding these deaths turned quickly into discussions about the officer's character and the victim's actions. Was the officer a racist and was that racism responsible for the death? Or did the victim act in ways that could be considered threatening and dangerous?

This chapter argues that focusing attention on these issues of character ignores the mechanisms of contemporary bias and severely limits efforts at racial progress. Copious scientific evidence reveals that subtle mental processes can produce racially discriminatory behaviors even absent conscious racial bias. These processes are predictable and pervasive. This chapter discusses how racial "suspicion cascades," waves of decision-making errors that can warp the perceptions of even the most egalitarian individuals,[14] may create instances of suspicion regardless of an individual's

---

Significant portions of this chapter were originally published as *Interrogating Racial Violence*, 12 Ohio St. J. Crim. L. 115 (2014).

conscious racial attitudes and beliefs. Additionally, the chapter suggests that grappling with the social science of contemporary bias—the science behind our theory of "suspicion cascades"—is a necessary step toward racial progress and elevating dialogue about racial inequality.

In sum, our examination of racial violence through the lens of suspicion cascades reveals that this violence is an inevitable and foreseeable consequence of current policing strategies and culture that together entrench racial subordination and thus, racial violence. Thus, solutions to the problems of racialized violence police must move beyond discussions of character and any specific individual police-citizen interactions. Rather, reducing violence requires corrective structural and institutional interventions.

Suspicion Cascades

The phrase "suspicion cascades" references the multiple waves of decision-making errors that can warp perceptions and lead to racial biases. Importantly, these errors do not require that someone hold consciously racist beliefs. Research consistently demonstrates that even individuals who hold egalitarian beliefs are subject to basic psychological processes that cause errors in perception and judgment.[15] Consequently, racial discrimination can exist even absent racial bigotry; in other words, "racism without racists."[16] In this sense, suspicion cascades are a psychological "racial trap" that people fall into under some circumstances.[17] As discussed in the next section, these traps can occur as a result of both unconscious racial biases and self-threats.

The framework of suspicion cascades provides a lens through which to understand how race can influence our perceptions and actions even absent racial bigotry. Importantly, we are not suggesting that racist attitudes are never the problem. They are. Therefore, bigotry should not be dismissed simply because racial attitudes have gentled over the past half-century. Rather, the phrase "suspicion cascades" provides a language for talking about racist outcomes even when bigotry is absent. This is a necessary advance at a time when conscious racial prejudice has genuinely declined.

Implicit Racial Bias

Our minds make automatic associations between two concepts in order to save time. In a world full of information overload, it is efficient for our minds to, for instance, have the word "doctor" call to mind the word "hospital" unconsciously and automatically. Implicit racial biases refer to the automatic associations connected with social groups. For instance, one might associate "elderly" with "wise," and "lawyers" with "expensive." Automatic associations are not, in and of themselves, problematic. However, a significant body of literature now demonstrates that these automatic associations can influence perceptions and subsequent behaviors.[18] Consequently, the automatic association of "blacks" with "criminal" may cause people to interpret ambiguous behaviors by a black citizen as more criminal than identical behavior by a white citizen.

Importantly, these racially biased judgments do not require traditional conscious racial animus. Rather, the unconscious association between blacks and criminality can cause individuals to interpret behaviors in line with the activated association—even if they are committed antiracists and even if they are black themselves. These associations exist because throughout our nation's sordid racial history, black individuals have been variously construed as violent, hypermasculine, animal-like, criminal, and unintelligent, to name a few of the racial stereotypes that exist.[19] Thus, these racial constructions are now deeply embedded in our history and culture and are easily called to mind, even unbidden. Social psychologists have demonstrated that because these stereotypes are so well rehearsed, they can influence perceptions and behaviors below the level of conscious awareness, even when people are committed to being racially egalitarian.

Implicit racial biases can have a number of pernicious effects. Research demonstrates that they can cause individuals to interpret identical facial expressions as more hostile on black faces than on white faces,[20] and to perceive identical ambiguous behaviors as more aggressive when engaged in by blacks as opposed to whites.[21] Researchers also have found that thoughts of crime or criminals prompt individuals to look for black male faces and to ignore white male faces.[22] This unconscious racial profiling is automatic and unrelated to individuals' explicit racial attitudes.[23] Similarly, racial stereotypes are implicated in the work of several researchers who demonstrate that black suspects are more likely to be mistakenly shot than are whites in simulated "shooter" tasks and to misidentify innocuous items as weapons under time pressure.[24] Thus, situations in which criminality is salient are ripe for the unconscious application of stereotypes. This is likely to lead perceivers to expect a more negative interaction with nonwhites than with whites, to interpret ambiguous cues as more threatening, and to behave in assertive ways to reduce the danger of those threats. With both perceptions and behaviors, the role of stereotyping need not rise to the level of explicit prejudice. Rather, merely being aware of stereotypes can infiltrate one's experience of the world and influence one's actions in it, possibly with negative and racially disparate outcomes.

More recently, Phillip Atiba Goff and colleagues found evidence that implicit dehumanization, a term Goff and colleagues coined to refer to the tendency to unconsciously associate blacks with beasts, particularly apes,[25] not only facilitates racial violence, but can also help people feel more comfortable with it. In one study, they examined the effects of implicit dehumanization on police uses of force by comparing officers' implicit dehumanization scores with their actual use-of-force history against juveniles. What they found was that officers who held the association more strongly were also more likely to have used force on the street against black as opposed to white youth.[26] Importantly, explicit bias did not predict officer use of force.

In another study, Goff and colleagues had participants watch a video of a brutal police beating of a suspect and asked them to rate whether or not the use of force was justified.[27] Participants who were exposed to the image of apes immediately prior to watching the video were more likely to find the beating of a black suspect more acceptable than the use of identical force against a white suspect.

The implications of implicit dehumanization for policing are disturbing. Regardless of officers' conscious racial attitudes, their unconscious association between black suspects and apes can lead them to be more likely to use physical force against blacks. Equally important, it can lead them and/or the public to believe that their use of force is justified. This is not to say that the use of force is necessarily unjustifiable from a doctrinal standpoint. The law allows officers to use force when they reasonably believe that it is necessary, even if their beliefs are mistaken.[28] Rather, what is problematic is that black suspects may be targeted for force more often than white suspects despite engaging in identical behaviors.

Recent research suggests that it is possible to counteract implicit dehumanization and restore some humanity to social targets.[29] For instance, imagining what another person's life is like makes it easier to imagine their human responses.[30] Thus, rethinking policing practices in order to foster closer relationships between the police and the non-white communities they serve holds some promise of reducing implicit dehumanization and the racial violence that results.

Thus far, our discussion has focused on how implicit racial biases can facilitate racial violence in the absence of racial animus. However, this violence can also arise in response to self-threats. "Stereotype threat" is discussed next.

Stereotype Threat

Stereotype threat refers to the concern with confirming or being evaluated in terms of a negative stereotype about one's group.[31] For instance, a woman professor may worry about being stereotyped as intellectually inferior, and a Muslim civilian may fear being perceived as a terrorist. The concern with being negatively stereotyped often provokes anxiety, leading to physical and mental reactions that are difficult if not impossible to volitionally control, such as increased heart rate, fidgeting, sweating, averting eye gaze, and cognitive depletion—often leading to a reported inability to think clearly.[32] Unlike implicit racial bias, people often have conscious access to their feelings of stereotype threat.[33]

Stereotype threat is most frequently used to explain racial and gender disparities in academic performance.[34] However, recent innovations demonstrate that majority group members and powerful individuals often experience concerns with being negatively stereotyped in terms of their advantageous group position.[35] In the context of intergroup contact, this can translate into whites being concerned with being stereotyped as racist, leading them to avoid interracial contact.[36] The concern of dominant group members with appearing racist can cause negative outcomes for minority group members.[37] This is because the anxiety felt about being stereotyped as racist ironically produces behaviors—such as physical distancing, avoiding eye contact, cognitive depletion, and general nervous behaviors—that foster negative interactions. Next, we demonstrate how stereotype threat can provoke racial disparities in police use of force by discussing research conducted within the San Jose Police Department.

In 2009, the San Jose Police Department voluntarily participated in research to determine, among other things, the role that an officer's biases might play in causing racially inequitable outcomes.[38] As part of the research, a group of nearly 100 officers volunteered to complete a battery of psychological instruments including measures of explicit racial bias, implicit racial bias, and stereotype threat. Researchers were also given access to each participating officer's performance file, including his use-of-force history. This allowed researchers to match the officer's history with his psychological profile. After controlling for a wide variety of factors, including the district that officers patrolled as well as years on the force, researchers performed a multiple regression model designed to identify possible relationships between psychological predictors and police behaviors.

What researchers found was that explicit racism did not predict overall rates of force used across officers or racial disparities in the use of force. However, researchers did find a counterintuitive relationship between the use of force and stereotype threat. They discovered that the more officers were concerned with appearing racist, the more likely they were to have used force against black suspects, but not suspects of other races, throughout the course of their careers.

Why might an egalitarian officer's concern with being evaluated as a racist be associated with greater use of force against black citizens? While this result may appear surprising, there are several reasons to expect this relationship. First, attitudes are relatively weak predictors of behavior.[39] Consequently, it is unsurprising that explicit prejudice was not a robust predictor of racial disparities in police behavior. Second, self-threats tend to figure more heavily in propensities toward violence than biases directed toward others.[40] Finally, these findings are more easily understood when accompanied by an understanding of standard officer safety training. Most officers agree that safety is the most important component of academy and continuing training for officers on patrol.[41] This is why officer safety trainings are among the most popular voluntary trainings and the most diverse continuing education options available for patrol officers.[42] A basic tenet of nearly all trainings is the need for officers to maintain physical and psychological control of a situation in order to preserve personal safety.[43] In other words, officers are trained to believe that threats to their authority constitute an immediate threat to their safety.

Further, officers are instructed that they have two forms of authority with which to maintain that control. The first, moral or legal authority, should be employed whenever possible.[44] The second, coercive or physical authority, should serve only as a last recourse or as a response to an immediate physical threat.[45] Although officers should rely first on moral or legal authority, they may feel unable to rely upon their moral authority to control the situation if they fear that a citizen will judge them to be racist. They may fear that because the citizen may view them as racist, the citizen will deem them to be unworthy of respect. Thus, officers will believe that they have no moral authority in the eyes of the citizen, and consequently their moral authority is no longer sufficient to control the situation. As a result, officers may be quicker to use force to control the situation than they would be in a situation where they feel they can rely upon their moral authority. In this way, concerns with appearing racist reduce the options officers believe are available to them. In other words, fear of being seen as racist promotes reliance on coercive authority, that is, force. Importantly, while it is possible that in any given incident, accusing someone of racism may provoke aggression in response to the simple act of name calling, the research conducted in San Jose demonstrates that it is the individuals who are most concerned with appearing racist that tend to demonstrate the highest rates of disparities in the application of force.

In sum, an officer's concerns with appearing prejudiced can have the ironic effect of causing racially disparate treatment of individuals within the communities they are sworn to protect. In addition, stereotype threat also provokes the kind of regulatory demands that lead people to use stereotypes in their decision making in the first place. Thus, the ironic outcome is that one's concerns with appearing prejudiced can produce increased reliance on stereotype-laden thinking—thinking that triggers the implicit biases discussed earlier—which then compounds racially disparate outcomes.

A stereotype threat approach to interracial contact does not locate racial problems in the "hearts and minds" of prejudiced agents. Rather, it demonstrates that certain features of the external situation in which individuals find themselves can exacerbate the insecurities that lead to racial violence. When it comes to police violence, what this suggests is that it is important to interrogate whether certain aspects of current policing practices exacerbate stereotype threat in egalitarian police officers. For instance, certain police tactics such as stops and frisks may foster the stereotype that officers are racist, without any corresponding crime control benefit. And, even if some crime control benefit exists, this benefit should be balanced against the increased risk of hegemonic racial violence. Since it may be possible to reduce officers' insecurities that they will be judged as racist by revising existing policing practices, it is imperative that police departments begin to explore these possibilities. Otherwise, it signals acceptance of the pernicious effects of stereotype threat in producing racial violence. Next, we attend to another self-threat that can lead to racial violence, namely, masculinity threat.

Masculinity Threat

Masculinity threat refers to the fear of being judged as insufficiently masculine. The previously discussed San Jose Police Department research examined the relationship between masculinity threat and police use of force. The officers involved in the study completed several measures of masculinity threat.[46] Then, their scores were compared to their record of force for the previous two years.[47] The results demonstrated that the more officers were insecure in their masculinity, the more likely they were to use greater force against blacks relative to other racial groups.[48] In other words, masculinity threat predicted whether officers had actually used force against black men in the previous two years. However, masculinity threat was not associated with the use of force against men of other races. Additionally, neither explicit racism nor implicit bias was associated with the use of greater force.[49] Even egalitarian-minded officers were more likely to have used force against noncompliant black suspects if the officers were highly insecure in their masculinity.

What might explain this result? Young black men in poor urban environments are stereotyped, both consciously and unconsciously, as violent, criminal, dangerous, and animal-like. These images are so deeply embedded in our culture that they have "become common-sense 'truths.'"[50] Earlier, we demonstrated how these unconscious stereotypes can cause disparate racial effects even in the absence of conscious racial animus. In the context of masculinity threat, these negative racial stereotypes likely do additional work by helping to construct black men as more masculine in relation to other men. In fact, empirical evidence confirms that black men are viewed as more masculine vis-a-vis other races.[51]

Regardless of an officer's conscious racial attitudes, then, black men pose the greatest threat to an officer's masculinity, especially if their actions are perceived as noncompliant and thus, disrespectful or challenging to an officer's masculine authority. We use the phrase "perceived as noncompliant" because there are circumstances where officers may view actions to be noncompliant when they are not. Perceived noncompliance is a sign of disrespect that poses a masculinity threat.[52] Since aggression is often a consequence of threats to masculinity in hyper masculine environments, black men are more vulnerable to police violence as officers attempt to defend or prove their masculinity not only to themselves and to the victim, but also to any fellow officers who might be present. Disturbingly, all this can occur without conscious racial bigotry on the part of the officer.

Importantly, we are not suggesting that aggression and violence are the only ways to respond to masculinity threats. However, such responses are more likely in hypermasculine environments, like police departments, because these responses are recognized as acceptable ways of establishing one's manhood.[53] Hypermasculinity among the rank and file is encouraged, reinforced, and policed in numerous ways. For one, hierarchies among the rank and file often are defined by the amount of aggression and violence perceived to be necessary to perform the job.[54] Furthermore, hypermasculinity is continuously reaffirmed through the subordination and harassment of women[55] and gay men.[56] Thus, the hypermasculine setting of police departments places young black men at greater risk of racial violence, even if they are acting identically to young white men in similar situations and even if the officer who confronts them is consciously egalitarian.

Implications

The theory of suspicion cascades can inform our thinking about racial violence. Suspicion cascades reveal that nonwhites face a greater risk of death or serious bodily injury at the hands of those who honestly, but mistakenly, fear them. These erroneous judgments about the need to act in self-defense can occur regardless of the actor's conscious racial attitudes. All that is required to trigger the cascade is knowledge of racial stereotypes. Suspicion cascades further demonstrate that officers' insecurities are just as consequential as both conscious racism and unconscious racial bias in causing pervasive racial disparities in police violence.

Importantly, these effects are not inevitable. Suspicion cascades result in racial violence in contexts that facilitate them, and these contexts can be changed. Thus, the state should have a responsibility to scrutinize its policing practices to determine whether they cultivate the psychological processes that lead to racial disparities in the use of force by the police. Once these problematic practices are identified, the state should take steps to change them. In sum, the state must protect all of its citizens from state perpetrated violence, regardless of whether that violence results from the intentional animus of its agents or not.

As we discussed, current policing strategies and culture help sustain and exacerbate suspicion cascades, leading to racial violence. Next, we briefly explore one promising avenue of reform, community policing, and suggest that the conversation surrounding community policing would be enriched by engagement with issues of power and privilege. However, in recognition of the fact that transformation of current policing practices and culture cannot take place overnight, we also discuss some interim remedies for reducing racial violence.

Community Policing

As our previous discussion suggests, racial violence will flourish under policing practices that make it easier for officers to dehumanize the communities they police, that foster beliefs that police officers are racists, and that encourage hypermasculinity. One potentially promising approach to policing that can avoid these problems is community policing.

In theory, community policing embraces the idea that the social work aspects of policing are important.[57] Under the ideal model, officers and communities work closely to address the underlying causes of crime and disorder. The focus is on crime prevention, not on making arrests and maintaining order. In theory, officers engaged in community policing "listen closely to and empathize with residents, . . . disentangle disputes that exist within communities, and . . . allow themselves to exist in deeply cooperative relationships."[58]

While most departments represent that they are engaged in community policing,[59] the reality is far from the ideal.[60] Instead, policing largely remains mired in practices that were ushered in during the so-called "professionalism era" that began in the 1930s and 1940s primarily in response to concerns over police corruption.[61] One major change to policing that occurred during this period was that officers began patrolling neighborhoods in cars instead of on foot, which distanced officers from the communities they policed.[62] Some departments went even further to "depersonalize policing" by frequently reassigning officers to new neighborhoods to patrol.[63]

Additionally, the professionalism model narrowed police functions to crime control rather than social work[64] and taught officers to view themselves as experts who did not need community input to inform their practices.[65] Furthermore, response times to calls for service and the number of arrests made became the primary methods for measuring officer success.[66] These data-driven aspects of policing continue today. In fact, this preoccupation with numbers has resulted in aggressive, proactive law enforcement practices that alienate communities from the police[67] and foster an "us versus them" mentality that encourages officers to view themselves as soldiers in a war against the residents of indigent, minority neighborhoods.[68] Despite the asserted commitment to community policing in many departments, the professionalism model remains predominant.

Community policing in its ideal form could potentially mitigate the violence associated with implicit dehumanization, stereotype threat, and masculinity threat. First, the current policing model fosters dehumanization by encouraging arms-length relationships between the police and citizens that prevent the development of understanding and close engagement. By promoting closer relationships, community policing could reduce implicit dehumanization since it is more difficult to dehumanize people with whom one is familiar.

Second, to the extent that community policing nurtures the community's trust in the police and improves perceptions of police legitimacy, it can also reduce stereotype threat in egalitarian officers. That is because improved police-citizen relationships may reduce an officer's anxiety that community members will prejudge him to be racist. Furthermore, as officers and neighborhood residents become familiar with each other, an egalitarian officer may become more comfortable and less likely to fear that his actions will be interpreted as being racially motivated.

Third, community policing can also disrupt hypermasculinity among the rank and file. By focusing on cooperative relationships instead of aggressive crime fighting, community policing "elevat[es] 'feminine' skills such as empathy, caring, and connection that historically were unacceptable to the male culture of traditional policing."[69] As sociologists Susan Miller and Emily Bonistall write:

> Community policing ... challenges the masculinized ethos by prioritizing connections and cooperation between police officers and community members in addressing crime and other social problems ... a more informal, relational, and conciliatory style of policing is encouraged. Roles that were previously denigrated as feminine, and too "soft" or emotional for "real" police work, have become the ideal qualities for community police officers to possess.[70]

By devaluing hypermasculinity, community policing can reduce the masculinity threat that results in racial violence. Although male police officers would still "do" gender, their performance of masculinity would not be tied to physical aggression but rather to their ability to solve problems through creativity and innovation.

Furthermore, a shift to community policing could help upset the coding of policing as hypermasculine. This, in turn, might attract different types of recruits, including more women[71] and others who may not currently be drawn to policing because of its hypermasculine identity. Conversely, those who are currently attracted to policing because of its reputation for violence and aggression might no longer be interested in joining the force.

While community policing holds great promise for reducing racial violence, there is reason for some caution. The idea of community can be deeply problematic if not informed by an analysis of power and privilege. For instance, officers may privilege the voices of the powerful elite within a community at the expense of the voices of the least powerful, that is, those members of the community most likely to bear the brunt of aggressive policing practices. In this situation, these more-privileged members can work with the police to implement policies that increase state control over subordinated groups. If community policing works in this way, it can perpetuate racial subordination by favoring dominant voices and values at the expense of the minority. As Roberto Unger once observed, "By its very nature, community is always on the verge of becoming oppression."[72] There are many other unresolved issues that deserve study, including how community should be defined, who can or should speak on behalf of the community, and whether genuine partnerships between subordinated groups and the police can exist.[73] It is beyond the scope of this chapter to consider these issues more closely, but, given the potential promise and perils of community policing, the question deserves further inquiry.[74]

Interim Solutions

While moving toward community policing to reduce racial violence is the goal, such a change cannot be effected overnight. Indeed, the current model of policing is so entrenched that even suggesting change can meet resistance. In the meantime, racial violence will continue unabated unless some changes are made. Here, we accordingly consider some promising interim solutions to address and reduce racial violence.

First, we urge scholars and practitioners to work closely with police departments and social scientists to identify interventions to reduce racial violence. There is already precedent for these partnerships. As previously discussed, Goff worked with the San Jose Police Department to identify some causes of racial disparities in policing and to develop solutions. Additionally, his organization, the Center for Policing Equity, has collaborated with a wide array of police departments across the country to conduct original research in order to foster the equitable delivery of police services. Thus, it is possible to build fruitful and successful collaborations with police departments.

Second, police departments should make changes to their training practices, both in the police academy and in the department. Frank Rudy Cooper has already proposed some changes to police training in order to address the problems posed by masculinity contests, including teaching officers to rely less on physical aggressiveness in response to disrespect.[75] We endorse his suggestions and would go even further. There is evidence that "police work rarely entails the aggressiveness celebrated by the masculinist cop,"[76] and that the "reality of police work . . . involves much tedium and paperwork and relatively little crime fighting or violence."[77] If this is accurate, police training should focus more attention on teaching skills that foster creative problem solving and collaborative decision making and less on physical strength and aggressiveness. The former is associated with community policing while the latter encourages hypermasculinity.[78] Furthermore, while officer safety is always a concern, there is some evidence that displays of force are not as effective as less confrontational strategies for defusing tense situations.[79]

Third, departments should revise incentive structures to reward skills related to an officer's demonstrations of creative problem solving, ingenuity, and interpersonal skills as opposed to hypermasculine behaviors such as making arrests. Otherwise, officers will continue to prioritize practices associated with hypermasculinity.

Finally, departments should abandon practices that show little effectiveness in reducing crime but that exacerbate community tensions. That is because these tensions foster racial violence for at least three reasons. For one, officers tend to view neighborhoods that are "antipolice" as more dangerous, and thus, as more masculine.[80] As a result, for police officers seeking to prove their masculinity through displays of aggression and daring, these neighborhoods are ideal locales. Hence, "[t]o enact masculinism is thus to reinforce a racialized pattern that yields aggressive patrolling in minority-dominated neighborhoods."[81]

Additionally, community-police antagonism helps foster the "us versus them" mentality that can lead to implicit dehumanization. Furthermore, police practices that exacerbate tensions within urban, minority neighborhoods promote and sustain the view that officers are racist. As discussed, police officers are aware of these views, and for egalitarian officers, the fear of confirming this stereotype can lead to racial violence.

One practice that should be abandoned is stop and frisk. This policing strategy creates significant anger and resentment within minority communities while its crime control benefits continue to be debated. A recent report from the New York Attorney General's Office concluded that although millions of nonwhite citizens were targeted by the New York City Police Department for stops and frisks between 2009 and 2012, only 0.1 percent of stop and frisk arrests resulted in a conviction for weapons possession or a crime of violence,[82] and almost one-half of all arrests made after a stop and frisk did not result in any conviction at all.[83] For those that did result in a conviction, "more than 40% were for 'quality of life' offenses, such as graffiti and disorderly conduct."[84] Furthermore, the anger and resentment produced by the practice makes it more difficult to detect and solve crime because the police lose legitimacy in the eyes of the community, resulting in decreased cooperation with the police.[85]

An additional problem with stops and frisks is that the practice contributes to police-citizen tensions, leading officers to view these neighborhoods as antipolice. As discussed, this facilitates racial violence both because these neighborhoods become ideal sites for masculine gender performances and because this antagonism fosters the alienation that facilitates implicit dehumanization. Finally, stops and frisks contribute to the view held by many residents in poor, urban, minority communities that officers are racist.[86]

These interim suggestions are preliminary and deserve more development than we are able to provide in this chapter. However, there is reason for optimism that departments will implement at least a few of them. As previously discussed, some departments are already working voluntarily to reduce racial disparities in policing practices. Furthermore, there are likely allies to be found within departments. For instance, police unions representing nonwhite officers and women may be supportive of some of these proposals. Additionally, egalitarian officers likely will be disturbed to learn about stereotype threat and its possible effects on their behaviors and thus may be motivated to implement changes to policing practices that exacerbate its effects.

Conclusion

Suspicion cascades reveal how racism has become normalized within institutions and systems and, thus, does not require individual or collective racial animus to support subordination. Thus, we focused our analysis on transforming systems of policing that continue to reproduce racial disparities in police violence. Importantly, however, existing legal doctrine is also inadequate to address racial violence. A new doctrinal framework is necessary to address it and we offer a couple of observations here.

First, any new approach must abandon the law's current reliance on demonstrating racial animus and must embrace a race-conscious approach. That is because racial animus cannot account for the fact that unconscious racial biases and perpetrator insecurities both result in unconscionable racial disparities in police violence. Approaches for reducing the effects of both unconscious biases and self-threats require that attention be paid to race.[87]

Second, we envision a new legal regime that places the onus on the state to remedy the institutional factors that exacerbate racial violence. The state has a duty to ensure that police officers use force equitably. Thus, it should have a concomitant duty to intervene when incontrovertible evidence of disparate treatment by its agents, the police, exists. The state's failure to act by revising policing strategies when evidence exists that these strategies facilitate racial disparities is culpable, at least when the state has the ability to act and its actions could remedy the problem. This conception rests culpability not on the demonstration of racial animus, but on the state's failure to remedy the racial subordination that is built into existing systems and practices. Consequently, just as the law makes a distinction between intent to do harm and negligence resulting in harm, one can imagine a legal system—better informed by the mind sciences—that likewise punishes the state for failing to take affirmative steps to protect all of its citizens from violence when the duty and means to do so exist.

Lastly, this chapter calls upon legal scholars to broaden their consideration of psychological science beyond a focus on implicit racial bias. For legal scholarship to take seriously the charge of behavioral realists[88] to translate what science knows about the human condition to the rules that govern human behavior, a more inclusive and integrative approach to importing that science is required. In the case of racial disparities in law enforcement, that integration should lead scholars to focus extensively on the ways that self-threats—and not only unconscious racial biases—predict unequal applications of the law. In sum, the manner in which we regulate the consequences of the wars inside each of us is not only a matter for poets and philosophers, but also for governance and jurisprudence. Thus, the breadth of the human experience that legal scholars must endeavor to understand is broader, still, than we have previously acknowledged.

Notes

1. *See, e.g.*, Annie Sweeney & Jason Meisner, A Moment-By-Moment Account of What the Laquan McDonald Video Shows, Chicago Tribune, Nov. 25, 2015, http://www.chicagotribune.com/news/ct-chicago-cop-shooting-video-release-laquan-mcdonald-20151124-story.html; Jonathan Cohn, *Darren Wilson Walks: No Indictment for Michael Brown's Killer*, New Republic, Nov. 24, 2014, http://www.newrepublic.com/article/120395/ferguson-grand-jury-makes-issues-no-charges-officer-wilson.

2. *See, e.g.*, Emma G. Fitzsimmons, *Video Shows Cleveland Officer Shot Boy in 2 Seconds*, N.Y. Times, Nov. 26, 2014, http://www.nytimes.com/2014/11/27/us/video-shows-cleveland-officer-shot-tamir-rice-2-seconds-after-pulling-up-next-to-him.html.

3. *See, e.g.*, J. David Goodman & Al Baker, *Wave of Protests after Grand Jury Doesn't Indict Officer in Eric Garner Chokehold Case*, N.Y. Times, Dec. 3, 2014, http://www.nytimes.com/2014/12/04/nyregion/grand-jury-said-to-bring-no-charges-in-staten-island-chokehold-death-of-eric-garner.html?_r=0.

4. Catherine E. Shoichet & Nick Valencia, *Cops Killed Man at Walmart, then Interrogated Girlfriend*, CNN, Dec. 16, 2014, http://www.cnn.com/2014/12/16/justice/walmart-shooting-john-crawford/.

5. Jennifer Medina, *Man Is Shot and Killed by the Police in California*, N.Y. Times, Aug. 13, 2014, http://www.nytimes.com/2014/08/14/us/man-shot-and-killed-by-los-angeles-police-officer.html?_r=0

6. Philip Caulfield, *Father of 5 Dies after Getting Tased by Police during Attempted Burglary Arrest*, N.Y. Daily News, Aug. 15, 2014, http://www.nydailynews.com/news/national/father-5-dies-tased-police-arrest-article-1.1904577.

7. Alan Blinder, *New Outcry Unfolds after St. Louis Officer Kills Black Teenager*, N.Y. Times, Oct. 9, 2014, *available at* http://www.nytimes.com/2014/10/10/us/st-louis-police-shooting-protests.html.

8. Reuters, *Police Account of the Fatal Shooting of Walter Scott Greatly Differs from Footage of the Actual Shooting*, Yahoo! News, https://uk.news.yahoo.com/video/police-account-fatal-shooting-walter-165558061.html.

9. Tony Briscoe, Protesters Criticize Judge, Alvarez after Cop's Acquittal in Shooting Death, Chi. Tribune, Apr. 21, 2015, http://www.chicagotribune.com/news/local/breaking/ct-rekia-boyd-protest-met-0422-20150421-story.html.

10. AP, *Freddie Gray's Death Was a Homicide*, N.Y. Times, June 23, 2015, http://www.nytimes.com/2015/06/24/us/freddie-grays-death-was-homicide-autopsy-says.html; *see also Freddie Gray Dies after Spine Injured in Police Custody: Lawyer*, NBC News, Apr. 20, 2015, http://www.nbcnews.com/news/us-news/healthy-baltimore-man-dies-after-being-restrained-police-n344506.

11. David Montgomery, *Texas Trooper's Behavior Called "Catalyst" in Sandra Bland's Death*, N.Y. Times, July 30, 2015, http://www.nytimes.com/2015/07/31/us/texas-troopers-behavior-called-catalyst-in-sandra-blands-death.html.

12. Richard Pérez-Peña, *University of Cincinnati Officer Indicted in Shooting Death of Samuel DuBose*, N.Y. Times, July 29, 2015, http://www.nytimes.com/2015/07/30/us/university-of-cincinnati-officer-indicted-in-shooting-death-of-motorist.html.

13. Jodi M. Brown & Patrick A. Langan, U.S. Dep't of Justice, Bureau of Justice Statistics, Policing and Homicide, 1976–98: Justifiable Homicide by Police, Police Officers Murdered by Felons (2001), http://www.bjs.gov/content/pub/pdf/ph98.pdf (studying killings between the years 1976 and 1998).

14. For a more detailed description of suspicion cascades, see L. Song Richardson & Phillip Atiba Goff, *Self-Defense and the Suspicion Heuristic*, 98 IOWA L. REV. 293 (2012).

15. Patricia Devine, *Automatic and Controlled Processes in Prejudice: The Role of Stereotypes and Personal Beliefs*, in ATTITUDE STRUCTURE AND FUNCTION 181–212 (Anthony R. Pratkanis et al. eds., 1989); John F. Dovidio, *On the Nature of Contemporary Prejudice: The Third Wave*, 57 J. SOC. ISSUES 829–49 (2001); Phillip A. Goff et al., *The Space between Us: Stereotype Threat and Distance in Interracial Contexts*, 94 J. PERSONALITY & SOC. PSYCHOL. 91–107 (2008); Anthony Greenwald et al., *Measuring Individual Differences in Implicit Cognition: The Implicit Association Test*, 74 J. PERSONALITY & SOC. PSYCHOL. 1464–80 (1998).

16. *See, e.g.*, EDWARDO BONILLA-SILVA, RACISM WITHOUT RACISTS: COLOR-BLIND RACISM AND THE PERSISTENCE OF RACIAL INEQUALITY IN AMERICA (2003); Goff et al., *supra* note 15.

17. Phillip A. Goff, Presentation at the W.K. Kellogg Foundation America Healing Conference: Identity Traps: The Shape of Contemporary Discrimination through the Lens of Law Enforcement (Apr. 24–27, 2012); Phillip Goff & L. Song Richardson, *Running from Race in Our Minds*, HUFFINGTON POST, Mar. 24, 2012, http://www.huffingtonpost.com/phillip-atiba-goff/trayvon-martin-race_b_1376621.html.

18. *See, e.g.*, L. Song Richardson, *Arrest Efficiency and the Fourth Amendment*, 95 MINN. L. REV. 2035, 2043–56 (2011) (citing sources).

19. Phillip Atiba Goff et al., *Not Yet Human: Implicit Knowledge, Historical Dehumanization, and Contemporary Consequences*, 94 J. PERSONALITY & SOC. PSYCHOL. 292 (2008); Phillip Atiba Goff, Margaret A. Thomas, Matthew C. Jackson, *"Ain't I a Woman": Towards an Intersectional Approach to Person Perception and Group-Based Harms*, 59 SEX ROLES 392 (2008); Patricia G. Devine & Andrew J. Elliot, *Are Racial Stereotypes Really Fading? The Princeton Trilogy Revisited*, 21 PERSONALITY & SOC. PSYCHOL. BULL. 1139 (1995).

20. Kurt Hugenberg & Galen V. Bodenhausen, *Facing Prejudice: Implicit Prejudice and the Perception of Facial Threat*, 14 PSYCHOL. SCI. 640 (2003).

21. Birt L. Duncan, *Differential Social Perception and Attribution of Intergroup Violence: Testing the Lower Limits of Stereotyping of Blacks*, 34 J. PERSONALITY & SOC. PSYCHOL. 590 (1976).

22. Jennifer L. Eberhardt et al., *Seeing Black: Race, Crime, and Visual Processing*, 87 J. PERSONALITY & SOC. PSYCHOL. 876 (2004).

23. *Id.*

24. Joshua Correll et al., *The Police Officer's Dilemma: Using Ethnicity to Disambiguate Potentially Threatening Individuals*, 83 J. PERSONALITY & SOC. PSYCHOL. 1314 (2002); Correll et al., *The Influence of Stereotypes on Decisions to Shoot*, 37 EUR. J. SOC. PSYCHOL. 1102 (2007); Keith Payne, Prejudice and Perception: The Role of Automatic and Controlled Processes in Misperceiving a Weapon, 81 J. PERSONALITY & SOC. PSYCHOL. 181 (2001); Michelle Peruche & Ashby Plant, *The Correlates of Law Enforcement Officers' Automatic and Controlled Race-Based Responses to Criminal Suspects*, 28 BASIC & APPLIED SOC. PSYCHOL. 193 (2006); Ashby Plant & Michelle Peruche, *The Consequences of Race for Police Officers' Responses to Criminal Suspects*, 16 PSYCHOL. SCI. 180 (2005); Ashby Plant et al., *Eliminating Automatic Racial Bias: Making Race Non-Diagnostic for Responses to Criminal Suspects*, 41 J. EXPERIMENTAL SOC. PSYCHOL. 141 (2005).

25. Goff et al., *supra* note 19, at 292, 293; *see also* Susan Opotow, *Moral Exclusion and Injustice: An Introduction*, 46 J. SOC. ISSUES 1, 10 (1990).

26. Phillip Atiba Goff et al., *The Essence of Innocence: Consequences of Dehumanizing Black Children*, 106 J. PERSONALITY & SOC. PSYCHOL. 526, 533–35 (2014).

27. Goff et al., *supra* note 19, at 292, 302.

28. Graham v. Connor, 490 U.S. 386, 388 (1989).

29. Antonio T. Fernando III & Nathan S. Consedine, *Beyond Compassion Fatigue: The Transactional Model of Physician Compassion*, 48 J. PAIN & SYMPTOM MGMT. 289–98 (2013).

30. Nicholas Epley et al., *On Seeing Human: A Three-Factor Theory of Anthropomorphism*, 114 PSYCHOL. REV. 864–86, 880 (2007).

31. Claude M. Steele, *A Threat in the Air: How Stereotypes Shape Intellectual Identity and Performance*, 52 AM. PSYCHOL. 613, 614 (1997).

32. Richardson & Goff, *Interrogating Racial Violence*, 12 OHIO ST. J. CRIM. L. 115, 125–26 (2015).

33. Goff et al., *supra* note 15, at 101–04.

34. Claude M. Steele & Joshua Aronson, *Stereotype Threat and the Intellectual Test Performance of African Americans*, 69 J. Personality & Soc. Psychol. 797 (1995); Steven J. Spencer et al., *Stereotype Threat and Women's Math Performance*, 35 J. Experimental Soc. Psychol. 4 (1999).

35. *Id. See also* Jennifer A. Richeson & J. Nicole Shelton, *When Prejudice Does Not Pay: Effects of Interracial Contact on Executive Function*, 14 Psychol. Sci. 287 (2003); Jacquie D. Vorauer et al., *How Do Individuals Expect to Be Viewed by Members of Lower Status Groups? Context and Implications of Meta-Stereotypes*, 75 J. Personality & Soc. Psychol. 917 (1998).

36. Goff et al., *supra* note 15.

37. *Id.*; Richeson & Shelton, *supra* note 35.

38. Phillip Atiba Goff, Karin Danielle Martin & Meredith Gamson Smiedt, Protecting Equity: The Consortium for Police Leadership in Equity Report on the San Jose Police Department 3 (2012) [hereinafter San Jose Report].

39. Dovidio, *supra* note 15, at 840–41.

40. San Jose Report, *supra* note 38, at 11.

41. Geoffrey P. Alpert, Roger G. Dunham & John M. MacDonald, *Interactive Police-Citizen Encounters That Result in Force*, 7 Police Q. 475 (2004).

42. *Id.*

43. *Id.*

44. Phillip Abita Goff, Brooke Allison Lewis Di Leone & Kimberly Barsamian Kahn, *Racism Leads to Pushups: How Racial Discrimination Threatens Subordinate Men's Masculinity*, 48 J. Experimental Soc. Psychol. 1111 (2012).

45. *Id.*

46. San Jose Report, *supra* note 38, at 5–6.

47. *Id.* at 4.

48. *Id.* at 11.

49. *Id.*

50. Patricia Hill Collins, Black Sexual Politics: African Americans, Gender, and the New Racism 151 (2005).

51. Phillip Atiba Goff, Margaret A. Thomas & Matthew Christian Jackson, *Ain't I a Woman?*, 59 Sex Roles 392, 403 (2008).

52. Frank Rudy Cooper, *"Who's the Man?": Masculinities Studies, Terry Stops, and Police Training*, 18 Colum. J. Gender & L. 671 (2009). For a more complete discussion of masculinity threat and its influence on policing, see L. Song Richardson & Phillip Atiba Goff, *Interrogating Racial Violence*, 12 Ohio St. J. Crim. L. 115 (2014).

53. For a general discussion, see Angela P. Harris, *Gender, Violence, Race, and Criminal Justice*, 52 Stan. L. Rev. 777 (2000); Angela P. Harris, *Heteropatriarchy Kills: Challenging Gender Violence in a Prison Nation*, 37 Wash. U. J.L. & Pol'y 13, 20 (2011).

54. Steve Herbert, *"Hard Charger" or "Station Queen"? Policing and the Masculinist State*, 8 Gender, Place & Culture 55, 59 (2001) (noting that detectives and management "are regularly disparaged by patrol officers; they are not 'real men' because they avoid the test of masculinity that the danger of the street presents").

55. Susan L. Miller, Kay B. Forest & Nancy C. Jurik, *Diversity in Blue: Lesbian and Gay Police Officers in a Masculine Occupation*, 5 Men & Masculinities 355, 365 (2003); R.W. Connell & James W. Messerschmidt, *Hegemonic Masculinity: Rethinking the Concept*, 19 Gender & Soc'y 829, 844 (2005).

56. Dean Lusher & Gary Robins, *Hegemonic and Other Masculinities in Local Social Contexts*, 11 Men & Masculinities 387, 387 (2009) ("Hegemonic masculinity controls a hierarchy of masculinities set up in a way to maintain these gender relations. So hegemonic masculinity has dominance not just over women but also over subordinate masculinities, such as gay or academically inclined.").

57. Herbert, *supra* note 54, at 63.

58. *Id.*

59. Wesley G. Skogan, *The Promise of Community Policing, in* Police Innovation: Contrasting Perspectives 27, 27 (David Weisburd & Anthony A. Braga eds., 2006).

60. *See generally* STEVE HERBERT, CITIZENS, COPS, AND POWER: RECOGNIZING THE LIMITS OF COMMUNITY (2006).

61. George L. Kelling & Mark H. Moore, *The Evolving Strategy of Policing, in* COMMUNITY POLICING: CLASSICAL READINGS, at 97, 101–02 (Willard M. Oliver ed., 1999).

62. *Id.* at 104.

63. Samuel Walker, *"Broken Windows" and Fractured History: The Use and Misuse of History in Recent Police Patrol Analysis, in* COMMUNITY POLICING: CLASSICAL READINGS, *supra* note 61, at 328.

64. Kelling & Moore, *supra* note 61, at 103; George L. Kelling & William J. Bratton, *Implementing Community Policing: The Administrative Problem, in* COMMUNITY POLICING: CLASSICAL READINGS, *supra* note 61, at 261.

65. Herbert, *supra* note 54, at 62.

66. Kelling & Moore, *supra* note 61, at 105–06.

67. Barbara E. Armacost, *Organizational Culture and Police Misconduct,* 72 GEO. WASH. L. REV. 453, 495 (2004).

68. *Id.* at 501.

69. Susan L. Miller & Emily Bonistall, *Gender and Policing: Critical Issues and Analysis, in* ROUTLEDGE HANDBOOK OF CRITICAL CRIMINOLOGY 319 (Walter S. DeKeseredy & Molly Dragiewicz eds., 2012). *See also* Herbert, *supra* note 54, at 63.

70. Miller & Bonistall, *supra* note 69, at 318.

71. Importantly, we are not saying that women will necessarily perform differently than men in the role of patrol officers. However, there is evidence that seems to suggest that this is true. For instance, at least one study demonstrated that female officers are less likely than male officers to use force. James P. McElvain & Augustine J. Kposowa, *Police Officer Characteristics and the Likelihood of Using Deadly Force,* 35 CRIM. JUST. & BEHAV. 505, 521 (2008). *See also* Herbert, *supra* note 54, at 60; Miller & Bonistall, *supra* note 69, at 317.

72. ROBERTO M. UNGER, KNOWLEDGE AND POLITICS 266 (1975).

73. *See, e.g.,* JANE J. MANSBRIDGE, BEYOND ADVERSARY DEMOCRACY 61–62 (1980) (noting that the well educated were more confident in speaking publicly).

74. Richard Delgado, *Law Enforcement in Subordinated Communities: Innovation and Response,* 106 MICH. L. REV. 1193 (2008) (book review).

75. Cooper, *supra* note 52.

76. Herbert, *supra* note 54, at 60.

77. Anastasia Prokos & Irene Padavic, *"There Oughtta Be a Law against Bitches": Masculinity Lessons in Police Academy Training,* 9 GENDER, WORK & ORG. 439, 442 (2002).

78. Herbert, *supra* note 54, at 59 (noting that police training "focuses heavily on managing violence and only lightly on resolving interpersonal disputes").

79. Jennifer Brown, Anita Maidment & Ray Bull, *Appropriate Skill-task Matching or Gender Bias in Deployment of Male and Female Police Officers?,* 3 POLICING & SOC'Y 121, 124 (1993); Tom R. Tyler, *Trust and Law Abidingness: A Proactive Model of Social Regulation,* 81 B.U. L. REV. 361, 369 (2001).

80. Herbert, *supra* note 54, at 57, 59–60; Thomas Nolan, *Behind the Blue Wall of Silence,* 12 MEN & MASCULINITIES 250, 252 (2009).

81. Herbert, *supra* note 54, at 57.

82. *Id.* at 3.

83. *Id.* at 1, 9.

84. *Id.* at 1, 3.

85. Bennett Capers, *Crime, Legitimacy, & Testilying,* 83 IND. L.J. 835 (2008); Delgado, *supra* note 74.

86. Jeffrey Fagan, Tom Tyler & Tracey Meares, Street Stops and Police Legitimacy in New York (Sept. 22, 2011) (unpublished manuscript) (on file with the John Jay College of Criminal Justice, http://johnjay.jjay.cuny.edu/files/Fagan_Tyler_and_Meares_Street_Stops_and_Police_Legitimacy_in_New_York.pdf).

87. For a general discussion, see Phillip Atiba Goff et al., *The Perils of White Stereotype Threat* (on file with author); *see also* Cynthia Lee, *Making Race Salient: Trayvon Martin and Implicit Bias in a Not Yet Post-Racial Society,* 91 N.C. L. REV. 1555 (2013).

88. Behavioral realists argue that judges should base their theories of human behavior on the best empirical scientific evidence that exists. Behavioral realists have to date relied primarily on the social science of implicit social cognition. *See, e.g.*, Linda Hamilton Krieger & Susan T. Fiske, *Behavioral Realism in Employment Discrimination Law: Implicit Bias and Disparate Treatment*, 94 CAL. L. REV. 997, 1002 (2006); Jerry Kang & Mahzarin R. Banaji, *Fair Measures: A Behavioral Realist Revision of Affirmative Action*, 94 CAL. L. REV. 1063, 1064 (2006).

Chapter 3

The Prosecution, the Grand Jury, and the Decision Not to Charge*

*Katherine Goldwasser***

For most of us, shooting and killing an unarmed man in broad daylight on a public street, as Darren Wilson did to Michael Brown, would result in almost certain arrest on the spot and swift prosecution. But the law treats police officers differently. In recognition of the nature and unique demands of the work they do, police are given more leeway to use deadly force, sometimes even against a person who is unarmed. The leeway is broad enough that most instances of police use of deadly force against an unarmed civilian are handled much as Wilson's was—that is, police are called to the scene, but there is not an immediate arrest.

Of course, just because police typically do not immediately arrest a fellow officer who has shot and killed someone does not mean the shooting is not a crime. Moreover, although whether to arrest at the scene is largely up to the police, whether a formal charge will be brought and the matter pursued criminally will be determined, not by the police, but by a prosecutor. Thus, when Darren Wilson shot and killed Michael Brown, it fell to the chief prosecutor for the jurisdiction where the shooting took place,

---

*As many are aware, several months after the grand jury referred to in the title to this chapter voted not to indict Darren Wilson for killing Michael Brown, the U.S. Department of Justice [DOJ] issued a report on the federal criminal investigation regarding the same incident. *See* U.S. Dep't of Justice, Report Regarding the Criminal Investigation into the Shooting Death of Michael Brown by Ferguson, Missouri Police Officer Darren Wilson (Mar. 4, 2015), http://www.justice.gov/sites/default/files/usao-mdpa/legacy/2015/03/18/DOJ%20Report%20on%20Shooting%20of%20Michael%20Brown.pdf. The report concluded, inter alia, that "Wilson's actions [did] not constitute prosecutable violations under the federal criminal civil rights statute." *Id*. at 5. Although the DOJ report shed important light on what happened between Wilson and Brown in the moments leading up to the shooting, it did not address the state criminal process in the Wilson case, which is what this chapter is about.

** I am grateful to Beverly Beimdiek, Kathleen Cash, Caterina DiTraglia, Ellen Goldwasser, Peter Joy and Ann Shields for their comments and suggestions; to Brian Hall, Nick Papadimitriou and Jenny Terrell for their research assistance; and to my dear friend Kimberly Norwood for inviting me to participate in this important project.

St. Louis County Prosecuting Attorney Robert P. McCulloch, to decide what criminal charges, if any, would be brought against Wilson.

Missouri law gave McCulloch three options: (1) he could decide on his own to bring charges against Wilson;[1] (2) he could decide on his own that no charges would be brought;[2] or (3) he could decide not to make the determination himself and instead put the matter in the hands of a grand jury.[3] Within days of the shooting, McCulloch announced that he was going to go the grand jury route.

The Grand Jury Proceedings

The grand jury that heard the Wilson case had already been serving and hearing routine cases presented by prosecutors from McCulloch's office for nearly four months by the time the presentation of evidence in the Wilson case got underway.[4] McCulloch's opening words to the grand jurors took note of their prior experience: "I want to tell you how this is going to proceed. Obviously, it is going to be different from a lot of the other cases that you've heard ... during your term."[5] And indeed it was very different—not just from this particular grand jury's other cases, but from how state grand jury proceedings are ordinarily handled.[6]

Differences from the Grand Jury "Norm"

One aspect of the Wilson proceedings that differed markedly from the usual grand jury proceeding was the scope of the prosecution's presentation, in terms of the number of witnesses and volume of evidence presented and, as a result, the length of time it took to complete it. In a typical case, the prosecution calls one or two witnesses at most and presents few if any exhibits. Each witness gives a bare-bones account of the key facts of the case—the facts that, in the prosecution's view, are sufficient to establish the requisite probable cause to believe that a crime was committed and that the suspect (often called the "target") committed it.[7] As a result, whole cases are often presented in well under an hour.[8] In the Wilson case, by contrast, the grand jury met for about 70 hours over a three-month period, on 25 separate days, during which time the prosecution called 60 witnesses, played hours upon hours of video and audio recordings, and presented hundreds of photographs, maps, diagrams, reports, and other exhibits.[9]

Another major difference from the usual was that the prosecution purported to take a "neutral" stance as to whether any charges should be brought in the case. Ordinarily, a prosecutor presents a grand jury with proposed charges, in the form of an indictment; the grand jury decides if the charges are supported by probable cause; and, if so, they vote to return the indictment or bring the proposed charges (also called returning "a true bill"). If a prosecutor is not convinced that charges should be brought, then the prosecutor simply does not present the matter to a grand jury.[10]

Two other differences, both also significant departures from the grand jury norm, worked in tandem. First, the "target"—here, Darren Wilson—testified before the grand jury and gave his version of the relevant events; and second, through Wilson and other witnesses, the prosecution presented extensive testimony in support of Wilson's claimed legal justifications for killing Brown. For a multitude of reasons, the target of an investigation rarely testifies before the grand jury. In Missouri, as in most jurisdictions, there is no right to do so, even if one is the grand jury's target.[11] If a target wants to testify (assuming they are even aware of the investigation), the most they can do is ask. Even if the prosecution is amenable, defense attorneys ordinarily counsel their clients against testifying, on the theory that the legal risks associated with doing so are simply too great.[12]

As rare as it is for a target to testify before the grand jury, it is even more unusual for the prosecution to present evidence favorable to the target, especially evidence that, if believed, would establish a complete defense to any possible charge. Although prosecutors in possession of such evidence do have a constitutionally imposed duty to disclose it to the defense for use at trial,[13] in most jurisdictions, including Missouri, there is no comparable duty to present it to the grand jury.[14] This is in keeping with the widely accepted view that the purpose of a grand jury is "not to determine guilt or innocence, but to assess whether there is adequate basis for bringing a criminal charge."[15]

Cause for Concern

Of course, just because the grand jury presentation in the Wilson case differed markedly from the usual grand jury presentation does not mean there was anything wrong with it. For other reasons, however, several aspects of the presentation were quite troubling.

McCulloch's Cryptic Message

Prosecuting Attorney McCulloch's opening words to the grand jury about how the case was "obviously . . . going to be different from" the grand jury's previous cases got the proceedings off to a questionable start.[16] Recall that this grand jury had been hearing cases for months. Although the facts of each case were different, the prosecution's approach in all of them was basically the same. Now here was the prosecuting attorney himself, telling the grand jurors that this next case would "obviously" be "different." But what did he mean that it was going to be "different?" And in what sense was the difference "obvious?" More importantly, what message did it send to the grand jurors that the prosecution viewed it that way?

Prosecution-Created Confusion

McCulloch's cryptic message aside, the grand jurors' task was also complicated by certain of the prosecution's choices as to what would and would not be presented to the grand jury—choices that made the presentation far more muddled, unfocused, and difficult to follow than it would have been had the prosecutors handled it in their usual way. McCulloch made the plan for the presentation clear at the outset: "Absolutely everything will be presented to the grand jury, every scrap of paper that we have, every photograph that was taken, every bit of physical evidence that has been gathered, every video clip, anything that we can get."[17] Left unsaid was an important corollary: presenting "[a]bsolutely everything" to the grand jury meant there would not be any of the sort of filtering that prosecutors usually do in order to help grand juries make sense of the cases they hear.

As a result of the decision to present "absolutely everything," the grand jury heard testimony that no prosecutor who was actually trying to help them do their job—that is, trying to help them determine whether there was probable cause to believe that Darren Wilson had committed a crime when he killed Michael Brown—would ever present. With the law enforcement witnesses who investigated the shooting, for example, the prosecutors elicited testimony, not just about the shooting and the surrounding circumstances, but also about the general step-by-step procedures and protocols (sometimes described in excruciating and mind-numbing detail) that they customarily followed in their jobs.[18] Even when prosecutors did elicit testimony about the case, their presentation was unfocused. In one instance they had a witness separately show the grand jury and testify about every one of the 161 crime scene photos the witness had taken. It was almost as though the prosecutors had thought to themselves, *why select only some of the photos to show to the grand jury—for example, the clear ones, or the important ones, or the most helpful ones—when we can just have them look at all 161 photos instead?*[19] The prosecutors went so far with their no-filtering stance that even when they knew witnesses were deliberately lying, they presented the perjured testimony to the grand jury anyway.[20]

Not everything that made the grand jury presentation so confusing was attributable to the prosecution's everything-but-the-kitchen-sink approach; prosecutors also created confusion about the applicable law. One of the most glaring instances occurred shortly before Darren Wilson began testifying, when prosecutors gave the grand jurors copies of the Missouri statute that specifies when police are justified in using deadly force to make an arrest.[21] A portion of the statute purports to authorize conduct that the U.S. Supreme Court ruled decades ago is unconstitutional.[22] Although prosecutors eventually told the grand jurors that there was a problem with the statute, they waited for over two months to mention it.[23] For that entire two-month period, the grand jurors were left to believe that the problematic statute stated the rule for when Wilson could use deadly force to arrest Brown. Even when the prosecutors finally told the grand jury about the statute issue, their explanation of the problem and how the grand jury should deal with it was confusing: they simply distributed their own statement of the law to replace the original handout and told the grand jurors, "So the statute [we] gave you [before], if you want to fold that in half just so that you know don't necessarily rely on that because there is a portion of that that doesn't comply with the law."[24]

The prosecutors also created confusion about the law by waiting until the last day of the proceedings to give the grand jurors the Missouri homicide statute.[25] The statute was essential: it specified the various charges to be considered, and set forth the legal requirements governing the probable cause determinations that the grand jury needed to make for each one in deciding whether to indict Wilson. It also could have helped the grand jurors throughout the proceedings in determining what information was relevant and thus what questions to ask the witnesses when they testified. The prosecutors clearly understood how much more difficult the grand jury's job would be without the statute, and early on they assured the grand jurors that a copy would be provided:

> [N]ormally when we've charged somebody with an offense, you have the charge in front of you, and you don't have that in this case. . . . [T]hat kind of leaves you not sure how you are supposed to look at this evidence. So after this morning session, [we]

will sit down and . . . come up with statutes for you on the various degrees of homicide and . . . some other relevant statutes on the use of . . . deadly force . . . and possibly self-defense, so you will have [those] by . . . next time. We'll have that for you so you can kind of at least understand the law as you are hearing this evidence.[26]

Although prosecutors did provide a copy of the use-of-deadly-force statute in time for the grand jurors to be able to "understand the law as [they were] hearing the evidence,"[27] not so with the homicide statute. Thus, they informed the grand jury of a defense that Wilson might be able to raise before informing them of any crimes he might have committed.

Anti-Indictment Bias

Quite apart from the problems discussed thus far, the grand jury presentation was seriously compromised because it was driven from start to finish by a Darren-Wilson-should-not-be-indicted bias so pervasive and powerful that a "no true bill" vote was inevitable. To be clear, this is not a judgment about the actual intent of the prosecutors who made the presentation, nor is it a judgment about the correctness of the grand jury's decision not to indict. Rather, the point is simply that whether consciously or unconsciously, the prosecutors conducted the grand jury proceedings in a way that made fair consideration of the option of returning an indictment against Darren Wilson virtually impossible.

The prosecution's decision to grant Wilson's request to appear before the grand jury benefited him greatly, but even after deciding that much, prosecutors still had complete control over when in the proceedings he would testify and what the grand jurors would see and hear before they heard from him. Most prosecutors who know that a grand jury target is going to testify would postpone the testimony until at or near the end of the proceedings, on the theory that hearing other (and often conflicting) accounts beforehand puts the grand jury and the prosecutor in a better position to scrutinize the testimony critically and with appropriate skepticism, and then question the target accordingly. Here, though, prosecutors took a different tack.

Wilson was allowed to testify relatively early in the proceedings—he was ninth of the 60 witnesses presented by the prosecution—and the proceedings leading up to his appearance could not have set the stage for his testimony any better had he planned them himself. Seven of the eight witnesses who testified ahead of him, although not themselves present for any of the events surrounding the shooting, either had taken a statement from Wilson about those events or had spoken to someone else who did, and prosecutors had all seven of them recount for the grand jurors what Wilson had said. As a result, by the time Wilson testified, the grand jury had repeatedly heard all or parts of his version of the events leading up to the shooting—including, for example, Wilson's claims: (1) that Michael Brown had "assaulted and attempted to kill him" when Wilson was just sitting in his car;[28] (2) that when Brown first started running away Wilson chased him because "he knew Brown would assault another responding officer or witness" and he "did not want Brown to cause injury or death to anyone else;"[29] and (3) that when Brown suddenly turned around and charged directly at Wilson, Wilson thought his life was in danger and so felt he had no choice but to kill Brown.[30]

The grand jurors did hear one account that differed from Wilson's before Wilson testified—namely, that of Dorian Johnson, the young man who had been with Michael Brown in the hours leading up to the shooting—but prosecutors took various measures to blunt the impact of his testimony. Chief among these measures was the playing of and questioning Johnson about a surveillance video that was at least somewhat unfavorable to Johnson and highly unfavorable to Brown.[31] The video, taken on the morning of the shooting at a local convenience store known as the Ferguson Market, showed Brown taking items without paying and pushing a store clerk in the process[32]—an incident that came to play a prominent role in Wilson's account of the events leading to his shooting of Brown.[33]

Also by the time Wilson testified, the grand jurors had heard favorable things about him and the opposite about Michael Brown. Wilson, they heard, "always ha[d] a smile on his face," and was "very easy going" "a good officer," and not one to "go . . . look[ing] for trouble" or start a fight with a suspect.[34] Concerning Brown, by contrast, in addition to hearing repeated references to Wilson's account of his aggressive conduct leading up to the shooting; the grand jurors were told that he came from a neighborhood that was "known for violence, guns, gangs and drugs;"[35] they watched the Ferguson Market video; and they heard one of the prosecutors characterize Brown's behavior in the video as "brash," "threatening," and "intimidating."[36] Then, having painted these starkly contrasting pictures of Wilson and Brown, shortly before Wilson testified, prosecutors distributed copies of the previously discussed Missouri use-of-deadly-force statute.[37] From Wilson's perspective, coming as it did shortly before he began his testimony about his own use of deadly force against Brown, the timing of the distribution could not have been better. Granted, the grand jurors were told months later that there was a problem with the statute, but as far as they knew when they heard from Wilson, the statute appeared to set forth a complete defense that Wilson could rely on to defeat any criminal charge the grand jury might vote to bring in connection with Wilson's use of deadly force against Brown.

With the stage thus set, enter Wilson. At the risk of stating the obvious, no witness had a bigger stake in the outcome of these grand jury proceedings than he did. As a practical matter, his testimony raised two questions for the grand jurors: first, was his version of events believable; and second, even assuming he was telling the truth about what happened, was his conduct reasonable?[38] Although the prosecutors presumably had their own views on both questions, as they themselves understood, legally, the grand jurors' views were the only ones that mattered.[39] Thus, it was up to the prosecutors to put aside any views of their own and conduct an examination of Wilson aimed at helping the grand jurors answer the believability and reasonableness questions for themselves. Certainly, any prosecutor would appreciate that to examine Wilson effectively they would need to scrutinize his testimony carefully and actively challenge what he said; otherwise, as one of these very prosecutors put it, "you don't get to the truth."[40] At almost every turn, however, the prosecutors simply failed to do their job. Two examples, each applicable to one of the questions the grand jury needed to resolve, will help make this point.

On the believability question, Wilson claimed that he knew about the earlier Ferguson Market stealing incident before he encountered Michael Brown and Dorian Johnson on the day of the shooting. This was an integral part of his version of events.[41] Although he said it was the two men walking in the middle of the street that had initially drawn his attention, Wilson described how that initial encounter had morphed into something more serious when he noticed that Brown was carrying cigarillos (the items reportedly taken from the Ferguson Market) and that Johnson was wearing a black shirt (clothing reportedly worn by one of the suspects), and it "clicked for [him]" that "these [we]re the two from the stealing."[42]

But what if it did not happen that way? More specifically, what if Wilson truly did not know anything about the stealing incident when he encountered Brown and Johnson? Certainly, there was some basis for thinking he might not have. The very first person Wilson spoke to after the shooting, a Ferguson police sergeant who was Wilson's supervisor at the time, testified that Wilson told him then and in subsequent conversations that he (Wilson) knew nothing about the Ferguson Market incident when he spotted the two men, and that everything had unfolded from their refusal to walk on the sidewalk.[43] The prosecutors seemed surprised by this testimony and inquired again several times, but the sergeant was emphatic: *Wilson said he did not know anything about the stealing incident.*[44] That is a significant discrepancy: either the sergeant was mistaken and Wilson really did mention having realized the connection to the stealing incident, or Wilson's story changed. Either way, once the sergeant testified that Wilson *did not* know about the incident, the prosecutors owed it to the grand jury to try to "get to the truth" by challenging Wilson's subsequent testimony that he *did* know about it. But that never happened; in fact, the prosecutors never even mentioned the discrepancy to Wilson.

Regarding the reasonableness of Wilson's conduct, Wilson's decision that he "had to kill [Brown]"[45] was an obvious topic for inquiry. There were many missed opportunities, but one in particular came relatively early in Wilson's testimony, when one of the prosecutors questioned him about the various weapons he had with him on the day of the shooting and asked specifically about a Taser:

Q. Did you carry a Taser?

A. No.

Q. Why not?

A. I normally don't carry a Taser. We only have a select amount. Usually there is one available, but I usually elect not to carry one. It is not the most comfortable thing. They are very large, I don't have a lot of room in the front for it to be positioned.

Q. Had you been trained on how to use a Taser?

A. Yes, ma'am.

   * * *

Q. You prefer not to have a Taser?

A. Correct.[46]

Here again, the prosecutors owed it to the grand jury to do more than they did. Instead of simply confirming Wilson's preference ("You prefer not to have a Taser?"), for example, they might have asked questions aimed at establishing (1) that Wilson could have been carrying a

Taser that day but decided not to; (2) that a Taser enables a police officer to subdue a dangerous person without having to use deadly force
like a gun; (3) that not carrying a Taser increases the risk of having to
use deadly force to subdue someone; and (4) that Wilson understood
all of this, yet opted not to carry a Taser anyway, mainly for reasons of
personal comfort.

Likewise, consider Wilson's subsequent testimony about Brown
hitting him in the face through Wilson's open car window when Wilson was seated in his car. Wilson said that from his perspective,
that assault by Brown made Wilson's gun a legitimate "deadly force
option"; in other words, he felt that Brown's hitting him in the face was
enough to justify shooting Brown.[47] The prosecutor's response? "Okay,
all right. So then you go to the [police] station?"[48]

Where was the scrutiny? Why not establish through Wilson the relatively minor nature of his facial injuries as a result of the hitting,[49] and
then challenge the reasonableness of his judgment that the hitting justified deadly force? And why not also ask Wilson whether he would
have reached the same conclusion about the appropriateness of using
his gun if he had been carrying a Taser at the time? Might the grand
jurors have wondered, if Wilson had been carrying a Taser, maybe
Michael Brown would be alive today?[50]

There were numerous instances of similar prosecutorial ball-dropping
throughout the proceedings, and of course we all know what happened
in the end: on November 24, 2014, nearly four months after Darren Wilson shot and killed Michael Brown, prosecuting Attorney McCulloch
called a nighttime press conference to announce that the grand jury
had voted not to indict Wilson. Later that night and over the next few
weeks, McCulloch released literally thousands of pages of grand jury
documents and transcripts—an almost unheard-of action, but one he
had said he would take for the sake of "transparen[cy]" in the event
that Wilson was not indicted.[51] The release of the transcripts, in turn,
brought to light what had gone on behind the closed doors of the
grand jury room, including the problems previously discussed.

Ignoring Race (the Elephant in the Grand Jury Room)

In addition to the problems just noted, there was one other problem
that was painfully evident from the grand jury transcripts: race mattered in this case, and yet its role was never even acknowledged in the
grand jury, let alone discussed. As evidence for the proposition that
race mattered here, we have, inter alia, the March 2015 Department of

Justice report on the Ferguson Police Department,[52] the available empirical evidence (scant as it is) about police shootings of unarmed African American men and boys,[53] a large body of social science research on the subject of implicit (unconscious) racial bias,[54] and, most importantly, accounts from African Americans about the experience of being Black in this country[55] and, even more to the point, accounts from African American men about their interactions with police.[56]

The Justice Department report paints a picture of how the Ferguson police were policing Ferguson on August 9, 2014, the day Michael Brown was killed. And Darren Wilson's grand jury testimony reveals the lens through which Wilson was viewing Michael Brown that day. Although prosecutors did not question Wilson directly about his racial attitudes, research concerning the phenomenon of implicit bias suggests that his answers probably would not have been as informative on the point as other aspects of what he said.[57]

Implicit bias refers to the negative attitudes and stereotypes that influence our perceptions, decisions, and actions at the subconscious level, without any intent or awareness on our part.[58] With implicit racial bias in particular, studies suggest that most of us are influenced at some level by messages we constantly receive in various ways that stereotype Black men as violent, dangerous, and inclined toward criminality.[59] According to one study, just over 40 percent of White Americans believe that "many" or "almost all" Black men—men like Michael Brown—are violent.[60] Studies also indicate that views about the dangerousness of Black men are often associated with views that Black people are superhuman, nonhuman, and/or less susceptible to pain—all of which, taken together, serve to increase the perceived danger, which in turn, warrants greater fear.[61]

Before the grand jury, Wilson testified that at one point he tried to grab Brown, [but] "*the only way I can describe it is I felt like a five-year-old holding onto Hulk Hogan.*"[62] A short time later, according to Wilson, Brown "*looked up at me and had the most intense aggressive face. The only way I can describe it, it looks like a demon, that's how angry he looked.*"[63] After Wilson fired his first round of shots, Brown "*made like a grunting, like aggravated sound.*"[64] When Wilson fired another round, "*it looked like he was almost bulking up to run through the shots, like it was making him mad that I'm shooting at him. And the face that he had was looking straight through me, like I wasn't even there, I wasn't even anything in his way.*"[65]

Wilson also testified that after Brown hit him in the face twice, "I felt that another one of those punches in my face could knock me out or worse. I mean it was, he's obviously bigger than I was and stronger and the, I've already taken two to the face and I didn't think I would, the third one could be fatal if he hit me right."[66] Bearing in mind the stereotype of the superhuman Black man, what is significant about this testimony is how poorly it fits with the nature and extent of Wilson's *actual* injuries as a result of his encounter with Brown: some scratches on his neck and a contusion on the right side of his face[67]—not nothing, to be sure, but arguably also not enough to reasonably fear that a third punch might kill him.

The prosecutors in some ways contributed to Wilson's portrayal of Brown as out of control and frightening by suggesting that Brown's prior marijuana use (as shown by a toxicology report) might have caused his extreme aggression toward Wilson (as described by Wilson). They had one witness testify that paranoia, hallucinations, and even psychosis are possible from marijuana use, and that there was no way to know from testing whether Michael Brown was experiencing any of those in the time just before Wilson shot him.[68] They also questioned several witnesses about a highly concentrated and potent marijuana product known as "wax," and about Michael Brown's possible use of it (although their basis for asking is unclear, as there seems to have been no evidence that Brown had ever used it and actually some evidence suggesting that he had never heard of it).[69]

The reason all of this matters is that the reasonableness of Darren Wilson's assessment of Brown's dangerousness is a factor that the grand jury needed to consider in determining whether Wilson should be criminally charged for shooting Brown.[70] Indeed, the reasonableness of police assessments of danger, and hence their fear, is an issue in many police use-of-force cases.[71] Unless we are going to say that it is always reasonable for police officers to fear Black men because Black men are dangerous (which makes race a proxy for danger and an automatic trigger for the lawful use of deadly force), grand jurors will sometimes need to consider the role of race in an officer's assessment of danger in determining whether the assessment was reasonable.[72] Prosecutors can play a key role in all of this. Conversations about race can be difficult, especially among strangers. Prosecutors, by first informing themselves and then educating grand jurors about implicit bias, by their questioning of witnesses, and by their decisions regarding what witnesses to call are in a position to help grand jurors discuss issues of race openly and honestly.[73] In the Darren Wilson case, unfortunately, that did not happen; in fact, in some instances, even if unconsciously, the prosecutors did just the opposite.

The prosecution's marijuana theory, which lent support to Wilson's negative portrayal of Brown, is one example of this, but some of the clearest examples occurred in connection with the questioning of various witnesses about Canfield, the overwhelmingly African American apartment complex where Michael Brown was shot and killed. The very first witness who testified, an investigator for the medical examiner's office who was called to the scene of the shooting shortly after it occurred, was asked whether he was frightened when he was at Canfield.[74] Another witness, a Ferguson police sergeant, was asked, "Didn't people at Canfield hate police?" The witness responded that it was a "business relationship."[75] Apparently not satisfied with the witness's answer, the prosecutor pressed further: "So there was no understanding that the residents just hated the police, it wasn't like that?"[76] (Interestingly, there was no comparable inquiry concerning how the police felt about the Canfield residents.)

When Wilson testified, the prosecutor raised the subject again:

Q. Did you guys have a volatile, well, how can I put this. Did you not really get along well with the folks that lived in [Canfield]?

A. It is an antipolice area for sure.

Q. And when you say antipolice, tell me more?

A. There's a lot of gangs that reside or associate with that area. There's a lot of violence in that area, there's a lot of gun activity, drug activity, it is just not a very well-liked community. That community doesn't like the police.[77]

One might ask, what were the prosecutors trying to convey to the grand jurors through this line of questioning? More importantly, what would the grand jurors have understood it to mean?

The Decision to Use a Grand Jury

With so much to criticize about the grand jury presentation in this case it is well to remember that under Missouri law, Prosecuting Attorney McCulloch did not have to use a grand jury at all; rather, he could have made the charging decision on his own. If he decided not to bring charges, he simply could have announced his decision; if he decided to go forward with charges, he could have brought them himself by filing a complaint, presenting evidence at a preliminary hearing, and, if the judge made the necessary probable cause determination, filing an information against Wilson and proceeding to trial.[78] The significance of the choice McCulloch made—presenting the case to a grand jury instead of to a judge at a preliminary hearing—would be difficult to overstate. A preliminary hearing is an adversary proceeding (both prosecution and defense are represented), held before a judge in a courtroom that is open to the public, at the conclusion of which the judge decides, based on the evidence presented, whether the probable cause standard has been met. A grand jury proceeding, by contrast, is nonadversarial (prosecutor only; no defense counsel, no judge), it is held in secret, and the decision maker is a group of lay people who, not being law-trained and having neither the authority nor the means to do their own investigating, are completely dependent on the prosecutor. When McCulloch chose to use the grand jury for Wilson, he was opting for a process that he knew would ensure secrecy, near-complete prosecutorial control, and a setting in which Wilson could safely present his version of what happened, including his claimed justifications for shooting Brown, free from cross-examination and any real-time public or media scrutiny. McCulloch also knew that the grand jury process would offer him political cover because, strictly speaking, the final decision would be the grand jury's and not his own. And although his after-the-fact release of grand jury documents was unusual, it did nothing to alter the essential nature of the secret, prosecutor-controlled proceedings that resulted in the decision not to bring criminal charges against Wilson for killing Michael Brown.

Lessons Learned?

The St. Louis County criminal justice system's treatment of the Wilson case followed what has become a depressingly familiar pattern: a police officer (usually White[79]), while acting in the course of the officer's police duties, kills or seriously injures an unarmed Black man or boy; the local prosecutor puts responsibility for deciding whether criminal charges should be brought against the officer in the hands of a local grand jury; and, after a secret, prosecution-controlled presentation of evidence, the grand jury votes not to indict.[80] Recently, however, the Wilson case and a string of other well-publicized police killings have put a spotlight on the virtual immunity from prosecution that police seem to have been granted in these cases.[81] Public awareness of the pattern has prompted widespread skepticism about the fairness and impartiality of the system that has been producing it,[82] and that in turn has sparked calls for change in how the cases are handled.

The calls for change have focused on two points in particular: (1) the people who are making all the key charging-related decisions in these cases—namely, local prosecutors—work hand-in-hand with the police officers whose use of force is ostensibly being examined for possible prosecution;[83] and (2) the presentations to the grand jury (handled by these same local prosecutors) are made in secret, out of public view.[84]

Some have argued that oversight of these cases should be taken out of the hands of local prosecutors and shifted to a prosecuting authority that does not have such close ties with local police.[85] The theory is that an inherent conflict of interest exists whenever local prosecutors are called on to decide whether to bring criminal charges against the very police officers whose cooperation, help, and goodwill the prosecutors depend on in order to do their work. The prosecutors who presented the Wilson case to the grand jury were laboring under just this sort of conflict, and while we cannot know for sure, the likelihood that it played a part in the bias they showed throughout the presentation—including, above all, their kid-glove treatment of Wilson—seems inescapable.

Others, focusing on the use of grand juries and the secrecy that attends them, have urged the use of a less secretive and more open charging process, if not in all cases, then at least in police lethal force cases.[86] Secrecy breeds suspicion, all the more when it conceals something that seems so clearly the public's business as the determination at issue in these cases—that is, whether a public servant who has used lethal force to kill an unarmed member of the very public supposedly being served at the time should be charged with a crime. Particularly for those who have little or no confidence in the fairness of the criminal process to begin with, chief among them the Black men and boys who are so disproportionately the victims when police kill, the secrecy only serves to confirm their sense that the fix is in.

Less often mentioned in discussions of how to reform the charging process in police lethal force cases is dealing with the subject of race when the person the police have killed is a Black man. For years, it has been standard operating procedure for prosecutors to ignore race in these cases, as though race were irrelevant. The Wilson case is a perfect example. But if we did not know better before, surely we do now. Instead of ignoring race, as was done in the Wilson case, there is a need for measures designed to help the various decision makers in the charging process address the special issues of race that these cases present. Whatever else the measures may entail, at a minimum, they should include familiarizing everyone—preliminary hearing judges, grand jurors where grand juries are used, and above all, prosecutors—with the phenomenon of implicit racial bias, and encouraging them to hold honest conversations about race.

Notes

1. Missouri permits felony charges to be brought by grand jury indictment or by complaint and information, and allows prosecutors to choose which way to proceed. *See* Mo. Rev. Stat. § 545.010. When a prosecutor chooses the latter, the process begins with the filing of a written complaint, Mo. R. Crim. P. 22.01, after which a hearing is held to determine if there are sufficient grounds (probable cause) to hold a trial on the charges, Mo. R. Crim. P. 22.09(a). If probable cause is found, in order to proceed with the prosecution, the prosecutor must file a formal written charge, called an "information." Mo. R. Crim. P. 23.03. Both the initial complaint and the subsequent information are signed by, and subject to the sole control of, the prosecutor.

Not all prosecutors have the option of bringing charges on their own. In federal criminal proceedings, for example, the Fifth Amendment requires that felony charges be brought by grand jury indictment. U.S. Const. amend. V. Although that right does not apply in the states, Hurtado v. California, 110 U.S. 516, 538 (1884), nearly half the states have similar requirements under their own constitutions and/or laws. *See* Susan Brenner & Lori Shaw, *Grand Jury Functions*, Fed. Grand Jury Website, http://campus.udayton.edu/~grandjur/stategj/funcsgj.htm.

2. American prosecutors have "virtually unlimited discretion not to proceed with a case." Gerard E. Lynch, *Prosecution: Prosecutorial Discretion, in* 3 Encyclopedia of Crime & Justice 1248 (Joshua Dressler ed., 2d ed. 2002).

3. Mo. Rev. Stat. §§ 545.010, 545.031; Mo. Const. art. I, § 17. A grand jury is a panel of citizens convened to determine whether evidence presented by a prosecutor is sufficient to bring criminal charges against the supposed perpetrator and hold a trial. Grand jury proceedings are held in secret without a judge and without defense counsel; only the prosecutor, the witnesses chosen by the prosecutor, and the grand jurors (and sometimes a stenographer) are permitted to attend. *See* Mo. Rev. Stat. §§ 540.130, 540.320. This is to be distinguished from a trial jury, which comes into play later in the process, only after criminal charges are brought, whether by a grand jury or by a prosecutor acting alone.

Some favored yet another option, which would have involved replacing McCulloch with a special prosecutor, whether by having him voluntarily recuse himself or by having Missouri Governor Jay Nixon remove him involuntarily. Those advocating this option questioned McCulloch's ability to handle the case against Wilson impartially, based in part on his close family ties to local police, but even more on his record of failing to prosecute police in similar cases. *See* Jaeah Lee, *Ferguson Cop Darren Wilson Is Just the Latest to Go Unprosecuted for a Fatal Shooting*, Mother Jones (Nov. 24, 2014), http://www.motherjones.com/politics/2014/11/darren-wilson-grand-jury-decision-ferguson-police-prosecutions. Ultimately, however, efforts to get a special prosecutor appointed were unsuccessful: the situation did not fit Missouri's requirements for replacing the regular prosecutor, *see* Mo. Rev. Stat. § 56.110; Governor Nixon declined to get involved, *see* Jo Mannies, *Nixon Sticking with McCulloch, Who Has No Plans to Step Out of Ferguson Case*, St. Louis Pub. Radio (Aug. 19, 2014), http://news.stlpublicradio.org/post/nixon-sticking-mcculloch-who-has-no-plans-step-out-ferguson-case; and McCulloch rejected calls for him to recuse himself voluntarily, Interview by McGraw Milhaven with Robert McCulloch, Prosecuting Attorney for St. Louis County, MO, KTRS.com (Aug. 20, 2014), http://www.ktrs.com/mcculloch-tells-nixon-to-man-up-and-make-decision/.

4. *See* Christine Byers, *Grand Jury Now Has until January to Decide Whether to Charge Ferguson Officer*, STLTODAY.COM (Sept. 16, 2014), http://www.stltoday.com/news/local/crime-and-courts/grand-jury-now-has-until-january-to-decide-whether-to/article_aa4111fc-2952-54c9-8316-76c4867dea48.html.

5. Transcript of: Grand Jury vol. 1, 5 (2014) [hereinafter Tr. vol. __, __ (2014)], http://apps.stlpublicradio.org/ferguson-project/evidence.html.

6. Allegations about some of these differences and how noticeable they were to the grand jurors were central to an unusual lawsuit brought by one of the grand jurors after the proceedings in the Wilson case had concluded. *See* Complaint ¶¶ 19–22, Grand Juror Doe v. McCulloch, No. 4:15-cv-00006, 2015 WL 47623 (E.D. Mo. Jan. 5, 2015), *dismissed on abstention grounds*, 2015 WL 2092492 (E.D. Mo. May 5, 2015). Brought first in federal court, dismissed there "to allow Missouri courts to address . . . [the unsettled state law issues raised by the lawsuit]," Grand Juror Doe v. McCulloch, 2015 WL 2092492, at 1 (E.D. Mo. May 5, 2015), and then brought in state court, *see* Grand Juror Doe v. McCulloch, 15SL-CC01891 (Mo. Cir. Ct. 21st Cir. June 2, 2015), the suit (still pending as of this writing) seeks release from the secrecy obligations normally imposed on grand jurors under state law to allow the plaintiff to speak out about her or his experience as a grand juror and participate in public discussions about issues in the case, especially issues involving race relations, *see* Compl. ¶¶ 1, 3, 4, 33, Grand Juror Doe v. McCulloch, 15SL-CC01891 (Mo Cir. Ct. 21st Cir. June 2, 2015).

7. *See* 19 MISSOURI PRACTICE, CRIMINAL PRACTICE & PROCEDURE § 12:2 (3d ed. 2013).

8. *See* Tr. vol. 2, 7 (2014).

9. Robert McCulloch, Prosecuting Att'y for St. Louis Cnty., MO, Missouri Grand Jury Decision Announcement (Nov. 24, 2014), C-SPAN, http://www.c-span.org/video/?322925-1/ferguson-missouri-grand-jury-decision-announcement.

10. Although some commentators posited that the prosecution's neutral stance was appropriate because the Wilson grand jury was not serving as a "regular (or indicting) grand jury," but as an "investigative grand jury," *see, e.g.*, Matt Hodapp & Dan Margolies, *Attorneys in Missouri Debate Role of Grand Jury*, KCUR.ORG (Dec. 5, 2014), http://kcur.org/post/attorneys-missouri-debate-role-grand-jury, Missouri law does not recognize this distinction or even mention anything about different types of grand juries, "investigative" or otherwise, *see* MO. REV. STAT. § 545.031; MO. CONST. art. I, § 17.

11. *See* 19 MISSOURI PRACTICE: CRIMINAL PRACTICE & PROCEDURE § 12:8 (3d ed. 2013).

12. *See* William Glaberson, *New Trend before Grand Juries: Meet the Accused*, N.Y. TIMES, June 20, 2004, http://www.nytimes.com/2004/06/20/nyregion/new-trend-before-grand-juries-meet-the-accused.html (noting as one of the main risks "the potential use of grand jury testimony to poke holes in a defendant's account of events at trial").

13. Brady v. Maryland, 373 U.S. 83, 87 (1963).

14. State v. Easter, 661 S.W.2d 644, 645 (Mo. Ct. App. 1983).

15. United States v. Williams, 504 U.S. 36, 51 (1992).

16. *See supra* text accompanying note 5.

17. Robert McCulloch, Prosecuting Att'y for St. Louis Cnty., MO, Press Conference, KSDK.COM (Aug. 13, 2014), http://www.ksdk.com/story/news/local/2014/08/13/st-louis-county-bob-mcculloch-press-conference-ferguson-shooting/14019205.

18. *See, e.g.*, Tr. vol. 2, 21–37 (2014).

19. *Id.* at 61–175 (2014).

20. Interview by McGraw Milhaven with Robert McCulloch, Prosecuting Att'y for St. Louis Cnty., MO, KTRS.COM (Dec. 19, 2014), http://www.ktrs.com/st-louis-prosecuting-attorney-bob-mcculloch-breaks-silence/.

21. *See* Tr. vol. 5, 5 (2014). Darren Wilson testified that he shot Brown while trying to arrest him, *see id.* at 232, thus making the statute, MO REV. STAT. § 563.046 (1979), potentially relevant.

22. The problematic portion is MO REV. STAT. § 563.046 (3)(2)(a) (1979), which says that police are justified in using deadly force to arrest a fleeing felon even if the person fleeing is unarmed and seemingly not otherwise dangerous. This contravenes the Court's decision in *Tennessee v. Garner*, 471 U.S. 1 (1985), which struck down as unconstitutional a similar Tennessee statute. *Id.* at 10.

23. Prosecutors distributed the statute on September 15, *see* Tr. vol. 5, 5 (2014), but did not mention the problem until November 21, *see* Tr. vol. 24, 134 (2014).

24. Tr. vol. 24, 135 (2014).

25. *See id.* at 131–33 (2014).

26. Tr. vol. 2, 14–15 (2014). The assurance came on Day 2 of the proceedings; the homicide statute was not distributed until Day 25. *See* Tr. vol. 24, 132–33 (2014).

27. *See supra* text accompanying note 21. Of course, the understanding provided by the statute was itself problematic. *See supra* note 22 and accompanying text.

28. Tr. vol. 5, 31 (2014).

29. *Id.* at 33–34.

30. *Id.* at 164.

31. Tr. vol. 4, 13, 31–37 (2014). Other measures included impeaching Johnson with prior inconsistent statements, *see id.* at 5, and questioning him about past encounters with the law, *see id.* at 171–76.

32. *See id.* at 31–37.

33. *See infra* text accompanying notes 41 & 42.

34. Tr. vol. 5, 74 (2014).

35. *Id.* at 170.

36. Tr. vol. 4, 84–86 (2014).

37. *See supra* text accompanying note 21.

38. The believability question is one that would apply to any witness. The reasonableness question ties in with certain of the potential charges against Wilson (specifically, both voluntary and involuntary manslaughter, *see* Mo Rev. Stat. §§ 565.023.1, 565.024.1), and with both affirmative defenses that prosecutors told the grand jurors were applicable, law enforcement use of force to arrest, *see id.* § 563.046, and self-defense, *see id.* § 563.031.1.

39. *See* Tr. vol. 24, 142 (2014).

40. *Id.* at 141 (quoting in full: "We want you to understand as attorneys it is our job to challenge witnesses' statements and that sometimes, you know, you don't get to the truth unless you challenge a witness statement.").

41. Tr. vol. 5, 202, 209 (2014).

42. *Id.* at 206–07, 209.

43. *See id.* at 52–53, 57–58, 31.

44. *See id.* at 52–53, 57–58

45. *Id.* at 236.

46. *Id.* at 205–06.

47. *See id.* at 236–37.

48. *Id.* at 237.

49. Wilson's injuries consisted of some scratches on his neck and bruising and swelling of his right jaw, resulting in jaw pain, for which an anti-inflammatory and ice were prescribed. *See* Tr. vol. 22, 77, 89–90 (2014).

50. In fairness, one of the prosecutors did initiate one reasonableness-related inquiry, concerning why Wilson did not remain in his car and wait for backup instead of trying to handle Brown on his own, *see id.* vol. 5, 261 (2014), but after a few questions on the subject the other prosecutor intervened with a different line of questioning and the matter was dropped, *see id.* at 261–62.

51. *Id.* vol. 1, 21 (2014). Whether McCulloch's release of the documents was legal is far from clear—it relied on a highly questionable interpretation of Missouri's Sunshine (open government) Law, Mo. Rev. Stat. §§ 610.020 et seq. (1973)—but no one came forward to object so the issue was never litigated.

52. Civil Rights Div., U.S. Dep't of Justice, Investigation of the Ferguson Police Department (Mar. 4, 2015), http://www.justice.gov/sites/default/files/opa/press-releases/attachments/2015/03/04/ferguson_police_department_report.pdf (finding, inter alia, that "Ferguson's approach to law enforcement both reflects and reinforces racial bias, including stereotyping[,]" . . . that this "disproportionately

. . . [harms] African Americans, and [that] there is evidence that this is due in part to intentional discrimination on the basis of race," *id.* at 4).

53. Data on deaths and serious injuries caused by police use of deadly force is woefully incomplete. *See* Carl Balik, *A New Estimate of Killings by Police Is Way Higher—And Still Too Low*, FiveThirtyEight.com (Mar. 6, 2015), http://fivethirtyeight.com/features/a-new-estimate-of-killings-by-police-is-way-higher-and-still-too-low/ (discussing various databases and their shortcomings). Mindful of the limitations, researchers and statisticians have nonetheless found what they believe to be reliable evidence of racial disparities. All agree, for example, that Black people are more likely than White people to be shot and killed by police, with estimates of the disparity ranging from three times more likely, *see, e.g.*, Mapping Police Violence, http://mappingpoliceviolence.org/ [hereinafter Mapping Police Violence 2014 Study]; Kimberly Kindy (reported by Julie Tate, Jennifer Jenkins, Steven Rich, Keith L. Alexander & Wesley Lowery), *Fatal Police Shootings in 2015 Approaching 400 Nationwide*, Wash. Post, May 30, 2015, http://www.washingtonpost.com/national/fatal-police-shootings-in-2015-approaching-400-nationwide/2015/05/30/d322256a-058e-11e5-a428-c984eb077d4e_story.html [hereinafter Wash. Post 2015 Study] to as high as 21 times more likely, *see* Ryan Gabrielson, Ryan Grochowski Jones, & Eric Sagara, *Deadly Force, in Black and White*, ProPublica (Oct. 10, 2014; updated Dec. 23, 2014), http://www.propublica.org/article/deadly-force-in-black-and-white. Two that have looked specifically at situations where police on duty have shot and killed *unarmed* individuals, as in the Wilson case, have found even more pronounced disparities: just over one-half of all of these involved Black victims according to one of the studies, *see* Mapping Police Violence 2014 Study; two-thirds according to the other, *see* Wash. Post 2015 Study.

54. *See, e.g.*, Kirwan Inst. for the Study of Race & Ethnicity, *State of the Science: Implicit Bias Review 2015*, http://kirwaninstitute.osu.edu/implicit-bias-review/, and sources cited therein.

55. *See, e.g.*, Kimberly Norwood, *Why I Fear for My Sons*, CNN (Aug. 25, 2014), http://www.cnn.com/2014/08/25/opinion/norwood-ferguson-sons-brown-police/; Arienne Thompson, *Voices: The Exhausting Task of Being Black in America*, USA Today Dec. 4, 2014, http://www.usatoday.com/story/life/people/2014/12/04/the-exhausting-task-of-being-black-in-america/19894223/.

56. *See, e.g.*, Stan Chu Ilo, *Being a Black Male in America: Racism and the Police*, Huffington Post, Blackvoices (Apr. 10, 2015), http://www.huffingtonpost.com/stan-chu-ilo/being-a-black-male-in-ame_b_7035468.html.

57. This is not to rule out the possibility of *explicit* (conscious) racial bias, but such views are sufficiently unacceptable under current social norms that a person holding them is unlikely to admit it, at least when talking to strangers.

58. *See* Kirwan Inst. for the Study of Race & Ethnicity, State of the Science: Implicit Bias Review 2013, at 7, http://kirwaninstitute.osu.edu/initiatives/implicit-bias-review/.

59. *See, e.g.*, Jennifer L. Eberhardt et al., *Seeing Black: Race, Crime, and Visual Processing*, 2004 J. Personality & Soc. Psychol. 876.

60. *See* John Sides, Trayvon Martin and the Burden of Being a Black Male, MONKEY CAGE (July 15, 2013), http://themonkeycage.org/2013/07/15/trayvon-martin-and-the-burden-of-being-a-black-male/ (discussing study conducted with Ismail White). By comparison, only about 12 percent of Whites believe that "many" or "almost all" White men are violent. *Id.*

61. Adam Waytz, Kelly Marie Hoffman & Sophie Trawalter, *A Superhumanization Bias in Whites' Perceptions of Blacks*, 6 Soc. Psych. & Personality Sci. 352 (2015).

62. Tr. vol. 5, 212 (2014). (emphasis added)

63. *Id.* at 224–25. (emphasis added)

64. *Id.* at 227. (emphasis added)

65. *Id.* at 228. (emphasis added)

66. *Id.* at 216 (2014).

67. *See supra* note 49.

68. *See* Tr. vol. 19, 66–67, 70, 74 (2014).

69. *See, e.g.*, Tr. vol. 11, 100–04 (2014); Tr. vol. 12, 170–71 (2014); Tr. vol. 13, 99 (2014); Tr. vol. 19, 70–74 (2014).

70. *See supra* note 38.

71. *See* Carol D. Leonnig, *Current Law Gives Police Wide Latitude to Use Deadly Force*, WASH. POST, Aug. 28, 2014, http://www.washingtonpost.com/politics/current-law-gives-police-wide-latitude-to-use -deadly-force/2014/08/28/768090c4-2d64-11e4-994d-202962a9150c_story.html.

72. *See* Falguni A. Sheth, *Shoot First, Ask Later: Why the Concept of "Reasonable Fear" Is Anything but Reasonable*, SALON (Sept. 6, 2014), http://www.salon.com/2014/09/06/shoot_first_ask_later _why_the_concept_of_reasonable_fear_is_anything_but_reasonable/.

73. *See* Jerry Kang et al., *Implicit Bias in the Courtroom*, 59 UCLA L. REV. 1124, 1181–84 (2012) (discussing possible methods of educating *trial* jurors about implicit bias). Prosecutors, of course, are as susceptible to implicit biases as the rest of us. *See* Robert J. Smith & Justin D. Levinson, *The Impact of Implicit Bias on the Exercise of Prosecutorial Discretion*, 35 SEATTLE U. L. R. 795 (2012). Lest there be concern that talking about race in this context might be counterproductive, research on the subject suggests otherwise. *See* Kang et al., *supra*, at 1184 (addressing a similar concern about trial jurors, and discussing research suggesting that when jurors are encouraged to discuss race, "it is precisely this greater degree of discussion, and even confrontation, that can potentially decrease the amount of biased decision-making"). For a discussion of the research, see Alexander M. Czopp et al., *Standing up for a Change: Reducing Bias through Interpersonal Confrontation*, 90 J. PERSONALITY & SOC. PSYCHOL. 784 (2006).

74. Tr. vol. 1, 43 (2014).

75. Tr. vol. 5, 50 (2014).

76. *Id.* at 51.

77. *Id.* at 238.

78. *See supra* note 1.

79. Subconscious biases that cause people to associate Black men with violence and criminality are not the exclusive province of Whites. *See* Theodore R. Johnson, *Black-on-Black Racism: The Hazards of Implicit Bias*, ATLANTIC (Dec 26, 2014), http://www.theatlantic.com/politics/archive/2014/12/ black-on-black-racism-the-hazards-of-implicit-bias/384028/.

80. Sometimes prosecutors in police killing cases have decided on their own not to bring charges, thus skipping the grand jury step, but those cases still are similar enough to fit the pattern because (1) as with the grand jury cases, there was no public hearing into the circumstances of the killing; and (2) the cases reached the same "no prosecution" result.

81. Other highly publicized cases occurring at around the same time included the killings of Eric Garner (in New York), Tamir Rice (in Ohio), Walter Scott (in South Carolina), and Eric Harris (in Oklahoma). *See* Nicholas Quah & Laura E. Davis, *Here's a Timeline of Unarmed Black People Killed by Police over Past Year*, BUZZFEED (May 1, 2015), http://www.buzzfeed.com/nicholasquah/heres-a-time line-of-unarmed-black-men-killed-by-police-over#.oiV7XowlX.

82. *See* Susan Page, *Whites and Blacks Question Police Accountability*, USA TODAY, Aug. 25, 2014, *http://www.usatoday.com/story/news/nation/2014/08/25/usa-today-pew-poll-police-tactics-military -equipment/14561633/*.

83. *See, e.g.*, Walter Katz, *Commentary: Enhancing Accountability and Trust with Independent Investigations of Police Lethal Force*, 128 HARV. L. REV. F. 235 (Apr. 10, 2015).

84. *See, e.g.*, Melody Gutierrez, *Calls Grow to Eliminate Grand Juries' Secrecy in Police Killings*, SFGATE (Dec. 14, 2014), http://www.sfgate.com/crime/article/Calls-grow-to-eliminate-grand-juries -secrecy-5956945.php.

85. *See, e.g.*, Katz, *supra* note 83.

86. *See, e.g.*, Gutierrez, *supra* note 84. This could be accomplished, even in jurisdictions where indictment by a grand jury is sometimes required, by prohibiting the use of a grand jury as the initial step in the charging process, and instead requiring that prosecutors either decide on their own not to bring charges or start the process with a complaint and a preliminary hearing in open court. *See supra* note 1.

Chapter 4

St. Louis County Municipal Courts, For-Profit Policing, and the Road to Reforms

Thomas Harvey and Brendan Roediger

Ferguson has been described as a microcosm of modern inequality and injustice in the United States.[1] If this is true, the St. Louis region is rich in microcosms. In St. Louis County, Ferguson is simply one of dozens of virtually identical predatory localized criminal justice systems. These municipalities routinely and disproportionately stop, charge, fine, and arrest the poor and people of color. Moreover, these municipalities often unconstitutionally close courts to the public and incarcerate people for failure to make monetary payments without providing them counsel. These destructive policies not only disrupt families, they push the poor further into poverty; prevent the homeless from accessing housing, treatment, and jobs they desperately need to regain stability in their lives; and violate the Constitution.

Other ongoing violations of the most fundamental guarantees of the U.S. Constitution in St. Louis County municipal courts include denial of counsel, denial of pretrial release, and the operation of de facto debtor prisons. This destructive system has existed for decades, prompting municipalities to structure budgets around court fines while attorneys profit and the poor suffer. The St. Louis region is just now, in the wake of the tragic killing of Michael Brown, beginning the task of examining and reforming these practices.

The Structure of St. Louis County Police Departments and Courts

A detailed and comprehensive description of the municipal structure of St. Louis County and its historical development is beyond the scope of this chapter. It is a tragic and sordid history, from the Reconstruction Era split between the county and the city to the present. To this day, St. Louis City remains a completely independent "charter city" with no legal relationship to St. Louis County and its 90 municipalities.[2] By and large, each St. Louis County municipality, Ferguson included, was founded and incorporated as a segregated community.[3] State law encouraged this proliferation of independent political entities with minimal state oversight by requiring virtually no prerequisites to incorporation.

As a result of this history, St. Louis County is now home to 90 distinct municipalities but only 58 independent municipal police departments.[4] The vast majority of these police departments are not accredited nor meaningfully monitored by state government.[5] Incredibly, in October of 2014, in the midst of a nationwide movement demanding police accountability and vigorous local debate over police training and oversight, the small St. Louis County municipality of Flordell Hills formed yet another St. Louis County police department. Just three miles from Ferguson, Flordell Hills is home to approximately 800 residents.[6] On the first official starting day of the Flordell Hills Police Department, an officer was arrested by the St. Louis County Police Department for the theft of prescription drugs from an evidence locker.[7]

The vast majority of St. Louis County municipalities have their own municipal court. As of 2015, there are a total of 81 independent municipal courts.[8] These are courts of "limited jurisdiction," hearing only cases involving violations of the municipal ordinances of the village or city in which the court sits. These municipal ordinances are largely duplicative of state law, meaning that most unlawful activity can be charged either as a state misdemeanor offense or a municipal ordinance violation. The discretion to charge unlawful activity as a state or municipal offense is left primarily to municipal police officers at the time of arrest or citation. Fines resulting from municipal ordinance violations are paid into general revenue for the municipality. Fines resulting from state offenses are paid to the state school fund. For obvious reasons, municipal police officers overwhelmingly choose to charge individuals with municipal ordinance violations.

The position of judge or prosecutor in these municipal courts is a part-time position. In most municipalities, judges and prosecutors are hired directly by the mayor, with the consent of the city council or village trustees. Although 81 of the 90 towns have their own court, there are not 81 different judges and 81 different prosecutors for each of these towns. Only 55 people work as judges in the 81 municipalities that have courts.[9] Similarly, although there are 81 prosecuting attorney positions available in St. Louis County, only 54 different people fill those roles.[10] Many attorneys and firms serve multiple roles, with some serving as judges, prosecutors, and defense attorneys. Some are full-time prosecutors for felony and misdemeanor cases during the day and municipal judges during the evening. These conflicts not only run contrary to best practices, they are normally prohibited by the judicial cannon. Missouri has exempted part-time judges from those portions of the cannon and has developed no specific standards for prosecutorial conflicts.[11]

Not surprisingly, these courts do not reflect the communities in which they sit or the defendants brought before them. Of the 55 judges serving in St. Louis County municipal courts, only five are African American.[12] Of the 54 prosecutors, only seven are African American.[13]

The Municipal Court Experience for Defendants

All 81 St. Louis County municipal courts are part-time courts. Some meet only once per month while others meet weekly. The vast majority of court dates or "docket calls" are in the evening. These evening sessions are designed to process as many cases as possible, most often through guilty pleas. Often times there are more defendants scheduled for court on a given night than the space could conceivably accommodate. It is not uncommon for defendants to wait outside for significant periods of time before being allowed to enter the court, including during winter months where temperatures are commonly below freezing.[14]

It is difficult to adequately describe the typical night court session in St. Louis County. As mentioned, many of the villages, towns, and cities have no adequate space to hold court. Court sessions are held in police stations, gymnasiums, closed elementary schools, and even a church basement. Many of these courts are within walking distance from one another. On one stretch of Natural Bridge Road (a major east-west road in St. Louis County), you can drive through eight towns in just three miles and be subject to the jurisdiction of each of those courts. This means that if you have expired license plates, you run the risk of being cited for that infraction eight times within a span of three miles. One town, Charlack, is so small that "its police department, city hall, and jail are all contained in one modified single-family house. In fact, you can stand on the front lawn of the Charlack City Hall, look across Midland Boulevard, and see the Vinita Park City Hall across the street."[15]

When faced with a traffic ticket or other petty offense, a middle-class person will typically resolve it by hiring an attorney and paying fines. If a person has the means to hire an attorney, that attorney enters his or her appearance and requests a recommendation for disposition of the charge from the prosecutor. In these situations, the prosecuting attorney almost always recommends that the charge be amended from a moving violation (such as a speeding ticket) to a nonmoving violation (such as littering) upon the payment of a fine and court costs that go directly to the municipality. For a simple speeding ticket, an attorney is paid $50–$100, the municipality is paid $150–$200 in fines and court costs, and the defendant avoids points on his or her license, as well as any possible increases in insurance costs. The process works for those with wealth: the attorney is paid for easy work, the town profits from the fines, and the defendant maintains a clean driving record. Often, neither the attorney nor the defendant even attends court. However, if a person cannot afford an attorney or pay the fines, prosecutors do not make any amendments and the outcomes are markedly different.

In contrast to middle-class people, people living in poverty can neither afford an attorney nor pay a fine. When faced with a traffic ticket or other petty offense, many poor people often end up pleading guilty, taking a conviction, having points assessed, and owing money. While some courts allow payment plans, others require immediate payment of all fines and costs. If a person cannot pay the amount in full before the court date listed on a ticket, he or she must appear in court again. Furthermore, under state law, failure to pay a fine within the time dictated by the municipal judge results in an automatic license suspension. The inability to pay the full amount, transportation issues, or the inability to secure child care or a night off from work can often lead to missed payments. Missed court dates and payments lead to an arrest warrant. As a result of the automatic license suspension, the next police stop likely results in incarceration on the arrest warrant and a new charge of driving with a suspended license.

Civil Rights Violations in St. Louis County Municipal Courts

Although indigent defendants routinely inform the court that they are unable to hire a lawyer or pay fines due to their poverty, few municipalities provide lawyers for those who cannot afford counsel. As a result, unrepresented defendants commonly plead guilty without knowing that they have right to consult with a lawyer. Defendants are also sentenced to probation and to the payment of unreasonable fines without a knowing, voluntary, and intelligent waiver of their constitutional right to counsel. The lack of counsel also eliminates any meaningful adversarial testing of the cases that come before a court. Individuals routinely plead guilty to offenses such as "sagging pants" or "manner of walking" that would never pass constitutional muster. These pretextual stops that are the hallmark of racial profiling are never challenged.

Under existing Missouri law, defendants are entitled to a hearing to determine their ability to pay if they raise the issue of their poverty to the court.[16] Further, prior to any finding of contempt or revocation of probation for failing to pay, defendants are again entitled to an inquiry into their ability to pay. In *Bearden v. Georgia*, the U.S. Supreme Court held that courts are required to make an affirmative finding that a person has the ability to pay a fine before it may impose incarceration for a person's failure to pay.[17] Despite the clear legal requirements, these hearings rarely occur. As a result, defendants are regularly incarcerated for their poverty. In fact, the practice of incarcerating debtors is at the core of the St. Louis County municipal court system. Individuals are threatened, abused, and left to languish in confinement at the mercy of local officials until their frightened family members can produce enough cash to buy their freedom or until officials decide, days or weeks later, to let them out for free. As previously mentioned, no municipality holds court on a daily basis, and some courts meet only once each month. A person who cannot pay the bond and is arrested on a warrant in one of these jurisdictions may spend as much as three weeks in jail waiting to see a judge.

Conditions of Incarceration

Once locked in jail, impoverished people owing debts to municipal courts endure grotesque treatment. Imprisoned persons report the following:

- Defendants are kept in overcrowded cells and denied toothbrushes, toothpaste, and soap.
- Holding cells smell of excrement and refuse and walls are smeared with mucus and blood.
- Women are not given adequate hygiene products for menstruation.
- Defendants are unable to change clothes and are without access to laundry. They are forced to wear the same underwear for weeks on end.
- Defendants endure days and weeks without being allowed to use a shower that is covered in mold and has gnats emanating from the drain.
- Defendants must step on top of other inmates, whose bodies cover nearly the entire uncleaned cell floor, in order to access a single shared toilet.
- Defendants huddle in cold temperatures with a single thin blanket even as they beg guards for warm blankets.
- The food has virtually no nutritional value and inmates lose significant amounts of weight.
- Defendants suffer from dehydration out of fear of drinking foul-smelling water that comes from an apparatus on top of the toilet.
- Defendants develop illnesses that go untreated and ignored as well as infections in open wounds that spread to other inmates.
- Defendants are routinely denied vital medical care and prescription medication, even when their families beg to be allowed to bring medication to the jail.
- Defendants must listen to the screams of other inmates languishing from unattended medical issues as they sit in their cells without access to books, legal materials, television, or natural light.
- Perhaps worst of all, defendants have no knowledge of when they will be allowed to leave or see a judge.

These physical abuses and deprivations are accompanied by other pervasive humiliations. Jail guards routinely taunt impoverished people when they are unable to pay for their release, telling them that they will be released whenever jail staff "feels" like letting them go. Jail guards also routinely and pervasively laugh at the inmates and humiliate them with discriminatory and degrading epithets.[18]

The "Muni Shuffle"

The "muni shuffle" is a term used locally to describe being transferred from one town's jail to the next as a direct result of poverty and the inability to pay large fines for petty violations. It is common for the poor in the St. Louis region to have warrants for their arrest in multiple jurisdictions as a result of their inability to pay these fines. When they are arrested on one of these warrants for allegedly failing to appear to pay their fines, they are held by that town until it extracts as much money as possible from them, and then they are subsequently released, most often without ever seeing a judge. The amount needed to secure release is often negotiated and reduced over a period of days with the police, jailers, or court clerks. The form of this extraction is "cash bond" but it is important to note that this is not bond in the traditional legal sense.

This "release" is in name only because upon being told the first town is finished with them, defendants are informed that the next town has a warrant for their arrest or "hold." This warrant, again, is not for a new offense but rather for the failure to pay fines. Instead of being freed from incarceration, they are simply moved from one jail to another until every town with the means to hold them has squeezed as much money from them as is possible. In this sense, the "release" from custody is simply the beginning of a Kafkaesque journey through the debtors' prison network of St. Louis County.

Justice by the Numbers: Planning for Warrants and Counting on Revenue

Municipal governments, police, courts, and jails are each active components of the localized criminal justice systems that destroy the possibility of trust between citizens of St. Louis County and their government. Nationally, advocates have drawn increased attention in recent years to the dangers of an increasing profit motive in the criminal justice system. In the St. Louis area there can be no doubt that policing and fining is largely motivated by revenue. City officials encourage this practice by prospectively budgeting for increased revenue from fines.[19] There are no police in the room when elected officials set the budget, over the course of the year the police issue the requisite number of tickets so that the courts can assess the requisite amount of fines to reach the budgeted figure. Likewise, judges increase fines and "court fees." Implicitly or explicitly, police and courts respond to meet the numbers.

None of this is lost on the community. Local wisdom is always ahead of the game. The people who have suffered under this system for the past 50 years do not need to look at the town budget or the attorney general's racial disparity report. They know that police work has come to mean issuing tickets, not investigating or preventing serious or violent crimes. They know they are being stopped, ticketed, and fined in order to fund their very own town. The Department of Justice Pattern and Practice Report on the Ferguson police and municipal court was not news to the hundreds of thousands of individuals who have had to navigate this system.

And it is not only the citizens who know this. Former St. Louis County Police Chief Tim Fitch has said on more than one occasion that he knows there are tiny towns requiring police to meet quotas.[20] While he blames government leaders instead of the police, the point remains: the problem starts with the city leaders setting a budget, continues when law enforcement overpolices a region for profit, and culminates in the courts where judges and prosecutors legitimize this system.

Policing and fining for revenue, combined with the fact that cities hire poorly trained officers and fail to demand any level of accountability, leads to a toxic mix when police stop African Americans in St. Louis County. While the population of the city of Ferguson is 67 percent Black, 85 percent of all vehicle stops, 93 percent of all arrests, 88 percent of the use of force cases, and 92 percent of all warrants issued involved African Americans.[21] Racial profiling data from the attorney general demonstrates definitively that Black drivers are targeted by police throughout St. Louis County.[22] Ferguson is the rule and not the exception. Police interactions with the community are further exacerbated by a court system that fails to provide counsel and routinely produces guilty pleas, ensuring that the actions of officers will never be scrutinized.

All of this leads to there being over 700,000 active warrants for arrest in a region of approximately 1.2 million people.[23] There are currently over 450,000 outstanding warrants for arrest in St. Louis County alone, which has a population of just over 900,000.[24] By comparison, there are just over 40,000 warrants for arrest in Cook County, Illinois, a region that comprises the city of Chicago and whose population exceeds 5 million.[25]

At the time of Mike Brown's death, there were more warrants for arrest than people living in the city of Ferguson. In 2013, the municipal court in Ferguson issued 32,975 arrest warrants for nonviolent offenses, mostly driving violations.[26] That is equivalent to 90 arrest warrants issued per day.

The stops, arrests, fines, and warrants all add up to a substantial revenue source for the region. Overall, it is estimated that St. Louis's municipal courts earn over $50 million in revenue per year. In Ferguson, fines and court fees comprise the second largest source of revenue for the city, a total of $2,635,400.[27] Budget documents show that this was an increase of more than 40 percent from 2010.

Missouri places a statutory limit of 30 percent on the amount of revenue individual municipalities can earn from their courts. In spite of that, several courts exceed that limit and do so with impunity. Eight communities exceed the limit, one collecting as much as 66 percent of its revenue from fines and fees.[28] When asked by the press about the reliance on fines and fees to fund their government, officials routinely respond by claiming the enforcement of these ordinances is about public safety, not revenue.

Inside the Numbers in Other St. Louis County Municipalities

As noted, Ferguson is far from the exception. Here is a summary of data from other select St. Louis County municipalities:

Pine Lawn

The city of Pine Lawn has a population of 3,275 people and a poverty rate of 38.7 percent.[29] 1.5 percent of the city's population is considered white, 96.4 percent of the population is considered African American, 0.09 percent of the city's population is considered Asian, and 2.02 percent of the city's population is considered as "other."[30] Out of the city's 3,908 vehicle stops, 841 stops were of white drivers and 2,982 of the vehicle stops were of African Americans over one year. Many drivers are not residents.[31] The search rate among whites was 4.88 percent and among African Americans it was 5.94 percent. The contraband hit rate was 19.51 percent among whites and 10.17 percent among African Americans.[32] The arrest rate was 5.95 percent among whites and 10.4 percent among African Americans.[33]

The city of Pine Lawn has revenue from fines and fees totaling $1,841,985. The cost to the city to run its municipal court was $453,125, with net revenue of $1,388,860 dollars from fines and fees.[34]

For the 2014 fiscal year, 708 warrants were issued. Outstanding warrants total 20,525.[35]

St. Ann

The city of St. Ann has a total population of 13,020 residents with a poverty rate of 14.6 percent.[36] Of its population, 69.52 percent of the residents are white, 22.11 percent are African American, 2.2 percent are Asian, and 6.16 percent are classified as "other."[37] There were 7,331 vehicle stops among whites and 3,934 vehicle stops among African Americans over one year. The search rate among whites was 5.62 percent and among African Americans it was 14.16 percent. The contraband hit rate among whites was 16.02 percent, 10.23 percent among African Americans, 33.33 percent among Asians, and 7.14 percent among other groups.[38] The arrest rate among whites was 6 percent and among African Americans was 17.51 percent.[39]

The city of St. Ann has revenue from fines and fees totaling $3,415,671. The cost to the city to operate its municipal court is $332,313, leaving net revenue of $3,083,358 that the city derives from fines and fees.[40]

The total number of warrants issued by the city for the 2014 fiscal year was 5,964.[41]

Maplewood

The city of Maplewood has a population of 8,046 and a poverty rate of 19.9 percent.[42] 74.14 percent of the city's population is white, 17.2 percent African American, 3.47 percent Asian, and 5.18 percent of the population can be classified as other.[43] There were total of 2,011 vehicle stops among white residents and 1,647 vehicle stops among African American residents over one year. The search rate among whites was 2.88 percent and among African Americans was 6.8 percent.[44] The arrest rate among whites was 1.7 percent and among African Americans was 3.7 percent.[45]

The city of Maplewood has revenue from fines and fees totaling $837,774. The cost of the city's municipal court is $255,462, with net revenue from fines and fees totaling $582,312.[46]

The city of Maplewood issued 1,251 warrants in 2014 and 3,106 warrants remain outstanding.[47]

Municipal Court Injustice and Its Toll

As a result of collaboration with social workers, the authors have seen firsthand how charges stemming from poverty in municipal courts prevent homeless and poor clients from gaining access to housing and jobs, cause children to drop out of school or change school districts midyear, and create or exacerbate health concerns. Individuals who are not homeless routinely lose housing and jobs as a result of contact with the police and courts. When they are stopped by municipal police and detained on a warrant, they miss work. Those who are lucky enough not to be fired as a result of the missed shifts are often fired as a result of missing additional shifts to go to court. Once people on the margins are unemployed, it is only a matter of time before they lose housing. Even if they find a job two weeks later, the loss of income is enough to push them into poverty and homelessness.

While the damage to housing and jobs is grave, the psychological damage is truly devastating, leading to anxiety, depression, and even suicide. The case of Nicole Bolden, a client of the nonprofit law firm Arch City Defenders, is illustrative.[48] Bolden, a single mother of three and a resident of Florissant, was arrested after a traffic accident on unpaid debt owed to four different St. Louis municipalities. She had already resolved all of her cases but still owed money to the towns: Florissant, Hazelwood, Dellwood and Foristell for fines. When a police officer initially arrived on the accident scene, he determined that Bolden was not at fault but still arrested her for warrants stemming from the outstanding debt. She was first taken to Florissant, where she was told she would have to stay in jail until her debt was paid. Bolden's mother, who lives on a fixed income, paid Florissant, but because Hazelwood claimed that Bolden owed it $150 in unpaid debt, she was held in Florissant for an additional 22 hours. Desperate to leave, she paid Hazelwood $120 from her child support card. She still wasn't free, however, because she still owed money to both Dellwood and Foristell.

Authorities in Hazelwood transferred Bolden to the Dellwood police, who kept her at St. Louis County's jail for 20 hours because they don't have their own jail. Her cousin eventually gave them $150 but she still wasn't free to go home because she owed $1,758 to Foristell.

Foristell police finally came to St. Louis County jail days later at 4:00 am Sunday morning to pick her up. Foristell doesn't have a jail, so they held her in the St. Charles County jail. When she asked when her court date was, no one knew. When a caseworker asked how she was doing, she told them she was tired and "couldn't take it anymore." This earned her suicide watch. By the time Bolden finally got out of jail, she was despondent, and hadn't slept in days.

Every year, thousands of St. Louis County residents experience the same ordeal, buying or waiting their way out of jail after jail. Some never make it out. One man, 24-year-old Charles Anthony Chatman Jr., hanged himself in March 2013 after being held on traffic warrants in Jennings.[49] He was left unmonitored after being placed in solitary confinement. He was found dead 45 minutes later. Chatman was doing the muni shuffle. He and his family had paid $750 in bail to two municipalities but needed $850 more to be released from Jennings. Perhaps most cruelly, because Jennings rents jail space to towns too small to have their own jail, Chatman was "released" from Jennings' official custody but not the physical space of their jail after he paid the initial bond.

Similarly, 26-year-old Dejuan Brison attempted to hang himself in the Jennings city jail in October 2014.[50] Brison was arrested on a warrant for failing to appear in court in a shoplifting case and awaiting transfer to another municipal court. Bernard Scott, 44 years old, was found with a shoestring around his neck in a Pine Lawn holding cell in September 2014.[51] Scott was taken to the hospital, and recovered at a rehabilitation center. Scott had been held on warrants for failure to appear to pay fines. That same month, Jenny Newman, 37, was found unconscious in the Des Peres jail an hour after arrest on warrants for failure to appear to pay fines. She died three days later.[52]

Efforts at Transforming the System

Arch City Defenders' White Paper

On August 12, 2014, Arch City Defenders' white paper on St. Louis County municipal courts was initially posted to its website.[53] Providing the first comprehensive analysis of the broken municipal court system, it helped to shape a movement toward reform of the municipal courts that has come to include a comprehensive litigation strategy, policy advocacy, legislative proposals, and rule changes. This white paper was the foundation for the national exposure of this issue in a detailed report by the *Washington Post*.[54] The persistent protests in Ferguson demanding accountability and justice for the killing of Michael Brown brought increased attention to the myriad of injustices in the St. Louis region, including those discussed in the white paper.

Requesting Municipal Court Amnesty to City of Ferguson

Saint Louis University School of Law Legal Clinics and Arch City Defenders sent a letter to the mayor of Ferguson on August 22, 2014, requesting that he commute all pending charges and remit all fines and fees in the city of Ferguson as a "first step towards reconciliation" within his community. The letter presented the legal authority under which the city could implement the suggested policy. The mayor never responded directly to the letter, but publicly refused to consider amnesty.

Proposal to the Supreme Court of Missouri

In September of 2014, Arch City Defenders and Saint Louis University School of Law Legal Clinics articulated to the Supreme Court of Missouri one of their long-standing proposals to proportion fines to income at the outset of a case. Unlike the current practice, where no inquiry is made into a person's ability to pay fines, this rule change would require courts to make a determination of an individual's income at the time of assessment. This single important change could have an enormous impact on the lives of the poor in the St. Louis region and could save courts untold time from processing payments, issuing warrants, and unconstitutionally incarcerating people because of their inability to pay.

Litigation Attacking Illegal Fees

Arch City Defenders, Saint Louis University School of Law Legal Clinics, and the Campbell Law Firm filed class-action lawsuits against Ferguson as well as Beverly Hills, Fenton, Jennings, Pine Lawn, Wellston, St. Louis, Kansas City, and Velda City. The lawsuits call for a judgment that the fees violate state law, an accounting of who paid the illegal fees and how much, and reimbursement to defendants who were forced to pay the fees to avoid jail time or warrants. The suits also include a claim under the Missouri Merchandising Practices Act, the state's consumer fraud statute, alleging that the cities attempted to deceive defendants into paying the fees.

Writ of Prohibition

Under Missouri law, municipalities are prohibited from collecting more than 30 percent of their overall revenue from traffic-related adjudications in their municipal courts.[55] In order for the state to determine whether a municipality has exceeded the cap, municipalities are required to file a report with the state after the end of their fiscal year. Under a recent amendment to the law, any municipality that fails to timely submit such reporting "shall suffer an immediate loss of jurisdiction of the municipal court of said city, town, village, or county on all traffic-related charges."[56] Many municipalities ignored the law and exceeded the 30 percent threshold or failed to report.[57] Arch City Defenders and St. Louis University Legal

Clinics brought a writ of prohibition alleging that cases heard by the Village of Bel-Ridge Municipal Court after it failed to file a timely report were without jurisdiction. This matter is still pending as is a constitutional challenge to the law brought by the Missouri Municipal League.

Arch City Defenders and Saint Louis University School of Law Legal Clinics have also partnered to bring a class-action lawsuit against the city of Bel-Ridge, alleging it has been operating a court without jurisdiction since June of 2014 as a result of failing to timely file the required reports. Shortly after these cases were filed, the Missouri Attorney General brought a number of suits against other municipalities that were not in compliance and the Missouri State Auditor announced increased audits of municipal courts.

Debtors' Prisons Lawsuits

Equal Justice Under Law, Arch City Defenders, and Saint Louis University School of Law Legal Clinics joined together to bring class-action lawsuits against Ferguson and Jennings alleging violations of the First, Sixth, Eighth, and 14th amendments. The suits allege that indigent people were jailed solely for not being able to make a monetary payment and were held in deplorable conditions in the Cities of Ferguson and Jennings until they or their family scraped together enough cash to buy their freedom. These cases are ongoing.

The Ferguson Commission

The Ferguson Commission was established by the governor of Missouri, Jeremiah ("Jay") Nixon, in response to community demand to study and address the socioeconomic issues underlying community unrest following the killing of Michael Brown Jr. by Ferguson police officer Darren Wilson. The governor specifically charged the commission with investigating the municipal court system. The Municipal Courts Working Group, which included the authors of this chapter, was tasked with making recommendations for the broader commission with regard to the courts. Ultimately, the Commission adopted municipal court reform and consolidation as a primary call to action in its final report.

Missouri Legislature

The Missouri Legislature has thus far largely ignored the crises brought to light by the killing of Michael Brown and the evolving nationwide Movement for Black Lives. Even the most conservative reforms, such as updating the law on "use of force" to comply with the Constitution, were rejected. Municipal court reform was the exception. Legislation was passed eliminating the separate offense of "failure to appear" and automatic license suspension for minor traffic violations. The legislation further limits the percentage of revenue a municipality may retain from traffic fines. Although heralded as comprehensive reform, the legislation does nothing to stop municipalities from engaging in predatory policing practices and incarcerating defendants as a consequence of their poverty.

Missouri Supreme Court

The Missouri Supreme Court amended Rule 37, the Supreme Court rule governing municipal courts, to clarify that no person can be incarcerated for failing to pay in municipal court without a judicial determination that nonpayment was willful. Further, the court exercised its authority over the municipal courts and transferred Appellate Court Judge Roy Richter to preside over the municipal court of Ferguson. In March and April of 2015, the Missouri Supreme Court requested public comment on the municipal courts. In May of 2015, the court announced the formation of a Blue Ribbon Committee to make recommendations on municipal court reform.

Reforms in Individual Municipalities

There are some early signs of meaningful reforms by individual municipalities. The city of St. Louis recalled over 200,000 outstanding warrants and proportioned fines to income for the poor. St. Louis County Presiding Judge Maura McShane ordered municipal courts to no longer exclude the public, a practice that is in clear violation of the U.S. and Missouri Constitutions. Ferguson has eliminated two ordinances charging fees not authorized by state law, eliminated the warrant recall fee, and created a new docket to address people who are struggling to make their payments.

Department of Justice Investigation and Report

At this time, the Department of Justice remains in active negotiations with the city of Ferguson regarding the resolution of the Department's pattern and practice investigation.

Conclusion

From Reconstruction Era Black Codes through the Drug War and "broken windows" policing, the systematic overenforcement of petty offenses in Black communities has been an integral part of maintaining white supremacy in the United States. This practice is not limited to the present and it is not limited to the St. Louis region. The Department of Justice investigation, whatever its deficiencies, was historically significant in its recognition that police and local courts worked in concert to criminalize Black residents. While profit motive is certainly not a necessary component of this phenomenon, in Ferguson and elsewhere, it is apparent that there is money to be made from excessive fines, cash bail schemes, and exorbitant court costs. Progressive catchphrases such as "restorative justice" and "community policing" miss the point. In the St. Louis region the task will be to put an end to the policing of day-to-day life and to abolish profit-driven part-time courts.

Notes

1. Peter Dreier & Todd Swanstrom, *Suburban Ghettos Like Ferguson Are Ticking Time Bombs*, WASH. POST, Aug. 21, 2014, http://www.washingtonpost.com/posteverything/wp/2014/08/21/suburban-ghettos -like-ferguson-are-ticking-time-bombs/.

2. MO. CONST. art. VI, § 31.

3. Richard Rothstein, *The Making of Ferguson*, ECON. POLICY INST., Oct. 15, 2014, http://www.epi .org/publication/making-ferguson/#executive-summary.

4. BETTER TOGETHER, POLICE REPORT #1: REGIONAL OVERVIEW 5 (Apr. 2015), http://www.bettertogetherstl .com/wp-content/uploads/2015/04/BT-Police-Report-1-Full-Report-FINAL1.pdf.

5. BETTER TOGETHER, POLICE REPORT #1: LICENSURE AND ACCREDITATION 1–2 (Apr. 2015), http://www.bet tertogetherstl.com/wp-content/uploads/2015/04/BT-Police-Report-2-Licensure-and-Accreditation-Full -Report-FINAL1.pdf.

6. Jennifer S. Mann, *New Flordell Hills Police Force Off to Rough Star as Officer Is Charged with Stealing from Evidence Room*, ST. LOUIS POST-DISPATCH, Oct. 1, 2014, http://www.stltoday.com/news /local/crime-and-courts/new-flordell-hills-police-force-off-to-rough-start-as/article_09030df7-6488-587f -b122-0d5ff9df50f6.html.

7. *Id.*

8. BETTER TOGETHER, PUBLIC SAFETY—MUNICIPAL COURTS 5 (Oct. 2014), http://www.bettertogetherstl .com/wp-content/uploads/2014/10/BT-Municipal-Courts-Report-Full-Report1.pdf.

9. BETTER TOGETHER, PUBLIC SAFETY—MUNICIPAL COURTS JUDGES AND PROSECUTORS ADDENDUM 1 (Oct. 2014), http://www.bettertogetherstl.com/wp-content/uploads/2014/11/BT-Judges-and-Prosecutors-Report -FINAL1.pdf.

10. *Id.* at 10–12.

11. *See generally* MODEL CODE OF JUDICIAL CONDUCT.

12. PUBLIC SAFETY—MUNICIPAL COURTS JUDGES AND PROSECUTORS ADDENDUM, *supra* note 9.

13. *Id.*

14. Both authors routinely represent defendants in municipal court and have personally witnessed this.

15. Radley Balko, *How Municipalities in St. Louis County, MO., Profit from Poverty*, WASH. POST, Sept. 3, 2014, http://www.washingtonpost.com/news/the-watch/wp/2014/09/03/how-st-louis-county-missouri -profits-from-poverty/.

16. Hendrix v. Lark, 482 S.W.2d 427, 431 (Mo. 1972).

17. Bearden v. Georgia, 461 U.S. 660, 673–74 (1983).

18. The conditions of confinement as described by plaintiffs in *Fant v. Ferguson*, No. 4:15-CV-00253-AGF (E.D. Mo. filed May 26, 2015).

19. PUBLIC SAFETY—MUNICIPAL COURTS, *supra* note 8, at 3.

20. Ryan J. Reilly & Mariah Stewart, *Fleece Force: How Police and Courts around Ferguson Bully Residents and Collect Millions*, HUFFINGTON POST, Mar. 26, 2015, http://www.huffingtonpost.com/2015/03/26/st-louis-county-municipal-courts_n_6896550.html.

21. CIVIL RIGHTS DIV., U.S. DEP'T OF JUSTICE, INVESTIGATION OF THE FERGUSON POLICE DEPARTMENT 4, 62 (Mar. 4, 2015), http://www.justice.gov/sites/default/files/opa/press-releases/attachments/2015/03/04/ferguson_police_department_report.pdf.

22. *Id.*; Office of Mo. Att'y Gen. Chris Koster, Racial Profiling Data/2013, https://ago.mo.gov/docs/default-source/public-safety/2013agencyreports.pdf?sfvrsn=2.

23. MO. SUP. CT., MISSOURI JUDICIAL REPORT SUPPLEMENT: FISCAL YEAR 2014, at 309 (2015), https://www.courts.mo.gov/file.jsp?id=83236.

24. *Id.*

25. Cook County Sheriff Thomas J. Dart, Fugitive Warrants Unit, http://www.cookcountysheriff.com/sheriffs_police/ccspd_SpecialInvestigations_FugitiveWarrants.html (last visited May 28, 2015).

26. MO. SUP. CT., MISSOURI JUDICIAL REPORT SUPPLEMENT: FISCAL YEAR 2013, at 303 (2014), https://www.courts.mo.gov/file.jsp?id=68905.

27. INVESTIGATION OF THE FERGUSON POLICE DEPARTMENT, *supra* note 21, at 9.

28. Betsey Bruce, *Court Study Shows Fines Weigh Heavily on Towns with Larger African American Population*, FOX2NOW, Oct. 15, 2014, video from 1:20 to 1:39, http://fox2now.com/2014/10/15/study-many-north-st-louis-county-towns-balance-budgets-with-court-fees/.

29. U.S. Census Bureau, Community Facts, http://factfinder.census.gov/faces/nav/jsf/pages/community_facts.xhtml (last visited June 3, 2015).

30. Racial Profiling Data/2013, *supra* note 22, at 877.

31. *Id.*

32. *Id.*

33. *Id.*

34. BETTER TOGETHER, PUBLIC SAFETY—MUNICIPAL COURTS APPENDIX 10 (Oct. 2014), http://www.bettertogetherstl.com/wp-content/uploads/2014/10/BT-Municipal-Courts-Report-Appendix.pdf.

35. MISSOURI JUDICIAL REPORT SUPPLEMENT: FISCAL YEAR 2013, *supra* note 26.

36. U.S. Census Bureau, State and County Quick Facts, http://quickfacts.census.gov/qfd/states/29/2963956.html (last revised Apr. 22, 2015).

37. Racial Profiling Data/2013, *supra* note 22, at 1021.

38. *Id.*

39. *Id.*

40. PUBLIC SAFETY—MUNICIPAL COURTS APPENDIX, *supra* note 34, at 11.

41. MISSOURI JUDICIAL REPORT SUPPLEMENT: FISCAL YEAR 2013, *supra* note 26, at 309.

42. U.S. Census Bureau, State and County Quick Facts, http://quickfacts.census.gov/qfd/states/29/2945830.html (last revised Apr. 22, 2015).

43. Racial Profiling Data/2013, *supra* note 22, at 657.

44. *Id.*

45. *Id.*

46. PUBLIC SAFETY—MUNICIPAL COURTS APPENDIX, *supra* note 34.

47. MISSOURI JUDICIAL REPORT SUPPLEMENT: FISCAL YEAR 2013, *supra* note 28, at 309.

48. One of the authors, Thomas B. Harvey, is the co-founder and executive director of this firm.

49. Denise Hollinshed, *Man Found Dead in Jail Cell in Jennings*, ST. LOUIS POST-DISPATCH, Mar. 22, 2013, http://www.stltoday.com/news/local/crime-and-courts/man-found-dead-in-jail-cell-in-jennings/article_cd89f507-f07d-583f-950d-f6392527c594.html.

50. Joel Currier, *Jennings Hanging Attempt Is Latest in a Series of Area Jail Incidents*, ST. LOUIS POST-DISPATCH, Oct. 6, 2014, http://www.stltoday.com/news/local/crime-and-courts/jennings-hanging-attempt-is-latest-in-series-of-area-jail/article_a62642ad-141b-5b5c-9881-6ec2a67290f8.html.

51. *Id.*

52. *Id.*

53. Thomas Harvey et al., Arch City Defenders, Municipal Courts White Paper (2014), http://www.arch citydefenders.org/wp-content/uploads/2014/11/ArchCity-Defenders-Municipal-Courts-Whitepaper.pdf

54. Balko, *supra* note 15.

55. Mo. Ann. Stat. § 302.341 (West).

56. *Id.*

57. Jennifer Mann, *Koster Sues 13 St. Louis County Municipalities over Court Fees*, St. Louis Post-Dispatch, http://www.stltoday.com/news/local/crime-and-courts/koster-sues-st-louis-county-municipalities -over-court-fees/article_09652317-c932-55b3-ab1d-f1e0bc478c0b.html.

Chapter 5

Making Ferguson: Segregation and Uneven Development in St. Louis and St. Louis County

Colin Gordon

The questions that arose in the wake of Michael Brown's death, in some respects, were less about the chain of events than about their location. Why Ferguson? How and why were episodes of police violence and community response, unfortunately commonplace in modern American urban history, moving to the suburbs? The answers lie in a conspiracy of causal factors that contributed to a stark and sustained racial divide between north and south St. Louis, and to a stark—but ultimately more tenuous—divide between St. Louis and St. Louis County.

In the early and middle decades of the last century, realtors, developers, and white property owners erected elaborate obstacles to black property ownership and occupancy. These restrictions were, over time, adopted and formalized as an ethical obligation of private realtors, lenders, and insurers; as the organizing principle of both local zoning and federal housing policies; and as the key determinant of value whenever property was taxed, "blighted" for redevelopment, or redeveloped. The net effect was not just the spatial segregation of metropolitan St. Louis by race and class, but also a cascade of disinvestment and disadvantage in the City's northside residential neighborhoods, an uneven and fragmented pattern of residential development and land-use zoning, and a yawning racial gap in local wealth.

Against this backdrop, other public policies (or public policy failures) began to dislocate large swaths of the region's African American population. In the 1950s, large-scale, downtown urban renewal programs displaced thousands of families—some of whom were accommodated in new public housing projects, most of whom simply moved west and north ahead of the bulldozer. In the 1960s, St. Louis County launched a much more limited program of redevelopment, but also a much more pointed one—blighting and razing pockets of African American settlement now surrounded by new suburban development. Underinvestment, underzoning, and the erosion of public services on the City's northside also encouraged population flight—although the outmigration of African Americans did not really take off until civil rights jurisprudence began to prise open County housing markets. Finally, the abject failure of "big-box" public housing (the City's infamous Pruitt-Igoe towers were razed in 1972) created yet another anxious diaspora.

All of this converged on the inner St. Louis County suburbs crowded between the City's western border and the airport (an area known locally as North County), Ferguson foremost among them. An older and more modest residential base, combined with the sustained dislocation elsewhere of those with limited accumulated housing wealth or savings, made Ferguson a logical and necessary zone of racial transition. The patterns and mechanisms of segregation established on the City's northside both drifted into North County and were reinvented there. And, in the bargain, the consequences of segregation—including concentrated poverty, limited economic opportunity, a paucity of public services (except heavy-handed policing) and political disenfranchisement—moved to the inner suburbs as well.

The basic trajectory of this history is straightforward. The American urban crisis is marked by sustained losses in the local industrial and employment base, dramatic racial transition and depopulation, and a host of consequential economic and social challenges—including a collapsing tax base, a growing share of vacant or abandoned housing, rapid disinvestment, and spatially concentrated threats to public safety and public health. All of this was particularly severe in St. Louis. Midwestern "rustbelt" cities sat at the leading edge of urban decline, bearing the brunt of both demobilization after World War II and the deindustrialization of later years. Patterns of racial conflict and racial segregation were also especially pronounced in St. Louis. The national pattern of white flight and inner-city decay, as one observer noted, could be found in St. Louis "in somewhat purer and less ambiguous form than almost anywhere else." St. Louis retained (decade after decade) its dubious distinction as one of the nation's most segregated metropolitan areas.[1] And, for all these reasons, St. Louis was also the setting for a string of landmark civil rights litigation including *Shelley v.*

Kraemer (the 1948 Supreme Court decision that outlawed state enforcement of restrictive deed covenants),[2] *Jones v. Mayer* (the 1968 case that prohibited private discrimination in real estate transactions),[3] and *United States v. City of Black Jack, Mo.* (1974, one of the first "exclusionary zoning" cases).[4]

The private and public policies that shaped the urban crisis in greater St. Louis, in the inner suburbs of north St. Louis County, and in Ferguson both entrenched patterns of residential segregation and disrupted them. Over the middle years of the 20th century, these inner suburbs employed the same tactics—including legal restrictions, systematic discrimination in private realty, and exclusionary zoning—as their neighbors. Over time, however, those tactics failed. Both disinvestment in north St. Louis (and with it the failure of local public goods like schools) and the dislocation caused by urban renewal (shouldered overwhelmingly by African Americans) in the City and in St. Louis County created immense pressures on the older, relatively affordable housing stock in the inner suburbs. The net result, in settings such as Ferguson, was both racial transition and an uneasy balance—reflected in local politics, local schooling, and local policing—between past practices and present realities.

The Politics of Segregation in Greater St. Louis

The conditions of north St. Louis and its inner suburbs are deeply rooted in a history of private racism, public policy, and economic decline. Segregation, more specifically, was accomplished and enforced by private and public strategies of exclusion that overlapped and reinforced one another. At the center of this story was the local realty industry, which lobbied for explicitly racial zoning in the World War I era; pursued and enforced race-restrictive deed covenants into the middle years of the century; pioneered the practice of residential security rating that governed both private mortgages and public mortgage guarantees; and—as a central precept of industry practice—actively discouraged desegregation of the private housing market.

At a time when cities were first exploring the politics and legality of zoning, St. Louis was one of a handful of cities to propose formalizing racial segregation. The St. Louis law (1916) and others like it were subject to immediate political challenge—both on "equal protection" grounds and as an unwarranted intrusion of the local police power onto private property rights. The ordinance sat in legal limbo for about a year until it was struck down when the Supreme Court ruled against a similar Louisville law in *Buchanan v. Warley* (1917).[5] In the wake of *Buchanan*, local property and realty interests moved to segregate by other means (see Figure 5.1 in color insert). The solution was a combination of private realty practices and race-restrictive deed covenants (the boilerplate covenant drafted by the St. Louis Real Estate Exchange included "a restriction against selling, conveying, leasing, or renting to a negro or negroes, or the delivery of possession, to or permitting to be occupied by a negro or negroes of said property and properties of the other owners of properties"), which eventually formed a ragged quadrangle at the western boundary of the City's traditionally African American wards.[6]

In the middle 1940s, a flurry of challenges to restrictive agreements culminated in a St. Louis case that would ultimately end up in the Supreme Court: *Shelley v. Kraemer*. While the Missouri courts had sustained the agreement in question, the Supreme Court disagreed and decided in 1948 that "judicial enforcement by state courts of such covenants is inhibited by the equal protection clause." In the wake of the decision, private parties were free to draft such agreements but could not turn to the courts for their enforcement.[7] For its part, the Real Estate Exchange quickly "approved a recommendation of the Committee on the Protection of Property that no realtor shall sell to Negroes, or finance any transaction involving the purchase of a Negro of any property north of Easton Avenue and West of Marcus avenue, nor elsewhere outside of the established unrestricted districts,"[8] and turned to day-to-day practice of selling and leasing real estate to sustain segregation. St. Louis realtors routinely denied that apartments or houses were available, often pulling them off the market in response to expression of interest or offers to buy. "We never sell to colored," boasted one realtor in 1969. "When they ask for a specific house, we tell them there is already a contract on that house"—adding that office staff were routinely reminded that "a house is not to be shown to colored."[9]

All of this had a lasting and decisive impact on residential patterns and opportunities in greater St. Louis. During the peak years of African American migration to the St. Louis area, all but a handful of the City's neighborhoods were off limits. "Housing is desperately short-handed in St. Louis as it is in most other large cities," the St. Louis Urban League noted in the wake of World War II, "but the lack of housing facilities for Negroes in St. Louis is critical for peculiar reasons. Approximately 97% of the Negro population in St. Louis lives at the geographical heart of the city, surrounded on the east by commerce and business, and on the south, west, and north by neighborhood covenant agreements. There are no outlets to the open county for any kind of expansion. There is a complete circle of restriction."[10]

The importance of these agreements and practices should not be underestimated—both for their impact on residential patterns in greater St. Louis and for the ways in which they lived on in other forms of public policy. The practices and assumptions of private realtors distorted not only the market for housing but also local and federal public policies that subsidized and regulated that market.

Consider federal housing and mortgage policies. In the 1930s, the new Home Owners Loan Corporation (HOLC) and Federal Housing Administration (FHA) established the basic framework (low down payment, long-term amortization) for modern home ownership by offering federal insurance on qualifying mortgages. In order to rate local properties and neighborhoods, the FHA/HOLC turned to the architects of racial zoning and restrictive deed covenants, local realtors and lenders, and echoed their assumption that neighborhoods "invaded" or "infiltrated" by African Americans had lost all value. At the core of the FHA rating system, parroting the same juxtaposition of "nuisances" found in many St. Louis deed covenants was the prohibition of "undesirable buildings such as stables, pig pens, temporary dwellings, and high fences" and *"prohibition of the occupancy of properties except by the race for which they are intended"* (italics added). In local settings such as St. Louis, the FHA's guidelines were enshrined on a series of "residential security maps" (see Figure 5.2 in color insert) that documented the insidious "spread" of the black population and carved the City into risk-rated neighborhoods.[11]

Consider local zoning. Local governments interested in maintaining property values and in funding local services by taxing those properties have every incentive to sort the population by race and class in such a way as to maximize tax returns and minimize other demands on the public purse. Where local governance is fragmented (the St. Louis metropolitan statistical area includes over 260 incorporated municipalities, almost 100 of which are in St. Louis County alone), there is an exaggerated incentive and opportunity to use property zoning as a means of sorting and segregating populations. Outside the central city, the dominant practice (emerging in the middle years of the 20th century) was "exclusionary zoning": land-use controls that ensured a pattern of predominantly low-density single-family settlement through a combination of outright prohibitions (heavy industry, manufactured housing), effective prohibitions (no land zoned for multifamily housing), and area or density standards (size, setbacks, and building size). Older cities, by contrast, did not have the power to zone until long after local land use had been decided by private restrictions and market forces. Unable to compete with the suburbs for high-end residential development, central cities often ran in the other direction—designating large areas for commercial or industrial use, and often "clearing" low-return residential tracts as part of the bargain.[12] From a metropolitan perspective, the results have not been pretty. Exclusive and fragmented zoning in the suburbs (see Figure 5.3 in color insert) erased any semblance of residential diversity, sorting the white middle class into income-specific single-family enclaves on the periphery and leaving African Americans, the elderly, and the poor to filter into older and higher-density housing stock (much of it unprotected by local zoning) in the central city and inner suburbs.[13]

All of this was designed to sort the metropolis not just by income or family status but by race as well. Prospectuses for urban subdivisions typically lauded the "protection" afforded by restrictive deed covenants, which (for a time) the FHA not only accommodated but also recommended. Planning consultants marketed municipal zoning as means of extending those protections behind a veil of public policy. The deliberations of suburban city planning or zoning commissions, in turn, were invariably haunted by the specter of "the City"—a ghostly reminder of what might happen if residential density and racial occupancy were not controlled.[14]

Finally, consider urban renewal. The net effect of political fragmentation, real estate restrictions, and exclusionary zoning was the virtual devastation of north and central St. Louis. City planners began taking stock of these conditions (substandard housing, abandoned commercial property, aging infrastructure) as early as World War I, but all that really changed over the following decades were the terms—obsolescence, decadence, blight, ghettoization, decay—used to label them. The prescription, in St. Louis and elsewhere, was urban renewal—a tangled combination of federal money, state enabling laws, local initiative, quasi-public redevelopment corporations, and private investment.[15] Between 1954 and 2000, the City of St. Louis "blighted" hundreds of areas under Chapter 353, the Missouri

Urban Redevelopment law, and Chapter 99, the Missouri Land Clearance Act.[16] Although the condition of the residential northside was often used to make the case for urban renewal, those neighborhoods received virtually none of the subsequent political attention, private investment, or public subsidies. Most of the attention instead flowed to commercial development—stadiums, retail, convention centers—in the City's central corridor (see Figure 5.4 in color insert).

These policies only made things worse. The relocation pressures created by urban renewal (which uprooted nearly 75,000 St. Louis residents, most of them African American, between 1950 and 1970), created new demands on both the northside and North County. Indeed, slum clearance and public housing actually deepened local patterns of racial segregation, and pressed displaced residents—one step ahead of the bulldozer—further west in the City and ultimately into North County.[17] Urban renewal often created, or recreated elsewhere, the very conditions it purported to fight. More than a decade into its urban renewal program, the City concluded glumly that "the gap actually has increased between the quantity of substandard housing that must be replaced (or rehabilitated) and the supply of new or renewed housing."[18]

On balance, federal housing and renewal policies did little to address the paucity of safe low-income housing in greater St. Louis and actually *deepened* patterns of residential segregation. FHA mortgage insurance flowed primarily to the suburbs, subsidizing white flight. Federal public housing assistance flowed primarily to the inner city, cementing the region's spatial organization of race and poverty. Indeed, when the federal government—in the context of protracted litigation over school desegregation—set out to prove that the St. Louis Board of Education was defying the mandate of the 1954 *Brown* decision, both local officials and expert witnesses identified federal housing policies as the prime culprit. "The segregated black community was left to fester," as a City official observed, "while developers aided by the federal government rushed out to build new white enclaves on the city's edge."[19]

Making Ferguson

As we recenter our attention from the broader metropolitan patterns to the particular patterns of North County and of Ferguson, four elements of the story stand out: First, systematic discrimination and disinvestment in black neighborhoods produced a stark (and growing) disparity between black and white wealth. Those barred from equal access to housing, federal subsidies, and home finance in the middle years of the 20th century also lost the ability to pass housing equity on to the next generation. Second, in the developmental and demographic history of greater St. Louis, the inner suburbs of North County (including Ferguson) had an uncertain and liminal status. They were, as enclaves of white flight, much like the other suburbs that sprawled west from the City border. But they were, in their patterns of residential development and zoning, more like the City itself. Third, decline and disinvestment on the northside and redevelopment projects in the City and in the County generated immense pressures on affordable housing stock in the inner suburbs. And finally, the racial premises of both development and redevelopment created and sustained a particular pattern of population movement in greater St. Louis, marked by "white flight" into St. Louis County (and beyond) beginning in the 1940s, and by black flight into North County a generation later. As a result, the black-white divide between north and south St. Louis extended out into St. Louis County, and local segregation was replicated in transitional neighborhoods—like Ferguson—in North County. Let's look at each of these in turn.

By almost any economic metric (unemployment, job quality, wages, incomes) the gap between white and black Americans is sustained and substantial,[20] but the starkest gap, in this respect, is in wealth. While the median black worker earns about three-quarters of the wages of his or her white counterpart and the median black household claims about two-thirds the income of its white counterpart, the gap in wealth—with black net worth stuck at about 10 percent of white net worth—is dramatically wider.[21] The racial gap in wealth reflects gaps in the rate of homeownership,[22] in the tenure of homeownership,[23] and in the terms of homeownership.[24] Facing systematic discrimination in both private realty and private lending, fewer African Americans entered the housing market, they entered it later in life, and they entered it on relatively unfavorable terms. Federal incentives and subsidies sorted opportunity by race—not only for homeownership but also for the intergenerational accumulation of equity and wealth, and the other advantages (public services, good schools) that flow from homeownership.[25]

Income, wealth, and inequality are embedded in places; in the neighborhoods (deeply segregated across our history) where families buy homes, raise families, and pass assets and opportunities to the next

generation.[26] Even as civil rights and fair housing legislation and litigation curbed the worst of these practices, substantial obstacles—
including continued discrimination, attenuated disadvantage, and late
access to housing markets—slowed progress. What this meant, in
St. Louis and its suburbs, was that a long history of discrimination and
segregation effectively "lived on" in the form of the black-white wealth
gap. So when housing markets did open up after the 1970s, segregation by wealth (and income) both displaced and sustained segregation
by race. Where African Americans would or could live was determined
less by the legal triumphs of the civil rights era than by the limited
supply of affordable housing—much of it abandoned (in the City and
its inner suburbs) by white flight.

Where was that affordable housing? As we traced above, private
development pressed westward, especially after World War II, relatively unrestrained by local or state restraints on what we now call
"sprawl." Like most Midwestern cities, St. Louis faced few geographic
obstacles to growth. And, among Midwestern settings, Missouri was
notoriously lax in exerting any regulatory control over the incorporation of new municipalities. Against a backdrop of systematic segregation, these background conditions had three important consequences:
First, it meant that private development generally preceded municipal
incorporation, so that incorporation (and zoning) simply cemented
private development patterns and choices. Second, it meant that such
patterns sustained segregation—hardly surprising given that municipal
incorporation was largely animated by the desire to seal exclusionary
patterns of land use. And third, it meant that the municipal organization (especially in St. Louis County) was remarkably fragmented, with
each of those fragments paying a particular role in sustaining and regulating patterns of land use and occupancy.

Ferguson, just to the northwest of the City border in St. Louis County,
was not a conventional suburb. It was incorporated in 1894, an out-
growth of rail-based development, and grew dramatically in the middle
years of the 20th century. But this growth and development was unlike
the larger-footprint suburban tracts spreading west through central
county municipalities such as Clayton, Ladue, and Creve Coeur. There,
private development generally preceded incorporation or annexation,
so that the latter (and the zoning laws that accompanied them) simply
sealed patterns of exclusive land use established by private developers. By contrast, the infrastructure and residential development of Ferguson came earlier, the lots and houses were generally smaller, and

the land use was less restrictive than in the County's more conventional suburban development (see Figure 5.5 in color insert).

All of this set a clear and starkly uneven pattern of housing development and housing opportunity. Median home values in North County, at $88,000 in 2012, are almost 40 percent less than the figure for the whole of St. Louis County ($144,000). From 2005 to 2011 (including the housing crash and recovery), most properties in Central, West, and South County showed a slight increase in assessed values; in most areas of North County, assessed values fell. Of the County's 24,000 foreclosures (2005–2012), fully 70 percent (17,000) were in North County.[27] And just as low values, foreclosures, and vacancies are concentrated in North County, so too are the region's multifamily rental units. This is an artifact of both early and uneven suburban development, and of less-exclusionary zoning in North County's inner suburbs—characterized by the rental complexes strung along Maline Creek in south Ferguson and in Kinloch.[28] As a result, much of the region's affordable and rental housing is concentrated in North County: of 6,600 tax credit units that are part of large properties (50 or more units) in the County, 63 percent are in North County.[29]

The net result left Ferguson in an unusually vulnerable position. Much of its midcentury residential development rested on the same motives and restrictions and subsidies that marked "white flight" suburbanization elsewhere in the region. But, because such development was crowded next to the City, it proved less exclusive and more transitional. Because these municipalities were older and their footprints generally smaller (especially in North County), they suffered both higher costs and lower fiscal capacity as they aged. And, because land use was less exclusive and lots were smaller in these inner suburbs, they served as the logical destination not just for the white working class fleeing the city in the 1940s and 1950s, but for African Americans displaced by disinvestment and urban renewal a generation later. In St. Louis County, 83 percent of public housing units and 93 percent of housing vouchers units are occupied by African Americans (the rate for both is only 3 percent in outlying Franklin and Jefferson Counties).[30]

This uneven development was accompanied by unrelenting pressures on the region's affordable housing stock. The City's population peaked at just over 850,000 in 1950, at which point it claimed just under half (47.9 percent) of the population of the metropolitan area. With each new census, the City's population dropped farther (750,000 in 1960, 622,000 in 1970, 453,000 in 1980, 397,000 in 1990, 348,000 in

2000, 318,000 in 2010), as did its share of the metropolitan area. The City lost an average of just under 10,000 persons a year between 1950 and 2013. The housing shortage of the 1940s and 1950s gave way to chronic vacancy and abandonment: by 1978, St. Louis had the highest vacancy rate (just under 10 percent) of all central cities. More important than the dimensions of this decline was its racial profile: in the 1940s, 1950s, and 1960s, the City experienced dramatic "white flight" to the suburbs. In the 1970s and after, this was followed by an equally dramatic pattern of black flight—as civil rights victories began to open County housing markets and whites began moving west again from the inner suburbs.

Just as blacks fled the residential northside (for the same reasons as whites but a generation later) they were also being expelled from neighborhoods targeted for urban renewal. These programs generally equated black occupancy with "blight" and viewed "slum clearance" as their primary goal. The City's first major projects were accompanied by cynical and haphazard plans for relocated residents. Urban renewal authorities simply expected dislocated residents to fend for themselves and vastly inflated (for the consumption of federal officials) their ability to accommodate or assist those losing their homes. The relocation office of the Mill Creek project, for example, claimed it had housed all those displaced by initial land clearance (4,172 families) in decent housing. But a federal audit found that more than half of those eligible for relocation assistance received no help, and that most of the assisted relocations were to substandard dwellings. The haphazard movement of African Americans from cleared tracts—some into local public housing but most into neighborhoods to the west and north—deepened segregation in many central city neighborhoods, created new demands for redevelopment in neighborhoods accommodating the refugees from the latest round of renewal, and encouraged white residents of north St. Louis out into the inner and outer suburbs.[31]

While the City's redevelopment and public housing policies hardened segregation within St. Louis, those of the County and its municipalities hardened the racial divide between the City and its suburbs. Urban renewal in St. Louis County was often designed and pursued as a means of relocating suburban pockets of African American settlement "back" into the City.[32] Among these pockets was Kinloch, bordering Ferguson to the west. Kinloch had a peak population of over 6,500 at the 1960 census, but was targeted by surrounding municipalities (who worked to quarantine African American students into a separate and unequal school district), St. Louis County (which was looking to erase the last pockets of older African American occupancy in the name of redevelopment), and the St. Louis Airport (which was looking to expand in the Kinloch area). While the County's "Maline Creek" redevelopment scheme never got off the ground (in part because the County refused to contemplate building affordable housing for those displaced), airport expansion did eventually erase much of Kinloch—whose population had shriveled to fewer than 300 people by 2012.

Taken together, uneven metropolitan development, disinvestment in the central city, and City and County redevelopment policies drove racial transition and segregation in the inner suburbs of North County. Initially developed and populated by white working class migrants from north St. Louis, Ferguson now became the logical frontier for black flight—and for those displaced by urban renewal to the west and the east. In part, this transformation and transition reflected the tangle of factors previously described. In part, it reflected the slow erosion of formal restrictions on black occupancy, especially after *Jones v. Mayer* extended civil rights protections to private realty and the institutions of home finance (after the 1975 passage of the Home Mortgage Disclosure Act) followed suite. And, in part, it reflected the evolution of public housing—from large-scale central city projects (like St. Louis's Pruitt-Igoe towers) to portable "Section 8" vouchers.[33]

The impact and implications of these patterns were dramatic and, in some respects, devastating. Disparate patterns of white and black settlement, of white and black wealth, and of white and black flight, hardened racial segregation, and isolation. Black flight from the northside opened a class rift in the black community, concentrating poverty in the central city and eroding the middle-class institutions (hospitals, schools, churches) upon which that community depended. By the 1980s and 1990s, these losses were underscored and exaggerated by dramatic patterns of local economic decline, disinvestment, vacancy, and property abandonment. Taken together, these trends began to exact tremendous social costs—captured by any regional assessment of educational attainment, public safety, or public health.

The fragile line between white and black occupancy at the City-County line eroded over time, as white settlement looked further west, and the collapse of formal racial restrictions finally opened County housing markets. But the north-south divide between black and white occupancy largely held, so that whites leaving the City (or its inner suburbs) moved south and west, while blacks leaving the City (including the diaspora from the failure of the City's public housing projects) settled largely in North County. In effect, the "Delmar Divide" between north and south St. Louis pushed across the County, splitting University City and marking everything to the north—the 25 postage-stamp municipalities between the City boundary and Highway 170 and south of Lindbergh as a zone of racial transition (see Figure 5.6 in color insert).

At the same time, the patterns and mechanisms of segregation invented and sustained in the City of St. Louis migrated along this north-south line out into St. Louis County. This extended the contours of segregation so engrained in the City's history, and it also reinvented them in new settings (including Ferguson) in the inner suburbs. Here, segregation was spatial: African Americans have settled overwhelmingly in the apartment complexes (Suburban Heights, Northwinds, Canfield) along Maline Creek in south Ferguson and Kinloch, and in pockets of single-family housing east of West Florissant Avenue and south of I-270. And it was also political, especially in settings where the previous generation of white residents retained a stranglehold over local employment, local politics, and local services such as education or policing.

And with racial transition came a replication and extension of the tangled disadvantages long-faced by African Americans on the City's northside. Income inequality, measured as a share of the metropolitan median, spread out into North County after the 1970s. Inflation-adjusted average earnings (for those employed) fell by one-third between 2000 and 2012. In 1990, median household income for North County was 3 percent greater than that of the region as a whole; now it is 13 percent lower.[34] Poverty rates rose dramatically: between 2000 and 2013, the poor population of Ferguson doubled—by which point about one in four residents lived in poverty.[35] Ferguson's unemployment rate almost doubled between 2000 and 2010, and still sits at over 12 percent. Localized inequality, racial segregation, and concentrated poverty multiply the problems faced by both communities and poor families.[36] Such circumstances underlie social disorganization, increased crime, threats to public health, and further flight of population, investment, and resources. As population flees and property values plummet, local tax capacities collapse—a combination that yields baser public services, deteriorating public schools, *and* higher tax rates; all of which makes new investment less likely and old investment less secure. The school districts of North County, including Ferguson-Florissant (shown in Figures 5.7 and 5.8 by the blue border in color insert) combine property values well below the metro average with tax rates well among the county average (see Figure 5.7 in color insert). To add insult to injury, the collapse of the local property tax base has also encouraged struggling North County communities to backfill public coffers with court costs and fines (see Figure 5.8 in color insert)— a tactic that underlies the dismal state of community-police relations in North County and created the backdrop for the shooting of Michael Brown.

As a border city, greater St. Louis bears a dual legacy: its race relations are essentially southern, rooted in the institutions and ideology of Jim Crow. But its organization of property—reflected in private realty and in public policy—follows a northern pattern in which the institutions and mechanisms of local segregation are particularly stark. In such a setting, race relations are always most fragile on the frontier of racial transition. And when that frontier sits in a struggling inner suburb—its citizens mostly black, its police almost exclusively white— the fuse is always lit. The surprise in Ferguson is not what happened, but why it does not happen more often.

Put another way, the death of Michael Brown may have struck the match in Ferguson, but it was these conditions of sustained and localized inequality, segregation, and discrimination that kept the tinder dry and ensured the fire would catch. As long as patterns of economic inequality remain intact, the contrast between a largely black populace and overwhelmingly white political and police rule is jarring—but largely symbolic. Winning power, as a generation of African American mayors and city councilors can attest, is small solace when local resources and local fiscal capacity make effective governance nearly impossible. And affirmative recruiting in the Ferguson Police Department will address a thin tendril of segregation but not its root.

The cascading wage and income and wealth gap, and its racial and spatial logic, is a much starker challenge. Its deep historical roots and lasting impact lie behind the case for reparations made so powerfully by the Atlantic's Ta-Nehisi Coates last summer.[37] In greater St. Louis, at least partial redress would begin with a stronger sense of metropolitan responsibility for the local legacy of segregation and the local inequalities it has sustained. If we can agree that sewers and transportation planning only work on a metropolitan basis, it's no great leap to say the same for property taxation, zoning, or economic development.[38] Only then can we dampen the incentive and opportunity to leave the city, and its inner suburbs, behind.

Figure 5.1. Racial real estate restrictions, 1916–1945.

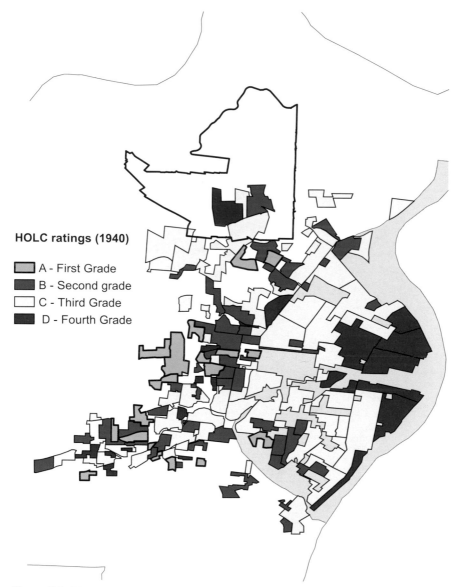

HOLC ratings (1940)

■ A - First Grade
■ B - Second grade
☐ C - Third Grade
■ D - Fourth Grade

Figure 5.2. Home Owners' Loan Corporation "Residential Security Ratings" (1940).

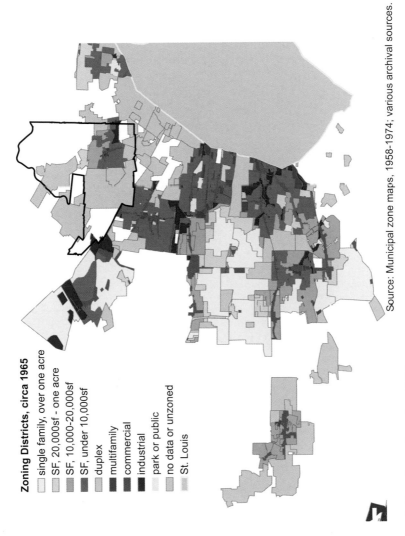

Zoning Districts, circa 1965

single family, over one acre
SF, 20,000sf - one acre
SF, 10,000-20,000sf
SF, under 10,000sf
duplex
multifamily
commercial
industrial
park or public
no data or unzoned
St. Louis

Source: Municipal zone maps, 1958-1974; various archival sources.

Figure 5.3. St. Louis County zoning, circa 1965.

Chapter 99 land clearmace
Chapter 353 tax abatements
Chapter 100 (planned industrial expansion)
tax increment financing
Enterprise zones

Source: Various LCRA, CDA reports; Collins (1974); Urban
Land Institute (1985); City ordinances and parcel data; UR Map
in Mercantile Library, UMSL

Figure 5.4. Urban redevelopment in Greater St. Louis, 1950–2000.

8000 sf

200 sf

Figure 5.5. Residential square footage, St. Louis County, 2003.

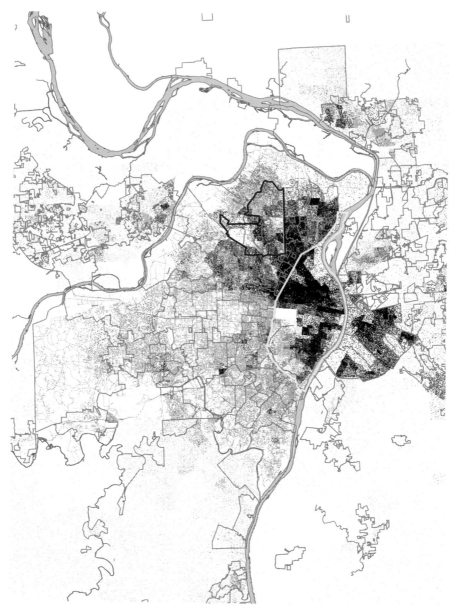

Figure 5.6. Racial occupancy by block group, 2010.
(green dot=1 white person; black dot=1 black person)

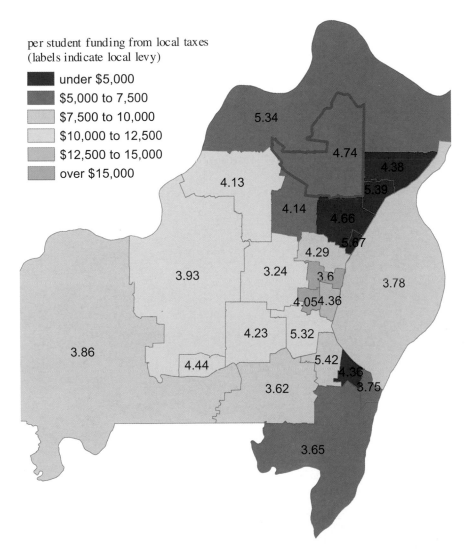

per student funding from local taxes
(labels indicate local levy)

- under $5,000
- $5,000 to 7,500
- $7,500 to 10,000
- $10,000 to 12,500
- $12,500 to 15,000
- over $15,000

5.34

4.74

4.38

4.13

5.39

4.14

4.66

5.67

4.29

3.93

3.24

3.6

3.78

4.05 4.36

4.23

5.32

3.86

4.44

5.42

4.36

3.62

3.75

3.65

Figure 5.7. Fiscal capacity and school levy, St. Louis County school districts
(2013).

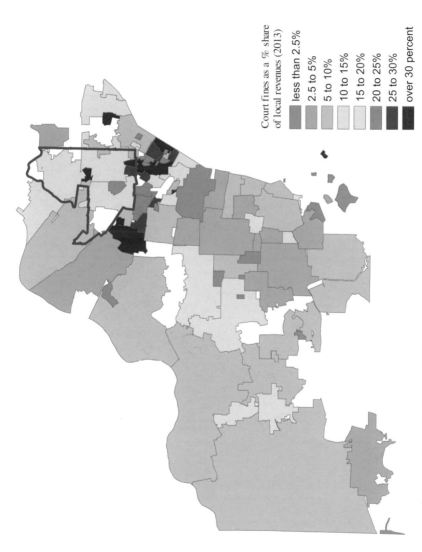

Court fines as a % share
of local revenues (2013)

less than 2.5%
2.5 to 5%
5 to 10%
10 to 15%
15 to 20%
20 to 25%
25 to 30%
over 30 percent

Figure 5.8. Revenue policing in St. Louis County, 2013.

Additional Reading

Charles Jaret, Lesley Williams Reid & Robert Adelman, *Black-White Income Inequality and Metropolitan Socioeconomic Structure*, 25:3 J. URBAN AFFAIRS 305–33 (2003).

John F. Kain, *Housing Segregation, Negro Employment, and Metropolitan Decentralization*, 82:2 Q. J. ECON. 175–97 (1968).

John F. Kain, *The Spatial Mismatch Hypothesis: Three Decades Later*, 3:2 HOUS. POLICY DEBATE 371 (1992). Robert E. Manley, *School Desegregation in the North: A Post-Milliken Strategy for Obtaining Metropolitan Relief*, ST. LOUIS U. L.J. 601 (1976).

MO. ADVISORY COMM'N TO THE U.S. COMM'N ON CIVIL RIGHTS, SCHOOL DESEGREGATION IN THE ST. LOUIS AND KANSAS CITY AREAS (Jan. 1981).

Gary Orfield, The Housing Issues in the St. Louis Case, Report to Judge William Hungate, U.S. Dist. Court (St. Louis, Mo.), Liddell v. Board of Education (1981).

Myron Orfield, St. Louis Metropolitics: A Regional Agenda for Community and Stability, Report to the Metropolitan Congregations United for St. Louis (Metro. Area Research Corp. Aug. 1999).

Alison Schertzer, Tate Twinam & Randall P. Walsh, *Race, Ethnicity, and Discriminatory Zoning* (NBER Working Paper No. 20108, 2014). U.S. Census Bureau, American Community Survey, Demographic and Housing Estimates, http://factfinder2.census.gov/faces/nav/jsf/pages/community_facts.xhtml (2013).

WASH. U. & ST. LOUIS U., FOR THE SAKE OF ALL: A REPORT ON THE HEALTH AND WELL-BEING OF AFRICAN AMERICANS IN ST. LOUIS AND WHY IT MATTERS FOR EVERYONE (2014).

WILLIAM JULIUS WILSON, THE TRULY DISADVANTAGED: THE INNER CITY, THE UNDERCLASS, AND PUBLIC POLICY (1987).

JOHN YINGER, CLOSED DOORS, OPPORTUNITIES LOST: THE CONTINUING COSTS OF HOUSING DISCRIMINATION (Russell Sage Found. 1995).

Notes

1. JOHN LOGAN, SEPARATE AND UNEQUAL: THE NEIGHBORHOOD GAP FOR BLACKS, HISPANICS AND ASIANS IN METROPOLITAN AMERICA (US2010 Project, 2011); John Logan et al., US2010 Project, City Sorting, http://www.s4.brown.edu/us2010/SegCitySorting/Default.aspx.

2. Shelley v. Kraemer, 334 U.S. 1 (1948).

3. Jones v. Alfred H. Mayer Co., 392 U.S. 409 (1968).

4. United States v. City of Black Jack, Mo., 508 F.2d 1179 (8th Cir. 1974).

5. COLIN GORDON, MAPPING DECLINE: ST. LOUIS AND THE FATE OF THE AMERICAN CITY 69–71 (U. Pa. Press 2008).

6. *Id.* at 78.

7. *Id.* at 81–83.

8. *Id.* at 84.

9. *Id.* at 86–87.

10. *Id.* at 78.

11. *Id.* at 89–91.

12. *Id.* at 112.

13. *Id.* at 131.

14. *Id.* at 145–46.

15. *Id.* at 153.

16. *Id.* at 164–67.

17. *Id.* at 194–200.

18. *Id.* at 206.

19. *Id.* at 98–99.

20. Robert Fairlie & William Sundstrom, *The Emergence, Persistence, and Recent Widening of the Racial Employment Gap*, 52:2 INDUS. & LABOR RELATIONS REV. 252–70 (1999); Kevin Lang & Jee-Yeon K. Lehrman, *Racial Discrimination in the Labor Market: Theory and Empirics*, 50:4 J. ECON. LITERATURE 959–1006 (2012); Kenneth Couch & Robert Fairlie, *Last Hired, First Fired? Black-White Unemployment and the Business Cycle*, 47:1 DEMOGRAPHY 227–47 (2010).

21. PAUL TAYLOR ET AL., WEALTH GAPS RISE TO RECORD HIGHS BETWEEN WHITES, BLACKS AND HISPANICS (Pew 2011). THOMAS SHAPIRO ET AL., THE ROOTS OF THE WIDENING RACIAL WEALTH GAP: EXPLAINING THE BLACK-WHITE ECONOMIC DIVIDE (Inst. Assets & Soc. Pol'y 2013).

22. William Collins & Robert Margo, *Race and the Value of Owner-Occupied Housing, 1940–1990* (Levy Inst. Working Paper 310, 2000); William Collins & Robert Margo, *Race and Home Ownership: A Century-Long View*, 38:1 EXPLORATIONS ECON. HISTORY 68–92 (2001); Daniel Fetter, *How Do Mortgage Subsidies Affect Home Ownership? Evidence from the Mid-Century GI Bills*, 5:2 AM. ECON. J.: ECON. POL'Y 111–47 (2013); IRA KATZNELSON, WHEN AFFIRMATIVE ACTION WAS WHITE (Norton 2005); Thomas A. Hirschl & Mark R. Rank, *Homeownership across the American Life Course: Estimating the Racial Divide* (Ctr. for Soc. Development Working Paper 06-12, 2006), http://csd.wustl.edu/Publications/Documents/WP06-12.pdf.

23. SHAPIRO, *supra* note 21.

24. Fetter, *supra* note 22; William Collins & Robert Margo, *Race and Home Ownership from the Civil War to the Present* (NBER Working Paper 16665, 2011).

25. KATZNELSON, *supra* note 22; THOMAS SHAPIRO & MELVIN OLIVER, BLACK WEALTH/WHITE WEALTH: A NEW PERSPECTIVE ON RACIAL INEQUALITY (Routledge 1996).

26. PATRICK SHARKEY, STUCK IN PLACE: URBAN NEIGHBORHOODS AND THE END OF PROGRESS TOWARD RACIAL EQUALITY (2013); PAUL JARGOWSKY, POVERTY AND PLACE: GHETTOES, BARRIOS, AND THE AMERICAN CITY (Sage 1997).

27. St. Louis Cnty. Dep't of Planning, Office of Cmty. Dev., St. Louis Cnty. Hous. Study (2012).

28. One St. Louis, Fair Housing Equity Assessment (Metro. St. Louis Equal Opportunity & Hous. Council 2013).

29. St. Louis Cnty. Dep't of Planning, *supra* note 27.

30. One St. Louis, *supra* note 28.

31. GORDON, *supra* note 5, at 206–11.

32. *Id.* at 100–01.

33. Dennis Judd, *The Role of Governmental Policies in Promoting Residential Segregation in the St. Louis Metropolitan Area*, 66:3 J. NEGRO EDUC. (1997).

34. St. Louis Cnty. Dep't of Planning, *supra* note 27; see also EAST-WEST GATEWAY COUNCIL OF GOVERNMENTS, WHERE WE STAND (6th ed., update #9, September 2014).

35. Elizabeth Kneebone, *Ferguson, Mo. Emblematic of Growing Suburban Poverty, in* 2015 THE AVENUE: RETHINKING METROPOLITAN AMERICA (Brookings Inst. 2014).

36. WILLIAM JULIUS WILSON, MORE THAN JUST RACE: BEING BLACK AND POOR IN THE INNER CITY (2009); WILLIAM JULIUS WILSON, WHEN WORK DISAPPEARS: THE WORLD OF THE NEW URBAN POOR (1996); DOUGLAS S. MASSEY & NANCY A. DENTON, AMERICAN APARTHEID: SEGREGATION AND THE MAKING OF THE UNDERCLASS (Harvard Univ. Press 1993); THE URBAN UNDERCLASS (Christopher Jencks & Paul Peterson eds., Brookings Inst. 1991).

37. Ta-Nehisi Coates, *The Case for Reparations*, ATLANTIC (June 2014).

38. Colin Gordon, *Patchwork Metropolis: Fragmented Governance and Urban Decline in Greater St. Louis*, 34:1 SAINT LOUIS UNIV. PUB. L. REV. (2014).

Chapter 6

From *Brown* to Brown: Sixty-Plus Years of Separately Unequal Public Education

Kimberly Jade Norwood

"Do you know how hard it was for me to get him to stay in school and graduate? You know how many Black men graduate?"

—Lesley McSpadden, Michael Brown's mother[1]

On August 9, 2014, Michael Brown, an 18-year-old Black teenager, was killed by police officer Darren Wilson. Brown had just graduated from a public high school in the Normandy School District (Normandy Schools) located in Normandy, Missouri. He was scheduled to attend a for-profit college in Missouri a few days after his death.[2] For all of his life, Normandy Schools were predominately Black, poor, and in academic distress. Take away the year 2014 and leave the words *Brown*, *education*, and *segregation*, and one would immediately think of a different time: the 1950s. One of the most famous decisions in U.S. Supreme Court history, *Brown v. Board of Education*,[3] decided in 1954, outlawed segregated and unequal education. Over 60 years later, the battle for integrated, quality education continues. This chapter examines the school district Michael Brown graduated from and situates its place in the *Brown* legacy.

A Segregated and Unequal Past

Unequal access to education for Black Americans began long before *Brown*. Almost from the beginning of African enslavement in this country through the end of the Civil War, laws existed in most of the colonies, and later the states, making it a crime to teach Blacks (in some cases whether enslaved or free) how to read or write.[4] With the Civil War's end and the beginning of Reconstruction in 1865, strong demands to overturn those laws and a positive movement toward obtaining a quality education became one of the first priorities for Blacks in America.[5] Freedom from bondage, citizenship, and the right to vote were eventually secured by the ratification of the 13th, 14th, and 15th Amendments. These gains were believed (and hoped) to be the beginning of the end of a 200-plus-year nightmare.[6] The post-Reconstruction era, however, saw the legalization of racial segregation as evidenced by the Supreme Court's holding in *Plessy v. Ferguson* that a standard of separate but equal was constitutional.[7] The decision in *Plessy*, combined with other laws in the nation at the time (e.g., peonage and convict lease laws) and the continued and escalating violence waged by the Ku Klux Klan, all worked to ensure that separate would not be equal.[8]

The collective Black community overwhelmingly believed, however, that education was the key to real freedom. Formerly enslaved Blacks were often mutilated and even killed if caught trying to learn how to read and write.[9] Both during Reconstruction, with the help of the Freedmen's Bureau—and thereafter once the Bureau was disbanded—these formerly enslaved people spent virtually all of their money to build schools and to obtain an education.[10] Although the right to an education was secured in many states, the quality of the education varied depending on the color of one's skin. Charles Hamilton Houston, born one year before *Plessy*, dedicated his life to changing that outcome. Using public education as his foundation, Houston proved, in cases spanning a 20-year period, that separate was not equal in the field of public education.[11] Though Houston did not live to see the culmination of his work in *Brown*, his protégé, Thurgood Marshall Jr., secured a unanimous Supreme Court vote completely accepting Houston's philosophy that segregation based on race was not, and could never be, equal.[12]

Following *Brown*'s announcement, and its second opinion a year later famously directing the nation to desegregate its schools with "all deliberate speed,"[13] there was tremendous pushback against the ruling, particularly in the South.[14] For two decades though, Supreme Court decisions suggested that integration was here to stay.[15] But White backlash was steadfast. Encouraged by racially discriminatory policies enacted by private banks, realtors, and even the federal and state governments, Whites fled urban areas as Blacks moved in.[16]

Urban school districts soon found very few Whites left in the cities with which to desegregate.[17] One district court in Michigan found its answer by allowing children to cross school district boundaries lines in order to desegregate schools. After finding that it was not enough that the State violated the constitution, the Supreme Court found that *individual school districts*, too, must be in violation of the constitution in order to be included in any remedy; in the case at hand, then, the crossing of school boundary lines was rejected.[18] This was the Court's first retreat from *Brown*. Over the next 20 years, the Court issued multiple opinions that virtually halted judicial efforts to undo hundreds of years of unequal and segregated education.[19] This occurred despite evidence that schools were not, in fact, being desegregated, much less integrated. Indeed, the Court held in 1991 that desegregation was no longer the goal. Rather, if a school could prove that it had acted in good faith to do what it could, "to the extent practicable," to desegregate, that was all that was required.[20] In 2007, the Court again revisited desegregation in public schools. In that year, the Court decided *Parents Involved in Community Schools v. Seattle School District No. 1.*[21] There the Court applied the most demanding constitutional standard, that is, the strict scrutiny test, to the question of whether race could be used by school districts to *voluntarily* desegregate schools. Answering no, the Court found that the use of race failed the second prong of the strict scrutiny test in the cases before it: the use of race was not narrowly tailored to achieve a compelling governmental interest.[22]

Racial Inequality in Public Schools

Segregated and unequal schools thrive throughout the United States.[23] *Brown*'s vision of both integrated and quality education for all students has been lost and indeed may be impossible to fulfill in the 21st century. Under racially segregated systems pre-*Brown*, most Black students were not receiving quality education; most White students were. *Brown* envisioned that if the students were desegregated and assigned to schools without regard to the color of one's skin, not only would the goal of integration be met—which many believe in and of itself is a form of education—but also that all students would receive a quality education. Quality education in an integrated setting was possible in the decades following *Brown*, but this dual goal is no longer possible.

It is not simply that public schools today are more racially segregated than 40 years ago, although this is true.[24] And it is not simply that Black, Asian, and non-White people of Latin American descent make up a majority of the students in public schools today (thus the term "majority minority"), although this is also true.[25] But, we must consider two other key factors: (1) White student enrollment in public schools has decreased over the years and (2) White births have declined significantly over the years.[26] All of these realities challenge any goal to integrate schools as that term was defined in *Brown*.

Notwithstanding the challenges facing racial integration of schools today, we must not abandon the *other* goal of *Brown*: that all children, no matter their skin color, receive access to quality education. This is really what *Brown* stood for. *Brown* viewed education as the mechanism to enable full citizenship in American society.[27] Indeed, Brown specifically acknowledged that without an education, it is virtually impossible to execute the rights of citizenship.[28] And yet, today, for millions, this goal has also been largely abandoned.

Public schools in the United States have been falling and failing for many years.[29] They have also become more unequal in terms of the quality of education and this can be racially tracked. Black, non-White Hispanic students, and American Indian/Alaska Native or Native American students are at the greatest academic disadvantage as compared to non-Hispanic White/Caucasian students and Asian/Pacific Islander students.[30] Blacks, and Black males in particular, are at the bottom of the academic ladder. Consider the following:[31]

Graduation

The national public school graduation rate for Black males in 2012–2013 was 59 percent. The percentage was 80 percent for White males. Worse still, the graduation rates for Black males in large urban school districts during that same period were far lower. Missouri's graduation rate for Black males in 2012–2013, for example, was 66 percent. Yet, for its largest urban school district, St. Louis Public School District (SLPSD), the graduation rate for this subgroup was 33 percent. These results were not unique to St. Louis. Atlanta graduated 38 percent of Black males; Cleveland, 28 percent; Detroit, 20 percent; Miami, 38 percent; New York, 28 percent; Philadelphia, 24 percent; and Milwaukee, 43 percent.[32] The announcement in 2015 by the Department of Education that U.S. students are graduating from high school at rates higher than ever before[33] rings hollow for some.

Literacy

Graduation is undoubtedly important but literacy is even more so. Indeed, one can graduate from high school but be unable to read.[34] Large achievement gaps exist between Black and Latino student performance and that of White and Asian students.[35] Of all subgroups, Black males are at the bottom of all performance levels.

The National Assessment of Education Progress (NAEP) has three academic achievement levels: Basic, Proficient, and Advanced.[36] NAEP's performance data reveals huge racial disparities. For example, in the 2012–2013 school year, the national percentage of Black males who scored at proficient or above in 8th-grade reading was 12 percent. The same figure for White males was 38 percent. For 8th-grade mathematics, the national figure for Black males in 2012–2013 was 13 percent at or above proficiency, compared to 45 percent for White males.[37]

Although NAEP tracks three achievement levels, many states add a fourth level: below basic (or level 1). This level is *below* grade level.[38] In New York State, for example, 2014 English Language Arts assessments for grades 3–8 showed that 46 percent of Black students scored below basic, compared to 25 percent of White students; in mathematics, the figures were 47 percent and 21 percent respectively.[39] In the nation's capital, 15 percent of Black students in 8th grade performed below basic in both reading and math categories as compared to 1 percent of White students.[40] In some of these Washington, D.C., school districts, the below basic percentage of Black students was as high as 61 percent for 8th-grade reading and 59 percent for 8th-grade math.[41]

Resources

If you compare schools where the student body is predominately Black and Latino to schools where the student body is overwhelmingly White and Asian, it is immediately apparent that a different type of education is taking place in each space.[42] In October of 2014, the Department of Education, Office of Civil Rights Division (OCR), issued a report demonstrating the different educational experiences of children depending on the racial makeup of their school. A sample of some of the findings contained therein revealed that schools attended by predominately Black and/or non-White Hispanic students

- were less likely to offer advanced and/or gifted courses and where offered, the students were less likely to be recommended to or enrolled in those classes.

- were less likely, at least in the case of predominately Black schools, to offer Advanced Placement (AP) courses.
- had newer, more inexperienced teachers.
- had teachers who made less money than similarly credentialed teachers in predominantly White school districts.
- were older and poorly maintained, with inadequate heating, ventilation, air conditioning, and lighting.
- were more likely to be overcrowded and lack essential educational facilities like science laboratories, auditoriums, and athletic fields.
- had fewer computers and other mobile devices and computers were of lower quality and capability; indeed, even the *speed* of Internet access varied.

These disparities were not limited to a simple comparison of inner-city and poor schools with wealthier suburban schools. Rather, even for schools in the same school district, schools with primarily White populations were shown to have more and better resources.[43] Michael Brown attended what are sometimes referred to as 'apartheid schools,' schools whose students are almost all Black and/or non-White Hispanic, and often usually poor.[44] These schools struggle in every way and at every level imaginable. As demonstrated below, Michael Brown attended one of these schools.

Normandy Schools

Michael Brown attended schools located in Normandy, Missouri. Incorporated in 1945, Normandy was originally a White suburb of St. Louis City. As Blacks started moving into Normandy and other similar suburbs near St. Louis city, Whites fled.[45] By 1978, Normandy Schools had the second-highest percentage of Black students in the St. Louis metropolitan area. SLPSD had—and still has—the highest percentage in the area.[46]

Born in 1996, Michael Brown started kindergarten in a district that had not been "accredited" since 1991.[47] The Missouri Department of Elementary and Secondary Education (DESE) is required by law to annually review school performance to evaluate which schools (and students) need improvement.[48] DESE follows an accountability system for reviewing schools. The system "outlines the expectations for student achievement with the ultimate goal of each student graduating ready for success in college and careers."[49] DESE considers various standards in attempts to determine if a school is on target to achieve its goal. Based on evaluation of these standards, a district can be unaccredited, provisionally accredited, accredited, or accredited with distinction. A 14-point scale was used (this system has since been replaced) to evaluate the effectiveness of school districts. A minimum of 6 points were required for accreditation.[50] During Michael Brown's tenure in the district, Normandy Schools *never* received more than 5 points.[51] Normandy Schools were not labeled as unaccredited during this time, as they should have been, but were allowed to operate as a provisionally accredited district. Though the district was finally, oficially labeled as unaccredited in 2013, the lengthy stay as provisionally accredited prevented the type of attention and focus on the district and on the children in that district that it surely needed.

To add insult to this injury, in 2009 DESE took another all-Black, poor, and unaccredited district, the Wellston School District (Wellston)—which was then the worst performing district in the state—dissolved it, and placed all of its students in technically-unaccredited-but-nonetheless-labeled-provisionally-accredited Normandy Schools.[52]

Serious questions remain as to why DESE placed students from Wellston into the struggling Normandy Schools. Granted, Normandy Schools were in close proximity to Wellston, but nothing required Wellston students to be placed in the district closest to them.[53] More importantly, given that Normandy Schools were, for all intents and purposes, technically unaccredited, it was a horrible choice. Indeed, there were two accredited districts near Wellston where those children could have been assigned. Those two districts, the Clayton School District (Clayton) and the Ladue School District (Ladue), were 3.2 miles and 7.6 miles away respectively, from Normandy Schools. (See Figure 1.) Not only were these two districts close to Normandy Schools *and accredited* but they were actually very high-performing districts. (See Appendix.) As the data in the Appendix reveals, both Clayton and Ladue outperformed Normandy Schools academically in all categories. The Wellston children could have easily been reassigned to schools in Clayton and Ladue, thus avoiding the unneeded pressure on the already frail Normandy Schools.

But DESE did not assign the Wellston children into these higher-performing districts. Many believe race and class were the underlying reasons. Clayton and Ladue are both affluent and virtually all-White school districts. Wellston and Normandy Schools both were then predominately Black, poor, and academically struggling. Missouri Board of Education

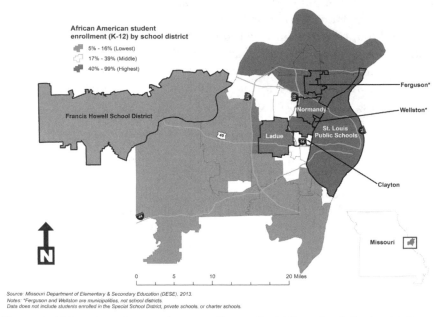

Figure 1. African American student enrollment (K–12) by school district, 2013.

Vice President Michael Jones said it best: "The [Wellston] students were not going to be absorbed into any of the high-performing, mostly White districts nearby. You'd have had a civil war."[54] There likely was a power dynamic going on as well. Two struggling and poor districts—Wellston and Normandy Schools—simply did not have the political clout of the wealthier Clayton and Ladue districts. Thus, by placing the Wellston children into already faltering Normandy Schools, political peace was maintained but it came at the cost of the demise of Normandy Schools.

And just like that, three years after Wellston was merged into Normandy Schools, Normandy collapsed. In September of 2012, DESE announced that, effective January of 2013, Normandy Schools would be unaccredited. This announcement triggered a Missouri law, known as the transfer law. This law provides that if a Missouri school was rendered unaccredited, the pupil residents in that district could opt to attend another accredited school in the same district, or could attend an accredited school in another district of the same or an adjoining county. The statute further mandated that the unaccredited district pay tuition for the transferring pupil to the accredited school and mandated that the unaccredited district choose a district for which it would also provide transportation.[55]

The Missouri transfer law dates back to 1931 but it was not until a 1993 amendment that the right of children in unaccredited schools to transfer to accredited schools was provided.[56] Interestingly, the sponsor of the transfer law never imagined it would actually be triggered. The statutory terms were to be used as a stick to force struggling districts to improve. "It was meant to be harsh. It was a wake-up call to clean up your situation and get it fixed."[57] In 1993, then, had Normandy Schools—with its 5 out of 14 points—been labeled unaccredited, parents might have taken advantage of the benefits of the transfer law. But DESE did not label Normandy Schools as unaccredited in 1993 or at any time during the 1993–2012 school years. This failure to label the district unaccredited for *almost 20 years* prevented parents from transferring their children to better schools. Twenty years. An entire generation of children were trapped in a failing district and deprived of their right to fully perform their citizenship.

Even when it was prepared to acknowledge Normandy Schools' unaccredited status in 2012, DESE still got it wrong. It announced *in September of 2012* that Normandy Schools would become *unaccredited in January of 2013.* This delayed effective date of the change to unaccredited status again prevented parents from transferring their children into accredited schools at the start of the 2012 school year. Because the statute is not triggered until a school and/or district is officially labeled unaccredited, parents could not take their children out of the failed schools until the middle of the school year. Anyone knows that transferring a child in the middle of a school year is rarely in the child's best interest.

Because of DESE's manipulation of the timing of Normandy Schools' unaccreditation, Normandy Schools did not experience the full impact of the transfer rule until the start of the 2013–2014 school year. In preparing for parents to exercise their children's right to transfer under the law, Normandy Schools chose to provide transportation to the nearly all-White Francis Howell School District (Francis Howell), approximately 23 miles (and a very long bus ride) away. (See Figure 1.) Recall that there were two highly performing districts less than eight miles away from Normandy Schools. Not only were Clayton and Ladue substantially closer than Francis Howell to Normandy Schools, but Clayton and Ladue were also stronger academic districts. In virtually every category, Clayton and Ladue outperformed Francis Howell. (See Appendix.) Yet Normandy Schools chose the further, lower-performing district for its students.

Transfers were effective for the 2013–2014 school year. Of the approximately 4,100 students in Normandy Schools, 1,100 elected to transfer to various school districts. Approximately 430 selected Francis Howell because that was the district to which Normandy Schools would provide transportation.[58]

In the weeks and months after Normandy Schools announced its decision to provide transportation to Francis Howell, anyone who picked up a St. Louis newspaper would have thought they were reading stories from the 1950s. They told of interviews with parents in Francis Howell, social media comments, and town hall meetings where parents in Francis Howell worried about Normandy Schools children being a bad influence on the Francis Howell children. They worried about compromising their test scores and accreditation; despite the higher drug use in the district, they worried about increased drug use and the need for drug sniffing dogs. Some comments referred to the Normandy School's children as trash, thugs, slum kids, and rapists.[59] One comment summed it up this way: "Too bad this country places such an emphasis on publically subsidizing the least qualified citizens to reproduce. I wonder how much things would improve if instead of WIC and other such nonsense, the govt gave out vouchers for free abortions."[60] Additional similar comments posted on the Francis Howell website and Facebook page were so troubling that the district had to disable the comment feature. Of course many of these comments also denied that race and class had anything to do with their conclusions. Safety was touted as the number one concern. The local newspaper in St. Louis did a story highlighting Normandy as the "most dangerous school in the area."[61] The comments, though, clearly went beyond concerns for safety. Race was often front and center. And indeed, for those who believe otherwise, one need only read the comments that did explicitly cover race and unabashedly admitted that they did not want their children to attend schools with black children.[62]

Nonetheless, the transfers proceeded, and pursuant to statute, despite some parents' concern that Normandy would not pay and would just suck their district dry, Normandy Schools wrote tuition checks to the tune of *$1.5 million per month* to the various transferee school districts, including Francis Howell.[63] Three interesting things happened as a result of those transfers:

1) *Not one* of the perceived fears of the Francis Howell parents manifested.[64]

2) Although the transfer law contained no such limitation, DESE advised all districts to set class size limitations that were in the range of already acceptable limitations, and districts followed this advice.[65] Schools did not have to deal, then, with hiring more teachers or finding additional classroom space. Some additional expenditures were necessary for extra books, art supplies, and such, but larger expenses like teacher salaries often were not.[66] Thus, only a portion of the money paid by Normandy Schools to the transferee districts was used to cover additional expenses and in some cases, *none* of the tuition money was spent on the Normandy children.[67]

3) The payments virtually bankrupted Normandy Schools.[68]

The situation became so dire that on May 20, 2014, the State Board of the Department of Education used its statutory power to dissolve Normandy Schools. It then proceeded to create what it said was a new district, appointed a new school board for the district, and announced that the new district would be operated under direct state oversight. This, the State Board said, would provide the district with a new beginning. It did not accredit the "new" Normandy Schools but labeled it as a "'State Oversight District'" *without an accreditation status* for up to three years."[69] This new district, then, would be *not-unaccredited*. And, this meant that the transfer statute would no longer apply. The new district, now called the Normandy Schools Collaborative (NSC), went into effect on July 1, 2014. Days later Francis Howell announced that it would not accept children from NSC. This decision was odd. After all, Francis Howell still had over a million dollars in tuition from NSC *that it had not spent*. There also were no concerns about drugs, violence, or crime. Nonetheless, the district stated that because NSC was no longer unaccredited, the statute no longer applied.[70] Several parents who wanted their children to continue to attend Francis Howell filed a lawsuit for injunctive relief to force that district to accept the students. A hearing was held on August 6, 2014, the first day of school in Francis Howell.

In the meantime, schools in NSC were scheduled to begin classes on August 11, 2014. Many children who lived near the Canfield Green Apartments, where Michael Brown was killed just 48 hours earlier, attended school in NSC. Emotions and tensions were high. Readers will recall the protests and civil unrest, tear-gas-filled air, military-style tanks, and police with assault rifles pointed and ready to shoot that marked Ferguson streets for the days and weeks after the Brown killing. In the midst of that turmoil and a week and a half after school had already begun in Francis Howell, a judge in St. Louis County enjoined Francis Howell from preventing the plaintiff children from coming back. Finding NSC *"abysmally unaccredited,"* the judge stated that irreparable harm would occur if the students, who wished to transfer and had done everything necessary to effectuate their right to transfer under the law, were not permitted to return to the district.[71]

To put the judge's statement that NSC was *"abysmally unaccredited"* into perspective, consider the following: In 2013, DESE adopted a new measure of performance based on a 140-point scale. A district needs 50–60 percent of those points to be accredited.[72] In 2013 NSC earned a total of 11.1 percent. By the time Michael Brown graduated one year later, it had earned just 7.1 percent.[73] This was the worst academic record in the state.[74] The court noted that under these circumstances, any attempt to recognize NSC as anything other than unaccredited would "completely def[y] logic."[75]

Even after the judge's order, however, Francis Howell required each student who wanted to return to have his or her own uniquely signed court order *in hand.* Thus another fight ensued for parents who thought the August 15 court order was enough. The court's preliminary injunction became final in February of 2015. Although it took some time (critical time, in fact, for a parent wanting to return to Francis Howell), Francis Howell finally, albeit begrudgingly, accepted the students. All of this uncertainty and instability, two things no child ever needs, were happening in the midst of the turmoil and unrest of Ferguson in the aftermath of the Michael Brown killing. Michael Brown's youngest sister attended school in this very district. This gives you a sense of how close the students in the school were to the issues simultaneously going on outside of the schoolhouse doors. The stress load on many parents and children alike was often too great to bear.

Thus, only about 110 of the 430 students who transferred to Francis Howell the prior year took advantage of the court victory. There were many students who, once the district stated that they could not return, did not fill out the proper "intent to return" documents. When Francis Howell tried to enforce the deadline, another fight was had, and the parents again won. Many parents, though, were simply tired of their children being batted about like balls in a ping pong game. The stress load in the community was already on overload. And a lingering question remained: Would the children be able to stay in Francis Howell once and for all, or would they be going through similar battles in the foreseeable future? In other words, if Normandy regained accreditation the next year or the year after, would Francis Howell push those children out and force them to return to their home school district or allow them to stay and graduate from their new school? Most parents decided to keep their children in Normandy Schools. Tanks and tear gas on the streets, fights with the Francis Howell school district, angry White parents in Francis Howell, two-hour-long one-way bus commutes, and the uncertainty of being able to stay in and graduate from high school in Francis Howell forced many parents to choose the devil they knew.

At the time of this writing, NSC continues to send tuition payments out to school districts including Francis Howell. It continues to have a student body that is over 97 percent Black, over 90 percent on free or reduced lunch, and struggling with tremendous academic issues. There are also behavioral challenges with the Normandy Schools children.[76] And, as discussed *infra,* NSC continues to have challenges with curriculum offerings, resources, and teacher expectations. The district is segregated by race, unequal on almost every measurable level, and there is no relief in sight.

What Is Left of *Brown?*

Nine months after Michael Brown's killing, the *St. Louis Post-Dispatch* ran a story on his former high school.[77] The story was written from the vantage point of Cameron Hensley, then a senior honors student. Hensley, unlike a number of his high-achieving classmates, had opted not to exercise his rights under the transfer statute, choosing instead to remain at NSC.[78] The story revealed no new beginning, as promised by state education officials; no expectations, few books, no homework, and no attempt to educate. Specifically, readers learned that at Normandy High School, there were: zero honors courses; seniors reading on a third-grade level; a physics teacher who had not planned a lesson in months; substitute teachers who had been substituting the same class since the beginning of the school year; unsupervised and unattended students sleeping in class, taking pictures, practicing dance routines, all in front of teachers who were in the classroom but not teaching; an AP English class taught by an instructor not certified to teach it; rooms that smelled like mildew and lacked adequate air conditioning; no school books to take home; and virtually nonexistent homework.[79] For students like Michael Brown and Cameron Hensley, who opted to stay in their home schools, no tangible benefits of the victory in *Brown* over 60 years earlier could be seen in their schools. They attended racially segregated schools, overwhelmingly poor schools, and extremely underperforming (and thus unequal) schools. Supreme Court precedents kept them in segregated schools, compulsory attendance laws required their attendance in segregated and underperforming schools, and despite that compulsory attendance, they were virtually ignored once inside the building.

Normandy Schools are reflective of many public schools throughout the nation. Dysfunction, racial segregation, and unequal education plague Black, Brown, and poor children in public schools.[80] Normandy Schools are not an anomaly. What is happening there, what has happened there, is reflective of a national story.[81] Indeed, public schools remain "so separate and vastly unequal that *Plessy v. Ferguson*, not *Brown v. Board of Education*, might as well be the law of the land."[82] Historical segregation and discrimination have laid the foundation for what we continue to see today. But it is the current trappings of poverty and unequal access to opportunity and resources, that is, the legacies of *Plessy*, that continue to smother the academic achievement of poor students, of Black students, of Brown students, and even of Native American students.

What Now?

For 60-plus years, we have defined integration in terms of White and Black. We can no longer do this given declining White births, increasing births among non-White Hispanic populations, and continued White flight from public schools. It is becoming harder to integrate, if integration is defined in Black and White. Of course, the benefits of diversity have been well established, so although increasingly difficult to implement, we should continue to work to integrate schools in spaces where that is still possible. But integration based on the Black/White model can no longer be the goal.

There remain real structural barriers to quality education. Racial isolation, class and housing segregation, unemployment and underemployment, concentrated poverty, inadequate access to nutritional food, inadequate health care and access to health care, and criminalization are just a part of the vicious cycle keeping people and their children trapped in dysfunction, inequity, and inequality.[83] Many children also come from communities afflicted with drugs, violence, and gangs. Family support structures are not always present. Many come from single-parent homes and homes where the students may have to care for younger siblings or work themselves to help the family survive. Many parents are uneducated themselves, coming from the same dysfunctional school systems their children attend. Consider too practices that prey on the working poor, like the failure to pay living wages, higher rents and food prices, predatory loans and interest rates, and municipal court abuses as reflected earlier in chapter 3. All of these certainly have negative repercussions on the lives of the children who live in these communities and on their cognitive development, learning capability, and attentiveness in school. Imagine trying to attend school and learn and thrive with this weight on your shoulders. Michael Brown's mother is often quoted for asking a reporter shortly after her son's death: "Do you know how hard it was for me to get him to stay in school and graduate?"[84] Maybe we can see a little of what she meant now.

Systemic educational deficiencies are part of the problem as well. Many children do not receive the critical early childhood education that they need to set their foundation for future learning. Despite the evidence of the importance of early childhood education, many districts in poor communities do not have early childhood education programs. Children without this access begin kindergarten behind the starting line.[85] We must find the funding for these proven means of providing the educational foundation children need. Early childhood interventions can and should also include work with parents and other care providers.[86] Schools should receive adequate funding to provide wraparound services to meet the needs of the students, the parents, and the community. Consider the work of Superintendent Tiffany Anderson in the Jennings School District, in close proximity to Normandy Schools. Superintendent Anderson was recognized by Education Week in 2015 as one of "the nation's 16 most innovative district leaders" in its 2015 Leaders to Learn From report. Despite a predominately Black, poor, and academically struggling district, Superintendent Anderson has implemented a variety of social services that reach into her district's community and therefore reaches her students. And her academic numbers have consistently improved over the past few years.[87]

Schools also need basic resources: textbooks, desks, chairs, science laboratory equipment, chalk. Schools need certified, qualified, degreed, well-paid, diverse, and empathetic teachers who care about their students and who have expectations of them. Recall from the

OCR report cited earlier that the best teachers do not gravitate to poor districts and it is not uncommon that many of the teachers in these districts are less experienced and hold fewer degrees than teachers in more affluent districts, and some have little or no expectations of their students.[88] Diverse teachers also are lacking despite the overwhelmingly Black and Brown student populations.[89] Explicit and implicit racial biases negatively inform and often taint teacher assumptions and conclusions about students and exacerbate the school to prison pipeline.[90] All of this can be addressed and remedied.

We must also rethink how schools are funded. Most public schools are funded by property taxes under the guise of local control. Such limited funding not only hurts the educational prospects for children who live in property-poor districts,[91] but also works to keep schools segregated.[92] Indeed, affluent communities often fight efforts to bring affordable housing to their communities.[93] And, as long as housing is segregated and schools are assigned by neighborhoods, schools will continue to be segregated based on class and/or race.[94] But there is an answer to this. We could change the way students are assigned to schools. Legislatures can remedy this deficiency by reassigning schools based on factors other than zip codes. For example, socioeconomic status is an acceptable way of assigning students to schools and its benefits are well known.[95] This has been suggested as a factor that should be considered when assigning schools.[96] Similarly, the Obama administration has recommended that schools consider multiple factors like household income, educational attainment of the adults in the household, and racial and economic demographics of a neighborhood when assigning children to schools.[97]

What Now for Normandy?

For Normandy Schools, the question of "what now?" is still uncertain. The governor of Missouri announced a plan for the state and surrounding school districts to support Normandy Schools and fellow struggling district Riverview Gardens. The state will provide $500,000 in reading and literacy funding, while neighboring districts will lend varying support: curricula design assistance, teacher training, cost reductions from pooled purchasing power, reading and math specialists, and in some districts reductions in tuition for transfer students.[98] Is this a step in the right direction or another Band-Aid? I think the latter. For decades now, Normandy children have been trapped in a failing and dying district. And they are not alone in the greater St. Louis area.[99]

The efforts previously mentioned at reforming unaccredited schools are not evidence of anything more than piecemeal and partial feel-good attempts at change. $500,000 and a little support by other districts is just feel good salve for the doers. It will not change the educational trajectory of the thousands of students in Normandy Schools or other failing districts. Sure, temporary relief might be had. But what is needed is more than temporary relief. We need systemic change. It is time to completely restructure how children are being educated in Missouri (and indeed, in public schools throughout America). But first, neighborhoods, like people, must be nourished. Communities need adequate housing, health care, and employment, for example. Districts must also meet children where they are. Recall the work of Superintendent Anderson in the Jennings School District, a district with near identical demographics to Normandy. There teachers are provided with dismantling racism training, poverty simulations, cultural and ethnic competency classes. Washers and dryers are made available for students. They have a health clinic in the school, parenting classes, and a food pantry. The district has a shelter for its homeless children. As the Superintendent says, it is impossible to teach if the child is cold, hungry, unhealthy, and has no place to live. Educating the child means treating the whole child and that requires meeting the child where the child is.[100] States, including Missouri, need to reconsider the way it assigns children to schools. Clearly children are receiving a different quality of education depending on where they live. (See Appendix.) This can and must be changed. Of course in order to do this in Missouri, we would need to consider consolidation of school districts. Currently the metropolitan area comprises 24 school districts. The districts would have to be consolidated into several larger groups or one large district, and children would need to be assigned along socioeconomic lines or a combination of other factors along the lines discussed earlier.

The solution of one unified school district in the St. Louis metropolitan area, at least, has been suggested before.[101] And, while it has been rejected time and time again, it seems to be the only way to assure that every child in Normandy Schools and the other failing school districts can be assured of the opportunity of a quality education without regard to their zip code.[102] It is the only way to ensure that every taxpayer, every teacher, every politician, and every parent is invested in the education of all. It is the only path on the road to full citizenship. It is the thing we have not tried.

Michael Brown attended school. He graduated. Given what you now know of the school district he graduated from, you might agree the road ahead of him would have been difficult had he lived. Indeed, underperforming schools, "a dearth of successful models, lack of networks that lead to jobs, unsafe streets, recurrent multi-generational family dysfunction, or the general miasma of depression that can pervade high poverty contexts may inhibit the success of even the most motivated."[103]

St. Louis NAACP City Chapter President Adolphus Pruitt once noted that "if the districts cannot find a way to properly educate their children, they might as well put a gun to their head and kill them. . . . The outcome of failing to get a good education is ruining their lives. I make that statement because it is that serious of an issue. *It impacts everything.*"[104] While the statement regarding guns to the head is merely hyperbole, we know that the rest of the statement is certainly true.

At the time of this writing, it is one year after Michael Brown's death. A new school year has just begun. Welcome Back signs greet students in Normandy everywhere. The question now is, Welcome back to what?

Notes

1. Julie Bosman & Emma G. Fitzsimmons, *Grief and Protests Follow Shooting of a Teenager: Police Say Michael Brown Was Killed after Struggle for Gun in St. Louis Suburb*, N.Y. Times, Aug. 10, 2014, http://www.nytimes.com/2014/08/11/us/police-say-mike-brown-was-killed-after-struggle-for-gun.html.

2. *Id.* Michael Brown was scheduled to attend Vatterott College, a for-profit school interested in "the UN-DER world: [the] Unemployed, Underpaid, Unsatisfied, Unskilled, Unprepared, Unsupported, Unmotivated, Unhappy and Underserved." *See* Nikole Hannah-Jones, *School Segregation, the Continuing Tragedy of Ferguson*, ProPublica, Dec. 19, 2014, http://www.propublica.org/article/ferguson-school-segregation. Hannah-Jones conducted a very powerful interview on the Normandy School system in a segment of *This American Life*. It is worth the time to listen. Go to: http://www.thisamericanlife.org/radio-archives/episode/562/the-problem-we-all-live-with.

3. Brown v. Bd. of Educ., 347 U.S. 483 (1954) (*Brown I*).

4. *Slavery and the Making of America*, PBS (broadcast Feb. 9 & 16, 2005), http://www.pbs.org/wnet/slavery/experience/education/docs1.html.

5. *See generally* W. E. Burghardt Du Bois, Black Reconstruction in America: 1860–1880 (1935).

6. *See, e.g.*, John Hope Franklin, From Slavery to Freedom, Third Edition: A History of Negro Americans (1971).

7. Plessy v. Ferguson, 16 S. Ct. 1138 (1896).

8. *See generally* Michelle Alexander, The New Jim Crow, Mass Incarceration in the Age of Colorblindness (The New Press 2012); Douglas A. Blackmon, Slavery by Another Name: The Re-Enslavement of Black Americans from the Civil War to World War II (2009).

9. *See, e.g.*, Janet Duitsman Cornelius, When I Can Read My Title Clear (1991); Ira Berlin, Marc Favreau & Steven F. Miller, Remembering Slavery (2013).

10. Heather Andrea Williams, Self-taught 106–08 (2005).

11. This story is documented in *The Road to Brown* (Cal. News Reel 2004). Some of the cases leading up to the Brown decision included *Pearson v. Murray*, 169 A.2d 478 (1936) (University of Maryland

School of Law ordered to admit Black male student); *Mo. ex rel. Gaines v. Canada*, 305 U.S. 337 (1938) (University of Missouri School of Law ordered to admit Black male student); *Sweatt v. Painter*, 339 U.S. 629 (1950) (University of Texas ordered to admit Black male student); *Sipuel v. Board of Regents of the University of Oklahoma*, 332 U.S. 631 (1948) (University of Oklahoma School of Law obligated under the equal protection clause to provide Black female plaintiff same educational opportunity as provided to White students); and *McLaurin v. Oklahoma State Regents for Higher Education*, 339 U.S. 637 (1950) (segregation of Black male student in University of Oklahoma's doctoral program violated equal protection clause).

12. *Brown I*, 347 U.S. at 493.

13. Brown v. Bd. of Educ., 349 U.S. 294 (1955) (*Brown II*).

14. *See, e.g.*, PBS, The Supreme Court: Expanding Civil Rights, Primary Sources, Southern Manifesto on Integration (Mar. 12, 1956), http://www.pbs.org/wnet/supremecourt/rights/sources_docu ment2.html (19 senators and 77 members of the House of Representatives signed the "Southern Manifesto," promising to use all lawful means to bring about a reversal of *Brown*). In 1957, Elizabeth Eckford, one of the Little Rock Nine, famously walked through a mob of angry White protestors in order to desegregate Central Rock High School. James T. Patterson, Brown v. Board of Education: A Civil Rights Milestone and Its Troubled Legacy (2001). Prince Edward County closed all public schools from 1959 to1964 in lieu of desegregating them. *Id.* In 1960, federal marshals escorted six-year-old Ruby Bridges into her new all-White school. *Id.* In 1963 then Alabama Governor George Wallace famously blocked the entrance to the University of Alabama, refusing to allow two Black students—Vivian Malone and James Hood—to enter the school. B.J. Hollars, Opening the Doors: The Desegregation of the University of Alabama and the Fight for Civil Rights in Tuscaloosa (2013).

15. *See* Green v. Sch. Bd. of New Kent Cnty., 391 U.S. 430 (1968); Swann v. Charlotte-Mecklenburg Bd. of Educ., 402 U.S. 1 (1971); Keyes v. Sch. Dist. No. 1, Denver, 413 U.S. 189 (1973).

16. Colin Gordon, Mapping Decline: St. Louis and the Fate of the American City (2009).

17. Milliken v. Bradley, 418 U.S. 717 (1974). *See also* Cedric Merlin Powell, *Milliken, "Neutral Principles," and Post-Racial Determinism*, 31 Harv. J. on Racial & Ethnic Just. 1 (Spring 2015).

18. *Milliken*, 418 U.S. at 752.

19. *See, e.g., Milliken*; Bd. of Educ. of Okla. City Pub. Sch. v. Dowell, 498 U.S. 237 (1991); Freeman v. Pitts, 122 S. Ct. 1430 (1992); Missouri v. Jenkins, 115 S. Ct. 2038 (1995).

20. *Dowell*, 498 U.S. at 638.

21. Parents Involved in Cmty. Sch. v. Seattle Sch. Dist. No. 1, 551 U.S.701 (2007) (PICS).

22. *Id.* at 726. The Court left undisturbed prior rulings that race could be considered to remedy the effects of past discrimination and to diversify the student body in higher education. *Id.* at 720–22.

23. Gary Orfield et al., Brown at 60 (Civil Rights Project May 15, 2014), http://civilrightsproject .ucla.edu/research/k-12-education/integration-and-diversity/brown-at-60-great-progress-a-long -retreat-and-an-uncertain-future/Brown-at-60-051814.pdf [hereinafter Brown at 60].

24. Erica Frankenberg, Chungmei Lee & Gary Orfield, A Multiracial Society with Segregated Schools: Are We Losing the Dream (Civil Rights Project Jan. 2003), http://civilrightsproject.ucla.edu/research/k -12-education/integration-and-diversity/a-multiracial-society-with-segregated-schools-are-we-losing -the-dream/frankenberg-multiracial-society-losing-the-dream.pdf. *See also* Brown at 60, *supra* note 23.

25. Valerie Strauss, *For the First Time Minority Students Expected to Be Majority in U.S. Public Schools This Fall*, Wash. Post, Aug, 21, 2014, http://www.washingtonpost.com/blogs/answer-sheet /wp/2014/08/21/for-first-time-minority-students-expected-to-be-majority-in-u-s-public-schools-this-fall. Most public school students today are also poor, qualifying for free and reduced lunch, the educational predictor for poverty. *See* Lyndsey Layton, *Majority of U.S. Public School Students Are in Poverty*, Wash. Post, Jan. 16, 2013, http://www.washingtonpost.com/local/education/majority-of-us-public -school-students-are-in-poverty/2015/01/15/df7171d0-9ce9-11e4-a7ee-526210d665b4_story.html.

26. *See* William H. Frey, *Shift to a Majority Minority Population in the U.S. Happening Faster than Expected*, Brookings Inst., June 19, 2013, http://www.brookings.edu/blogs/up-front/posts/2013/06/19-us -majority-minority-population-census-frey; Brown at 60, *supra* note 23, at 6.

27. Linda Sheryl Greene, *The Battle for Brown*, 68 Ark. L. Rev. 131, 132 (2015).

28. *Brown I*, 347 U.S. at 493.

29. Edward Graham, *"A Nation at Risk" Turns 30: Where Did It Take Us?*, NEA (Apr. 25, 2013), http://neatoday.org/2013/04/25/a-nation-at-risk-turns-30-where-did-it-take-us-2/. *See also* U.S. Dep't of Educ., Performance of U.S. 15-Year-Old Students in Mathematics, Science, and Reading Literacy in an International Context (2014), http://nces.ed.gov/pubs2014/2014024rev.pdf.

30. *See, e.g.*, U.S. Dep't of Educ., Averaged High School Graduation Rates of Public Secondary Schools (2014), http://dashboard.ed.gov/statecomparison.aspx?i=e&id=6&wt=40 (state-by-state comparison of average freshman graduation rates from public secondary schools for the various racial/ethnic groups).

31. This chapter does not address school discipline matters, which also plague public schools with glaring racial disparities. See Daniel Losen et al., *Are we Closing the School Discipline Gap?*, Civil Rights Project 1 (Feb. 2015), http://civilrightsproject.ucla.edu/resources/projects/center-for-civil-rights-remedies/school-to-prison-folder/federal-reports/are-we-closing-the-school-discipline-gap/Are WeClosingTheSchoolDisciplineGap_FINAL221.pdf; U.S. Dep't of Educ., Civil Rights Data Collection Data Snapshot: School Discipline (Mar. 2014), https://www2.ed.gov/about/offices/list/ocr/docs/crdc-discipline-snapshot.pdf; Kimberlé Williams Crenshaw with Priscilla Ocen and Jyoti Nanda, *Black Girls Matter: Pushed Out, Overpoliced and Underprotected*, African Am. Pol'y Forum, http://www.atlanticphilanthropies.org/sites/default/files/uploads/BlackGirlsMatter_Report.pdf.

32. Black Lives Matter: The Schott 50 State Report on Public Education and Black Males (Schott Found. 2015) [hereinafter BlackLivesMatter Report].

33. Press Release, U.S. Dep't of Educ., U.S. High School Graduation Rate Hits New Record High, Feb. 12, 2015, http://www.ed.gov/news/press-releases/us-high-school-graduation-rate-hits-new-record-high.

34. *See, e.g.*, Kimberly Jade Norwood, *Adult Complicity in the Dis-Education of the Black Male High School Athlete & Societal Failures to Remedy His Plight*, 34 Thur. Mar. L. Rev. 21 (2008). *See also "Cheated" Out of an Education: Book Replays UNC's Student-Athlete Scandal*, NPR (broadcast Mar. 23, 2015, 6:46 PM), http://www.npr.org/2015/03/23/394884826/cheated-out-of-an-education-book-replays-unc-s-student-athlete-scandal.

35. *See, e.g.*, Nat'l Ctr. for Educ. Statistics, NAEP Data Explorer: Reading Grade 12, http://nces.ed.gov/nationsreportcard/naepdata/report.aspx?app=NDE&p=3-RED-2-20133%2c20093%2c20053%2c20023%2c19983%2c19982%2c19942%2c19922-RRPCM-GENDER%2cSDRACE-NT-MN_MN-J_Y_0-1-0-37 (last visited July 13, 2015).

36. Nat'l Ctr. for Educ. Statistics, NAEP Glossary of Terms (2015), https://nces.ed.gov/nationsreportcard/glossary.aspx?nav=y#proficient.

37. BlackLivesMatter Report, *supra* note 32, at 39.

38. The New York State Department of Education defines level 1 as follows: NYS Level 1: Students performing at this level are well below proficient in standards for their grade. They demonstrate limited knowledge, skills, and practices embodied by the New York State P–12 Common Core Learning Standards for Mathematics that are considered insufficient for the expectations at this grade. N.Y. Dep't of Educ., Definitions of Performance Levels (2014), http://www.p12.nysed.gov/irs/ela-math/2014/2014-MathDefinitionsofPerformanceLevels.pdf.

39. N.Y. Dep't of Educ., 3–8 ELA Assessments (2014), http://data.nysed.gov/assessment38.php?year=2014&subject=ELA&state=yes. The assessments for mathematics were nearly identical (47 percent Black students as compared to 21 percent White students). *See* 3–8 ELA Assessments (2014), http://data.nysed.gov/assessment38.php?year=2014&subject=Mathematics&state=yes.

40. D.C. Pub. Sch., DCPS Data Sets, http://dcps.dc.gov/DCPS/About+DCPS/DCPS+Data/DCPS+Data+Sets (last visited July 13, 2015).

41. *Id.*

42. *See, e.g.*, San Antonio Indep. Sch. Dist. v. Rodriguez, 411 U.S. 1 (1973). In 2006, Oprah Winfrey aired a special report titled "Schools in Crisis." Although the report focused on many inferior public school buildings in inner cities throughout America, one particular experiment revealed in the report is worth noting. A group of students from a poor inner-city school in Chicago with a graduation rate of 40 percent traded places for a day with a group of students from an affluent suburban school 35 miles west of the city and with a graduation rate of 99 percent. The students from the inner-city school were overwhelmingly Black while the students from the affluent suburban school

were predominately White. The physical structure of the two facilities were vastly different, with the inner-city school barely structurally sound and the suburban school a multimillion-dollar facility. Inside, the buildings continued to reflect the vast differences in resources. Working computers with keyboards (with all keys intact), instruments for music classes, award winning music programs, fully functional science laboratories, state of the art—and thus actually working—exercise equipment, cardio rooms, and water-filled pools, to name a few amenities, were all available in the suburban school, but completely absent in the inner-city school. Even the level of expectation from teachers and rigor in classrooms were vastly different between the schools. An "A" student in math from the inner-city school sat in on a comparable class in the suburban school and later remarked: "I was looking at the math problems that they're doing and I was like what language is that? Soon as I get to college, I'mma be lost." *The Oprah Winfrey Show: Oprah's Special Report: American Schools in Crisis* (Harpo Prods. Inc. television broadcast Apr. 12, 2006).

43. Letter from Catherine E. Lhamon, Assistant Sec'y for Civil Rights, to colleagues (Oct. 1, 2014), http://www2.ed.gov/about/offices/list/ocr/letters/colleague-resourcecomp-201410.pdf (emphasis added).

44. "Apartheid schools" is a term used to describe schools that are 90% or more Black and/or brown. *See, e.g.,* Lilly Workneh, March 26, 2014, Study: NY schools most segregated in US labeling some "apartheid schools;" http://thegrio.com/2014/03/26/study-ny-schools-most-segregated-in-the-us-labeling-some-apartheid-schools/; *see also* Jonathan Kozol, Shame of the Nation 19 (2005). This frequently also means that the school is likely a high poverty one. *See, e.g., supra* note 25.

45. For studies in the history of the White communal beginnings of the suburbs immediately surrounding St. Louis City, see GORDON, *supra* note 16.

46. *See, e.g.,* Hannah-Jones, *supra* note 2. From 1972 through 1999, SLPSD was at the center of the largest voluntary desegregation lawsuit (and settlement) in the country. Minnie Liddell, a Black parent who resided in the City of St. Louis, filed a lawsuit in 1972 against SLPSD and the state of Missouri to force those entities to comply with the mandate of *Brown*. The lawsuit eventually ballooned to include over 20 suburban school district defendants. Settlement included transportation of some Black students from the city schools into largely White suburban schools and the transfer of some White suburban children into city magnet schools. This arrangement did not allow transfers *between* county schools. Normandy Schools, a county school district, was not a defendant in the case. Not being a party to the lawsuit, it could not benefit from the settlement. More importantly, even had it been a defendant, as a county district, it would not have been eligible to transfer students from its primarily Black school district to any of the largely White county school districts. *See, e.g.,* GERALD W. HEANEY & SUSAN UCHITELLE, UNENDING STRUGGLE: THE LONG ROAD TO AN EQUAL EDUCATION IN ST. LOUIS (2004). I explored areas that unfolded after this book's publication. *See* Kimberly Jade Norwood, *Minnie Liddell's Forty-Year Quest for Quality Public Education Remains a Dream Deferred*, 40 WASH. U. J.L. & POL'Y 1 (2012).

47. E-mail from Carol D. McCauley, Custodian of Records for the Normandy Schools Collaboration (June 8, 2015, 17:48 CST) (on file with author).

48. *See, e.g.,* MO. CODE REGS. ANN. tit. 5, § 20-100.105.

49. MO. DEP'T OF ELEMENTARY & SECONDARY EDUC., COMPREHENSIVE GUIDE TO MISSOURI SCHOOL IMPROVEMENT PROGRAM 1 (May 2012), http://dese.mo.gov/sites/default/files/MSIP-5-comprehensive-guide.pdf.

50. Norwood, *supra* note 46, at 32.

51. E-mail from Kelli Dickey (June 4, 2015, 11:05 CST) (on file with author). *See also* Mo. Dep't of Elementary & Secondary Educ., 2012 School District Performance and Accreditation: A Presentation to the State Board of Education 109 (Sept. 18, 2012) (on file with author); Mo. Dep't of Elementary & Secondary Educ., What Happens When a School District Becomes Unaccredited? (May 2012).

52. Leah Thorsen, *School Merger Draws Fire at Forum That Draws More Than 400 People; Wellston District Residents Question Whether Normandy Schools Are Much Better*, ST. LOUIS POST-DISPATCH, Dec. 15, 2009, http://www.stltoday.com/news/school-merger-draws-fire-at-forum-that-draws-more-than/article _a713f679-717d-526b-bb7c-4b792d335237.html.

53. Children have a right to free education in Missouri. MO. CONST. art. IX, § 1(a). State statutes require that school aged children from a lapsed district be reassigned to another school district or

districts. Mo. Ann. Stat. § 162.081 (West 2015). *See also* Mo. Ann. Stat. § 167.121 (West 2015) (setting forth the residency requirements to register a pupil in a school district); Mo. Ann. Stat. § 167.121 (West 2015) (noting circumstances of hardship under which students may be assigned to a district other than that of residence).

54. Hannah-Jones, *supra* note 2.

55. Mo. Rev. Stat. §167.131 (2000). For additional analysis of this law, see Norwood, *supra* note 46.

56. Norwood, *supra* note 46, at 40–42.

57. Elisa Crouch & Jessica Bock, *School Transfer Issue Spawns Logistical Headaches and Legal Questions*, St. Louis Post-Dispatch, Aug, 4, 2013, http://www.stltoday.com/news/local/education/school-transfer
-issue-spawns-logistical-headaches-and-legal-quetions/article_d3942b4b-24ee-5246-9743-77fed0b8579a
.html.

58. Massey v. Normandy Schs. Collaborative, No. 14SL-CC02359 (St. Louis Cnty. Ct. Feb. 11, 2015) (Findings of Fact, Conclusions of Law, Final Order, and Judgment).

59. *See, e.g.*, Chris McDaniel, *Francis Howell Parents Express Outrage over Incoming Normandy Students*, St. Louis Pub. Radio, Jul 12, 2013, http://news.stlpublicradio.org/post/francis-howell-parents-express
-outrage-over-incoming-normandy-students.

60. FB Post to Francis Howell Facebook Page by Todd Breer, July 11 at 8:39 am.

61. Elisa Crouch, May 5, 2013, Normandy High: The most dangerous school in the area, http://www
.stltoday.com/news/local/education/normandy-high-the-most-dangerous-school-in-the-area/article_49a1b
882-cd74-5cc4-8096-fcb1405d8380.html.

62. All comments are on file with the author.

63. Elisa Crouch, *Efforts to Improve Normandy Schools Have Fallen Short, State Board Admits*, St. Louis Post-Dispatch, May 19, 2015, http://www.stltoday.com/news/local/education/efforts-to-improve
-normandy-schools-have-fallen-short-state-board/article_65d7b44b-6407-5c94-96b9-1b5a62d09856.html.

64. Jessica Bock, *Francis Howell Officials Say 'No' to Normandy Students*, St. Louis Post-Dispatch, June 21, 2014, http://www.stltoday.com/news/local/education/francis-howell-officials-say-no-to-nor
mandy-students/article_fad2b8bd-3631-5b51-9c58-e31ccf5d2a22.html.

65. Elisa Crouch, *Missouri Offers Some Relief on Impending School Transfers*, St. Louis Post-Dispatch, June 20, 2013, http://www.stltoday.com/news/local/education/missouri-offers-some-relief-on
-impending-school-transfers/article_bca34ac8-c8ad-51d3-8a90-e60a3aacbaeb.html. In the *Guidance for Student Transfer from Unaccredited Districts to Accredited Districts*, DESE also imposed arbitrary time limits on when students could sign up to transfer, *see* Mo. Dep't of Elementary & Secondary Educ., Guidance for Student Transfer from Unaccredited Districts to Accredited Districts, STLToday.com, http://www.stltoday.com/guidelines-for-student-transfers/pdf_7760177a-6fbf-5e35-b702-b05bc557d53f
.html.

66. *See also* Elisa Crouch & Jessica Bock, *Money Being Paid by Normandy, Riverview Gardens to Other Districts Not Being Spent*, St. Louis Post-Dispatch, Feb. 10, 2014, http://www.stltoday.com/news
/local/education/money-being-paid-by-normandy-riverview-gardens-to-other-districts/article_f2ae823
3-bf03-57b3-9270-dcc5366de090.html.

67. *Id.*

68. Dale Singer, *Normandy Not Bankrupt Now, but Its Future Remains Cloudy*, St. Louis Pub. Radio, Mar. 31, 2014, http://news.stlpublicradio.org/post/normandy-not-bankrupt-now-its-future-remains-cloudy.

69. *Massey, supra* note 58.

70. Bock, *supra* note 64.

71. *Massey, supra* note 58.

72. Today districts are "accredited with distinction" if they obtain at least 90 percent of all possible points (126–140 points); "accredited" if they have 70–89.9 percent of the possible points (98–125 points); "provisionally accredited" if they have between 50 and 69 percent of the relevant points (70–97 points). If the district has less than 50 percent of the points (0–69 points), the district is unaccredited. Mo. Dep't of Elementary & Secondary Educ., MSIP 5 Questions and Answers, http://dese
.mo.gov/sites/default/files/msip5-faq.pdf.

73. Mo. Dep't of Elementary & Secondary Educ., LEA Summary for Annual Performance Report–Public, http://mcds.dese.mo.gov/guidedinquiry/MSIP%205%20%20State%20Accountability/LEA%20Summary %20for%20Annual%20Performance%20Report%20-%20Public.aspx?rp:Year=2014&rp :District= 096109.

74. *See* Mo. Dep't of Elementary & Secondary Educ., Normandy School District Report Card 2000– 2014, http://mcds.dese.mo.gov/guidedinquiry/School%20Report%20Card/District%20Report%20Card .aspx?rp:SchoolYear=2014&rp:SchoolYear=2013&rp:SchoolYear=2012&rp:SchoolYear=2011&rp:Dist rictCode=096109. *See also* Mo. Dep't of Elementary & Secondary Educ., Normandy School District Demographic Data 2005–2014, http://mcds.dese.mo.gov/guidedinquiry/District%20and%20Building %20Student%20Indicators/District%20Demographic%20Data.aspx?rp:Districts=096109&rp:SchoolYear =2014&rp:SchoolYear=2013&rp:SchoolYear=2012&rp:SchoolYear=2011.

75. *Massey, supra* note 58.

76. *See* Elisa Crouch, *Behavior Problems Boil Over at Normandy Schools*, St. Louis Post-Dispatch, Sept. 12, 2014, http://www.stltoday.com/news/local/education/behavior-problems-boil-over-at-normandy -schools/article_dd9f1f26-06cb-5326-bcfa-3eec77e6f9c1.html; Elisa Crouch, *Normandy High: The Most Dangerous School in the Area*, St. Louis Post-Dispatch, May 5, 2013, http://www.stltoday.com/news /local/education/normandy-high-the-most-dangerous-school-in-the-area/article_49a1b882-cd74-5cc4 -8096-fcb1405d8380.html.

77. Elisa Crouch, *A Senior Year Mostly Lost for a Normandy Honor Student*, St. Louis Post-Dispatch, May 4, 2015, http://www.stltoday.com/news/local/education/a-senior-year-mostly-lost-for-a -normandy-honor-student/article_ce759a06-a979-53b6-99bd-c87a430dc339.html.

78. As detailed elsewhere in this book, living in the Normandy School District during the time of Michael's Brown's death was incredibly stressful. Canfield Green Apartments was just five miles away. Not only were there psychic traumas as a result of the killing of Michael Brown, the leaving of his body in the street for four hours, the protests, the militarized police response, and the violence, but there were tremendous uncertainties among Normandy residents about whether accredited school districts would follow the court's August 15 order. The Francis Howell School District fought the transfers as long as it could and even once it relented, parents in Francis Howell were not happy with the transfers and Normandy Schools parents did not know when/if Normandy Schools would declare bankruptcy and if so, what would happen to their children. Moreover, transfers only applied to unaccredited districts. What would happen a year or two or three down the road for a Normandy Schools child attending school in Francis Howell if Normandy Schools regained accreditation? Would the child be able to finish school in Francis Howell or be uprooted once again? Given these uncertainties, many parents opted to have their children stay in Normandy Schools. Staying meant that the children would be surrounded by a known and familiar environment and would be close to home. This also meant receiving an education in the worst district in the state. A year after Michael Brown's death, these issues remain. Elisa Crouch, *Normandy Transfer Students Left in the Lurch*, Aug. 4, 2015, http://www.stltoday.com/news/local/education/normandy-transfer-students-left-in-the-lurch /article_3f127024-1997-55d5-8219-7a057b7ee259.html.

79. Crouch, *supra* note 77.

80. Analysis of Census Bureau data shows that while the percentage of children living in poverty declined for Hispanics, Whites, and Asians, the number remained steady for Black children, with poverty among Black children registering at almost 40 percent. This is the first time the number of Black children living in poverty surpassed the number of White children living in poverty. This is significant because there are three times as many White children as Black children in the United States. *See* Eileen Patten and Jens Manuel Krogstad, *Black Child Poverty Rate Holds Steady, Even As Other Groups See Declines*, Pew Res., July 14, 2015, http://www.pewresearch.org/fact-tank/2015/07/14 /black-child-poverty-rate-holds-steady-even-as-other-groups-see-declines/.

81. As cities become more segregated, schools follow. *See, e.g.*, Brown at 60, *supra* note 23. Even in completely integrated cities, segregated education thrives. *See, e.g.*, N.R. Kleinfield, *A System Divided: "Why Don't We Have Any White Kids?,"* N.Y. Times, May 13, 2012, at MB1.

82. Jonathan Kozol, Shame of the Nation 216 (2005) (quoting Jack White, reporter for Time Mag.).

83. *See, e.g.*, Richard Rothstein, *For Public Schools, Segregation Then, Segregation Since: Education and the Unfinished March*, Econ. Pol'y Inst., Aug. 27, 2013, http://www.epi.org/publication/unfinished -march-public-school-segregation/; Alexander, *supra* note 8.

84. Bosman & Fitzsimmons, *supra* note 1.

85. Eduardo Porter, *Investments in Education May Be Misdirected*, N.Y. Times, Apr. 2, 2013, http:// www.nytimes.com/2013/04/03/business/studies-highlight-benefits-of-early-education.html?_r=0.

86. Lynn A. Karoly, M. Rebecca Kilburn & Jill S. Cannon, *Proven Benefits of Early Childhood Interventions*, (RAND 2005), http://www.rand.org/pubs/research_briefs/RB9145.html.

87. Rebecca Klein, *How One Superintendent Is Improving Her Community by Improving Her Schools*, Huffington Post, Feb. 27, 2015, http://www.huffingtonpost.com/2015/02/27/tiffany-anderson -jennings_n_6770446.html.

88. *See, e.g.*, Appendix. *See also* Barbara Glesner-Fines, *The Impact of Expectations on Teaching and Learning*, 38 Gonz. L. Rev. 89 (2003); Linda Gorman, *Good Teachers Raise Student Achievement*, NBER Digest 4 (Aug. 2005), http://www.nber.org/papers/w11154.pdf.

89. Jesse J. Holland, *Studies Highlight Teacher-Student Diversity Gap*, Bos. Globe, May 5, 2014, https:// www.bostonglobe.com/news/nation/2014/05/04/teachers-nowherenot-diverse-their-students/Wq6n M4XOyoMwlOYJLtfL3L/story.html.

90. *See* Aleasa M. Word, *Unconscious Bias and the School to Prison Pipeline*, Good Men Project, Sept. 29, 2015, http://goodmenproject.com/featured-content/unconscious-bias-and-the-school-to-prison -pipeline-wrd/.

91. *How Do We Fund Our Schools?*, PBS (Sept. 5, 2008), http://www.pbs.org/wnet/wherewestand /reports/finance/how-do-we-fund-our-schools/?p=197.

92. *See, e.g.*, Ericka K. Wilson, *Toward a Theory of Equitable Federated Regionalism in Public Education*, 61 UCLA L. Rev. 1416, 1439 (2014).

93. *See generally* Sheryll Cashin, The Failures of Integration: How Race and Class Are Undermining The American Dream, ch. 3 (2004); John Eligon, *An Indelible Black-and-White Line: A Year after Ferguson, Housing Segregation Defies Tools to Erase It*, N.Y. Times, Aug. 9, 2015, http://www.nytimes.com/2015/08/09 /us/an-indelible-black-and-white-line.html?hp&action=click&pgtype=Homepage&module=first-column -region&region=top-news&WT.nav=top-news&_r=0.

94. Heather Schwartz, Housing Policy Is School Policy (Century Found. 2010), https://www.tcf.org /assets/downloads/tcf-Schwartz.pdf.

95. Richard D. Kahlenberg, The Future of School Integration: Socioeconomic Diversity as an Education Reform Strategy (Century Found. 2012). See also Sheryll Cashin, *Place, Not Race: Affirmative Action and the Geography of Educational Opportunity*, 47 U. Mich. J. L. Reform 935 (2014); Amy Stuart Wells & Erica Frankenberg, *The Public Schools and the Challenge of the Supreme Court's Integration Decision*, 89(3) Phi Delta Kappan 178–88 (2007). *See also,* Erica Frankenberg, *The Promise of Choice, in* Educational Delusions? Why Choice Can Deepen Inequality and How to Make Schools Fair 75–78 (Gary Orfield & Erica Frankenberg eds., 2013).

96. *See, e.g.*, U.S. Dep't of Ed., Guidance on the Voluntary Use of Race to Achieve Diversity and Avoid Racial Isolation in Elementary and Secondary Schools (2012), http://www2.ed.gov/about/offices/list/ocr /docs/guidance-ese-201111.html.

97. Derek Black, *Middle-Income Peers as Educational Resources and the Constitutional Right to Equal Access*, 53 B.C. L. Rev. 1 (2012).

98. Jessica Bock, *22 School Districts Offer to Help Normandy and Riverview Gardens Schools*, St. Louis Post-Dispatch, June 23, 2015, http://www.stltoday.com/news/local/education/school-districts -offer-help-to-normandy-and-riverview-gardens-schools/article_e01a8007-6e76-59bd-9790-d3d f36cf80b1.html.

99. Elisa Crouch & Walter Moskop, *Poverty and Academic Struggle Go Hand in Hand*, St. Louis Post-Dispatch, May 17, 2014, http://www.stltoday.com/news/local/education/poverty-and-academic-struggle -go-hand-in-hand/article_944bf0f6-c13f-5bbc-9112-9ab9ae205607.html.

100. The Superintendent Who Turned Around A School District, http://www.npr.org/2016/01/03 /461205086/the-superintendent-who-turned-around-a-school-district?utm_source=npr_newsletter&utm _medium=email&utm_content=20160105&utm_campaign=npr_email_a_friend&utm_term=storyshare.

101. D. Bruce La Pierre, *Voluntary Interdistrict School Desegregation in St. Louis: The Special Master's Tale*, 1987 Wis. L. Rev. 971, 992 (1987).

102. Tony Messenger, Editorial, *Time for the Spainhower Solution: Unify St. Louis Schools*, St. Louis Post-Dispatch, Feb, 18, 2014, http://www.stltoday.com/news/opinion/columns/the-platform/editorial -time-for-the-spainhower-solution-unify-st-louis-schools/article_93dee4a2-f573-5a6e-919d-c97e7942f703 .html. *See also* Elisa Crouch, *Black Leadership Roundtable Proposes City-County School District*, St. Louis Post-Dispatch, Nov. 15, 2014, http://www.stltoday.com/news/local/education/black-leadership-round table-proposes-city-county-school-district/article_6dd6c4fd-bc9b-5474-9525-3715e85cc807.html.

103. Cashin, *supra* note 95, at 940.

104. Crouch & Bock, *supra* note 57 (emphasis added).

Appendix

Public School District Characteristics

Characteristic	Clayton			Ladue			Francis Howell			Normandy		
	2012	2013	2014	2012	2013	2014	2012	2013	2014	2012	2013	2014
Graduation rate (%)	98.7	99.5	96.7	96	97.8	98.7	90.0	89.0	93.6	61.7	56.9	61.7
African Americans	100	100	93.8	93.8	96.6	95.7	79.6	91.4	87.5	62.1	57.5	63.4
Whites	98.1	100	97.9	95.8	98.1	99	90.0	92.2	94.7	25*	50*	0*
8th grade math (below basic) (%)	8.5*	4.8*	7.2*	6.2*	21.8*	6.7*	8.1	11.9	4.1	40.4	52	59.5
African Americans	36.2*	14.6*	14.6*	21.7*	28.2*	17.2*	28.6	26.8	29.9	39.9	52.4	58.3
Whites	0.8*	2.2*	2.4*	3.9*	16.7*	4.3*	6.5	10.1	10.4	71.4*	n/a	n/a
8th grade math (basic) (%)	20.9	17.9	19.7	15.3	43.7	11	27.3	40.4	40.4	48.5	39.4	36.5
African Americans	36.2*	41.7	35.4*	28.3*	66.7	24.1*	36.3	50	42.3	49.3	39	38
Whites	19.5	11.1*	15.3*	12.6	27.8*	7.4*	26.4	39.6	40.4	14.3*	n/a	n/a
8th grade math (proficient) (%)	24.6	33.8	26.9	24.8	8*	32.3	33.3	37.5	34.5	9.8	8.6	3.5*
African Americans	23.4*	39.6*	31.3*	19.6*	2.6*	36.2	23.1	19.5	21.2	9.4	8.6	3.1*
Whites	25.8	34.8	28.2	26.2	11.1*	31.9	34.8	39.6	37.7	14.3*	n/a	n/a
8th grade math (advanced) (%)	46	43.5	46.2	53.7	26.4	50	31.3	10.2	11.1	1.3*	0*	0.5*
African Americans	4.3*	4.2*	18.8	30.4*	2.6*	22.4*	12.1	3.7*	6.6	1.4*	0*	0.5*
Whites	53.9	51.9	54	57.3	44.4*	56.4	32.2	10.8	11.5	0*	n/a	n/a

Characteristic	Clayton			Ladue			Francis Howell			Normandy		
	2012	2013	2014	2012	2013	2014	2012	2013	2014	2012	2013	2014
3rd grade ELA (below basic) (%)	2.1*	1.6*	4.9*	2*	3.6*	6.3	3.2	4.5	4.3	19.3	17.6	21.4
African Americans	9.4*	0*	13.3*	3.3*	10.5*	20.3*	10.8*	12.5*	13*	19.2	18.1	21
Whites	0.8*	2.2*	4.1*	1.8*	3.1*	4*	2.4*	3.8	3.5	37.5*	n/a	n/a
3rd grade ELA (basic) (%)	31.9	24.9	32.1	31.4	25.8	31	34.7	31.5	35.6	57.1	57.5	60.7
African Americans	59.4*	53.8*	56.7*	53.3*	50*	49.2	49.5	40.9	52.8	57.5	57.2	61.3
Whites	25.4	22.8	27.3	31.3	24.2	28.5	33.4	30	33.8	25*	n/a	n/a
3rd grade ELA (proficient) (%)	36.7	29.5	30.4	33.7	32	32.7	30.3	32.1	32.5	14.5	18.8	11.1
African Americans	25*	26.9*	23.3*	30*	18.4*	18.6*	24.7	30.7	19.4	13.9	18.4	11.1
Whites	38.5	28.7	33.1	35	32	35.5	30.9	32.1	33.4	37.5*	n/a	n/a
3rd grade ELA (advanced) (%)	29.3	44	32.6	33	38.6	30.1	31.8	31.9	27.6	9.1	6.2	6.8*
African Americans	6.3*	19.2*	6.7*	13.3*	21.1*	11.9*	15.1*	15.9*	14.8*	9.4	6.3	6.6*
Whites	35.2	46.3	35.5	31.8	40.7	32	33.3	34	29.2	0*	n/a	n/a
ACT composite scores	25.9	25.3	25.7	26.4	25.1	25.9	22.8	22.7	23.2	16.1	16.8	16
Free & reduced priced lunch (%)	15.4	15.6	15	11.7	11.8	12.3	17.6	18.6	19.9	91.8	91.8	91.5
Average teacher salary ($)	69,111	70,715	71,205	60,610	61,967	62,386	56,345	57,567	58,233	61,083	60,170	59,560
Teachers with master's degree (%)	88.6	91.5	94.1	70.9	74.2	74.1	80.8	81.2	80.3	65.9	61.5	61.5

Source: Missouri Department of Elementary and Secondary Education (DESE)

*Percentage with a numerator less than 20. Data does not include students enrolled in the Special School District, private schools, or charter schools. ELA—English Language Arts; ACT—American College Testing; Below basic—Percent of students with an Achievement Level of Below Basic; Basic—Percent of students with an Achievement Level of Basic; Proficient—Percent of reportable students who scored Proficient; Advanced—Percent of reportable students who scored Advanced.

Chapter 7

If Michael Brown Were Alive, Would He Be Employable?

Terry Smith

Michael Brown, an 18-year-old black teenager, was shot dead by a white police officer who owed his job in part to Ferguson, Missouri's mercenary penchant for raising city operating revenue off petty municipal code violations.[1] Among those violations was the one that brought Officer Darren Wilson into contact with Brown in the first place, jaywalking, or as known under the Ferguson municipal code, Brown's "manner of walking along the roadway."[2] Brown and his companion did not readily oblige Wilson's order to stop walking in the street, and tragedy ensued, though the precise concatenation of events remains in dispute.[3] Although death from such encounters with law enforcement is hardly the norm, a more compliant citizen of Ferguson still might have suffered outsized consequences for such a minor offense.

The deaths of five other unarmed black males at the hands of police and one black female in police custody followed in short order after Michael Brown's shooting, provoking national outcries and indignation, but little reform. Eric Garner was accosted by police in Staten Island, New York, on suspicion of evading state tax laws by selling loose cigarettes. Police placed Garner in an illicit chokehold while wrestling him to the ground to arrest him. Ignoring his pleas of "I can't breathe," police continued to maintain Garner in the chokehold to the point he was deprived of oxygen. Garner's death was ruled a homicide by the coroner's office.[4]

In Cleveland, Tamir Rice, merely 12 years of age, was shot to death by a white officer who purportedly mistook a pellet gun in the boy's possession for a handgun. Whether Rice was given any warning before being shot in the abdomen remains a matter of dispute, but the video that captured the shooting cast considerable doubt on police claims that he was. The officer who fired the fatal shot had not been properly vetted; he had resigned from a previous police department after a "dangerous loss of composure" during firearms training.[5]

A few months later in North Charleston, South Carolina, Walter L. Scott was shot in the back by a white officer as Scott fled the scene of a traffic stop for a broken taillight.[6] A few months later, riots would erupt in Baltimore after the death of Freddie Gray, who was forcibly arrested by police and placed in a van without proper restraints. Gray suffered a "high-energy injury" to his spine during the ride to the police precinct and died one week later.[7] Indictments were made in the Scott and Gray incidents, but these charges did not deter further apparent police abuses. Describing a recent University of Cincinnati police officer's shooting of an unarmed black man, Samuel DuBose, as "a senseless, asinine shooting," the Hamilton County prosecutor obtained a murder indictment against the white officer.[8] In Prairie View, Texas, Sandra Bland, an African American woman, became a gender outlier to the pattern of police encounters that led to black deaths when Bland was pulled over by a white state trooper for failing to use her signals and subsequently threatened with a Taser for not following the trooper's order to extinguish her cigarette.[9] After spending three days in jail following this encounter, Bland was found dead in her jail cell. The coroner has ruled her death a suicide, a finding that is being contested by Bland's family.[10]

In the first eight months of 2015, 24 unarmed black men were shot dead by police.[11] Black men account for 40 percent of all unarmed deaths caused by police shootings, despite constituting just 6 percent of the U.S. population.[12] Unarmed black males are seven times more likely than unarmed white men to die from a police shooting.[13] These violent tragedies and others have fueled the movement known as Black Lives Matter, a hashtag and popular incantation that sprang from the acquittal of George Zimmerman, who shot and killed an unarmed teen, Trayvon Martin, during a confrontation that Zimmerman himself had instigated. If black lives matter, however, they now seem to matter more in death than during life itself. Black lives, particularly those of black men, are stained by a socioeconomic marginality that renders black people society's most suitable candidates for police abuse, judicial exploitation, and, yes, even death by the state. This chapter explains the deaths of Brown, Garner, Rice, Scott, Gray, DuBose, and many others as products of the interaction of socioeconomic marginality, most especially in the labor market, with police abuse and misconduct and mercenary judicial practices. While the public's attention has been riveted to the deaths of these individuals, the less spectacular "slow violence" against black lives—socioeconomic marginality—occurs with far less fanfare even though it is so often an a priori condition of black death at the hands of the police.[14] More importantly, for the vast majority of blacks who encounter the criminal justice system and escape the fast violence of death, their very engagement with the criminal justice system reinforces—and in many cases renders permanent—the same socioeconomic marginality that made them grist for the system in the first place.

The Enterprise of Criminalizing Black Lives

Ferguson, Missouri, is two-thirds African American, yet blacks account for 95 percent of those charged with an unlawful "manner of walking along the roadway," or jaywalking.[15] Similar racial disparities abound in myriad other code violations, all redounding to the financial benefit of the City of Ferguson.[16] The notion of any government criminalizing a segment of its citizens in order to maintain its operation as a government is repugnant to modern ideals of democracy and due process. Yet Ferguson's for-profit model of policing has historical precedent in the United States and exists throughout the country in some degree or another. To be sure, profit does not appear to animate the entirety or even most of the American criminal justice system. But the intersection of local and state governments' thirst for revenue in a period of increasing austerity and the vestiges of the nation's centuries-old history of racial bias has been brought into sharp relief by events in Ferguson, Missouri. Moreover, the intersection has highlighted the social toll of petty-crimes law enforcement. Even setting aside the risk of escalation that accounted for the deaths of Michael Brown and others, for every petty-crimes arrest or citation, there is a high potentiality of leaving the criminal subject with a record that diminishes his employment prospects and increases the likelihood that he will be trapped in the structural socioeconomic conditions that facilitate his engagement with the criminal justice system in the first place. Any reasonable society would weigh these costs against the putative benefits of enforcement. As Ferguson demonstrates, however, this cost-benefit analysis is seldom performed and is unlikely to be when pecuniary motives on the part of the government enter the calculation.

Under post-Reconstruction Black Codes, former slaves were sub-jected to an elaborate battery of legal strictures the infraction of which resulted in continued involuntary servitude.[17] Black peonage was a pre-ferred recourse of former Confederate states wishing to maintain white dominance after the emancipation of four million slaves.[18] The Black Codes and peonage laws comprehensively criminalized the ex-slaves' very existence, though the peonage laws were not always drafted in explicitly racial terms.[19] The codes criminalized unemployment or the failure to enter employment contracts; they made it a crime to quit a job while under contract; they allowed for the "apprenticing" of the children of former slaves by probate courts; and they fined indigents for petty crimes and contracted out the impoverished convicts to pri-vate employers to work off their fines.[20] To achieve the goal of contin-ued white dominance in the South, the codes were selectively enforced against blacks.[21]

A striking feature of black peonage during the period of Redemption of white southern dominance over blacks and into the 20th century was its pecuniary motivations, not merely on the part of private-sector employers but those of state and local governments. The Civil War had left the governments of the South encumbered by debt and burdened with decimated economies.[22] Former Confederate states were incentiv-ized to arrest and convict as many black men as possible in order to lease convicts to private employers for a profit to the state.[23] Police practices in Ferguson, Missouri, and surrounding municipalities in St. Louis County bear a remarkable resemblance to an animating principle of post-Reconstruction black peonage: the criminalization of blacks for profit to the state. This historical analogy, moreover, is not at all limited to the pecuniary motives shared by Ferguson and post-Reconstruction governments of the South. Rather, just as peonage rebranded the badges of slavery upon newly emancipated blacks, Ferguson's gratu-itous criminalization of its black citizenry has done much the same, with one startling modern difference: Peonage subjugated the ex-slaves to work for private employers against their will; Ferguson's criminalization of its black citizens has the effect of making work of any kind difficult to impossible for them to obtain. When one considers the economic costs of disabling citizens from work, peonage ironically seems more rational than the for-profit policing of Ferguson and a multitude of other jurisdic-tions throughout the United States.

Despite a population of only 21,000 residents, between July 1, 2010, and June 30, 2014, the City of Ferguson issued nearly 90,000 citations and summonses for municipal code violations.[24] That is more than four citations and summonses for each resident of Ferguson. Moreover, despite stable incident levels of serious crime, Ferguson's citations rate increased by more than 50 percent from June 30, 2013, to July 1, 2014.[25] Between July 1, 2010, and June 30, 2014, despite constituting only 67 percent of Ferguson's population, African Americans composed 85 percent of Ferguson Police Department (FPD) traffic stops, 90 percent of FPD citations, and 93 percent of FPD arrests.[26] Following a traffic stop, African Americans were 2.07 times more likely to be searched than non-African Americans; 2.00 times more likely to receive a citation; and 2.37 times more likely to be arrested.[27] These statistically significant disparities can occur randomly less than one time in 1,000.[28]

African Americans residing in Ferguson were viewed as grist for fines. In 2013, more than half of blacks who received citations from the FPD received multiple citations during a single encounter compared to only 26 percent of nonblacks.[29] The more discretionary the charge, the greater the racial disproportionality. The disparity in speeding tickets between African Americans and non-African Americans increased by a statistically significant 48 percent when the ticket was issued based on an officer's visual conclusion rather than a speed detection device.[30] Similarly, Ferguson's 67 percent black population was disproportionately represented in an array of charge categories that lend themselves to significant officer discretion and hence abuse: Manner of Walking in Roadway (95 percent); Failure to Comply (94 percent); Resisting Arrest (92 percent); Peace Disturbance (92 percent); Failure to Obey (89 percent).[31] Across ten different offense categories, including the latter highly discretionary charges, African Americans were more likely to be assessed a higher fine than nonblacks.[32] Moreover, African Americans were 68 percent less likely than others to have their cases dismissed and three times less likely than others to have their cases voided.[33]

Ferguson's criminalization of African Americans has been lucrative. Fine and court fees accounted for more than 12 percent of the city's general fund revenue in 2010 and are projected to account for more than 23 percent of its fiscal 2015 general revenue funds.[34] Yet 25 percent of the city's population lives in poverty, making the aggressive levying of fines all the more troubling. Still, Ferguson maintains some of the highest fines in St. Louis County and has sought to increase fines for "high volume offenses" as part of revenue enhancement.[35]

The City of Ferguson is not unique in relying on traffic and similar fines for operating revenue. Faced with declining sources of traditional revenue, officials in cities large and small have been incentivized to deploy traffic ticketing as a source of revenue independent of safety motives.[36] Indeed, since the Great Recession of 2008, 48 states have created new civil and criminal court fees, increased existing ones, or both.[37] In 2011, 325,000 residents of Philadelphia (approximately one in five residents) owed court-related fees or fines, with a median debt of $4,500. In New York City in 2014, there were 1.2 million outstanding warrants, a substantial number of which were for unpaid court fees or fines.[38] It is estimated that nearly $10 billion in fines and fees are owed in California, where 4 million licenses have been suspended for failure to pay fines for traffic infractions.[39]

Ferguson, then, is but one case study in the collateral consequences of petty-crimes law enforcement, not the least of which is the death of Michael Brown, who was initially approached by Officer Darren Wilson only because he was jaywalking. As elsewhere, the human toll of the 90,000 citations and summonses meted out by Ferguson between July 1, 2010, and June 30, 2014, can amount to death of a different kind—a civil death that renders these citizens less able or even unable to find or maintain work and to therefore participate in mainstream life.[40]

Although the egregiousness and pervasiveness of their practices compel a despairing hope that the FPD and the Ferguson municipal court are aberrational, evidence suggests otherwise.[41] Similar to Ferguson's conflict of interest in increasing its enforcement of minor violations when doing so also enriches the city's coffers, New York City collects $800 million annually from court, criminal, and administrative fines,[42] making vigorous enforcement an alluring proposition. Examining policing for profit in a somewhat different context, in New Orleans, Louisiana, criminal district courts, most violations punishable by only a fine end up having arrest warrants issued for failure to pay.[43] Judges deciding fines in New Orleans criminal courts face personal and structural conflicts of interest because these courts are substantially funded by the fines judges assess against convicted defendants.[44] The existence of a plausible population to pass off as criminally inclined (African Americans) and a scarcity of dollars from traditional revenue sources conspire across the country to make the criminalization of black lives not only acceptable but indeed a perceived financial imperative.

Structural Inequality and Petty-Crimes Law Enforcement

To understand the real magnitude of the violence brought against African Americans by Ferguson-style justice and other injurious police and court practices, it is essential to examine the structural inequality and systemic and individual discrimination under which black lives are lived. Structural inequality denotes vestigial impediments to economic and educational equal opportunity that effectively create castes within the American social structure. Structural inequality and its racial correlative are predictive of the likelihood of one becoming engaged with the criminal justice system, for the poor are disproportionately represented in the criminal justice system, and African Americans are disproportionately represented among the poor.[45] Once engaged with the criminal justice system, racial discrimination in the labor market interacts with the collateral consequences of their engagement to bind blacks more inescapably to the structural inequality that facilitated the engagement in the first place.

Although structural inequality cabins the potential for success of African Americans as a whole, its effects on black men have been especially devastating. For every 100 nonincarcerated black females between the ages of 25 and 54, there are only 83 nonincarcerated black males within the same age range.[46] Adult black males disproportionately fall out of society primarily due to incarceration and early death, with the incarceration rates since 1980 accelerating to more than offset the decreasing rates of early death.[47] No such gender gap exists among whites, where for every 100 nonincarcerated white females between the ages of 25 and 54, there are 99 similarly situated white men.[48] Among blacks in Ferguson, Missouri, the gap is even more yawning: for every 100 black female cohorts, there are just 60 black men.[49] Indeed, Ferguson boasts the largest gap of any jurisdiction with 10,000 or more blacks.[50] All told, there are 1.5 million "missing" black men in the United States.[51]

Life for those black men who are not among the missing can be notably bereft, especially for young black men. A 2015 Gallup-Healthways well-being survey of more than 97,000 men found that black men under the age of 35 had the lowest well-being index score of any group, a difference that was statistically significant.[52] Conditions in Ferguson are a microcosm of the reasons for this group's bleak outlook. Forty-seven percent of black males ages 16 to 24 are unemployed in St. Louis County, Missouri, which encompasses Ferguson.[53] By contrast, 16 percent of white men in this age cohort are unemployed.[54] Across the nation, young black men as a group face heightened unemployment, diminished graduation rates, higher incarceration rates, and less access to healthcare—a despairing brew that cripples socioeconomic mobility, if not hope itself.[55]

The economic violence of everyday black life is, of course, a condition shared across genders, even if gender itself may in some circumstances exacerbate the condition. The unemployment rate for blacks nationally was 9.5 percent as of June 2015, compared to 4.6 percent for whites.[56] By recent history, blacks in St. Louis County have tended to fare worse than blacks nationally, having had an unemployment rate that was 2.8 times that of area whites in 2013, compared to a national black unemployment rate that was 2.2 times the rate for whites.[57] The 2013 poverty rate for blacks nationally was 27 percent, compared to 10 percent for whites.[58] The disparity was even greater in St. Louis County, where blacks were more than three times as likely to live in poverty compared to whites.[59] Nationally, in 2013, white households had an annual income that was 1.7 times greater than black households. Here again, black residents of St. Louis County fared worse; white household incomes were on average double that of blacks.[60] Whatever the relative conditions of blacks in Ferguson and St. Louis County vis-à-vis blacks nationally, however, it clear that black economic conditions overall vis-à-vis those of whites are distressed. Moreover, these conditions do not reflect eddies of cyclical boom and bust but are instead structural in nature.[61]

The meme of black slothfulness is a convenient one with which to dismiss the statistical data, and Ferguson officials were quick to repair to it in citing a lack of "personal responsibility" on the part of blacks in Ferguson as the reason for their problems with the criminal justice system.[62] These officials are hardly alone among whites in attributing blacks' lot to their trifling ways. A 2012 survey found that 40 percent of whites believed that blacks did not work as diligently as whites.[63] Forty-five percent of whites believed that blacks did not possess the motivation or will to remove themselves from poverty.[64] These stereotyped views of African Americans reinforce structural inequality by normalizing white advantage as the inevitable byproduct of merit and black disadvantage as a reflection of a lack of effort, or even worse, ability. The facts on the ground belie such a deprecating depiction of black resilience.

Although racial discrimination is an explanation for black structural inequality, social scientists have begun to redirect the discourse to patterns of group conduct that benefit in-group members without any active or even latent intent to exclude others. In her groundbreaking study of how white Americans obtain employment, sociologist Nancy DiTomaso documents the striking conclusion that most whites do not obtain their jobs through unbridled competition in the labor market but rather receive assistance from personal or extended connections who facilitate their gaining a position.[65] According to DiTomaso, whites deploy social capital—informal networks of friends, family, and casual acquaintances—to acquire jobs or skills for jobs with a frequency that they rarely acknowledge until prodded.[66] Because most whites' core networks do not include many if any African Americans, the opportunity hoarding created by the use of social capital to obtain jobs has a racially disparate effect—whites help other whites.[67] Although blacks help other blacks, "there are fewer social resources in their communities and fewer institutional sectors from which they can draw social resources."[68]

Opportunity hoarding among members of a particular demographic or social group is not, standing alone, illegal. Despite a manifest underrepresentation of black workers in *EEOC v. Chicago Miniature Lamp Works*, the Seventh Circuit Court of Appeals found no intentional discrimination or disparate impact against African Americans where the employer "relied almost exclusively on 'word-of-mouth' in order to fill its entry-level job openings."[69] The word-of-mouth system sustained by the court is a textbook example of the use of social capital to obtain positions and in-group opportunity hoarding: "Employees would simply tell their relatives and friends about the nature of the job—if interested, these persons then would come to Miniature's office and complete an application form."[70] A subsequent panel of the Seventh Circuit conceded that use of existing employees' informal networks to hire additional employees perpetuates existing homogeneity in an employer's workforce.[71] It nevertheless found these informal conduits both legal and salutary because of their potential to redound to the benefit of immigrant communities who are often "resented for their ambition and hard work."[72] Moreover, according to the court, reliance upon informal conduits for applicants was not only economically efficient but was more likely to produce a good work force because new employees are likely to have fuller information about the position when recruited by an existing employee and because existing employees naturally seek to preserve their good standing with an employer and therefore will carefully screen the persons they refer.[73]

Absent from the Seventh Circuit's analysis is any acknowledgement that while use of social capital may occasionally benefit certain minority communities, it more often retards the mobility of African Americans because social capital is not equally distributed across ethnic groups. As if to give legitimacy to the disparity in social capital, the court deploys a racial trope in pitting the "ambition and hard work" of immigrants against those who are excluded as a result of the employer's reliance on informal conduits for hiring. Whether the group against whom blacks are juxtaposed is whites or immigrants of color, the valorizing of the latter groups in relation to blacks reinforces structural inequality as surely as does opportunity hoarding among groups with greater social capital.[74]

Opportunity hoarding directly affects black representation in law enforcement. In New York City, for instance, many of the applicants who passed the police exam drop out of the application process, which is opaque and can drag on for years. This happens less often for white applicants, however, because "[w]hite applicants, who are far more likely than their black counterparts to have relatives, friends and neighbors on the force, often know someone who can help them navigate the bureaucracy."[75] Such forgone employment opportunities deprive the African American community of economic prowess for years and perhaps generations to come. For example, New York City police officers receive total compensation of $90,829 per year, excluding overtime pay, after five and a half years of service.[76] Thus, social capital often translates into financial capital, and, like social capital, financial capital tends to be exchanged among in-group members.[77] Given their advantage of greater social capital, whites accumulate far more financial capital than African Americans.[78] This wealth accumulation, in turn, positions whites to help children, relatives, and friends to a degree without parallel among blacks.[79] Indeed, about 50 percent of parents' income advantage is passed on to their children.[80] In more concrete terms, this means that the expected income of children raised in a family whose parents are in the 90th percentile of wages is *nearly three times* that of children raised in a family whose parents earn in the tenth percentile of wages.[81] These data denude refrains of "personal responsibility" for the empty clichés they often are and strongly suggest that blacks' disproportionate involvement with the criminal justice system is largely facultative.

Structural inequality, then, is the primary milieu in which policing of African Americans takes place. While this milieu makes especially noxious and predatory Ferguson-style policing for profit, it also poses fundamental questions about the ultimate utility of petty-crimes law enforcement as a standard police practice because such enforcement simply enshrines structural inequality by saddling primarily underprivileged black males with criminal records that impede their ability to become contributing members of society. As the next section demonstrates, when structural inequality is coupled with active discrimination in the labor market against blacks, the mark of a criminal record often becomes a death knell to social mobility. The American polity has yet to weigh and actively debate whether the benefits of petty-crimes law enforcement outweigh the social stagnation wrought by a criminal record.

Discrimination, Criminalization, and Employment Opportunity

Criminal records have a compounding negative effect on the employment prospects of African Americans because African Americans are already among the most likely victims of job discrimination to begin with.[82] Thus, in 2013, black college graduates were more than twice as likely to be unemployed as all other college graduates.[83] Recent studies using black and white testers with the same qualifications in Milwaukee and New York City document that black men were less likely to receive a job callback than their white comparator. In the case of Milwaukee, they were less than half as likely.[84] In addition, a series of recent studies using black and white testers have demonstrated that white men with recent criminal histories are more likely to receive job callback interviews than black men with no criminal history at all.[85] Research has also shown that job applicants with black-sounding names fare significantly worse than those with names traditionally associated with whites.[86] Racial discrimination affects job performance evaluations. One study demonstrated that law firm partners reading the same brief rated the quality of the brief lower when informed that its author was black than when told the author was white.[87] Discrimination is not only a barrier to African American access to labor markets and a determinant of their success, it also confines the type of work available to them. Regardless of age, black college graduates are more likely to be underemployed than nonblack graduates.[88]

The ease with which criminal records are generated in the United States is a subject worthy of disquisition beyond the scope of this chapter. In the past 20 years, law enforcement officials in the United States have made approximately a quarter billion arrests.[89] Nearly 77.7 million citizens are contained in the Federal Bureau of Investigation master criminal database, amounting to one in three adults. Most of the individuals in the database have committed nonviolent offenses.[90] That blacks bear a disproportionate brunt of the nation's overzealous law enforcement is largely beyond dispute. Although the City of Ferguson arrests blacks at three times the rate of other groups, at least 1,581 police departments of varying sizes arrest blacks at an even more disproportionate rate.[91]

At least 70 police departments in varied regions of the country arrested blacks at a rate of ten times that of other groups.[92] In Dearborn, Michigan, where blacks comprise only 4 percent of the city's residents and a quarter of the Detroit metropolitan area, the arrest rate for blacks compared to Dearborn's population is 26 times greater than for other groups.[93] These disparate arrest rates cannot be explained by greater criminal propensities among blacks: in the United States, blacks are arrested at a higher rate regardless of the seriousness of the crime.[94] Moreover, if black crime is targeted more often than that of other groups, the criminal-propensity explanation becomes self-fulfilling and thus inherently unreliable. Still, public officials repair with ease to the circular explanation of black criminal propensity, as did the mayor of North Charleston, South Carolina, the scene of the recent shooting of Walter L. Scott, an unarmed black man shot in the back by a white police officer. Mayor R. Keith Summey insisted that it made sense to concentrate patrols in the black sections of North Charleston because 83 percent of all people arrested were black.[95]

The human costs of a criminal record for those against whom society is already predisposed to discriminate can be devastating. Princeton University sociologist Devah Pager has conducted an "employment audit" using black and white testers posing as job applicants with criminal backgrounds.[96] Each tester was intelligent and well-spoken, and all were assigned identical credentials. The employment audit was conducted in Wisconsin, where employers are prohibited by law from basing a hiring decision on an individual's criminal background unless the past crimes are relevant to the position for which the individual has applied.[97] Whites with a criminal record were called back at a higher rate than blacks with no criminal record; only 5 percent of blacks with a criminal record were called back by employers.[98] Pager concludes, "The effect of race was very large, equal to or greater than the effect of a criminal record."[99]

Many laws compel the exclusion of those with criminal records from certain kinds of employment or afford significant discretion to licensing authorities to exclude those seeking employment in positions for which the government's imprimatur is required.[100] The American Bar Association has catalogued more than 38,000 statutes that mete out collateral consequences for those convicted of offenses; 80 percent of these provisions pertain to employment.[101] Given that one in every 15 black men are incarcerated, compared to one in every 106 white men,[102] the disparate effects of these statutes are self-evident. It is not just convictions, however, that mar individuals with criminal records. Criminal records can include arrests without conviction;[103] citations without conviction;[104] and arrest warrants.[105]

Most employers are averse to hiring applicants with a criminal background. Even males with only an arrest record but no conviction, once hired, earn less than those with no criminal history.[106] Moreover, once a prospective employer conducting a background check discovers a criminal history, an applicant's chances are only slightly better than even that he will be given an opportunity to explain a prior arrest.[107] When the government, itself, imposes barriers to employment and other benefits because of one's criminal activity, it is referred to as "civil death," a diminution of the individual's legal capacity as part of the (attenuated) punishment for his crime.[108] Civil death refers not only to employment-related restrictions but also a host of other impediments to full and equal participation in civil society, such as disenfranchisement.[109] Nor is civil death limited to felony convictions, as a multitude of legal restrictions may ensue from the commission of a misdemeanor.[110] Although it is historically and juridically accurate to attribute civil death to postconviction burdens or collateral consequences imposed by the state, it is clear that the alienation of ex-convicts (a class that includes both those who have and have not been incarcerated) from civil society is effectuated as much by private actors such as private-sector employers as it is by the state. Civil death in its broadest and most practical sense, then, encompasses the full array of postconviction disabilities visited upon on offender, whether imposed by the state or private action.

Disabling individuals with criminal histories from pursuing gainful employment lowers the nation's rate of employment and is estimated to reduce GDP by as much as $65 billion a year.[111] Most states view the imposition of private barriers to labor market participation as restraints on trade.[112] Yet many of these same jurisdictions impose employment barriers either directly through positive law or indirectly through law enforcement policies that swell the ranks of petty criminal offenders and thus grow a class of undesirable prospective employees. Public policy, then, is often at cross-purposes with itself. Although some legal recourse exists for those who are denied employment due to their criminal history, as explained next, none of these protections adequately addresses the intersection of racial discrimination in law enforcement, policing for profit, and racial discrimination in employment that places African Americans in the untenable position that many in Ferguson find themselves.

Expungement of Criminal Records

Professor Michael Pinard, one of the country's foremost experts on reentry of ex-convicts into civil society, has championed the expungement or sealing of criminal histories to allow individuals who have interacted with the criminal justice system the opportunity to redeem themselves.[113] Pinard argues that expungement or sealing is preferable to litigation against private employers that seeks to demonstrate that their consideration of applicants' criminal past works a disparate impact on racial minorities because these cases are difficult to prove, and, in any event, most individuals with a criminal background are unlikely to litigate their rejection by an employer.[114] Similarly, although several jurisdictions now "ban the box"—that is, they do not permit applications for employment to inquire into the applicant's criminal past, though such inquiry is permitted later in the application process —the enforcement of these laws by individual applicants with criminal records who are denied a job opportunity is impractical.[115]

Expungement and sealing of criminal records "actually take the criminal record off the table." Although they are controversial because an individual's criminal past becomes invisible to the general public, expungement and sealing acknowledge that individuals often transcend their past mistakes even as employers continue to attempt to saddle them with their criminal record.[116] Citing to studies that demonstrate that over time, those convicted of a crime become no more likely to commit a crime than those who have never been convicted, Pinard would make expungement and sealing available for "the bulk of offenses that have stretched criminal court dockets throughout the U.S. beyond capacity and to the point of dysfunction, particularly the non-violent drug offenses that have overwhelmingly fallen on poor individuals."[117] Expungement and sealing occur in several jurisdictions but vary considerably as to the types of convictions for which they are available, the conditions that an individual must meet to be eligible for this remedy, and the process he must undertake to secure expungement or sealing.[118]

Although clearly ameliorative, expungement and sealing, insofar as their adoption is optional for each state, do not address the Ferguson-type harm of the mass criminalization of a targeted segment of a municipality's citizenry. Where the disproportionate criminalization of African Americans and other people of color has been essentially made an enterprise of a local or state government, the federal government should compel expungement and sealing on pain of loss of federal funding for law enforcement activity. On this score, investigations like the Justice Department's investigation into the FPD and its municipal court are all too rare. The Justice Department's report exposed abusive police and court practices the systemic nature of which would otherwise remain invisible to the public. The Justice Department, however, is currently investigating only 20 of the nation's police departments, a figure that actually represents a doubling of the number of investigations since fiscal year 2010.[119] In fiscal 2015, out of a budget of $26 billion, a mere $12.2 million was allocated to staff deployment for "effective and democratically accountable policing."[120] In contrast, the prison system was allocated $6.9 billion.[121] Perhaps, then, local and state law enforcement agencies, themselves, should be responsible for conducting, at a minimum, the type of statistical analyses that the Justice Department performed in Ferguson. Revelations from such studies would inform both the moral and legal imperatives of expungement and sealing.

Antidiscrimination Laws

A few states, such as Wisconsin, have employment discrimination statutes that specifically ban the use of criminal records in employment decisions unless the employer can demonstrate a relationship between the crime for which an individual has been convicted and the at-issue job position.[122] Wisconsin requires a "substantial relationship."[123] These statutes, like "ban the box" provisions prohibiting initial inquiry into criminal backgrounds on an employment application, work at cross-purposes with many of these same jurisdictions' law enforcement policies and practices. These laws provide ex post remedies against private employers for their use of criminal records that at least in some instances, such as Ferguson, are the product of state predation. Thus, jurisdictions are, at once, creating the circumstances for mass convictions through petty crime and often predatory policing;

restraining trade in contravention of their general policy—embodied in the at-will employment rule, among other laws—of unfettered labor markets;[124] and demanding that employers justify the use of criminal records that the state saw perfectly fit to create in the first place.

Although federal antidiscrimination law does not expressly prohibit employer consideration of criminal records in employment decisions, the disparate impact doctrine of Title VII has been used to challenge employer practices that have a racially disparate effect and cannot be justified as job-related and necessary to the operation of the business.[125] The mixed results in these cases have led at least one commentator to propose relying more on the traditional doctrine of disparate treatment under Title VII, in which a plaintiff of color prevails by showing that similarly situated white applicants received more favorable treatment. Because social science evidence indicates that whites frequently link crime with race, "*whenever* a criminal record is contemplated, race is considered, at least unconsciously."[126] Given the frequent conflation of race and crime, a disparate treatment claim would focus on employers' discriminatory application in individual cases of their policies regarding criminal backgrounds.[127]

Eighth Amendment Concerns

State-imposed civil sanctions that flow from convictions of a crime are, themselves, generally not considered punishment and thus evade sanction under the Eighth Amendment's prohibition against "cruel and unusual punishment."[128] Yet in the operation of the highly regulatory state that the United States has become, the impact of a constellation of collateral consequences that have the result of denuding a convicted individual of his legal character may violate the Eighth Amendment.[129]

In addition, as evidenced by the practices of the municipal court in Ferguson, a citizen's interaction with the criminal justice system that begins with merely a finable petty offense can quickly escalate when payment is not received. Because courts often fail to consider a defendant's ability to pay, many jurisdictions have effectively turned indigent criminal defendants into permanent debtors.[130] Although the issue has not yet been settled by the Supreme Court,[131] the Eighth Amendment's prohibition against "excessive fines" can reasonably, and consistently with its historical genesis, be read to require courts to consider a defendant's ability to pay.

Neither of these salutary readings of the Eighth Amendment reach the private collateral consequences that both convicts and nonconvicts face in the labor market and elsewhere. Mass convictions, many for petty offenses pursued by jurisdictions for revenue as much as for public safety, are ultimately judged twice: once by the state when it metes out the punishment, then by private actors who are empowered to make a determination about what weight to give the state's mark in job, housing, and other decisions.

Conclusion

In *Bailey v. Alabama*,[132] the U.S. Supreme Court invalidated under the 13th Amendment and the federal antipeonage law a state provision that treated as an intent to defraud an employer a worker's failure to complete an employment contract without reimbursing the employer his advance. Violation of the state statute was a crime punishable by a fine equaling double the amount of the injury to the employer, up to $300. One half of the fine would go to the county, and one half to the injured party.[133] When Bailey was unable to satisfy the fine, he was sentenced to 20 days of hard labor in lieu of the fine and 116 days for court costs.[134] The Supreme Court refused to consider the race of the defendant, who was black, and noted that the statute was facially race-neutral.[135] As Benno Schmidt has written, however, "If peonage tended to ensnare some whites, it netted a far greater number of blacks; it was in origin, official contemplation, and public consciousness overwhelmingly an aspect of the victimization of blacks."

Today, Montgomery, Alabama, stands accused of targeting African Americans for traffic stops, enabling the city to collect three to four times the municipal traffic ticket revenue of other cities in Alabama.[136] Peonage in its strictest sense may have disappeared in the United States, but its remnant of racially targeting African Americans for petty crimes in order to enrich the state (and private actors such as probation companies)[137] has not.

Looking at the myriad offenses contained in the municipal code for a small town like Ferguson might lead one to believe that Ferguson is simply an outlier. Such low-level offenses, however, are in fact the grist of the American criminal justice system.[138] States and localities increasingly impose legal financial obligations on defendants to fund their criminal justice systems,[139] or, in cases like Ferguson, general city operations. The Supreme Court has required that judicial entities whose own budgets stand to benefit from the imposition of a fine on a criminal defendant must meet minimum standards of neutrality and individuation of the fine assessed in order to satisfy due process.[140] Yet there are not sufficient constraints on the police, themselves, whose exercise of vast discretion bring individuals into the criminal justice system in the first place.

Like the Court in *Bailey*, many Americans are undoubtedly inclined to portray the gaping racial disparities in arrest rates, criminal citation rates, and convictions as unrelated to racial discrimination by law enforcement and the judiciary. If the Justice Department's investigation of Ferguson proves anything, however, it is that we cannot credibly declare the absence of racial discrimination in the American criminal justice system unless we first look for it.

We will never know whether Michael Brown would be employed or employable had he lived, but chances are he would have faced long odds, as do so many young black men. Until we as a society stop permitting their lives to be laid to waste by structural inequality and discrimination, their untimely and senseless deaths will only multiply.

Notes

1. *See* Civil Rights Div., U.S. Dep't of Justice, Investigation of the Ferguson Police Dep't 1, 2 (2015) [hereinafter FPD Report], http://www.justice.gov/sites/default/files/opa/press-releases/attachments/2015/03/04/ferguson_police_department_report.pdf ("Ferguson's law enforcement practices are shaped by the City's focus on revenue rather than by public safety needs. This emphasis on revenue has compromised the institutional character of Ferguson's police department, contributing to a pattern of unconstitutional policing, and has also shaped its municipal court, leading to procedures that raise due process concerns and inflict unnecessary harm on members of the Ferguson community.").

2. U.S. Dep't of Justice, Department of Justice Report Regarding the Criminal Investigation into the Shooting Death of Michael Brown by Ferguson, Missouri Police Officer Darren Wilson 1, 12 (2015), http://www.justice.gov/usao/pam/Documents/DOJ%20Report%20on%20Shooting%20of%20Michael%20Brown.pdf.

3. *Id.* at 12, 15.

4. Joseph Goldstein & Marc Santora, *Staten Island Man Died from Chokehold during Arrest, Autopsy Finds*, N.Y. Times (Aug. 1, 2014), http://www.nytimes.com/2014/08/02/nyregion/staten-island-man-died-from-officers-chokehold-autopsy-finds.html.

5. Shaila Dewan & Richard A. Oppel, *In Tamir Rice Case, Many Errors by Cleveland Police, Then a Fatal One*, N.Y. Times (Jan. 22, 2015), http://www.nytimes.com/2015/01/23/us/in-tamir-rice-shooting-in-cleveland-many-errors-by-police-then-a-fatal-one.html.

6. Manny Fernandez, *North Charleston Police Shooting Not Justified, Experts Say*, N.Y. Times (Apr. 9, 2015), http://www.nytimes.com/2015/04/10/us/north-charleston-police-shooting-not-justified-experts-say.html.

7. Melanie Eversley, *Report: Freddie Gray Died of "High-Energy Injury" in Baltimore*, USA Today (June 25, 2015, 10:34 AM), http://www.usatoday.com/story/news/2015/06/23/freddie-gray-baltimore-autopsy/29179697/.

8. Richard Perez-Pena, *University of Cincinnati Police Officer Indicted in Shooting Death of Samuel DuBose*, N.Y. Times (July 29, 2015), http://www.nytimes.com/2015/07/30/us/university-of-cincinnati-officer-indicted-in-shooting-death-of-motorist.html?_r=0.

9. Katie Rogers, *Sandra Bland's Autopsy Details How She Died*, N.Y. Times (July 24, 2015), http://www.nytimes.com/2015/07/25/us/sandra-blands-autopsy-details-how-she-died.html.

10. *See id.*

11. Sandhya Somashekhar, Wesley Lowery & Keith L. Alexander, *A Year after Michael Brown's Fatal Shooting, Unarmed Black Men Are Seven Times More Likely Than Whites to Die by Police Gunfire*, Wash. Post (Aug. 8, 2015), http://www.washingtonpost.com/sf/national/2015/08/08/black-and-unarmed/?hpid=z6.

12. *Id.*

13. *Id.*

14. *See* Rob Nixon, Slow Violence and the Environmentalism of the Poor 1–45 (2011) (discussing the idea of slow versus fast violence in the context of environmental catastrophe).

15. FPD Report, *supra* note 1, at 62.

16. *See infra* notes 60–66 and accompanying text.

17. Benno C. Schmidt Jr., *Principle and Prejudice: The Supreme Court and Race in the Progressive Era, Part 2: The Peonage Cases*, 82 Colum. L. Rev. 646, 650 (1982).

18. Michelle Alexander, The New Jim Crow: Mass Incarceration in the Age of Colorblindness 27–28 (2010).

19. *See* Schmidt, *supra* note 17, at 646–47.

20. *Id.* at 650.

21. *See* Alexander, *supra* note 18, at 28.

22. *Id.* at 27.

23. *See* Schmidt, *supra* note 17, at 651 ("Because the demand for convicts by rich sawmill operators, owners of brick-yards, large farmers, and others [was] far in advance of the supply . . . the natural tendency is to convict as many men as possible.") (internal quotation marks omitted); Benno C. Schmidt Jr., *Juries, Jurisdiction, and Race Discrimination: The Lost Promise of* Strauder v. West Virginia, 61 Tex. L. Rev. 1401, 1411 (discussing the post-Reconstruction criminal justice system in the South: "The system of criminal law was further perverted by its function as a pipeline for forced labor. To William Archer, the profit the state derived from the sweat of the convict was the chief explanation for the rampant injustice against black defendants in Southern courts: 'Why let any pedantic rule of evidence or sentimental scruple of humanity deprive the commonwealth of a profitable serf?'").

24. FPD Report, *supra* note 1, at 6–7.

25. *Id.* at 7.

26. *Id.* at 62.

27. *Id.* at 65.

28. *Id.* at 65–66.

29. *Id.* at 66.

30. FPD Report, *supra* note 1, at 66–67.

31. *Id.* at 67.

32. *Id.* at 69.

33. *Id.*

34. *See id.* at 9–10.

35. *See id.* at 10 (quoting a report written by Ferguson's finance director).

36. *See* Thomas A. Garrett & Gary A. Wagner, *Red Ink in the Rearview Mirror: Local Fiscal Conditions and the Issuance of Traffic Tickets*, 52 J.L. & Econ. 71, 88 (2009) (examining counties in North Carolina and finding that in the year following a decrease in city revenue, police issue significantly more traffic tickets.).

37. Joseph Shapiro, *As Court Fees Rise, the Poor are Paying the Price*, NPR (broadcast May 19, 2014, 4:02 PM), http://www.npr.org/2014/05/19/312158516/increasing-court-fees-punish-the-poor.

38. *Id.*

39. Rex Nutting, *Opinion: It's a Crime to Be Poor in America*, MarketWatch (broadcast Apr. 9, 2015, 12:25 PM), http://www.marketwatch.com/story/its-a-crime-to-be-poor-in-america-2015-04-09?page=2.

40. *See infra* notes 103–112, 125–26, and accompanying text.

41. *See supra* notes 36–38 and accompanying text; *see also infra* notes 89–94 and accompanying text.

42. Jonathan Blanks, *The NYPD's Work Stoppage Is Costing the City Lots of Money. That's Great for New Yorkers*, Wash. Post (Jan. 7, 2015), http://www.washingtonpost.com/posteverything/wp/2015/01/07/the-nypds-work-stoppage-is-costing-the-city-lots-of-money-thats-great-for-new-yorkers/.

43. Micah West, *Financial Conflicts of Interest and the Funding of New Orleans's Criminal Courts*, 101 Cal. L. Rev. 521, 526–27 (2013).

44. *Id.* at 529–31.

45. *See* Ann Cammett, *Shadow Citizens: Felony Disenfranchisement and the Criminalization of Debt*, 117 Penn. St. L. Rev. 349, 369–70 (2012).

46. Justin Wolfers et al., *1.5 Million Missing Black Men*, N.Y. Times (Apr. 20, 2015), http://www.nytimes.com/interactive/2015/04/20/upshot/missing-black-men.html?_r=0&abt=0002&abg=0.

47. *Id.*

48. *Id.*

49. *Id.*

50. *Id.*

51. *Id.*

52. Dan Witters & Diana Liu, *Young Black Males in U.S. Suffer Well-Being Deficit*, Gallup (Mar. 13, 2015), http://www.gallup.com/poll/181952/young-black-males-suffer-deficit.aspx.

53. Phillip Bump, *How Ferguson Happened*, Wash. Post (Aug. 18, 2014), http://www.washingtonpost.com/news/the-fix/wp/2014/08/18/how-ferguson-happened/.

54. *Id.*

55. See Witters & Liu, *supra* note 52.

56. *Economic News Release: Table A-2. Employment Status of the Civilian Population by Race, Sex, and Age*, Bureau of Lab. Statistics, http://www.bls.gov/news.release/empsit.t02.htm (last modified Aug. 7, 2015).

57. *The Strategic Assessment of the St. Louis Region*, Where We Stand, 99, 100 (2015), http://www.ewgateway.org/pdffiles/library/wws/wws2015-RacialDisp.pdf.

58. *Poverty Rate by Race/Ethnicity*, Kaiser Family Found., http://kff.org/other/state-indicator/poverty-rate-by-raceethnicity/ (last visited Aug. 5, 2015).

59. *The Strategic Assessment of the St. Louis Region*, *supra* note 57, at 101.

60. *Id.*

61. *See* Terry Smith, Barack Obama, Post-Racialism, and the New Politics of Triangulation 90–91 (2013) (documenting the persistent economic disparities between blacks and whites even during the economic boom under President Bill Clinton).

62. FPD Report, *supra* note 1, at 44.

63. Reniqua Allen, *For Black Men, a Permanent Recession*, Al Jazeera Am. (Oct. 9, 2014), http://america.aljazeera.com/features/2014/10/for-black-men-a-permanentrecession.html.

64. *Id.*

65. Nancy DiTomaso, The American Non-Dilemma: Racial Inequality without Racism 70, 73 (2013).

66. *Id.* at 92 ("Getting help from family and friends is so taken for granted, so much a part of the way people get jobs, and so much in the background of consciousness that hardly anyone thinks to mention it when asked about their lives. Instead, they highlight the things they did in response to this help, not the help itself.").

67. *Id.* at 55.

68. *Id.*

69. EEOC v. Chi. Miniature Lamp Works, 947 F.2d 292, 295 (7th Cir. 1991).

70. *Id.*

71. *See* EEOC v. Consol. Serv. Sys, 989 F.2d 233, 235 (Conn. 1993) ("Of course if the employer is a member of an ethnic community . . . this stance [use of word-of-mouth] is likely to result in the perpetuation of an ethnically imbalanced work force.").

72. *Id.* at 238.

73. *Id.* at 236.

74. *See* Smith, *supra* note 61, at 10 (explaining the unfavorable comparison of blacks to Asians as racial triangulation intended to maintain a hierarchy among racial groups).

75. Rachel L. Swarns, *Black Police Applicant Frustrated by Opaque Hiring Process*, N.Y. TIMES (July 19, 2015), http://www.nytimes.com/2015/07/20/nyregion/black-police-applicant-frustrated-by-hiring -process.html?emc=eta1&_r=0.

76. *Id.*

77. See DiTOMASO, *supra* note 65, at 81.

78. *Id.* at 82.

79. *See id.*

80. *Economic Mobility in the United States*, PEW CHARITABLE TRUSTS & RUSSELL SAGE FOUND., 1, 4 (2015), http://www.pewtrusts.org/~/media/Assets/2015/07/EconomicMobilityintheUnitedStates.pdf?la=en .%20P.%201.

81. *Id.* at 5.

82. *See* Michael Pinard, *Criminal Records, Race and Redemption*, 16 N.Y.U. J. LEGIS. & PUB. POL'Y 963, 973 (2013) ("Even African-American men *without* a criminal record experience extraordinary difficulty in securing gainful employment. The difficulty, in substantial part, is due to negative employer attitudes about African-American men.").

83. Janelle Jones & John Schmitt, *A College Degree is No Guarantee*, CTR. ECON. & POL'Y RES. 1, 1 (2014), http://www.cepr.net/documents/black-coll-grads-2014-05.pdf.

84. *Id.* at 11.

85. *Id.*

86. *Id.* at 11–12.

87. *Id.* at 12.

88. *Id.* at 6.

89. Karen Dolan & Jodi L. Carr, *The Poor Get Prison: The Alarming Spread of the Criminalization of Poverty*, INST. POL'Y STUDIES, 1, 13 (2015), http://www.ips-dc.org/wp-content/uploads/2015/03/IPS-The -Poor-Get-Prison-Final.pdf.

90. *Id.* at 13.

91. Brad Heath, *Racial Gap in U.S. Arrest Rates: "Staggering Disparity,"* USA TODAY (Nov. 19, 2014, 2:24 PM), http://www.usatoday.com/story/news/nation/2014/11/18/ferguson-black-arrest-rates/19043207/.

92. *Id.*

93. *Id.*

94. *Id.* ("Blacks are more likely than others to be arrested in almost every city for almost every type of crime. Nationwide, black people are arrested at higher rates for crimes as serious as murder and assault, and as minor as loitering and marijuana possession.")

95. Alan Binder & Manny Fernandez, *Residents Trace Police Shooting a Crime Strategy Gone Awry*, N.Y. TIMES, Apr. 10, 2015, at A1.

96. Devah Pager, *The Mark of a Criminal Record*, 23(2) FOCUS 44 (2004).

97. *Id.*

98. *Id.* at 46.

99. *Id.*

100. *See* Pinard, *supra* note 82, at 973.

101. *Id.* at 973–74.

102. Dolan & Carr, *supra* note 89, at 13.

103. *See id.* at 12.

104. Amber Widgery, *Citation in Lieu of Arrest*, NAT'L CONFERENCE OF STATE LEGISLATURES (Mar. 3, 2013), http://www.ncsl.org/research/civil-and-criminal-justice/citation-in-lieu-of-arrest.aspx.

105. *See, e.g.*, Erin Murphy, *Paradigms of Restraint*, 57 DUKE L.J. 1321, 1338 (2008).

106. Dolan & Carr, *supra* note 89, at 13.

107. *Id.*

108. *See* Gabriel Chin, *The New Civil Death: Rethinking Punishment in the Era of Mass Conviction*, 160 U. PA. L. REV. 1789, 1790–91 (2012).

109. *Id.* at 1799.

110. *Id.*

111. *See* Dolan & Carr, *supra* note 89, at 13–14.

112. *See, e.g.*, David R. Trossen, *Edwards and Covenants Not to Compete in California: Leave Well Enough Alone*, 24 BERKELEY TECH. L.J. 539, 541 (2009) (comparing state laws on covenants not to compete in employment contracts and noting that state laws range from allowing such covenants only if reasonable to banning them outright, as California law does in section 16600: "Except as provided in this chapter, every contract by which anyone is restrained from engaging in a lawful profession, trade, or business of any kind is to that extent void.").

113. Pinard, *supra* note 82, at 989–93.

114. *See id.* at 992–94.

115. *See id.* at 985–86 & 991–92.

116. *Id.* at 991–92.

117. *Id.* at 994–96.

118. *Id.* at 989. For overview of state laws on expungement and sealing, *see Jurisdiction Profiles*, NAT'L ASS'N CRIM. DEF. LAWS., https://www.nacdl.org/ResourceCenter.aspx?id=25091 (last visited Aug. 7, 2015).

119. Michael Hirsh, *Tackling America's Police Abuse Epidemic: Can the Justice Department Keep Up with a National Systemic Problem?*, POLITICO (Apr. 9, 2015), http://www.politico.com/magazine/story /2015/04/north-charleston-shooting-americas-police-abuse-epidemic-116838.html#.VSreVvnF-AV.

120. *Id.*

121. *Id.*

122. Thomas M. Hruz, *The Unwisdom of the Wisconsin Fair Employment Act's Ban of Employment Discrimination on the Basis of Conviction Records*, 85 MARQ. L. REV. 779, 803–07 (2002) (surveying the jurisdictions with such laws).

123. *Id.* at 788.

124. *See supra* notes 22–44 and accompanying text.

125. *See* Alexandra Harwin, *Title VII Challenges to Employment Discrimination against Minority Men with Criminal Records*, 14 BERKELEY J. AFR.-AM. L. & POL'Y 2, 6–16 (2012) (discussing federal courts' and the U.S. Equal Employment Opportunity Commission's treatment of disparate impact cases challenging employers' use of criminal histories to exclude job applicants).

126. *Id.* at 18.

127. *See id.* at 19–20.

128. *See* Chin, *supra* note 108, at 1806–07 ("Courts have imposed few limits on creation and implementation of collateral consequences. . . . Accordingly, they are not evaluated for overall proportionality, nor is there significant scrutiny for reasonableness.").

129. *See id.* at 1826 ("Whether or not any individual collateral consequence is punishment, the overall susceptibility to collateral consequences is punishment. This is the case at least when, as now, there is a vigorous, existing network of collateral consequences."). *See also* U.S. CONST. Amend. VIII ("Excessive bail shall not be required, nor excessive fines imposed, nor cruel and unusual punishments inflicted.").

130. Nicholas M. McLean, *Livelihood, Ability to Pay, and the Original Meaning of the Excessive Fines Clause*, 40 HASTINGS CONST. L.Q. 833, 886–87 (2013).

131. *See id.* at 891–92 (noting that the Supreme Court's 14th Amendment jurisprudence forbids jailing a defendant solely for his inability to pay).

132. 219 U.S. 219 (1911).

133. *Id.* at 228.

134. *Id.* at 231.

135. *Id.*

136. *See* Hirsh, *supra* note 119.

137. *See* Dolan & Carr, *supra* note 89, at 16–18 (describing how states have turned over supervision of petty offenders to private probation companies at no cost to the state: "The cost of the service is passed onto the probationer in the form of monthly supervisory fees. When the probationer

cannot afford the cost to be supervised, he or she can face jail time. It is a vicious cycle. Once a person is released from jail, he is placed on probation, accruing additional supervisory fees imposed by the private probation companies. In fact, probationers usually end up paying more in additional fees than the actual debt they owe for the crime committed.") (citations and footnotes omitted).

138. *See* Wayne A. Logan & Ronald F. Wright, *Mercenary Criminal Justice*, 2014 U. ILL. L. REV. 1175, 1185 (noting that "low-level offenses, such as misdemeanors and infractions . . . dominate the criminal justice diet.") (footnote omitted).

139. *Id.* at 1176–77.

140. *Id.* at 1199–1200.

Chapter 8

The Geography of Inequality: A Public Health Context for Ferguson and the St. Louis Region

Jason Q. Purnell

Less than three months before the fatal shooting of Michael Brown in Ferguson, Missouri, a report was released to the St. Louis region titled *For the Sake of All: A Report on the Health and Well-Being of African Americans in St. Louis—and Why It Matters for Everyone*. The professionally designed, full-color cover of the report featured a photo of a black father looking down with pride at his young son as both peer out a bright, sunny window. It conveyed a sense of possibility and promise in the face of persistent challenges. The originators of the project, seven African American scholars from Washington University in St. Louis and Saint Louis University, had no way of knowing how timely their work would become after August 9, 2014.

As national and international news media descended on the small suburban town of Ferguson, several journalists looked to *For the Sake of All* for clues about the frustrations that fueled months of mostly peaceful protest and less frequent eruptions of looting and other destruction of property. Members of the St. Louis community, who had greeted the report's release with enthusiasm at a conference several weeks before the shooting, also began to look

I would like to acknowledge the assistance of Robert Fields in compiling the data, graphs, and maps presented in this chapter. I would also like to acknowledge all of the staff, colleagues, partners, and supporters who make the *For the Sake of All* project possible.

more closely at the detailed descriptions of educational, economic, and health disparities in the St. Louis region. At least initially, most searched for answers to the question *Why*? What could have caused a tiny enclave in North St. Louis County to become the center of national and international attention? What could have thrust St. Louis—known to most outsiders for its iconic monument to westward expansion and its sports teams—onto the world stage? Part of the answer they found in the report: decades of inequality, patterned along racial and geographic lines. Of course, this was a story bigger than Ferguson, older than St. Louis, a part of the American fabric. As time went on, a community in search of healing also began to consult *For the Sake of All* to answer the question, *What now?* The report offered recommendations in six major areas, providing a kind of blueprint for a way forward that was truly in the interests of everyone in the region.

This chapter endeavors to answer both the questions *Why?* And *What now?* The answers, though driven by data and evidence, will nonetheless be incomplete. History, the purview of which the events of August 9, 2014, and the ensuing months have become, is not a science. We do not know with certainty why a set of circumstances coalesces into a movement or how a generation comes to view itself as particularly situated for a given moment in time. And even historians hesitate to offer any definitive interpretation of events as fresh as these. The methods of social science and public health, upon which *For the Sake of All* is based, can at best point to a situation that many viewed as untenable before August 9 and that more came to see as unacceptable afterward. To the extent possible, this chapter offers a snapshot of Ferguson along the same lines that the St. Louis region (specifically St. Louis County and the City of St. Louis) was examined in the original report. It will describe the social, economic, and health characteristics of the population of Ferguson, and place this one of over 90 municipalities in the region within the context of that larger geography. What will emerge from this analysis is a stark picture of the geography of inequality. St. Louis itself also will be placed within the context of a nation that continues to struggle with racial inequality, long considered its primal flaw.

For the Sake of All—Background

With funding from the Missouri Foundation for Health, a project to report on the health and well-being of African Americans in St. Louis began without a formal name in March of 2013. *For the Sake of All* came from an unfinished 1915 composition by one of the city's most celebrated residents, "King of Ragtime," Scott Joplin. The incomplete *For the Sake of All* score was found with Joplin's papers after his death in 1917. Both the inclusiveness of the title and the symbolism of unfinished work fit the purposes of the project quite well.

One of the first tasks of the project team was to assemble a cross-sector, regionally representative community partner group that would actively engage with researchers in the process of presenting data and recommendations to the public and policy makers. The ultimate composition of that group included representatives from

- Both the City of St. Louis and St. Louis County health departments
- An organization composed of the region's federally qualified health centers
- Washington University's medical school and affiliated medical center
- An organization supporting the region's school districts
- The community investment division of the Federal Reserve Bank of St. Louis
- An organization of executives responsible for health benefits for the region's major employers
- A national developer of mixed-income and affordable housing based in St. Louis
- An organization of African American civic and community leaders
- The multi-award-winning African American weekly print newspaper in St. Louis
- An independent online journal focused on topics of importance for the St. Louis region

This diversity of perspectives, expertise, and experience made for a rich and vibrant academic-community partnership. It also forced the project team to take community engagement very seriously—even extending the original 12-month timeline by two months in order to ensure that key community stakeholders and community members had adequate opportunity to weigh in.

The community partner group also helped to refine the project goals. It was decided very early on that this project had to distinguish itself from earlier efforts to bring health disparities and racial inequality to the attention of the St. Louis region. More than an academic report, it needed to present data but also inspire hope and spur action. To that end the goals were to

1) Inform the public about the social determinants of health (e.g., education, economic status, neighborhood quality, segregation, etc.) as they impact African Americans, as one of the populations most impacted by health disparities in St. Louis.
2) Present the regional health and economic consequences of intervening (or failing to intervene) on social determinants of health.
3) Provide evidence of the impact of persistent disparities on all members of the region, regardless of race or socioeconomic status.
4) Influence the policy agenda on health disparities by broadening the conversation beyond personal responsibility and the delivery of medical care.

The main products would be five policy briefs authored by the project team in close consultation with the community partner group and key community stakeholders in the areas of education, poverty, mental health, residential segregation, and chronic disease and a final report summarizing the case for considering social and economic factors alongside health outcomes and making recommendations for policy and programmatic change to address disparities. Briefs were released between August and December of 2013. In March of 2014 community members had an opportunity to provide feedback on draft elements of the final report, which included data and recommendations from the briefs as well as additional material. Response to community feedback was incorporated into the final report released in May of 2014.

To the extent possible, indicators included in the final report for the City of St. Louis and St. Louis County are presented below along with any available updates and data specific to Ferguson. The project relied on publicly available secondary data sources. These included the U.S. Census and its American Community Survey (ACS), the Missouri Department of Health and Senior Services' Missouri Information for Community Assessment database, and the Missouri Department of Elementary and Secondary Education. Not all of the data available at the county level is available at the municipality or city level. Where sample sizes were too small to report reliable estimates, the presentation of certain data points and outcomes have been omitted. It was also necessary to aggregate some health data that is collected by zip code to the closest approximation of the geography of Ferguson. Notes included with each table and figure define the source and relevant geography of the data presented.

Historical and Demographic Context

One of the benefits of the timing of *For the Sake of All* was the ability to capitalize on several anniversaries during the project period. The first brief was released on August 28, 2013, exactly 50 years after Dr. Martin Luther King, Jr. delivered the "I Have Dream" speech at the March on Washington in 1963. Release of the report in 2014 also coincided with the 50th anniversary of the signing of the Civil Rights Act of 1964, the 60th anniversary of the landmark *Brown v. Board of Education* case ending segregation in public schools, and the 250th anniversary of the founding of the City of St. Louis. The report referenced these milestones by briefly surveying historical trends and current demographics. Of particular note were the trends in African American population size and place of residence, educational attainment, unemployment, poverty, and income.

Population and Place of Residence

In 1950, there were 170,350 African Americans in St. Louis County and the City of St. Louis combined,[1] which increased by 37 percent to 233,384 by 1960.[2] Most African Americans during this period lived in the City of St. Louis. In 1960, less than 3 percent (2.7 percent; 19,007) of the population of St. Louis County was African American, and 92 percent of the African American population resided in the City.[3] The African American population of Ferguson was less than 0.5 percent in both 1950 and 1960.[4] By 2012, African Americans made up 23 percent of the population of St. Louis County, nearly 50 percent of the City of St. Louis, and nearly 30 percent of their combined geography.[5] By that time, 60 percent of the African American population resided in St. Louis County. This follows the general trend of steady population loss for the City of St. Louis since its early-to-midcentury peaks.[6]

Educational Attainment

Education is one of the strongest and most consistent predictors of health outcomes like disease, disability, and death. Educational attainment grew quite rapidly between 1960 and 2010 for both whites and African Americans in St. Louis (see Figure 8.1). Though African Americans saw a fivefold increase in the percentage of the adult population 25 years and older with at least some college education, even these gains were not enough to close a 20-percentage-point gap with whites. That gap in educational attainment is relevant to health outcomes, as recent research shows a widening gap in life expectancy between those with high school or less education and those with some college or more.[7] One analysis found that between 1990 and 2000, those with some college or more education gained 1.6 years of life expectancy, while those with high school made no life expectancy gains.[8] Education has such a powerful impact on life expectancy that highly educated African Americans (e.g., with 16 years or more of education) can expect to live 7.5 years longer than whites with less than 12 years of education.[9] In 2013, estimates for adults 25 and older reveal that 73 percent of whites have some college or more education versus 48 percent for African Americans in the City of St. Louis.[10] Educational attain-

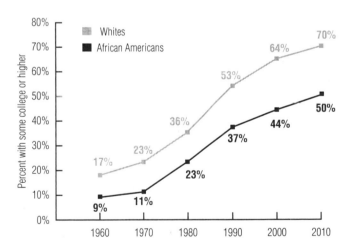

Source: Social Explorer Tables (SE), Census 1960, 1970, 1980, 1990, 2000, ACS 2010 (1-Year Estimates); Social Explorer & US Census Bureau.

Notes: Educational attainment among population 25 years and older; 1960 estimate of African Americans classified as "non-white" population

Figure 8.1. Educational attainment by race in the City of St. Louis and St. Louis County, 1960–2010.

Source: *For the Sake of All.*

ment is higher overall in St. Louis County, where 74 percent of whites and 63 percent of African Americans have at least some college education. In the combined geography, 74 percent of whites and 57 percent of African Americans have some college education or more.[11] In Ferguson, 65.8 percent of white adults 25 and older have at least some college education compared with 58.5 percent of African Americans.[12]

Unemployment

Employment confers a number of health benefits, the most basic, of course, being sufficient income to support oneself and one's family. Conversely, unemployment is associated with poorer health and higher rates of death.[13] Figure 8.2 shows unemployment by race between 1970 and 2010. Specifically, it shows an unemployment rate for African Americans that is two to three times or more the rate of whites over several decades. In 2013, African American unemployment in St. Louis County and the City of St. Louis combined was 17.6 percent, almost four times

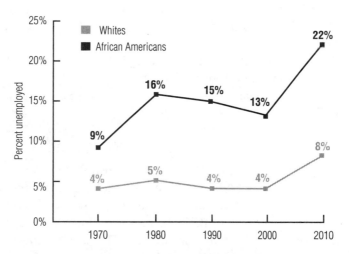

Source: Social Explorer Tables (SE), Census 1970, 1980, 1990, 2000, ACS 2010 (1-year estimates); Social Explorer & US Census Bureau.

Notes: Unemployment rates are among those 16 years or older in the civilian labor force

Figure 8.2. Unemployment by race in the City of St. Louis and St. Louis County, 1970–2010.

Source: *For the Sake of All.*

the rate for whites (4.6 percent).[14] The unemployment rate is higher for African Americans in the City (19.7 percent) than the County (16.4 percent), and in all geographies it is higher than the national African American unemployment rate (15.2 percent).[15] For African Americans in Ferguson, the unemployment rate is 16.1 percent compared with a rate of 5.5 percent for whites.[16]

Poverty

In light of persistent disparities in educational attainment and unemployment, it is not surprising that disparities in poverty and income also exist. Examining these three socioeconomic indicators over time, the widest and most consistent disparities are for poverty, with a rate for African Americans that is five to six times that of whites from 1980 to 2010 (see Figure 8.3). In 2013, African Americans in the City of St. Louis and St. Louis County combined had a poverty rate (28.8 percent) that was almost four times the white poverty rate (7.5 percent).[17] Though lower than the City rate of 36.3 percent (versus 15.9 percent for whites), the African American poverty rate in St. Louis County (23.9 percent) was more than four times the rate of whites in the County (5.8 percent).[18] The poverty rate for African Americans in Ferguson, at 29.7 percent, is nearly three times the white rate of 10.6 percent and is higher than the rate for African Americans in St. Louis County as a whole.[19] Poverty has a profound and lasting impact on health, through both the lack of material resources and the chronic stress that accompanies it.[20] It is particularly damaging to the long-term health of children, with adverse health outcomes often following them well into adulthood.[21]

Income

It is not only the poor who suffer worse health. A concept called the "socioeconomic gradient in health" notes that health outcomes are worse at every step down the income ladder.[22] There are several ways of looking at the structure of the income distribution for populations. One of the most popular is median income. Table 8.1 shows the estimated median household income (inflation adjusted in 2013 dollars) for the total population, African Americans, and whites in the City of St. Louis, St. Louis County, Ferguson, and the combined City and County geography in 2013. The lowest median income is for African American households in the City of St. Louis, which is roughly half (50 percent) the median household income of whites. Median income

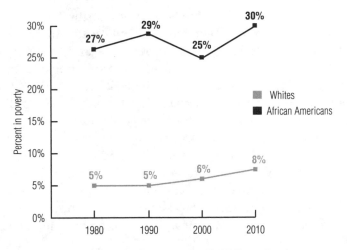

Source: Social Explorer Tables (SE), Census 1980,1990, 2000, ACS 2010 (1-year estimates);
Social Explorer & US Census Bureau.

Notes: Defined as individuals below poverty level among those for whom a poverty status was determined

Figure 8.3. Poverty rate by race in the City of St. Louis and St. Louis County, 1980–2010.

Source: *For the Sake of All.*

is higher across groups in St. Louis County, where African American median household income is 57 percent of white median household income. While median household income is slightly lower than St. Louis County for both groups, African American households in Ferguson have 60 percent of the median income of white households. In the City and County combined, African American households have half the median income of white households.

Table 8.1. Household Median Income by Race

	City of St. Louis[a]	*St. Louis County*[a]	*Ferguson*[b]	*City and County*[a]
Total	$34,488	$59,290	$38,685	$52,216
African American	$23,218	$38,294	$32,023	$31,763
White	$46,842	$67,346	$53,614	$63,153

[a] 2013 ACS 1-Year Estimates
[b] 2013 ACS 5-Year Estimates

Another way to look at income is the full distribution for all households. Figure 8.4 shows the income distribution for African American and white households in the City of St. Louis and St. Louis County combined. Some 40 percent of African American households in this combined geography subsist on less than $25,000 in annual income, and more than half (54 percent) have household income of less than $35,000. The federal poverty line for a family of four in 2013 was $23,550. By comparison, only 17 percent of white households in the City and County combined have income of less than $25,000, and only a quarter (25 percent) have household income of less than $35,000. Instead, white household income clusters around the top of the income distribution, with 61 percent having $50,000 or more of household income. Only 30 percent of African American households have incomes in that range.

Figure 8.5 shows the income distribution for Ferguson. The same proportion (40 percent) of African American households has less than $25,000 in income as in the City and County combined, and again, over

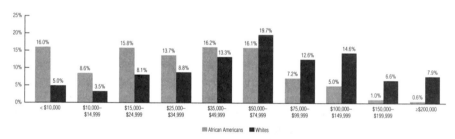

Figure 8.4. Income distribution by race in the City of St. Louis and St. Louis County, 2013.

Source: ACS 2013 1-Year Estimates.

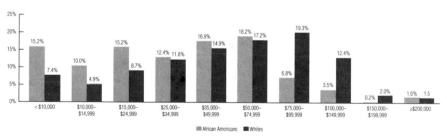

Figure 8.5. Income distribution by race in the City of Ferguson, 2013.

Source: ACS 2009–2013 5-Year Estimates.

half (53 percent) have household income of less than $35,000, compared with 21 percent and 33 percent of white households respectively. Also, in Ferguson there is greater parity in the $25,000 to $74,999 range of the income distribution. White households are much more likely to make between $75,000 and $199,999 (34 percent of white households versus 10.5 percent of African American households), but there are equivalent, though small, proportions of households making $200,000 or more in income.

Mapping Inequality

In light of the strong and consistent association between social determinants like education, employment, poverty, and income and health outcomes, it is striking to see a consistent pattern of disparities on these indicators. These data alone provide a sense of the unequal distribution of resources necessary for healthy and productive living in the St. Louis region, but they do not necessarily convey the geographic distribution of these factors. In fact, we know that place matters. Even when the socioeconomic status of households is held constant in analyses of health outcomes, lower socioeconomic status in neighborhoods continues to exert negative influence on health.[23] This makes where one lives, and the social and economic resources available to those with whom one lives, crucially important to health.

The series of maps of the City of St. Louis and St. Louis County that follow illustrate the geographic clustering of African American population, poverty, and high school dropout rates as social and economic factors and heart disease mortality, cancer mortality, and all-cause mortality rates as selected health outcomes. In these maps, the distribution of outcomes is divided into three groups of high (dark gray), moderate (light gray), and low (black) levels for each indicator. The geographic boundaries of the City of Ferguson in northeastern St. Louis County are also represented in each map.

Areas with the highest African American population (44–99 percent) are concentrated in the north and near south side of the City of St. Louis and the northeastern portion of St. Louis County (see Figure 8.6). Ferguson is included in this latter area. There is moderate African American population (6–43 percent) in the central corridor and southwestern portions of the City and the central east and northwestern portion of the County. Areas with the lowest levels of African American population (0–5 percent) include the far west and southern portions of

St. Louis County. Recent reports have ranked the larger St. Louis metropolitan area among the most segregated large metropolitan areas in the country.[24]

The area with the highest proportion of the population living in poverty (23–53 percent) encompasses the northern portion of the City of St. Louis, much of its central corridor, and the southeastern section along the Mississippi River; the northeastern portion of St. Louis County, including Ferguson, is also included in this area (see Figure 8.7). An analysis by the Brookings Institution noted an increase in the poverty rate in Ferguson between 2000 and 2010–2012 in line with a national trend toward the "suburbanization of poverty."[25] Much of the same area with the highest African American population also has the highest rates of poverty. Moderate rates of poverty (9–22 percent) are found in a small north-central area along the Mississippi and the southwestern section of the City of St. Louis and in portions of northwestern and southern St. Louis County. The lowest poverty rates are in a section of northwestern St. Louis County that also had a relatively high African American population as well as the central corridor, far west, and portions of the southwest and southeast.

The map of high school dropout rates is much more of a patchwork, but again some of the highest (6–17 percent) are found in the northern part of the City of St. Louis, and the northeastern part of St. Louis County that includes Ferguson (see Figure 8.8). These are also areas with high African American population and rates of poverty. Several of the areas with moderate poverty show some of the higher rates of high school dropout, though there are also areas of high poverty with moderate high school dropout rates (2–5 percent). Dropout rates are the lowest in areas that also have the lowest poverty rates.

Turning now to health outcomes, the number one leading cause of death in the United States, heart disease, has a mortality rate that is not equally distributed throughout the St. Louis region (see Figure 8.9). The highest heart disease death rates (250–345 deaths per 100,000) are in much of the northern portion of the City of St. Louis as well as the western edge of the central corridor and the southeast. In St. Louis County, portions of the northeast (including Ferguson), the northwest, and just south of the central corridor have the highest rates. Most of these areas in the City and County have moderate-to-high African American population, rates of poverty, and high school dropout.

Cancer is the second leading cause of death in the United States. Cancer deaths rates (see Figure 8.10) are the only indicator for which

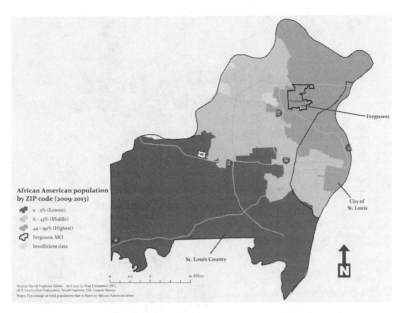

Figure 8.6. African American population by zip code in the City of St. Louis and St. Louis County, 2013.

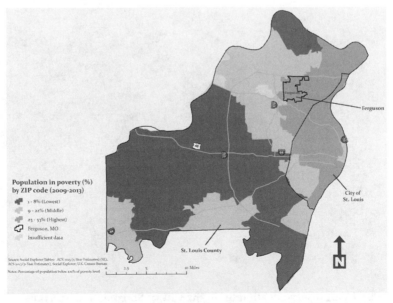

Figure 8.7. Poverty rates in the City of St. Louis and St. Louis County, 2013.

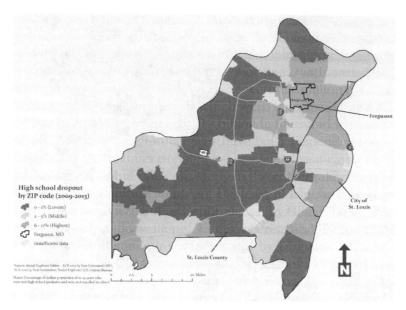

Figure 8.8. High school dropout rates in the City of St. Louis and St. Louis County, 2013.

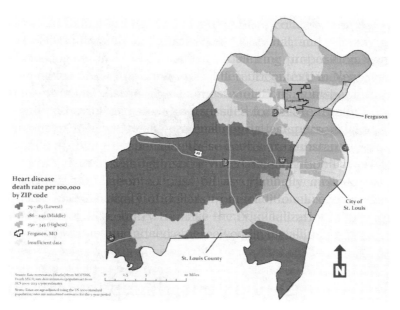

Figure 8.9. Heart disease death rates in the City of St. Louis and St. Louis County, 2013.

all but the eastern most portion of Ferguson is not included in the highest category (205–293 deaths per 100,000). However, much of the City of St. Louis and of St. Louis County affected by high rates of heart disease mortality also has high rates of cancer death. Moderate rates (162–204 deaths per 100,000) are found in the far north, central east, and southwestern sections of the City of St. Louis and northeastern and southeastern portions of St. Louis County. Mortality from all causes follows a similar and now familiar pattern (see Figure 8.11).

One particularly powerful way of encapsulating health outcomes for the St. Louis community is to examine life expectancy at birth by zip code. Indeed, a map such as this in the *For the Sake of All* report gained the most attention and reaction of any data point or figure in the document. It reported an 18-year gap in life expectancy at birth between the predominantly African American, high-poverty, highly unemployed zip code of 63106 in the northern part of the City of St. Louis and the largely white, affluent zip code of 63105 less than ten miles away in the suburban enclave of Clayton (see Figure 8.12). Figure 8.13 expands upon this original map to include additional zip codes, including zip codes in and near Ferguson. There is perhaps no more apt representation of the geography of inequality than this. It should be noted that Ferguson (63135) does not have the lowest life expectancy even among its neighbors in northeastern St. Louis County. However, at 77 years, there is still an eight-year gap between Ferguson and the highest life expectancy shown on the map (85 years in 63105).

When African Americans in the St. Louis region voice frustration, anger, and disappointment about systematically diminished prospects, theirs are not idle complaints; they are quite literally a matter of life and death. Long before the shooting death of Michael Brown, there was reason to question whether this was a region in which black lives mattered. From the moment of birth, substantial obstacles stand in the way of a large proportion of the African American population in St. Louis. Factors that are often considered separately, like education, employment, income, and neighborhood quality, actually interact to produce very different health and life outcomes by place and by race in the St. Louis region. Ferguson must be understood in the context of that larger St. Louis geography and the history of its development. And St. Louis must be understood in the context of a nation in which both health outcomes[26] and economic mobility trail many of the wealthy nations of the world, but where St. Louis also fares worse in terms of economic mobility than other large metropolitan areas in the United

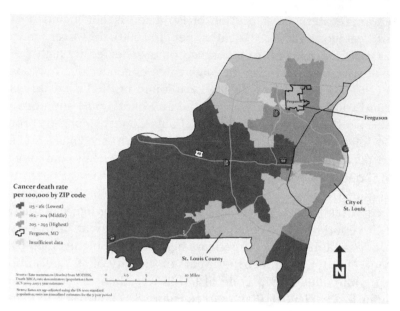

Figure 8.10. Cancer death rates in the City of St. Louis and St. Louis County, 2013.

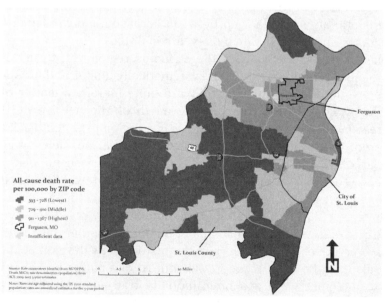

Figure 8.11. All-cause death rates in the City of St. Louis and St. Louis County, 2013.

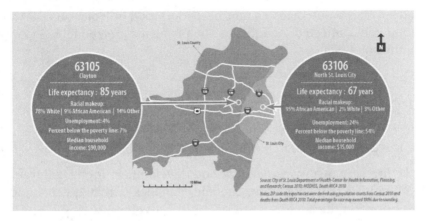

Figure 8.12. A tale of two zip codes.

Source: *For the Sake of All.*

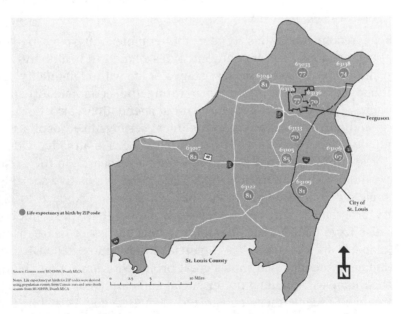

Figure 8.13. Life expectancy at birth by ZIP code (2012).

States.[27] These outcomes cannot be understood in isolation. They are very much connected. And just as the problems are connected, so too are the solutions.

Recommendations

There were six major recommendations offered in *For the Sake of All*, informed both by research evidence and community input:

1) Invest in quality early childhood development for all children.
2) Help low-to-moderate income families create economic opportunities.
3) Invest in coordinated school health programs for all students.
4) Invest in mental health awareness, screening, treatment, and surveillance.
5) Invest in quality neighborhoods for all in St. Louis.
6) Coordinate and expand chronic and infectious disease prevention and management.

These recommendations reflect the complex interplay between social and economic factors and outcomes related to health and well-being. Starting at the very earliest stages of life with high-quality early childhood development and incorporating the economic prospects of families and neighborhoods, the recommendations also deal with mental and physical health in both clinical settings like hospitals and community-based settings such as schools. There is already evidence that these approaches can work. For example, research in the area of early childhood development notes a wide range of positive social and economic outcomes in adulthood when children are exposed to high-quality programs,[28] and recent research shows that these interventions also have health benefits such as reduced risk of heart disease and diabetes in adulthood.[29] A financial intervention called a Child Development Account also shows great promise for impacting children and their families, including better social and emotional functioning in children who receive these subsidized savings accounts at birth and lower levels of symptoms of depression in their mothers.[30] Models also exist for integrating aspects of health promotion in schools, treating violence as a public health problem, and incorporating an analysis of health impacts of policies from a wide range of different domains.[31] This holistic approach to health in St. Louis is aligned with the national "culture of health" initiative that is being promoted by the Robert

Wood Johnson Foundation and the latest report from its Commission to Build a Healthier America.[32]

For the Sake of All data and recommendations also critically informed the deliberations and "signature priorities" of the Ferguson Commission, appointed by Missouri Governor Jeremiah Nixon to determine the "underlying social and economic conditions underscored by the unrest in the wake of the death of Michael Brown."[33] A presentation related to economic opportunity and health was made to the commission in February 2015. The Commission's report, released in September of 2015, prominently features calls to action from all six of the areas of recommendation in *For the Sake of All*.[34]

Now in its second phase, with an additional round of funding from the Missouri Foundation for Health, the *For the Sake of All* project team is focused on implementation of the recommendations by mobilizing the community and key stakeholders. In partnership with a local civic leadership development organization called FOCUS St. Louis, discussion guides and action toolkits are being developed for each of the six recommendation areas to help community members understand and share the information in the report and take practical steps toward making recommended changes.

Conclusion

The tragic death of Michael Brown has awakened the St. Louis region, and the nation, once again to the effects of racial inequality. As the data presented in this chapter show, that inequality extends beyond policing and criminal justice to encompass the educational, economic, and health outcomes of an entire population. Indeed, the data and recommendations presented in *For the Sake of All* even before national attention turned to Ferguson suggest that any real response to these inequities must be multifaceted and will involve multiple sectors of the community. With renewed energy and focus occasioned by the events of August 2014 and beyond, there may yet be reason to hope that much-needed change will finally come—for the sake of all.

Notes

1. U.S. Census Bureau, Social Explorer, http://www.socialexplorer.com/explore/tables (Census 1950, Race. St. Louis Cnty., Mo. & St. Louis City, Mo.).

2. U.S. Census Bureau, Social Explorer, http://www.socialexplorer.com/explore/tables (using Census 1960, Race. St. Louis Cnty., Mo. & St. Louis City, Mo.).

3. *Id.*

4. U.S. Census Bureau, Social Explorer, http://www.socialexplorer.com/explore/tables (using Census 1950 & 1960, Race. Census tracts SLC0010, SLC0011, SLC0012 in St. Louis Cnty., Mo.).

5. U.S. Census Bureau, Social Explorer, http://www.socialexplorer.com/explore/tables (using 2012 American Community Survey 1-Year Estimates, Race. St. Louis Cnty., Mo. & St. Louis City, Mo.).

6. C. Gordon, Mapping decline: St. Louis and the Fate of the American City (2008).

7. S.J. Olshansky et al., *Differences in Life Expectancy Due to Race and Educational Differences Are Widening, and Many May Not Catch Up*, 31(8): Health Aff. (Millwood) 1803–13 (Aug. 2012); E.R. Meara, S. Richards, D.M. Cutler, *The Gap Gets Bigger: Changes in Mortality and Life Expectancy, by Education, 1981–2000*, 27(2)Health Aff. (Millwood) 350–60 (Mar.–Apr. 2008).

8. Meara et al., *supra* note 7.

9. Olshansky et al., *supra* note 7.

10. U.S. Census Bureau, Social Explorer, http://www.socialexplorer.com/explore/tables (using 2013 American Community Survey 1-Year Estimates, Educational attainment for the population 25 years and over, (White alone) & (Black or African American alone)).

11. *Id.*

12. U.S. Census Bureau, Social Explorer, http://www.socialexplorer.com/explore/tables (using 2013 American Community Survey 5-Year Estimates, Educational attainment for the population 25 years and over, (White alone) & (Black or African American alone)).

13. M. Bartley & I. Plewis, *Accumulated Labour Market Disadvantage and Limiting Long-Term Illness: Data from the 1971–1991 Office for National Statistics' Longitudinal Study*, 31(2) Int. J. Epidemiol. 336–41 (Apr. 2002).

14. U.S. Census Bureau, Social Explorer, http://www.socialexplorer.com/explore/tables (using 2013 American Community Survey 1-Year Estimates, Unemployment rate for the population 16 years and over (White alone) & (Black or African American alone). St. Louis Cnty., Mo.; St. Louis City, Mo.; United States).

15. *Id.*

16. U.S. Census Bureau, Social Explorer, http://www.socialexplorer.com/explore/tables (using 2013 American Community Survey 5-Year Estimates, Unemployment rate for the population 16 years and over (White alone) & (Black or African American alone). Ferguson, Mo.; United States).

17. U.S. Census Bureau, Social Explorer, http://www.socialexplorer.com/explore/tables (using 2013 American Community Survey 1-Year Estimates, Poverty status in 2013 (White alone) & (Black or African American alone). St. Louis Cnty., Mo.; St. Louis City, Mo.; United States).

18. *Id.*

19. U.S. Census Bureau, Social Explorer, http://www.socialexplorer.com/explore/tables (using 2013 American Community Survey 1-Year Estimates, Poverty status in 2013 (White alone) & (Black or African American alone). Ferguson, Mo.; United States).

20. B.S. McEwen & P.J. Gianaros, *Central Role of the Brain in Stress and Adaptation: Links to Socioeconomic Status, Health, and Disease*, 1186 Ann. N.Y. Acad. Sci. 190–222 (Feb. 2010).

21. S. Cohen et al., *Childhood Socioeconomic Status and Adult Health*, 1186 Ann. N.Y. Acad. Sci. 37–55 (Feb. 2010); G.J. Duncan et al., *Early-Childhood Poverty and Adult Attainment, Behavior, and Health*, 81(1) Child Dev. 306–25 (Jan.–Feb. 2010).

22. P.A. Braveman et al., *Socioeconomic Disparities in Health in the United States: What the Patterns Tell Us*, 100 Suppl. 1 Am. J. Pub. Health S186–96 (Apr. 1, 2010).

23. A.V. Diez Roux & C. Mair, *Neighborhoods and Health*, 1186 Ann. N.Y. Acad. Sci. 125–45 (Feb. 2010).

24. East-West Gateway Council of Gov'ts, Where We Stand (2014).

25. E. Kneebone, *Ferguson, Mo. Emblematic of Growing Suburban Poverty, in* The Avenue: Rethinking Metropolitan America (Brookings Inst. 2014).

26. Nat'l Res. Council & Inst. of Medicine, Shorter Lives, Poorer Health (Nat'l Acads. Press 2013).

27. R. Chetty et al., *Is the United States Still a Land of Opportunity? Recent Trends in Intergenerational Mobility*, 104(5) Am. Econ. Rev. Paper & Proc.141–47 (2014); R. Chetty et al., Nat'l Bureau Econ. Res., Where Is the Land of Opportunity? The Geography of Intergenerational Mobility in the United States (2014).

28. J.J. Heckman, *School, Skills and Synapses*, 46 Econ. Inquiry 289–324 (2008).

29. F. Campbell et al., *Early Childhood Investments Substantially Boost Adult Health*, 343 Science 1478–85 (2014).

30. J. Huang et al., *Effects of Child Development Accounts on Early Social-Emotional Development: An Experimental Test*, 168(3) JAMA Pediatr. 265–71 (Mar. 2014); J. Huang, M. Sherraden & J.Q. Purnell, *Impacts of Child Development Accounts on Maternal Depressive Symptoms: Evidence from a Randomized Statewide Policy Experiment*, 112 Soc. Sci. Med. 30–38 (Jul. 2014).

31. R.W. Bostic et al., *Health in All Policies: The Role of the US Department of Housing and Urban Development and Present and Future Challenges*, 31(9) Health Aff. (Millwood) 2130–37 (Sept. 2012); J.A. Butts et al., *Cure Violence: A Public Health Model to Reduce Gun Violence*, Ann. Rev Pub. Health, Jan. 7, 2015; M.A. McNall, L.F. Lichty & B. Mavis, *The Impact of School-Based Health Centers on the Health Outcomes of Middle School and High School Students*, 100(9) Am. J. Pub. Health 1604–10 (Sept. 2010); Ctrs. for Disease Control, Coordinated School Health, http://www.cdc.gov/HealthyYouth/CSHP/ (last visited Mar. 9, 2015).

32. Robert Wood Johnson Found., Comm'n to Build a Healthier America, Time to Act: Investing in the Health of Our Children and Communities (2014).

33. STL Positive Change, http://stlpositivechange.org/ (official site of the Ferguson Commission).

34. Forward through Ferguson: A Path toward Racial Equity http://forwardthroughferguson.org/ (report of the Ferguson Commission).

Chapter 9

Media Framing in Black and White: The Construction of Black Male Identity

Candice Norwood

The Real Michael Brown

It started with what easily could have become a routine crime story. Just after noon on Saturday, August 9, 2014, shots rang out in Ferguson, Missouri, a predominantly African American, St. Louis suburb of about 21,000 residents. Eighteen-year-old Michael Brown lay face down in a pool of blood outside 2947 Canfield Drive, killed by Officer Darren Wilson of the Ferguson Police Department. Video captured by witnesses at the scene showed that Brown's motionless body remained in plain view on the street until 4 p.m. Within hours of the shooting, residents of Ferguson began to protest, attracting the attention of local news organizations, soon followed by national and international outlets. Protests began peacefully, with marches, music, and demands for justice. But a candlelight vigil the night after Brown's death quickly escalated into violence; looters vandalized dozens of neighborhood shops and set a QuikTrip convenience store on fire.

By the Tuesday after Brown's death, this average American town became the stage for the type of conflict most Americans associate with overseas politics. Images of St. Louis County police officers in riot gear aiming assault rifles at peaceful protesters and spraying tear gas into private backyards became fixtures on televisions and computer screens around the world. The question news media and audiences asked was: Who was the real Mike Brown? What events led to the shooting?

As details of the case surfaced, the news media presented different versions of Brown's identity. As cultural critic Touré Neblett wrote in an op-ed for the *New York Times*, "An information war is being waged in Ferguson, Mo., each salvo meant to shape public perceptions of Michael Brown and Darren Wilson."[1] Neblett discussed the most common depictions of Michael Brown: The first is the "gentle giant" on his way to begin college and pursue a career in the music industry. A second narrative—fueled by video footage showing Brown participating in the "strong-arm" robbery of cigarillos from a convenience store—characterized Brown as a thug. The third popular media construct was Brown as a drug user. This developed after the St. Louis County medical examiner reported evidence of marijuana in Brown's system at the time of the shooting.

The news coverage of Michael Brown's death is a compelling case study through which to identify and analyze techniques commonly used by media to frame African American men. These tactics have been used throughout African American history to construct a stereotypical representation of black male identity. They remain a prevalent part of mainstream media, particularly in recent news coverage of the high-profile police killings of unarmed black men.

A Brief History of Framing Theory and Techniques

The first thorough analysis of framing theory and its effects are attributed to Canadian sociologist Erving Goffman. His highly cited work *Frame Analysis* says that frames allow people to "locate, perceive, identify, and label" key problems as a way to organize and understand them.[2] Since the publication of *Frame Analysis*, modern scholars have sought to expand on Goffman's ideas.

One of the prominent voices of modern framing analysis is Robert Entman, professor of media and public affairs at George Washington University. Entman addresses framing as something the media does through a process of "selection and salience."[3] Organizations will select stories or issues that they value and then obscure or ignore certain facts in order to make the issues more salient, or important, to an audience.

> To frame is to select some aspects of a perceived reality and make them more salient in a communicating text, in such a way as to

promote a particular problem definition, causal interpretation, moral evaluation, and/or treatment recommendation for the item described.[4]

When used in media, frames come out as several types of biases. Distortion bias applies to news that fabricates or distorts reality. Content bias occurs when a news company fails to present a balanced account of a particular issue and instead favors or overemphasizes one side. Decision-making bias pertains to the mindset and intent of the journalists who create biased content.[5]

Gail T. Fairhurst and Robert A. Sarr identify five framing techniques in their book *The Art of Framing: Managing the Language of Leadership*. Though this book was designed as a guide to effective business management, the concepts it uses are applicable to news media framing techniques. *Metaphors* show likeness between objects. They help to redefine an issue by comparing it to something familiar to audiences. *Stories* grab attention by making the details of an event or case more tangible. Stories can include myths or legends and are used by the media to frame an issue in a memorable way. *Slogans*, *jargon*, and *catchphrases* enhance the meaning of a subject by attaching it to popular references or ideas. Similar to metaphors, these are specific words that people understand easily, thereby increasing the subject's value. *Contrast* can be used to highlight the shortcomings or strengths of a subject by placing it alongside an opposing object. This is perhaps the most prevalent technique used by media and legal teams during controversial criminal cases. The last technique is to *spin* a subject in a positive or negative way by obscuring certain details.[6]

News organizations' long-standing use of these tactics has reinforced widespread perceptions of African American men. Media coverage of the Michael Brown shooting is no exception to this history. As tensions escalated following Brown's shooting, a battle ensued between the news media, Ferguson police, Ferguson citizens, Brown's parents, and news audiences to establish an authentic representation.

"Michael Brown Remembered as 'Gentle Giant'"— *St. Louis Post-Dispatch (Aug. 11, 2014)*

Two days after Brown's death, the shock of the shooting captivated audiences and news organizations across the country. One source of frustration for Ferguson citizens was the lack of evidence that could establish a timeline of events leading to Brown's death. The St. Louis

County Police Department, which took over the investigation almost immediately, had yet to file an incident report or name Wilson as the shooting officer. According to police statements to the press at the time, Wilson shot Brown inside the officer's vehicle after a struggle over the officer's gun. Several Ferguson witnesses, however, claimed that Brown was several feet away—his hands in the air—when he was shot. News organizations and interested citizens were left to speculate. Which version was the truth? Did a decorated police officer target an innocent black teen? Or did a large, black teenager attack an officer in order to evade arrest?

Michael Brown was 6'4" and weighed more than 250 pounds. He liked to rap in his free time and wear pants that sagged. These facts were critical components of the narratives that played out in the news. Those who favor Wilson's account used Brown's size as a way to emphasize his (alleged) propensity to violence. Brown's family, friends, and supporters, on the other hand, used his size as a way to associate Brown with a common lovable archetype—the gentle giant. The gentle giant is a stock character, a stereotypical figure that reoccurs in literature or pop culture.

Throughout American history black stock character depictions have been used to shape public perception. Many of these depictions fixate on black men's physical size through the use of a "black brute" caricature. As a way to provoke fear of newly freed black men during the late 19th century, the "brute" caricature portrayed them as large, savage, and animalistic.[7] The brute lusted for helpless white women and violently took whatever he desired. The brute was a common subject for Reconstruction-era propaganda following the Civil War, including academic articles and illustrations in popular pulp fiction magazines. These images typically showed a frightened, frail white woman in the clutches of a strong, threatening black man. In the 1910 article "The Relation of the Whites to the Negroes," American educator George T. Winston painted a frightening image that was common at the time:

> When a knock is heard at the door, she [a white, Southern woman] shudders with nameless horror. The black brute is lurking in the dark, a monstrous beast, crazed with lust. His ferocity is almost demoniacal. A mad bull or tiger could scarcely be more brutal. A whole community is frenzied with horror, with blind and furious rage for vengeance.[8]

Early news coverage also reflected these depictions. A 1916 *New York Times* headline read: "Armed giant negro goes mad on liner."

A 1922 *New York Times* article said, "Seize giant negro, hide him for safety." These associations between black men and the giant, brute character still permeate American society today. We can see evidence of this in Officer Darren Wilson's own grand jury testimony in November 2014 about his fatal altercation with Brown. "And when I grabbed him, the only way I can describe it is I felt like a 5-year-old holding onto Hulk Hogan," Wilson said in one part of the testimony. He went on to say that Brown had the "most aggressive, intense face. The only way I can describe it, it looks like a demon, that's how angry he looked."[9]

Wilson's depiction of the scene is riddled with similar imagery to that of the brute caricature. Whether intentional or not, Wilson's testimony provides powerful evidence demonstrating that this culture steeped in stereotypical presentations continues to influence people.

The gentle giant is also a pop culture fixture. Though academic scholarship about this particular character is scarce, audiences confront gentle giants regularly in film and literature. Rubeus Hagrid from Harry Potter, King Kong, and John Coffey from Steven Spielberg's *The Green Mile* are just a few of countless examples. In these storylines, the giant initially frightens those who cross his path. The giant's shy disposition and kindness give him humanity and eventually win the hearts of audiences. A battle between the gentle giant archetype and the brute caricature often takes place during cases involving black men.

Eric Garner was a 43-year-old father of six in Staten Island described by a friend as the "neighborhood dad." Garner, who was illegally selling loose cigarettes, died in July 2014 after a New York City officer put him in a chokehold.[10] When a video of Garner's death went viral, news organizations including the *Associated Press*, *Time*, and the *Daily Beast* detailed Garner's life as a kind-hearted father trying to make money for his family. Articles discussed his friendships with people on Staten Island, his 25-year relationship with his wife, and his college-bound son.

A similar narrative surfaced in the aftermath of Brown's shooting. A story published by the *St. Louis Post-Dispatch* two days after his death introduced the "gentle giant" trope in connection with Brown, describing him as physically striking, but caring. Brown was two days away from beginning classes at Vatterott College, a for-profit training institute. He dreamed of going into the music business and eventually owning his own label.[11] Attaching these humanizing details to the "gentle giant" label is a strategy that illustrates Fairhurst and Sarr's *metaphor* and *catchphrase* techniques.

Brown's supporters used the positive qualities associated with this pop culture character to ingrain a reoccurring motif into the public's minds. It is important in high-profile cases to present a balanced narrative to the public; however, framing Brown as either a brute or a gentle giant does not effectively achieve this goal. Both depictions rob Brown of his complexities as a human being and emphasize a singular, stereotypical characteristic: his size. This method of framing objectifies Brown rather than successfully sharing his story. It perpetuates the idea that a black man's physical stature should be a factor in determining his personality or propensity to violence. Despite views expressed in news and social media, having a large size should not be comparable to having a lethal weapon.

"Surveillance Video of Strong-Arm Robbery Tied to Michael Brown"—Fox News (Aug. 16, 2014)

One week after Brown's shooting, tensions remained high between Ferguson residents and its police department. After requests from protesters and Missouri Governor Jay Nixon to release the name of the shooting officer, Ferguson police complied. During a press conference on August 15, Ferguson police chief Thomas Jackson identified Darren Wilson as the shooter. Wilson was a white, six-year police veteran with no prior history of disciplinary action. Despite this step toward a clearer picture of the shooting, many details remained unclear. The day after the press conference, Ferguson police released a video of Michael Brown participating in a strong-arm robbery at a convenience store just minutes before his altercation with Wilson. The video shows two men who fit the description of Michael Brown and his friend Dorian Johnson enter the store, and Michael Brown is shown grabbing snacks and a package of cigarillos. He pushes the sales associate aside before exiting the store without paying. A police incident report of the robbery corroborates the video footage and identifies Brown and Johnson as the primary suspects of the investigation.[12]

Critics said police released the video of the robbery in an attempt to shape public opinion. Whether this is the case, the release of the tape intensified support for Ferguson police and Officer Wilson. Facebook pages supporting Wilson received tens of thousands of "likes." Two separate pages posted to the crowdsourcing site GoFundMe raised more than $400,000 for the officer combined.[13] The release of the robbery footage sparked the beginning of the "thug-ification" of Michael Brown.

Portrayals of black men as violent and dangerous are nothing new in American media. The dissemination of "black brute" propaganda at the beginning of the 20th century established a foundation from which to devise modern ways to link black men to violence. The scope of this association between black men and violence expanded with the introduction of hip-hop culture in the late 1970s. More specifically, the rise of "gangsta rap" gave way to the "thug" persona that permeates modern media depictions of black men. Popular rap groups such as N.W.A. detailed life in the inner city, often characterized by gun violence, street gangs, and promiscuity. Guillermo Rebollo-Gil and Amanda Moras discuss the implications of these messages in their article "Black Women and Black Men in Hip Hop Music: Misogyny, Violence and the Negotiation of (White-Owned) Space."[14] As they mention, critics of hip-hop culture rarely discussed the problematic messages in some hip-hop music as a way to address problems within American society as a whole. Rather, hip-hop critics often single out black men as the sole perpetrators of violence and misogyny.

> Often, the treatment of black women in hip-hop is brought up only to highlight the alleged moral depravity of the artists or the wantonness of so-called Black ghetto culture rather than as a critical and necessary discussion of patriarchy and violence. It is used as yet another tool by which white American critics and politicians further stigmatize the black males as violent and/or criminal.[15]

This "thug-ification" has been one of the major sources of conflict when discussing the shootings of unarmed black men in America. Modern media "thug-ification" includes writing sensational headlines, publishing criminalizing photographs, and overemphasizing a victim's past indiscretions. With respect to the coverage of police violence, media "thug-fication" has targeted both the victims of this brutality and the protestors who speak out against it. Coverage of the protests in Ferguson, Baltimore, New York, and other cities around the country demonstrate how news reports differ when discussing unrest from white crowds versus unrest from black crowds. CNN, Fox News, and other news outlets have used the words "criminal" and "thug" to describe black demonstrators since the early Ferguson protests. Meanwhile, white sports fans who riot after a game, overturning cars and breaking windows, are frequently described with more positive language such as "young people" doing "stupid things." These discrepancies have been highlighted in opinion articles and social media campaigns.

The news media's emphasis on black crime and violence has been formally studied as well. A study by the nonprofit research organization Media Matters for America found that between August 18 and December 14, 2014, four New York City-based television stations reported on murder, theft, and assault cases with black suspects at a higher rate than black suspects were arrested for those crimes. Based on the report, 54 percent of murder suspects arrested in New York City between 2010 and 2013 were black. However, 74 percent of the murder suspects mentioned in the broadcasts of these four stations were black. Fifty-five percent of theft suspects arrested in New York between 2010 and 2013 were black, but 84 percent of the theft suspects in these broadcasts were black. Finally, 49 percent of assault suspects arrested in New York City during that time period were black, but 73 percent of the TV stations' assault reports mention black suspects.[16] Another study from 2002 found that news programming at three television stations in Orlando, Florida presented blacks and Latinos in more threatening contexts. According to the research, whites were more likely to appear as a role model figure in the news than as a criminal suspect. Alternately, blacks were 2.6 times more likely than whites to appear as criminal suspects. Latinos were 5.6 times more likely than whites to be represented as criminal suspects.[17] The rise of social media and cell phone imagery has allowed even more widespread dissemination and analysis of photos from a victim's past. These images often reinforce common perceptions of black men as violent and depraved.

Visual "thug-ification" was a prominent aspect of the murder of 17-year-old African American Trayvon Martin. Martin was shot and killed in his father's Florida neighborhood by neighborhood-watch captain George Zimmerman in 2012. During Zimmerman's trial, his defense team retrieved and presented a number of controversial images from Martin's cell phone. These photos were later widely distributed by news outlets, inevitably shaping public opinion on the case. Negative depictions of Zimmerman were limited to a single mug shot of him from a 2005 arrest for assaulting a police officer. Other photos of Zimmerman either showed him as a clean-cut high school graduate donning a cap and gown, or as a battered victim of Martin's alleged attack. Martin's character, on the other hand, was forced to hold up against a number of startling images. The pictures taken from Martin's phone included one that shows him flipping his middle fingers to the camera and another of a handgun alongside a detachable magazine holding bullets.

This same framing structure plays out in the tumultuous aftermath of Brown's shooting two years later. With the exception of a *New York*

Times feature, details of Officer Wilson largely focused on his commendable reputation as a police veteran. The most widely distributed image of Wilson came from a February 2014 Ferguson City Council meeting during which he received a commendation for his "extraordinary effort in the line of duty" in a felony drug arrest.[18] Rather than revealing any of Wilson's youthful indiscretions before joining the force, the focus remained on Brown's past. Within a week of his death, criminalizing photos leaked from Brown's social media accounts show him "flipping the bird" and allegedly flashing gang signs. Conservative documentarian Pat Dollard published these images on his website; they were subsequently circulated and analyzed by mainstream outlets such as the *Christian Science Monitor*. The media portrayals in both the Martin and Brown cases shed light on the important relationship between the *contrast* and *story* framing techniques discussed by Fairhurst and Sarr.

Grand jury hearings and trials often come down to stories. Prosecutors and defense teams share the narratives of a particular crime and it is the members of a jury's responsibility to decide which version of events they believe and whether that version suggests beyond a reasonable doubt that the defendant committed a crime. In theory the media bias should have no effect on a jury's decision to charge or convict a defendant. Jurors are often instructed to disclose any biases and to avoid outside information regarding their specific case. Despite this ideal, our country has a history of disseminating images in literature, film, music, and news that continually reinforce the idea that blacks frequently engage in criminal activity. The media have created a society that holds subconscious negative feelings about blacks based on their race and color. These subtle cognitive associations have become a popular area of study known as implicit bias. Studies suggest that these deeply rooted biases also affect courtroom procedure. One example is an empirical study published by researchers Justin D. Levinson and Danielle Young in 2010. The study explored how a group of mock jurors assessed trial evidence based on a defendant's skin tone.

> The perpetrator's skin tone in the photo significantly affected evidence judgments. Participants who saw the photo of the perpetrator with a dark skin tone judged ambiguous evidence to be significantly more indicative of guilt than participants who saw the photo of a perpetrator with a lighter skin tone.[19]

The research from this study provides strong evidence suggesting how bias can lead to the criminalization of certain racial groups.

Studies suggest that these biases factor into criminal justice. While we cannot definitively prove that the jury decisions in the Brown and Martin cases were influenced by racial prejudice, research supports the claim that jurors and public audiences are more likely to believe the stories that criminalize Brown, Martin, and other black men.

Contrasting images and details help to shape these stories. In Brown's case, the images that show him flipping his middle finger or displaying ambiguous hand signs help to illustrate the narrative that Brown is a thug. These images are then *contrasted* with images of Wilson proudly receiving a commendation for his police service. As Fairhurst and Sarr discuss in their analysis, the most problematic flaw with the contrast technique is that public perception varies based of the two images that are selected. For example, when placing a "thug" image of Mike Brown next to a heroic photo of Wilson, Brown might look capable of a vicious attack on the officer. When this same image of Brown is contrasted against an actual gang member or murderer, however, Brown looks like a typical rebellious teenager.

"Mike Brown Had Marijuana in System at the Time of Shooting"—*International Business Times (Aug. 18, 2014)*

On August 18, the *Washington Post* reported that the St. Louis County medical examiner's autopsy report concluded Brown was shot from the front six times. It also noted evidence of marijuana in his system at the time of the shooting.

Many reporters and observers of the case acknowledged that the presence of marijuana alone is not alarming, especially given new marijuana legislation throughout the country. Fox News, however, was one of several large news outlets to suggest that the marijuana may have been laced with more severe drugs such as PCP that could have produced an erratic response from Brown preceding the shooting.[20] As with the allegations in the strong-arm robbery, this narrative shifted the focus away from Wilson and placed responsibility on Brown. What did *he* do that would make a decorated officer shoot him? The possibility that Wilson might have misinterpreted or overreacted in the situation was generally ignored by many news organizations.

Discussing drug use as a way to criminalize black men is a subset of the "thug-ification" concept discussed in the previous section. Due to direct links between drug use and the incarceration rates of black men, the category merits a separate evaluation. An intensified "War on Drugs," launched by President Reagan in 1982, profoundly affected the black community. Crack cocaine began to ravage inner-city neighborhoods in 1984, shaping Americans' socioeconomic status as well as their mainstream media identity. Michelle Alexander explored the lasting effects of this campaign in her book *The New Jim Crow: Mass Incarceration in the Age of Colorblindness*:

> The Reagan administration hired staff to publicize the emergence of crack cocaine in 1985 as part of a strategic effort to build public and legislative support for the war [on drugs]. The media campaign was an extraordinary success. Almost overnight, the media was saturated with images of black "crack whores," "crack dealers," and "crack babies"—images that seemed to confirm the worst negative stereotypes about impoverished inner-city residents.[21]

The nation's prison population growth after 1985—with a majority of the inmates being people of color—continued to reinforce the criminal media depictions Alexander discussed in her book. In 1973 the U.S. penal population was approximately 200,000, but grew to about 2.23 million by 2012.[22] The majority of these convictions were for drug-related offenses. Despite evidence suggesting that blacks and whites are equally likely to use and sell drugs, blacks are 3.6 times more likely to be arrested for selling drugs and 2.5 times more likely to be arrested for using them.[23]

These statistics have shaped the public's connection between black men and illicit drug use, which often surfaces during racially charged court cases. A *Huffington Post* article from August 2014 produced a list of 16 news headlines from across the country that show major differences in the language used to describe black victims of crime versus whites who are suspected of major crimes. One headline in New York's *Staten Island Advance* about a white murder suspect read: "Son in Staten Island murders was brilliant, athletic—but his demons were the death of parents." A headline from Al.com in Alabama regarding a black shooting victim read: "Montgomery's latest homicide victim had history of narcotics abuse, tangles with the law."[24] These and many other examples given in the *Huffington Post* article show that outlets are more willing to use sympathetic language with white perpetrators of crime than they are with black victims. Whether the news sources intend to, their word choice puts a *spin* on the subjects of these cases. Their inclusion of positive or negative details about a subject—for example, describing a white suspect as "brilliant, athletic," or saying a black victim has abused narcotics—shape audience sympathy and attention. They perpetuate common stereotypes of white violence as an anomaly and black violence and drug abuse as the norm.

This is what we find in the Michael Brown case as well. Many news outlets have overemphasized the role marijuana might have played in the violent exchange, putting a negative spin on Brown that supports Darren Wilson's account of events. Though a number of studies have found no concrete correlation between marijuana and violence—after excluding alcohol and other drug use—critics in racially charged cases continue to emphasize its importance. In one particular example, Pat Robertson of the Christian Broadcast Network's *700 Club* program discussed Brown's drug use during the show on August 18, 2014. He was careful not to directly accuse Brown, stating: "We don't have the facts yet." But he adds that Brown's actions that day—robbing a store and later walking in the middle of the street where Wilson stopped him—suggest "he probably was high on something." This airing came a day after the *Washington Post* reported Brown's marijuana use. Though Robertson had access to a variety of information and could have given more specific details about the case, he used ambiguous language that left the extent of Brown's drug use open to interpretation.

Another black man killed in Beavercreek, Ohio, just days before Brown's death. On August 5, 2014, 22-year-old John Crawford III was shot and killed in an open carry state by two Beavercreek police officers in a Walmart while he was talking on his cell phone and holding a toy pellet gun sold by the store. Following Crawford's death several local news outlets, including the Dayton's WDTN News 2 station and the Dayton Daily News, chose to report that the coroner's office found evidence of marijuana in his system.[25] While they have every right to report this piece of factual information, without the proper context it can significantly damage Crawford's character. When reading these reports two crucial problems arise. The first is that despite Crawford's innocence, both news stories dedicate more time to a white victim, a 37-year old woman who also died from a heart attack after hearing the gun shots. Secondly, these stories reported Crawford's toxicology findings and left their readers to wonder about the importance of this information. Did the marijuana cause Crawford to behave erratically? Did potentially erratic behavior cause the officers to shoot him? Of course, the videotape footage from the store showed none of this. Yet, this kind of reporting raises questions about the victim and whether he did something to cause this extreme reaction. These are examples of the problematic questions that can surface when reporters provide piecemeal details surrounding the circumstances of a victim's drug use without further clarifying the relevance of the revelation. Walmart's video footage and eyewitness accounts, for example, do not suggest that Crawford was a threat to anyone in the store.

Indeed, police were initially called by a person who told the 911 operators that Crawford was loading and pointing the gun at customers. The videotape proves that this was an untrue statement and the witness later retracted his statements.

Despite widespread attention and criticism of this spin tactics following the Brown and Crawford deaths, news outlets continue to use it. About two weeks after the July 2015 shooting death of 43-year-old Sam DuBose by a white University of Cincinnati police officer, news reports surfaced about drugs found in his car at the time of the shooting. Cincinnati Police Department executed a search warrant after the shooting and discovered four bags and a jar of marijuana amounting to slightly less than the two pounds required to meet felony convictions.[26] Most of these reports of the marijuana discovery failed to include that the officer pulled DuBose over because he didn't have a front license plate—not because of suspected drug use. Video footage of the shooting recorded by a police body camera also contradicts the officer's claim that DuBose dragged him before the shooting. Even with these available facts, somehow the marijuana has been an important factor in shaping public opinion on this case.

We can see that the spin tactic can be an effective, but dangerous technique, because it allows individuals to cherry pick details that support a particular narrative. In cases that lack physical evidence—and even ones that have video footage—these select details of drug consumption often become very powerful. They can condemn black males in the eyes of the public.

Conclusion

Framing is a powerful tool used by governments, organizations, and media outlets to shape public knowledge, perception, and opinion. The use of framing in the aftermath of Michael Brown's shooting provides a case study through which to examine how the news media help to construct public identities of black men. Throughout U.S. history many whites sought to create fear of black men by presenting "evidence" demonstrating their propensity to violence. This took place using the "black brute" stock character during the Reconstruction period. The use of the "gentle giant" and the "brute" tropes to emphasize black men's sizes highlights the degree to which this factor shapes the public perception. In the cases of Michael Brown and Eric Garner, large size decreased the sympathy these victims received from mainstream audiences. A black victim's large size allows people to construct the aggressive, thug narrative that so often plays out in these cases.

Many mainstream and conservative media outlets continue to use the heavily ingrained stereotype for current cases. In the Michael Brown and Trayvon Martin cases, aggressive images of each victim were contrasted against dignified images of their respective shooters. The connection between drugs and black men further emphasizes the aggression stereotype. The war on drugs that began in 1984 has been a critical factor in the public's view of black men as illicit drug users. Media outlets emphasize illicit drug use more frequently in incidents involving black men, as seen in the negative identification of Michael Brown with marijuana and drug use. We can see that rather than helping the public make sense of complex legal issues, these framing techniques instead continuously reduce black men to a list of stereotypes that affect their social, economic, and legal treatment in American society.

Today in the United States, particularly after President Obama's election, people tend to push back against conversations about race and discrimination with claims that we live in a color-blind, postracial society. Yet we continue to see examples that contradict this postracial ideal. Studies show disheartening disparities between black and white arrests and convictions. We see that children of color are disproportionately punished in schools. Minorities experience more problems in the workforce and when trying to buy a house. Though Darren Wilson was not charged with Michael Brown's death, an investigation into the Ferguson Police Department by the U.S. Department of Justice found damning evidence of racial bias and discrimination by Ferguson police. Major problems continue to exist in many areas of American society. These problems have been a constant throughout black and white relations in the United States. Though legislation and ideas have improved since the transatlantic slave trade, decades of legalized discrimination and pervasive negative depictions of minorities continue to shape the cognitive framework of American society. The bias and discrimination that remain today are tricky to identify and solve. What American society needs to meet this goal is less legislative and more psychological. Our country needs to work on different levels to restructure the way we think about people of color.

It will not be an easy task, but an essential component of accomplishing this is bringing attention to bias in the news media. News organizations have tremendous influence on their audiences. We rely on them to tell us about significant events throughout the world. If people consistently face news reports of black-on-black crime or black drug use, then they will come to view these occurrences as normal. With budget constraints, today's 24-hour news cycle, and the constant demand for updated information, news organizations are under a lot of pressure. But even with these daily challenges news companies must make fair and balanced reporting their priority. This may take different forms depending on the organization and its structure, but each company should have a team that is responsible for looking at its news coverage, assessing its fairness, and suggesting ways it can improve. This certainly will not solve the problem, but it is an important and necessary place to start.

Notes

1. Touré Neblett, *Black America and the Burden of the Perfect Victim*, WASH. POST, Aug. 22, 2014, http://www.washingtonpost.com/opinions/black-america-and-the-burden-of-the-perfect-victim/2014/0 8/22/30318ec2-27d1-11e4-958c-268a320a60ce_story.html.

2. ERVING GOFFMAN, FRAME ANALYSIS: AN ESSAY ON THE ORGANIZATION OF EXPERIENCE 21 (Harper & Row 1974).

3. Robert M. Entman, *Framing: Towards Clarification of a Fractured Paradigm*, 43(4) J. COMMC'N 51, 52 (1993).

4. *Id.*

5. Robert M. Entman, *Framing Bias: Media in the Distribution of Power*, 57 J. COMMC'N 163, 163 (2007).

6. GAIL FAIRHURST & ROBERT A. SARR, THE ART OF FRAMING: MANAGING THE LANGUAGE OF LEADERSHIP 100 (Jossey-Bass 1996).

7. CATHERINE JUANITA STARKE, BLACK PORTRAITURE IN AMERICAN FICTION: STOCK CHARACTERS, ARCHETYPES, AND INDIVIDUALS 62 (Basic Books 1971).

8. George T. Winston, *The Relation of Whites to the Negroes*, 18 AM. ACAD. POLITICAL & SOC. SCI. 105, 109 (July 1910).

9. Transcript of Grand Jury, State of Missouri v. Darren Wilson, Aug. 20, 2014, http://graphics8 .nytimes.com/newsgraphics/2014/11/24/ferguson-assets/grand-jury-testimony.pdf.

10. Josh Sanburn, *Behind the Video of Eric Garner's Deadly Confrontation with New York Police*, TIME, July 22, 2014, http://time.com/3016326/eric-garner-video-police-chokehold-death/.

11. Elisa Crouch, *Michael Brown Remembered as a "Gentle Giant,"* ST. LOUIS POST-DISPATCH, Aug. 11, 2014, http://www.stltoday.com/news/local/crime-and-courts/michael-brown-remembered-as-a-gentle-giant /article_cbafa12e-7305-5fd7-8e0e-3139f472d130.html.

12. St. Louis Cnty Police. Incident Report No. 14-43984 (Aug. 9, 2014).

13. Matt Pearce, *Fundraising Web Pages for Ferguson Cop Still Closed; It's Unclear Why*, L.A. Times, Sept. 1, 2014, http://www.latimes.com/nation/nationnow/la-na-nn-ferguson-officer-fundraisers -20140831-story.html.

14. Guillermo Rebollo-Gil & Amanda Moras, *Black Women and Black Men in Hip Hop Music: Misogyny, Violence and the Negotiation of (White-Owned) Space*, 45.1 J. Popular Culture 118–32 (2012).

15. *Id.* at 118–19.

16. Daniel Angster, Salvatore Colleluori, & Todd Gregory, *New York City Television Stations Give Lopsided Coverage to Black Crime*, Media Matters, Aug. 26, 2014, http://mediamatters.org /research/2014/08/26/report-new-york-city-television-stations-give-l/200524.

17. Ted Chiricos & Sarah Eschholz, *The Racial and Ethnic Typification of Crime and the Criminal Typification of Race and Ethnicity in Local Television News*, 39.4 J. Research in Crime Delinquency 400–420 (2002).

18. Jason Sickles, *Photos: Ferguson Officer Darren Wilson Earned Police Honor before Fatal Shooting*, Yahoo News, Aug. 16, 2014, http://news.yahoo.com/photos-ferguson-officer-darren-wilson-received -police-award-earlier-this-year-021255893.html?soc_src=mediacontentstory.

19. Justin D. Levinson & Danielle Young, *Different Shades of Bias: Skin Tone, Implicit Racial Bias, and Judgments of Ambiguous Evidence*, 112.2 W. Va. L. Rev. 307, 337 (2010).

20. *Inside Private Autopsy of Michael Brown*, Fox News, Aug. 18, 2014, http://www.foxnews.com /on-air/on-the-record/2014/08/19/inside-private-autopsy-michael-brown.

21. Michelle Alexander, The New Jim Crow: Mass Incarceration in the Age of Colorblindness 5 (New Press 2010).

22. Jeremy Travis et al., The Growth of Incarceration in the United States 2 (Nat'l Acads. Press 2014).

23. Jonathan Rothwell, *How the War on Drugs Damages Black Social Mobility*, Brookings Inst., Sept. 30, 2014, http://www.brookings.edu/blogs/social-mobility-memos/posts/2014/09/30-war-on-drugs-black -social-mobility-rothwell.

24. Nick Wing, *When the Media Treats White Suspects and Killers Better than Black Victims*, Huffington Post, Aug. 14, 2014, http://www.huffingtonpost.com/2014/08/14/media-black-victims_n_5673291 .html.

25. Jill Drury, Coroner: Crawford had THC in system when shot at Walmart, News 2 WDTN, Sept. 26, 2014, http://wdtn.com/2014/09/26/coroner–williams–death–at–walmart–ruled–homicide/ and Thomas Gnau & Chris Stewart, New details in deaths of 2 at Walmart, Dayton Daily News, Sept. 24, 2014, http://www.daytondailynews.com/news/news/new–details–in–deaths–of–2–at–walmart/nhWF3/. See also Frank Vyan Walton, So Why Isn't Ronald Ritchie Being Charged with Manslaughter in Police Killing of John Crawford?, DAILY KOS (Sept. 10, 2014, 8:41 AM), http://www.dailykos.com/story /2014/09/10/1328519/-So-why-isn-t-Ronald-Ritchie-being-charged-with-Manslaughter-in-Police-Killing-of -John-Crawford.

26. Ben Petracco, *Search Warrant: Bags of Marijuana Found in Sam DuBose's Car*, Cincinnati's WLWT5, Aug. 5, 2015, http://www.wlwt.com/news/source-2-bags-of-marijuana-in-duboses-car-at-time -of-fatal-shooting/34533640.

Chapter 10

Psychic Pain: Residents, Protesters, Police, and Community

Kira Hudson Banks and Vetta L. Sanders Thompson

Introduction

This chapter provides a context for understanding the range of psychological responses experienced as a result of history, recent events, and efforts to produce systemic change in Ferguson, Missouri; Baltimore, Maryland; Chicago, Illinois; and similar communities. The community's response must be understood within the framework of systemic racism and discrimination occurring on individual, institutional, structural, and cultural levels. We discuss anticipated reactions based on exposure and proximity to events, as well as interpretive lens.

Given the history and social situation of Ferguson and indeed North St. Louis County, many residents were and are primed to experience trauma in response to the issues that began in early August, 2014.[1] Analyses and discussions of events in Baltimore and Chicago suggest that while there are differences in the racial history and composition of these cities, similar racial and social oppression predated and sparked unrest.[2] As recent scholarship has made clear, racism and racial discrimination have health,[3] psychological, and mental health impacts.[4] Therefore, the deleterious effects of racism as a stressor should be considered along with more severe stress responses. The extent to which the event and related encounters are considered stressful versus traumatic will be determined by the extent of engagement and the individuals' trauma history.[5]

The discussion of race-based trauma calls for analyses that move beyond the impact of individuals' acts to an understanding of how discrimination based on race is enacted through systems and occurs within a social structure that privileges a majority group, such that language, dress, norms, and other aspects of one group are considered superior and normative and for other groups are constrained or prohibited.[6] In addition to individuals experiencing the specific events of Ferguson directly (i.e., the shooting and subsequent protests) or vicariously (via media); institutional dynamics such as policing, housing, and education patterns set the stage for residents to be disparately impacted by the events of Ferguson. The federal housing and local real estate practices, planning, and zoning policies that influenced the racialized residential patterns of St. Louis City and the 90 municipalities in St. Louis County, as well as economic, educational, health, and other disparities are detailed by Colin Gordon[7] and others.[8] These and other historical dynamics are the fertile ground upon which the twitter organizing effort, #Ferguson, occurred. Therefore, the varied responses should be seen in that context, as potentially part of a larger narrative rather than "post" a specific traumatic event. For many directly affected by Ferguson, the trauma continues and it did not begin with the death of Mike Brown; therefore, the concept of "posttraumatic" is inaccurate. In the aftermath of the Michael Brown shooting, seven Black men in as many months were shot by law enforcement in the St. Louis area. These points suggest that to narrow our understanding of psychological responses to Ferguson solely to one event is to miss the forest for the trees.

Carter's discussion of the origins of the term racism, systematic advantage on the basis of race, is worth highlighting.[9] Carter notes that the term came into widespread use with the 1968 Kerner Commission report on unrest and riots in minority communities, which highlighted segregation, poverty, and discrimination in housing, education, employment, facilities, and services as contributing factors. Add to these observations police force composition and law enforcement policies that disproportionately impact people of color and the poor, and the parallels to Ferguson build. In that light, it should come as little surprise to learn the Department of Justice cited a pattern of racial bias in addition to derogatory and dehumanizing communications by the Ferguson Police Department in a report released in March of 2015.[10] The report can be seen as part of a series of reports connected to other data that preceded it. Ferguson did not occur in a vacuum and neither did the individual reactions to the events.

Shooting Reactions

Luckily, most adults, youth, and children will not experience acute stress, posttraumatic stress disorder (PTSD), depression, or anxiety as a direct result of Ferguson. Prior studies focusing on events such as the Oklahoma City bombing and the September 11, 2001, attacks, suggest that while individuals living in or near the area affected by traumatic events do experience traumatic reactions at higher rates than those living in unaffected areas, the vast majority of community members do not have clinical diagnoses.[11] However, while PTSD symptoms were higher among those directly affected by the 9/11 attacks, many people who were not directly affected by the attacks also met criteria for PTSD.[12] It is important to note that these symptoms seemed to resolve within in the first six months after the attacks,[13] and the impact on those not directly affected may have been related to media exposure.[14] Data obtained from New York City parents documented high rates of initial distress among children, with more than 60 percent of adults in households with children reporting that "1 or more children were upset by the attacks."[15] In a ten-year follow-up study of over 70,000 individuals affected by 9/11, those with the most exposure to the event were more likely to have symptoms of both PTSD and depression. Greater social isolation, experiencing trauma post-9/11, and unemployment were also correlated with increased prevalence of comorbidity.[16] The association between unemployment and increased prevalence of both PTSD and depression holds particular significance for residents of St. Louis City and North County who participated in protests.[17] The high rates of unemployment noted in these geographic areas suggest an increased potential for symptoms of both disorders.

Factors that affect response and coping include prior trauma and mental health, neighborhood quality, social support, and conflict following the event.[18] In the cases of Ferguson, Baltimore, and Chicago, the presence of ongoing protests, which could be construed as an indication of social conflict, may have increased the level of distress experienced by members of the community.[19] In addition, the largely African American community most directly affected experiences greater levels of poverty and deprivation than White Ferguson residents.[20] Research shows that family and community support are among the strongest buffers against developing difficulties. Specific to collective trauma—a psychological effect, with the potential for transgenerational transmission, experienced by a group—research on the aftermath of Hurricane Katrina suggests that attending to racial identity and the way perceptions differ across and within racial groups is important.[21] Taken together, it is important not to assert that responses to such community incidents are monolithic. Instead they are influenced by a number of factors that affect who, for whom, and when psychological distress surfaces.

Reviews of the literature indicate that the prevalence of PTSD among those with direct exposure to a community trauma ranges between 30 percent and 40 percent, with the range of PTSD in the general population expected to be between 5 percent and 10 percent.[22] The estimate for the experience of major depression was 9.7 percent.[23] The factors that determine the likelihood of PTSD are "degree of physical injury, immediate risk of life, severity of property destruction and fatalities."[24]

Given what we know, the death of Michael Brown may result in symptoms of acute stress or PTSD among a subset of the residents living in and around the Canfield Green Apartments. Adults and children alike may show signs of the stress that resulted from the shooting and the four and a half hours that the body remained in the street, along with blood and other relevant stimuli. These individuals might meet the stressor criteria for a clinical diagnosis[25] based on their actual exposure and proximity to the initial shooting and/or or their relationship to the young man who died at the hands of a Ferguson police officer Darren Wilson.

Acute stress is differentiated from PTSD by two issues. Acute stress can only be diagnosed if the traumatic event has occurred within one month, and dissociative symptoms, such as flashbacks, numbing, and reduced awareness, are more important to the diagnosis.[26] PTSD is diagnosed one month after the traumatic event and requires intrusion symptoms (thoughts, memories, or reactions including recurrent intrusive memories, nightmares, distress after contact with reminders, and physical reactions in response to trauma related stimuli); avoidance symptoms (effort made to avoid thoughts of contact with trauma reminders, situations, people); negative changes in thoughts and mood (isolation or lack of concern about others); negative, distorted beliefs about self and others, including self-blame; inability to recall aspects of the trauma; inability to experience positive emotions; and changes in arousal and reactivity (having trouble concentrating or making decisions, feeling jumpy, being easily startled, having sleeping difficulties, having irritable or aggressive behavior).[27]

A portion of individuals experiencing or witnessing these events can also be expected to report depression, anxiety, and less severe signs of distress. Symptoms of depression might include feeling down or sad, loss of interest in activities, lack of energy, changes in appetite and sleep, and feelings of hopelessness.[28] Anxiety might include more general fears, arousal, preoccupation with death, safety, what is going on, concern for and watching for danger, irritability, worry, and difficulty focusing on school or work.[29] Substance abuse or use may also occur in response to depression or anxiety; the use of substances may represent a way of coping with upsetting events. Individuals might drink too much or use drugs to numb and to try to deal with difficult thoughts, feelings, and memories related to the trauma. This response to the traumatic events might actually lead to more problems.

Protest Exposure

Similar reactions to those just described might also be noted among those adults, adolescents, and children who participated in or lived near the site of protests. These incidents are considered under the rubric of community violence.[30] The individuals with experiences in this category may have witnessed the police presence, tear gas, rubber bullets, flash bombs, pepper spray, and denigrating language. They might have also experienced the two nights with uncontrolled crowds that looted and committed arson, including the night the grand jury verdict was announced (November 24, 2014), which might provoke thoughts of death and concerns for safety required for trauma related diagnoses.[31] The protesters facing police officers pointing guns at them and calling them animals, experiencing or witnessing others being hit with flash bombs, tear gas, pepper spray, mace, acoustic weapons, rubber bullets, and at times multiple forms of violence, may be at greatest risk. Distress could also have stemmed from the contradiction in law enforcement standing by while criminal acts occurred rather than intervening to protect the right to protest.[32] The reactivity to these actions might be influenced by the extent to which individuals were previously aware of issues related to policing, mistrust of the system, or systemic racism more broadly.

In addition to issues of PTSD and other clinical diagnoses, we must remember that both daily hassles related to race, as well as more significant experiences of discrimination have psychological consequences for their targets and manifest and build whether or not affected individuals understand the relevant processes.[33] As Carter and Bryant-Davis note, there is cumulative impact of these experiences,[34] and, to the extent that they affect mental health, members of the Ferguson community who protested precisely because of experiences of police and judicial discrimination are at increased risk of trauma given their experiences while advocating for their rights. Carter's model of race-based traumatic stress suggests that when an individual experiences a race-related stressor, the response can range from anger, depression, avoidance, hypervigilance/arousal, intrusion, and low self-esteem to physical reactions. It is likely that individuals protesting and engaged in activism around Ferguson, Baltimore, and Chicago perceive such events as race-based, and they are subsequently at risk for the array of symptoms outlined by Carter.[35]

Youth Exposure

While not typically considered, the limited studies conducted following the Los Angeles riots in 1992 suggest that youth are vulnerable regardless of age. Preschool children directly exposed to the LA riots told stories and had narratives with more aggression, violent content, and unfriendly people than children in a control group with no riot exposure.[36] In a separate study of students, teachers reported on student behavior after the riots compared to two weeks before the riots. The teachers reported significant increases in students' aggression and decreases in their ability to get along with peers and in academic progress.[37] Despite this study and 9/11 data,[38] children who witnessed all or some parts of these events have the unlikely, but ongoing, expectation of functioning as normal in school.

The responses of concern among children and youth can include regressive behavior (thumb-sucking or bed-wetting, fears of darkness, clinging to parents, and speech difficulties) among preschoolers; whining, separation anxieties, aggressive behavior at home or school, school avoidance, withdrawal from peers, and poor concentration in school among children in early childhood; and rebelliousness (e.g., refusal to do chores), school problems (e.g., withdrawal, fighting), and physical problems (headaches, vague aches and pain, psychosomatic complaints, loss of interest in social activities with peers) among pre-adolescents and adolescents.[39] Children are also affected by a prior history of trauma—family abuse, neglect, community violence, natural disasters, accidents, injury, emotional problems, learning disabilities, or developmental disabilities. Finally, children who live with chronic stressors, such as those who live in poverty, are more vulnerable.[40] Despite these markers, it is a mistake to believe that children will not react because they do not fit into the categories of vulnerability described. Older youth may have had prior personal involvement with law enforcement or witnessed or been told about denigrating interactions. Younger children will have heard adults discussing events, and many youth will have seen Ferguson-related protests and violence on television and social media.

Distanced Exposure

Sometimes considered more distally are individuals who viewed events via traditional media, social media, or live stream. However, research suggests that prolonged viewing can be correlated with psychological outcomes. A study of over 2,000 U.S. viewers found that watching four or more hours of 9/11 and early Iraq war footage predicted PTSD symptoms two to three years later.[41] Similar trends were found in a study of children responding to 9/11, and a kidnapping and sniper incident from 2002.[42] Increased worry and change in activity were correlated with media exposure to these events with greater stress reported among 10–13 year olds, children of color, those in close proximity to the event, and those of lower socioeconomic status. These findings suggest that direct trauma exposure is not necessary to experience negative effects.

Another group not often considered at risk during incidents of community violence is media personnel. However, when a pilot study examining the potential impact of reporting on a disaster was completed in Australia, the study authors noted that those who are assigned to cover community violence, including the type witnessed in Ferguson, are "generally the youngest in the profession and have no training in dealing with either grief or trauma or interview techniques for distressed people."[43] They indicate that journalists covering these stories experience serious trauma, and symptoms persists for some.[44]

Police Reactions

This sequence of events also continues to impact police officers in their work, generally, and in distressed communities in particular. A study examining police response after the Los Angeles riots noted that

17 percent of the officers who responded to the scene experienced stress symptoms.[45] Results indicated a positive relationship between PTSD symptoms and cognitive avoidance, sense of resignation, and emotional discharge. Avoidance of situations and people associated with the traumatic events could have counterproductive repercussions for policing activities in affected communities. In addition, issues related to emotional regulation may affect police interactions with and relations within those communities. Furthermore, an inverse relationship between PTSD symptoms and seeking support and information among the police officers interviewed was observed, which has implications for officer recovery and policing ability and attitudes.[46]

In addition to issues of trauma, the psychological mindset of police officers going into communities must be considered. Research suggests that police officers might be prone to dehumanize African Americans they police as "apes," or as "violent."[47] In a sample of active duty police officers, the ages of Black children were significantly overestimated in felony scenarios more so than in misdemeanor cases. However, there were no estimated age differences in Latino and White children. Furthermore, Blacks were rated as significantly more culpable in the context of felonies compared to Whites connected to a felony. More troubling was the finding that police officers' history of the use of force against Black children compared to children of other races was associated with implicitly associating Blacks with apes.[48] This research suggests that the dehumanization of Blacks along with a decreased window of childhood innocence affect how police perceive and engage with Black youth, which might be exacerbated post-Ferguson, post-Chicago and post-Baltimore.

Implicit biases and stereotypes can reasonably be expected to increase as police officers and other officials interact with citizens in a context of heightened tension. Implicit biases are attitudes and stereotypes that operate outside of the awareness and control of the individual.[49] Empirical research suggests that implicit biases can result in behavior that is counter to a person's explicitly stated attitudes and beliefs toward others. In-group bias, the more frequent response, results in favoritism toward the groups with which one affiliates. Those perceived and treated as outsiders may note this differential treatment. Out-group bias results in direct negative reactions and responses to those who are perceived as different.[50] Empirical research suggests that where race is concerned, implicit biases increase perceptions of fear of African Americans among White Americans.[51] In addition, perceived protester defiance, taunting, and generally tense negative reactions may have the effect of confirming negative stereotypes and biases, regardless of officers' awareness or stated attitudes. Thus, in ambiguous situations these stereotypes and biases are more likely to affect responses than they might have prior to the events of Ferguson, Baltimore, and Chicago and may have a profound impact on interactions between police and the communities they serve in the near future.

Given the number of long hours and prolonged exposure to protest situations, another possible outcome for police officers is burnout. This feeling of exhaustion, withdrawal, or a negative attitude toward one's organization or client can occur as a result of prolonged stress. Research with Dutch and Canadian officers found that higher burnout scores were correlated with more physical and verbal force.[52] In a study of Swiss officers, those who were more cynical and emotionally exhausted also applied greater use of force.[53] These potential outcomes might be visible before an officer or police department is even aware that an officer is suffering from burnout. Unfortunately, the resort to or tendency to invoke greater use of force may precede other indications that an officer is suffering from burnout.

Not Just African Americans

The psychosocial costs of racism for Whites frequently go unacknowledged in the aftermath of events of civil unrest, such as that observed in Ferguson, Baltimore, and Chicago. Understandably, a great deal of attention should be paid to targets of systemic oppression; yet, agents play an important role that should also be examined. Research on the psychosocial costs of racism suggests that Whites potentially experience distress as a result of being in the dominant racial group.[54] Costs can include White guilt (i.e., feeling shameful about being White), White fear (i.e., distrusting people of different races), and White empathy (i.e., feeling angry or sad that racism exists). The events of Ferguson potentially served as a catalyst for an outpouring of White empathy. For some individuals, there was potentially an increase in White guilt, an awakening to the intensity of the inequities or a deepening of knowledge that was already present. Yet for others, a fear or distrust of African Americans likely emerged fueling White fear.

Previous research found that Whites' perceptions of racism in Katrina-related events predicted negative mental health symptoms, and that this relationship was mediated by White guilt.[55] These results highlight the potential need to support White residents of Ferguson and the wider region, as well as those living in and around Baltimore and Chicago, in acknowledging feelings of guilt and developing adaptive ways to focus energy and process affect as to avoid negative mental health outcomes. It is less clear the role other psychosocial costs of racism play in these types of community events; however, limited research suggests that White Americans are not immune to negative mental health outcomes in the context of such events.

Other Community Concerns

Regardless of the vantage point, Mike Brown's death and the subsequent activism has challenged our nation's attempt to be color-blind or "postracial." Being color-blind refers to the minimization of race, yet taking this perspective actually perpetuates racism.[56] Research suggests that greater adherence to the color-blind rhetoric is significantly related to greater levels of implicit and explicit bias.[57] In the wake of #Ferguson, #BlackLivesMatter, and President Obama's Taskforce on 21st Century Policing, there might be distress experienced by individuals who have bought into the myth of color blindness and who are attempting to make sense of recent events, the related history, and their own implicit biases.

Psychology has identified interventions that can help reduce implicit and in-group bias. In addition, there is a body of literature that can inform the development of cultural competencies. Such training should be offered within the community and be mandated for all government employees and encouraged for individuals in law enforcement, the legal field, education, healthcare, and helping professions. Despite the reality that we all have biases, these individuals should be held to a higher standard given their prominence in society and roles as policy makers or criminal justice practitioners who affect the lives of people from various demographics, backgrounds, and experiences.[58]

Finally, there must be concern for anticipatory community anxiety moving forward. As the Ferguson Commission[59] completes its work, it is clear that the issues that produced the response to the Michael Brown shooting have not been resolved. The commission cannot solve these issues but can be a mechanism for making recommendations and highlighting necessary steps the region must take to address the issues. Ongoing protests, some directed at key elected officials, are a reminder that tensions have not fully deescalated. In advance of the second Rodney King verdict, a small group of participants were asked to participate in a prospective study that assessed affective and behavioral responses.[60] Those who reported negative experiences with the 1992 Los Angeles riots reported experiencing more negative affect, avoided social contact except with known and familiar individuals, and were more likely to report expecting to travel at the time of the verdict announcement compared to those who did not have this prior experience.[61] Data suggested that contact with family and close friends and planning to be at home were associated with reductions in negative affect in response to the second verdict.[62] The avoidance of social contact in anticipation of civil unrest is a complicating factor in situations where there is a need for community dialogue focused on finding common ground. This finding[63] and more recent findings[64] suggest that those in and near the original protests are at risk for ongoing stress and mental health concerns until the issues that sparked unrest are resolved and a sense of community is restored.

Summary

Even as policy and regional change occurs, there will continue to be emotionally injured people who need counseling, therapy, and resources to heal. Data from other community level traumas suggest that rates of PTSD, while high among those directly affected, show a rapid rate of decline. However, there are still reasons for concern. Data also show that those not directly affected demonstrate psychological consequences and mental health needs. In addition, September 11 data suggest that symptoms may persist after criteria for PTSD are no longer met.[65] However, use of these data is limited in that the activism post-Ferguson has continued in a way that is unrepresented in these studies on community trauma. As previously mentioned, the term "post" is inaccurate given that Black men continue to be killed by police and protests keep the spirit of the #BlackLivesMatter movement relevant.

Research suggests that the psychological impact of Ferguson should remain a necessary focal point for at least the next decade. Mental health professionals and anyone concerned about the well-being of the region should consider the multitude of ways individuals might have been impacted and validate those who express distress regardless of their proximity to the events. In addition to attending to individual concerns, leaders of regional institutions must not be anachronistic in understanding reactions and charting subsequent actions post-Ferguson.

Notes

1. There have been several brief accounts of the social and racial history of Ferguson, Missouri, and surrounding suburbs. *See* Tanzina Vega & John Eligon, *Deep Tensions Rise to Surface after Ferguson Shooting*, N.Y. TIMES, Aug. 16, 2014, http://www.nytimes.com/2014/08/17/us/ferguson-mo-complex -racial-history-runs-deep-most-tensions-have-to-do-police-force.html; Peter Coy, *Injustice in Ferguson, Long before Michael Brown*, BLOOMBERG BUS., Aug. 21, 2014, http://www.bloomberg.com/bw/articles /2014-08-21/ferguson-economic-political-conditions-fuel-protest-fury; Tierney Sneed, *Ferguson's Problems Are Not Ferguson's Alone*, U.S. News & World Rep., Aug. 22, 2014, http://www.usnews.com/news /articles/2014/08/22/fergusons-racial-problems-are-not-unique-to-ferguson. Colin Gordon provides a detailed history and description of the federal, state, and local policies and politics forged the development of the 90 municipalities in the region, as well as how this history relates to tensions and distress observed in other urban communities across the United States. COLIN GORDON, MAPPING DECLINE: ST. LOUIS AND THE FATE OF THE AMERICAN CITY (U. Penn. Press 2008).

2. The civil unrest in Baltimore has been attributed to police brutality, as observed in the death of Freddie Gray, and high unemployment and poverty, which are markers of persistent inequality, observed in many cities across the United States. Dan Diamond, *Why Baltimore Burned*, FORBES, Apr. 28, 2015, http://www.forbes.com/sites/dandiamond/2015/04/28/why-baltimore-burned/.

3. D. R. Williams & Selina A. Mohammed, *Discrimination and Racial Disparities in Health: Evidence and Needed Research*, 32.1 J. BEHAVIORAL MED. 20–47 (2009).

4. V. L. Thompson Sanders, *Perceived Experiences of Racism as Stressful Life Events*, 32 CMTY. MENTAL HEALTH J. 223–33 (1996); V. L. Thompson Sanders, *Racism: Perceptions of Distress among African Americans*, 38 CMTY. MENTAL HEALTH J. 111–18 (2002); V. L. Thompson Sanders, *Coping Responses and the Experience of Discrimination*, 36(5) J. APPLIED SOC. PSYCHOLOGY 1198–1214 (2006); Robert T. Carter, *Racism and Psychological and Emotional Injury Recognizing and Assessing Race-Based Traumatic Stress*, 35.1 COUNSELING PSYCHOLOGIST 13–105 (2007); K. H. Banks & L. Kohn-Wood, *The Influence of Racial Identity Profiles on the Relationship between Racial Discrimination and Depressive Symptoms*, 33(3) J. BLACK PSYCHOLOGY 331–54 (2007); K. H. Banks, L. P. Kohn-Wood & M. S. Spencer, *An Examination of the African American Experience of Everyday Discrimination and Psychological Distress*, 42 CMTY. MENTAL HEALTH J. 555–70 (2006); Thema Bryant-Davis, *Healing Requires Recognition: The Case for Race-Based Traumatic Stress*, 35.1 COUNSELING PSYCHOLOGIST 135–43 (2007).

5. Carter, *supra* note 4; Bryant-Davis, *supra* note 4.

6. *Id.*

7. Gordon, *supra* note 1.

8. RICHARD ROTHSTEIN, THE MAKING OF FERGUSON: PUBLIC POLICIES AT THE ROOT OF ITS TROUBLES (Econ. Pol'y Inst. Report, Oct. 15, 2014), http://community-wealth.org/sites/clone.community-wealth.org/files/downloads /paper-rothstein.pdf; Vega & Eligon, *supra* note 1.

9. Carter, *supra* note 4.

10. U.S. DEP'T OF JUSTICE, INVESTIGATION OF THE FERGUSON POLICE DEPARTMENT (Mar. 4, 2015).

11. Sandro Galea et al., *Trends of Probable Post-Traumatic Stress Disorder in New York City after the September 11 Terrorist Attacks*, 158(6) AM. J. EPIDEMIOLOGY 514–24 (2003); Yuval Nerla, Arijit Nandi & Sandro Galea, *Post-Traumatic Stress Disorder Following Disasters: A Systematic Review*, 38.04 PSYCHOLOGICAL MED. 467–80 (2008); William E. Schlenger et al., *Psychological Reactions to Terrorist Attacks: Findings*

from the National Study of Americans' Reactions to September 11, 288.5 JAMA 581–88 (2002); Roxane Cohen Silver et al., *Coping with a National Trauma: A Nationwide Longitudinal Study of Responses to the Terrorist Attacks of September 11th*, in 9/11: MENTAL HEALTH IN THE WAKE OF TERRORIST ATTACKS 45–70 (Y. Neria et al. eds., 2006).

12. Neria, Nandi & Galea, *supra* note 11.

13. *Id.*; Schlenger et al., *supra* note 11.

14. Schlenger et al., *supra* note 11.

15. *Id.*

16. Kimberly Caramanica et al., *Comorbidity of 9/11-Related PTSD and Depression in the World Trade Center Health Registry 10–11 Years Postdisaster*, 27.6 J. TRAUMATIC STRESS 680–88 (2014), doi: 10.1002/jts.21972.

17. ROTHSTEIN, *supra* note 8; Vega & Eligon, *supra* note 1.

18. Silver et al., *supra* note 11.

19. *Id.*

20. ROTHSTEIN, *supra* note 8; Vega & Eligon, *supra* note 1.

21. Amy L. Ai et al., *Racial Identity–Related Differential Attributions of Inadequate Responses to Hurricane Katrina: A Social Identity Perspective*, RACE SOC. PROBLEMS 3, 13–24 (2011), doi: 10.1007/s12552-011-9039-1.

22. Neria, Nandi & Galea, *supra* note 11.

23. Galea et al., *supra* note 11.

24. Neria, Nandi & Galea, *supra* note 11.

25. AM. PSYCHIATRIC ASS'N, DIAGNOSTIC AND STATISTICAL MANUAL OF MENTAL DISORDERS (5th ed. 2013) [hereinafter DSM-5].

26. *Id.*

27. *Id.* The description here focuses on adult and adolescent diagnostic criteria. A more detailed description that includes symptoms particular to children and the specific diagnostic criteria for children six years of age and younger is available. PTSD response may be delayed.

28. DSM-5, *supra* note 25.

29. *Id.*

30. Jessica Hamblen & Carole Goguen, *Community Violence*, U.S. DEP'T OF VETERANS AFFAIRS, http://www.ptsd.va.gov/professional/trauma/other/community-violence.asp (last visited Dec. 21, 2014).

31. DSM-5, *supra* note 25.

32. Tom R. Tyler, *Enhancing Police Legitimacy*, 593.1 ANNALS AM. ACAD. POL. & SOC. SCI. 84–99 (2004).

33. *See* sources cited *supra* note 4.

34. *See* Carter, *supra* note 4; Bryant-Davis, *supra* note 4.

35. Robert T. Carter et al., *Racism and Psychological and Emotional Injury Recognizing and Assessing Race-Based Traumatic Stress*, PSYCHOLOGICAL TRAUMA: THEORY, RES., PRAC. & POL'Y 5, 1–9 (2013).

36. Jo Ann M. Farver & Dominick L. Frosch, *LA Stories: Aggression in Preschoolers' Spontaneous Narratives after the Riots of 1992*, 67.1 CHILD DEV. 19–32 (1996).

37. M. L. Stuber, K. O. Nader & R. S. Pynoos, *The Violence of Despair: Consultation to a Head Start Program Following the Los Angeles Uprising of 1992*, 33(3) CMTY. MENTAL HEALTH J. 235–41 (1997), doi:http://dx.doi.org/10.1023/A:1025089511722.

38. Schlenger et al., *supra* note 11; Silver et al., *supra* note 11.

39. Nat'l Child Traumatic Stress Network, Symptoms and Behaviors Associated with Exposure to Trauma, http://www.nctsn.org/trauma-types/early-childhood-trauma/Symptoms-and-Behaviors-Associated-with-Exposure-to-Trauma (last visited Aug. 2014).

40. William E. Copeland et al., *Traumatic Events and Posttraumatic Stress in Childhood*, 64.5 ARCH. GEN. PSYCHIATRY 577–84 (2007).

41. Roxane Cohen Silver et al., *Mental- and Physical-Health Effects of Acute Exposure to Media Images of the September 11, 2001, Attacks and the Iraq War*, 24 PSYCHOLOGICAL SCI. 1623–34 (Sept. 2013).

42. Kathryn A. Becker-Blease, David Finkelhor & Heather Turner, *Media Exposure Predicts Children's Reactions to Crime and Terrorism*, 9(2) J. TRAUMA & DISSOCIATION 225–48 (2008).

43. Cait McMahon, *Covering Disaster: A Pilot Study into Secondary Trauma for Print Media Journalists Reporting on Disaster*, Australian J. Emergency Mgmt. 16, 52–56 (2001).

44. *Id.*

45. T. Harvey-Lintz, *Psychological Effects of the 1992 Los Angeles Riots: Post Traumatic Stress Symptomatology among Law Enforcement Officers* (1994) (Ph.D. dissertation, University of California, Los Angeles).

46. *Id.*

47. Phillip Atiba Goff et al., *The Essence of Innocence: Consequences of Dehumanizing Black Children*, 106(4) J. Personality & Soc. Psychology 526–45 (2014), doi: 10.1037/a0035663.

48. *Id.*

49. Anthony G. Greenwald & Linda Hamilton Krieger, *Implicit Bias: Scientific Foundations*, Cal. L. Rev. 945–67 (2006).

50. *Id.*

51. Edward Donnerstein et al., *Variables in Interracial Aggression: Anonymity, Expected Retaliation, and a Riot*, 22(2) J. Personality & Soc. Psychology 236–45 (May 1972), http://dx.doi.org/10.1037/h0032597.

52. Martin C. Euwema, Nicole N. Kop & Arnold B. Bakker, *The Behavior of Police Officers in Conflict Situations: How Burnout and Reduced Dominance Contribute to Better Outcome*, 18(1) Work & Stress 23–28 (2005); G. Stearns & R. Moore, *Physical and Psychological Correlates of Job Burnout in the Royal Canadian Mounted Police*, 35(2) Canadian J. Criminology 127 (1993).

53. P. Manzoni & M. Eisner, *Violence between the Police and the Public; Influences of Work-Related Stress, Job Satisfaction, Burnout, and Situational Factors*, 33(5) Crim. Justice & Behavior 613–45 (2006).

54. L. B. Spanierman & M. J. Heppner, *Psychosocial Costs of Racism to Whites Scale (PCRW): Construction and Initial Validation*, 51 J. Counseling Psychology 249–62 (2004).

55. Alison Blodorn & Laurie T. O'Brien, *Perceptions of Racism in Hurricane Katrina-Related Events: Implications for Collective Guilt and Mental Health among White Americans*, 11(1) Analyses Soc. Issues & Pub. Pol'y 127–140 (Dec. 2011), doi: 10.1111/j.1530-2415.2011.01237.x.

56. E. Bonilla-Silva, Racism without Racists: Color-Blind Racism and the Persistence of Racial Inequality in the United States (Rowman & Littlefield 2003); V. C. Plaut, *Diversity Science: Why and How Difference Makes a Difference*, 21 Psychological Inquiry 77–99 (2010).

57. J. A. Richeson & R. J. Nussbaum, *The Impact of Multiculturalism versus Color-Blindness on Racial Bias*, 40 J. Experimental Soc. Psychology 417–23 (2004).

58. N. Ghandnoosh, Sentencing Project, Race and Punishment: Racial Perceptions of Crime and Support for Punitive Policies (2014), http://sentencingproject.org/doc/publications/rd_Race_and_Punishment.pdf.

59. The Ferguson Commission was appointed by Governor Jeremiah Nixon to study "the underlying social and economic conditions underscored by the unrest in the wake of the death of Michael Brown." The Ferguson Commission is charged with helping state and local leaders to develop a path to positive change. *See* Stephen Deere, *Ferguson Commission Picks a Managing Director and Receives a $150,000 Donation*, St. Louis Post-Dispatch, Dec. 23, 2014, http://www.stltoday.com/news/local/ferguson-commission-picks-a-managing-director-and-receives-a-donation/article_ba858ff4-dbdc-595f-a4d0-05ed83d8a9c4.html.

60. Joel David Swendsen & Sloan Norman, *Preparing for Community Violence: Mood and Behavioral Correlates of the Second Rodney King Verdicts*, 11(1) J. Traumatic Stress 57–70 (1998).

61. *Id.*

62. *Id.*

63. *Id.*

64. D. R. Garfin, E. A. Holman & R. C. Silver, *Cumulative Exposure to Prior Collective Trauma and Acute Stress Responses to the Boston Marathon Bombings*, Psychological Sci. (2015), doi:10.1177/0956797614561043.

65. Galea et al., *supra* note 11.

Chapter 11

Ferguson and the First Amendment

Chad Flanders

Introduction: Wilson-Brown as Metaphor

The release on the same day of the Department of Justice (DOJ) report declining to prosecute Darren Wilson and the DOJ report excoriating the Ferguson Police Department may have obscured the connection between the two documents.[1] One seemed, in rather stark terms, to condemn the whole Ferguson Police Department root and branch, while the other seemed to exonerate completely the actions of one Ferguson police officer, namely Darren Wilson. But if we take a broader view, the contradiction dissipates. While we may never know what exactly happened between Wilson and Brown, the DOJ report on Ferguson's police department showed that people's fears about how Brown's death happened —the "hands up, don't shoot" narrative, in part[2]—were in many ways predictable and even justified given the past relationship between the police and the City of Ferguson. What people worried might have happened between Wilson and Brown was going on already and repeatedly in comparatively smaller but still disturbing ways. Relations between people of Ferguson and the police were strained (to put it mildly) and rights were being consistently and routinely violated not as a matter of some "bad apples," but as a matter of departmental policy. Wilson acted against the background of a style of policing that probably made his resort to deadly force more likely, because tension between the police and

I am enormously grateful to the efforts of Joe Welling and Michael Hill, students at Saint Louis University School of Law, who offered numerous substantive and editorial suggestions and saved me from numerous mistakes. John Inazu, Christopher Bradley, Will Baude, and Kim Norwood offered extremely helpful comments on an earlier draft.

citizens in Ferguson was already at a breaking point.[3] In other words, we could read off of the Wilson-Brown encounter—and the reaction to it—a larger story about what was happening between the police and the community in Ferguson.

In this essay, I advance a related thesis: that in the police response to the protests after Michael Brown was shot, we could see played out on a wider scale a similar dynamic to that which was present, or at least thought to be present, in the encounter between Wilson and Brown.

In particular, I show that, just like Brown, protesters were told that they were walking in the wrong place and had to move, and that force was used against them as well—and also without warning.[4] I argue that the police response to the protesters, just like Wilson's response to Brown, reflected an attitude that saw the police-community relationship as one to be controlled by escalating the use of force rather than one to be managed by negotiating with the community. And I conclude by considering one of the more recent First Amendment lawsuits to emerge from Ferguson, based on a grand juror's claim that he should be able to speak about his experience on the Wilson grand jury without fear of punishment.[5] My overall thesis is that everything people *thought* went wrong between Brown and Wilson *did* go wrong in the police response to the protesters.

There are limits to the analogy between Michael Brown and the protesters. To take one difference, the protesters were shot at with rubber bullets, not real ones—and no protesters were killed, although some were injured.[6] But the response to the protesters' ability to speak did put at risk that thing which is the "lifeblood"[7] of a well-functioning democracy: speech and the promise that deliberation and discussion will rule rather than arbitrary force.[8] In what became an endlessly playing loop, the aggressive police response to protesters decrying injustice became an instance of the very injustice that the protesters were decrying. A clash between two people in turn became a clash between the police and the people of Ferguson, and what suffered, what kept being put back on its heels, were the First Amendment rights of the people.

I use the following capsule summary of the Brown-Wilson encounter as the outline for the rest of the chapter, to highlight the analogies between the story of Brown and the story of the protesters:

1) A man was told by a police officer to get out of the street, and to walk somewhere else.

2) When the man turned toward the police officer, there was a struggle, and the officer in response used a large amount of force against the man.

3) There was no reliable video of the event, and the police were selective in what they shared with the media.

4) In the days that followed, perceptions differed as to what happened: whether the man was mostly blameless or mostly to blame, and whether the force was excessive or proportional.

5) The deliberations of the grand jury were kept secret, but the prosecutor in a news conference and in subsequent public events got to tell his side of the story.[9]

6) A DOJ report released in March showed that aggressive policing tactics were long a part of Ferguson's history, and demands were made for reform.[10]

1. A Man Was Told by a Police Officer to Get Out of the Street, and to Walk Somewhere Else

The shooting of Michael Brown started with Darren Wilson yelling at Brown to get out of the street.[11] In the protests that followed Brown's death, there were also commands directed at protesters who were on sidewalks or streets that they needed to keep moving, to get out of the way, because they were not where they were supposed to be.[12] Particularly controversial was the so-called "five-second rule," where protesters could not be in the same place for more than five seconds.[13] They had to be constantly moving (difficult if you are a protester who is disabled or who has trouble walking), or risk getting arrested.[14] Simply standing still on a public street or sidewalk became a crime.[15]

Where exactly the policy to keep moving originated, or what it meant, never became entirely clear. Could protesters walk around in a circle? What if a protester had to tie his or her shoe? Attend to a crying baby in a stroller? Stand in line to use the bathroom? When did the five seconds begin to run in the officer's mind vis-à-vis the protester's mind? Was there any place they could stop and protest, or was the five-second rule applicable everywhere in Ferguson? Were there certain times when the policy was not in effect? How fast did they have to "keep moving"? Did it apply to small groups as well as large crowds?

Would protesters really be arrested if they didn't move? Officers did not know the answers to these questions, and it showed: sometimes the rule was enforced, sometimes it wasn't, and when it was enforced, it seemed to be enforced differently every time.[16]

The questions about the exact policy were important, not only as a matter of practicality, but as a matter of compliance with the First Amendment. Two foundational constitutional doctrines were at issue: the public-forum doctrine, and the requirement that laws not be vague—especially when it comes to laws concerning speech. The public-forum doctrine holds that the streets and the sidewalks belong to the people. They are the places, as the Supreme Court recently reaffirmed in *McCullen v. Coakley*, where people gather to meet, to express themselves, and to make their voices known, and so laws and policies that restrict access to and behavior in public forums are subject to careful scrutiny by courts.[17]

Relatedly, laws and policies that regulate people's ability to speak must be clearly laid out, for two reasons. First, policies have to be clear so that *people* know how to obey them, and second, policies have to be clear so that the *police* know how to enforce them. So if a command is hard to follow, that leads to these two obvious problems. People will be confused about what they are supposed to do, and police may have more discretion in applying the law, which they may abuse intentionally or unintentionally.[18]

Mustafa Abdullah wasn't strictly speaking a protester, but he was involved with the protests. He worked for the ACLU, and when he heard that police were telling protesters they couldn't stand still—even in the daytime, even when there was no violence[19]—he got involved. He filed suit against St. Louis County and the Missouri State Highway Patrol seeking an injunction prohibiting the further use of the policy.[20] He initially was denied a temporary restraining order (TRO) because a lawyer for the defendants informed the judge that an alternate "protest area" was being set up where people could meet and not be subject to the five-second rule.[21] What the judge didn't know at the time was that the protest area probably didn't exist in any meaningful form,[22] at least not until well after the TRO was denied.[23]

In the second round, however, Abdullah won. After a day-long hearing that included multiple witnesses, the court issued a preliminary injunction. The court found the policy confusing and nearly random, and held it was unconstitutionally vague.[24] What the policy was, Judge Perry concluded, was left up to the moment-to-moment decisions of the officers, and that was no good: protesters couldn't tell what they would have to do to avoid falling afoul of the policy.[25] The policy had neither definiteness nor clarity.

In addition, the judge held that the policy likely violated the First Amendment.[26] The streets are open to the people, and while this does not mean that the government can never regulate how and when people use the streets, it does mean that those restrictions have to be reasonable. The keep-moving rule was not reasonable. Under the policy, people couldn't stand on the sidewalks to protest without risking being arrested. And because suppressing speech, even for a small amount of time, is still a very real harm, the policy had to be stopped.[27] In response to the preliminary injunction, the city entered into a consent judgment that enjoined application of the policy.[28]

2. When the Man Turned toward the Police Officer, There Was a Struggle, and the Officer in Response Used a Large Amount of Force against the Man

After Darren Wilson told Michael Brown to get out of the street—to keep moving—things didn't proceed peacefully. Instead, there was (most accounts agree) a struggle and a confrontation between the two men.[29] Things quickly escalated, and ultimately Wilson shot multiple times at Brown, killing him. The question, in the Wilson case, turned from one about police keeping people out of the streets for jaywalking to one about the justifiability of using force against an unarmed person, force that was ultimately deadly. In the aftermath of Brown's death, with massive displays of force by the police against protesters— SWAT teams, armored vehicles, rifles, rubber bullets, tear gas, pepper spray—the question too turned from one about keeping people off the street to one about excessive force. Again, things escalated quickly, and the First Amendment rights of the protesters were in the balance.

The injunction against the five-second rule was granted, in part, because it involved the use of police power to threaten innocent and constitutionally protected activity: standing still and protesting. Police couldn't and shouldn't be able to tell people to keep moving when there is no real danger to their standing still. Even worse, the police justified the policy, at least initially, as necessary to avoid people "unlawfully assembling" to riot or commit other acts of violence.[30] But police were telling people to keep moving even when they had no evidence that the people assembling were doing it for any unlawful purpose. The police seemed to be anticipating violence that wasn't there.

There *was* eventually some violence mixed in with the protests in Ferguson.[31] And even the judge in the *Abdullah* case acknowledged that the police had a legitimate interest in maintaining order and protecting the public safety. She wrote, "Citizens who wish to gather in the wake of Michael Brown's tragic death have a constitutional right to do so, but they do not have the right to endanger lives of police officers or other citizens."[32] But there was also violence mixed in with the *policing* in Ferguson.[33] Things had not only escalated, they had broken down. Again, there were allegations of excessive force, just as there were in regard to the shooting of Brown, except this time it was on a larger scale: it was not a gun against a single person—it was armored vehicles and chemical agents used against a crowd. The images of a quasi-military takeover of Ferguson have now become as indelible as the image of Michael Brown's slain body on the street.

Tear gas was used against people in the protests immediately following Brown's death, and also after the announcement of the grand jury's decision in November. On December 10, protesters filed a lawsuit against the Unified Command,[34] claiming violations of the protesters' First Amendment rights.[35] The lawsuit alleged, in part, that officers acting under the Unified Command were using tear gas and pepper spray, and shooting protesters with "so-called 'less-than-lethal projectiles.'"[36] Regarding the use of tear gas, the protesters' point was simple: tear gas should not be used except as a last resort, and when it is used, there should be a clear warning given.[37] This was also an echo of the vagueness claim in the earlier lawsuit by Abdullah: if you are going to restrain protesters, at least make it clear what the rules are, and enforce them fairly. Anything less chills expression and clamps down on the right to protest in a public forum protected by the First Amendment.

Brittany Ferrell, Steven Hoffman, and Kira Hudson, all named plaintiffs in the lawsuit against the Unified Command, were near a coffeehouse that was remaining open past hours as a place of safety and rest for protesters.[38] In the lawsuit, they described what they saw in the late evening of November 24 and the early morning of November 25:

> Suddenly, Plaintiffs Ferrell, Banks and Hoffman observed police officers controlled by the Defendants speed north on Grand

towards Arsenal in a black armored personnel carrier vehicle which was fitted with a turret type attachment for the firing of tear gas. The vehicle rapidly approached without siren or other warning device. Without notice or warning, the vehicle began firing tear gas canisters at the unsuspecting Plaintiffs and others who were gathered in and around the area in front of MoKaBe's Coffeehouse and near the corner of Grand and Arsenal. Because there was no announcement or dispersal order prior to the administration of gas, Plaintiffs Ferrell and Banks were unable to put on adequate protective gear to escape the effects of the gas.[39]

The plaintiffs won a TRO against the police.[40] The judge agreed that the police had been authorized to use tear gas, but that they were using it against those who were not engaged in any violent activity and that they were using it without warning. In a striking passage, the judge wrote that the protesters' First Amendment rights of speech and assembly were being "encumbered" by a "law enforcement response that would be used if a crime were being committed."[41] That is, by their use of tear gas, the police were treating *all* protesters as presumptively criminal. If the police were going to use tear gas, the judge ordered, they would have to give a warning—a clear, unambiguous warning.[42] And they could not use tear gas merely to frighten, or punish, those who were exercising their constitutional rights.[43]

It was another victory for the First Amendment—the parties reached a settlement limiting police use of tear gas—but again, it came late. And this time, the victory was not against a haphazard policy that was stitched together on the fly, as the five-second rule possibly was.[44] Rather, this response came not only in the immediate aftermath of the Brown shooting, but also after the release of the grand jury's decision. It was the result of forethought and planning.

3. There Was No Reliable Video of the Event, and the Police Early on Were Selective in What They Shared with the Media

The public learned very little about the Brown shooting at first. The Ferguson Police Department was, to put it generously, reticent about the details of the shooting—perhaps suggesting that they had something to hide. They initially said that they would not identify the officer who had shot Brown, out of fears for his safety; a very long and tense seven days later they released the officer's name.[45] Rumors were floated and details leaked about what happened at the police vehicle and the extent of Darren Wilson's injury, some of which would turn out to be false.[46] No one captured video of the struggle or the shooting, although a phone happened to capture audio of the shots being fired.[47] The only video released by the Ferguson police was a grainy videorecording of Michael Brown earlier in the day, allegedly stealing from a liquor store.[48] This video was released simultaneously with the officer's name to the public and despite the chief of police's admission that Officer Wilson did not know of the confrontation between Brown and the store owner at the time he confronted Brown for jaywalking.[49] The whole affair seemed timed in such a way (many suggested) as to imply the police were trying to "spin" the narrative against Brown.[50]

The Supreme Court has held that the press as an entity has no uniquely special status relative to other speakers;[51] but as a matter of convention, the press has been thought to have the responsibility to report the news and to report it objectively.[52] This responsibility, in turn, gives it special privileges and special access to the news as it is happening. But as the story of Ferguson unfolded, reporters were routinely treated as poorly as the protesters. They were told to shut off cameras, to stop recording, and, as well, to keep moving.[53] Sometimes they were told these things by actions as well as by words. If the police were not going to shape the narrative positively, by sharing information, they would do their best to prevent a negative narrative about them from developing.

In a widely reported instance, both *Washington Post* reporter Wesley Lowery and *Huffington Post* reporter Ryan J. Reilly were harassed and, ultimately, detained by police.[54] According to Lowery, he was in the Ferguson McDonalds' recharging his phone when several police entered, and one asked him for identification. With Lowery refusing the request, the police began to turn away, but then came back and told him and Reilly to leave. Lowery started recording the police with his cell phone, and was immediately told to stop. Lowery resisted, asking if he didn't have the right to record the officers. The officer "backed off, but told [Lowery] to hurry up."[55] Lowery continued:

> So I gathered my notebook and pens with one hand while recording him with the other hand.

As I exited, I saw Ryan to my left, having a similar argument with two officers. I recorded him, too, and that angered the officer. As I made my way toward the door, the officers gave me conflicting information.

One instructed me to exit to my left. As I turned left, another officer emerged, blocking my path.

"Go another way," he said. As I turned, my backpack, which was slung over one shoulder, began to slip. I said, "Officers, let me just gather my bag."

As I did, one of them said, "Okay, let's take him."[56]

Lowery was put into plastic handcuffs and taken into custody, but not without having his face slammed into a soda machine first. Reilly, too, was arrested. They were both released within 15 minutes of arriving at the Ferguson Police Department after they were identified as credentialed members of the media. Reilly called the experience "dehumanizing."[57]

But the experiences of Lowery and Reilly weren't unique: reporters were asked to stay in the "press pen," were escorted away from protesters, and were sometimes arrested[58]—showing that the institutional press frequently worked under *greater* constrains than the general public. Early on, reporters had to sue to clarify that they were within their First Amendment rights to record the police and the police response to the protests. Mustafa Hussein, an activist and journalist, claimed in a suit against the Ferguson police that in the days after the death of Michael Brown, police officials "ordered everyone on the street to stop recording."[59] Upon hearing this, the lawsuit states, Hussein was "required to choose between surrendering his First Amendment right to record the action unfolding on the street before him or risking arrest or serious bodily injury inflicted by law enforcement officials if he continued recording"[60]—precisely the choice faced by Lowery and Reilly.

Hussein obtained an injunction against the police, preventing them from "interfering with individuals who are photographing or recording at public places but who are not threatening the safety of others or physically interfering with the ability of law enforcement to perform their duties."[61] In the DOJ report released in March of 2015, the policy of restricting recording of the police was picked out for special condemnation.[62] The right to record the police, the report stated, had been clearly established in the Eighth Circuit and nationwide.[63]

4. In the Days That Followed, Perceptions Differed as to What Happened: Whether the Man Was Mostly Blameless or Mostly to Blame, and Whether the Force Was Excessive or Proportional

In all of the three lawsuits just outlined, the police lost and the pro-testers and the media won. In each case, a federal judge enjoined the behavior of the police, holding that it represented a threat to the First Amendment rights of speech and assembly. What then explains the behavior of the police? We should note, first, that in each case the court didn't say that the interests of law enforcement were entitled to no weight. Indeed, in the longest opinion we have, Judge Perry went out of her way to explain the police's interest in maintaining order and pro-tecting the safety of the public. And in the orders enjoining the use of tear gas and the practice of preventing protesters from recording, the court said that the problem was not that these measures could *never* be used, but that they could not be used against people who do not rep-resent a threat to law enforcement. So there are values to be weighed against the First Amendment; the question is, when do those values trump the First Amendment? But the failure of the police in Ferguson points to a larger problem, because the policies and procedures the Unified Command used against the protesters weren't just instances of occasional mistakes. The need for injunctions revealed a pervasive fail-ure. It was not just that the police were at times misjudging the rights and interests of the protesters, whether on the spot or as a matter of policy. It was as if the First Amendment was never a consideration.

Sociologists and criminologists who study the relationship between protesters and the police speak broadly of two models: the "escalated force" model and the "negotiated management" model.[64] The two differ most strikingly in how they regard the First Amendment. In the escalated-force model, the First Amendment is treated at best as distraction and at worst a pretext for those who wish to disguise their criminal activ-ity. In the negotiated-management model, by contrast, protecting the First Amendment is treated as an important goal of successful policing. In the force model, the First Amendment rights of protesters and the police are treated as antagonistic. In the negotiation model, the inter-ests of the police and protesters are seen as converging.

The rhetoric surrounding the policing of Ferguson was heavily in the register of escalating force, and the practice of the Unified Command was practically textbook. Protesters were viewed as a hostile force that needed to be boxed in and contained. Each disruption, however minor, was used as a further excuse to swiftly ramp up the level of force. Little effort was made to communicate the aims and methods of the police to the protesters. Arrests were being made for activity that fell short of actual lawbreaking.

What is especially troublesome about the escalated-force model is that it can quickly become a self-fulfilling prophecy—and the events of Ferguson seem to bear this out. If you are primed to use force, you may use that force sooner rather than later. You may let the occasional instances of lawless activity stand in for the activity of the protesters in general. You will *see* things differently, and as a result *react* to them differently. Shows of force can antagonize the protesters, which lead to further shows of force—which in turn further antagonizes the protesters.[65]

In news conferences and other public speeches, Jon Belmar, the Chief of Police of St. Louis County presented the fact that no lives were lost as his main achievement—and as proof of the success of his tactics.[66] No one should deny that preventing the loss of lives is a worthy goal, but to present it as the *only* goal or the *primary* metric of success is symptomatic of the escalating-force model: to use whatever means are necessary to prevent the loss of life and destruction of property. The First Amendment is presented as a lower priority, if it stands as a value at all.

For a brief moment—the space of a few days—when Missouri State Highway Patrol Captain Ron Johnson took charge of the Unified Command, there were signs that a different model would be used.[67] Pictures of Johnson (who was from Ferguson) marching with the protesters raised hopes that the police would no longer fight the protesters, but help them.[68] These images suggested the use of the negotiated-management model—where police aren't there to stamp out protests but to facilitate their expression. If there is some minor lawbreaking, this can be tolerated, because the price of cracking down on lawbreaking can be too dear: the suppression of freedom of speech.[69] On the negotiated-management model, the police are there to moderate the inevitable disruption, not to make sure there is no disruption at all.[70]

But that moment of negotiated management faded quickly, and it was made clear that it was never really an option at all. As soon as things got a little out of hand, force was brought to bear again—swiftly and powerfully. Pictures of militarized vehicles and tear gas again dominated the media. Toleration for free speech meant toleration for disorder, and the First Amendment suffered.

Johnson's brief détente illustrates a limitation to the negotiated-management model. It cannot just be brought out at the time there is a crisis. Rather, the groundwork for negotiation must be laid much earlier, by a collaborative relationship between the police and the community they serve that fosters and preserves open lines of communication between them. [71] This prior, ongoing relationship is a necessary precondition for citizens' exercise of their rights. Both the tragedy of Michael Brown and the tragedy of the clash between protesters and the police have a deeper root in the many prior failures of governance that existed in Ferguson.

5. The Deliberations of the Grand Jury Were Kept Secret, But the Prosecutor in a News Conference and in Subsequent Public Events Got to Tell His Side of the Story

The grand jurors voted not to indict Wilson, and instead of this being the end of things, it was another beginning. Again protests erupted, and again force was used. Weirdly, though, the style of the police initially seemed to be hands-off, and property and businesses suffered badly. But soon enough, the police resorted to the same tactics that they had used for the first protests. If at first there was no force, it was clear soon enough that the police were more than willing to return to the use of force.

Meanwhile, Prosecutor Bob McCulloch held a news conference to explain why he thought the grand jury reached the conclusion it did, leading some to accuse McCulloch of acting more like Wilson's defense attorney than a prosecutor for the State.[72] McCulloch also stated that he would, shortly, release nearly all the evidence that was available to the grand jury as they made their deliberations.[73]

McCulloch and his supporters hailed what can only be called the "data dump" of grand jury witness testimony and evidence[74] as an instance of transparency—especially in comparison to the opacity of the Ferguson police in the aftermath of the shooting. But it was also clear that combing through all the documents would be a massive undertaking, one that would take weeks, if not months (if it was to be undertaken at all). Still, if the First Amendment values citizen knowledge and transparency about government decision-making, then the release of the transcripts from the grand jury must be rated as a plus for free speech. If there was not to be a trial with the openness and discovery that a trial requires, this may have been the next best thing.

But there was still something that McCulloch didn't and couldn't disclose: the actual deliberations of the grand jurors themselves. This became the basis of an additional First Amendment challenge. In the weeks following the release of the decision, one grand juror anonymously sued to be allowed to speak about her experiences on the grand jury.[75] Missouri law requires the jurors to swear an oath to secrecy, and prescribes certain penalties if they speak about what they learned as a grand juror.[76] If grand jurors could freely disclose what witnesses told them and what facts they learned as a grand juror, it might dissuade future witnesses from testifying in a grand jury. But, given McCulloch's disclosure of the grand jury records, there might not be a similar issue in this case. And the grand juror seemed to want to discuss not the reactions of the other grand jurors, but mainly his own feelings and impressions.[77] McCulloch was able to frame the narrative about what the grand jury found and did. One of those jurors wanted to provide her narrative.

The lawsuit tested an underlitigated area of the First Amendment. While the Supreme Court has held that *witnesses* can freely talk about what they told the grand jury,[78] case law is sparse about what grand jurors can tell about their own experiences. Moreover, the Ferguson grand juror's suit presents unique facts, where nearly all of the information supplied to the grand jury has already been disclosed, and the grand juror only wants to speak about her own subjective experience and thoughts and not release any facts about the actual deliberations of the grand jury—what other people said, or how they voted. The grand juror, in her lawsuit, claims her speech has been "chilled" because she cannot know for certain whether McCulloch will prosecute her for violating grand jury secrecy.[79]

The First Amendment implications of the battle are twofold, for not only is the speech of the grand juror at issue, so too is the right of concerned citizens for whom the information may help them make up their minds about why the grand jury decided as it did. The risk, as it was in the early days of information about Ferguson, is that a partial transparency—when we know only some information, and interested parties get to pick and choose which information we see—can sometimes be as distorting to debate as no transparency at all.

McCulloch moved to dismiss the lawsuit, arguing that while the federal court had equitable jurisdiction, it should abstain from exercising that jurisdiction when there was a possible state court remedy.[80] And a federal judge has granted McCulloch's order to dismiss, on the ground that the issue should be decided in state court, not in federal court.[81] As of this writing, this is where the lawsuit stands: in state court.[82]

6. A DOJ Report Released in March Showed That Aggressive Policing Tactics Were Long a Part of Ferguson's History, and Demands Were Made for Reform

"Officers expect and demand compliance even when they lack legal authority. They are inclined to interpret the exercise of free-speech rights as unlawful disobedience, innocent movements as physical threats . . . ."[83]

On March 4, 2015, the DOJ released two reports. The first concerned whether Darren Wilson violated Michael Brown's civil rights. The report found that Wilson's actions as an individual officer, acting within the scope of his job, "lack[ed] prosecutive merit."[84] The second DOJ report, describing a history of rights abuses in Ferguson, was a damning judgment of the Ferguson Police Department, of which Wilson was a member.[85] It is hard not to read the reports together, not as rendering a conflicting judgment, but as making an overall negative one: even if in this one instance Wilson might have behaved within the limits of the law, this was something of an exception and not the rule. By aggressive and revenue-oriented policing, the Ferguson Police Department had sown deep mistrust between law enforcement and the community.[86]

What the report on the Ferguson Police Department revealed in particular was that the practices used to enforce discipline and stifle dissent were not unique to the Brown protests; rather, they were set plays in the department's playbook. Long before the protests, Ferguson police were arresting people for their "manner of walking," for criticizing the police (so-called "contempt of cop"), and for record-ing officers.[87] They would do these things all in the absence of any evidence that arrests were necessary because of safety concerns.[88] Moreover, police behavior in these situations served only to heighten tensions.[89] Arrests of people simply exercising their rights, the report said, reflected the fact that the Ferguson police had no tools or training "for de-escalating emotionally charged scenes, even though the ability of a police officer to bring calm to a situation is a core policing skill."[90]

In the end, though, the report did not tell us anything we could not have already seen about the Ferguson police in how they responded to the protests after the shooting of Michael Brown: they were just responding to dissent and disruption as they always had—although this time, perhaps more systematically and on a larger scale, and in front of a larger audience. The City of Ferguson, and the voices of those in solidarity with the city, suffered.

Conclusion: History Keeps on Repeating Itself

It is a sad irony that the response to the protests may have made those protests that much more effective in getting their message across, and that much more persuasive. By displaying an aggressive pose, the police proved that what many feared had happened between Brown and Wilson in Ferguson surely could have happened, because something like it was happening to the protesters in Ferguson. And in the days and months that followed, more instances of police killings around the nation came to light, which were then followed by more protests. We now seem to be stuck in a recurring loop of action and reaction nationwide—police action and then reaction by protesters, followed by more police action, followed by more protests.[91]

We may, at times, despair whether anything is changing—and whether it *can* change. We may wonder whether the protests are doing any good and whether it is worth the cost. But if this is our attitude, we might look at one of the most necessary aspects of freedom of speech. It is not captured in some of the more popular metaphors justifying free speech—speech as a "safety valve" or speech playing a role in the "marketplace of ideas."[92] It is captured in something more fundamen-tal: the necessity of speaking truth to power. It is here that protest justifies itself as an end in itself.

Notes

1. U.S. DEP'T OF JUSTICE, DEPARTMENT OF JUSTICE REPORT REGARDING THE CRIMINAL INVESTIGATION INTO THE SHOOT-ING DEATH OF MICHAEL BROWN BY FERGUSON, MISSOURI POLICE OFFICER DARREN WISON (Mar. 4, 2015) [hereinafter DOJ REPORT], http://www.justice.gov/sites/default/files/opa/press-releases/attachments /2015/03/04/doj_report_on_shooting_of_michael_brown_1.pdf; U.S. DEP'T OF JUSTICE, INVESTIGATION OF THE FERGUSON POLICE DEPARTMENT (Mar. 4, 2015) [hereinater DOJ INVESTIGATION], http://www.justice.gov/sites /default/files/opa/press-releases/attachments/2015/03/04/ferguson_police_department_report_1.pdf.

2. *See, e.g.,* Eric Zorn, *"Hands up, Don't Shoot" Is a Lie Obscuring a Bigger Truth,* CHI. TRIB., Mar. 19, 2015, http://www.chicagotribune.com/news/opinion/zorn/ct-ferguson-brown-wilson-hands-up-shoot-holder -usdoj-perspec-0320-jm-20150319-column.html ("Wilson's exoneration is not tantamount to an exon-eration of American law enforcement in how it interacts with minority communities.").

3 *See* Christine Byers, *After Ferguson, Police Consider "Tactical Retreat" Instead of Force in Cer-tain Cases,* ST. LOUIS POST-DISPATCH, Jan. 24, 2015, http://www.stltoday.com/news/local/crime-and-courts /after-ferguson-police-consider-tactical-retreat-instead-of-force-in/article_7fa34fed-9770-5860-ad10 -4358b4523b76.html (suggesting that better training may have led to a "tactical retreat" by Wilson rather than to further confrontation).

4. Petition at 1–2, 4–7, Abdullah v. Cnty. of St. Louis, Mo., 52 F. Supp. 3d 936, 939 (E.D. Mo. 2014) (No. 4:14-cv-1436), http://www.aclu-mo.org/download_file/view_inline/1268/535/; Petition at 2–4, 7–13, Templeton v. Dotson, No. 4:14-cv-1436 (CEJ) (E.D. Mo. Dec. 8, 2014), http://www.documentcloud.org /documents/1378607-templeton-vs-dotson.html.

5. Petition at 1–2, Doe v. McCulloch, 4:15 CV 6 RWS, 2015 WL 2092492 (E.D. Mo. 2015) (Jan. 5, 2015), http://www.aclu-mo.org/files/4214/2047/0504/Grand_Jurur_Doe_Complaint_1-5-15.pdf.

6. There were, however, allegations that police did point their guns at protesters. Josh Levs, *Ferguson Violence: Critics Rip Police Tactics, Use of Military Weapons,* CNN (Aug. 15, 2015, 10:47 AM), http://www.cnn.com/2014/08/14/us/missouri-ferguson-police-tactics/.

7. Miss. Women's Med. Clinic v. McMillan, 866 F.2d 788, 796 (5th Cir. 1989) ("[I]n regulating free-dom of speech in a public forum, the Supreme Court has been reluctant to construe such regulations in such a way as to drain the life-blood of a democracy—'uninhibited, robust, and wide-open debate' on controversial public issues.").

8. Whitney v. California, 274 U.S. 357, 375 (1927) ("Those who won our independence believed that the final end of the state was to make men free to develop their faculties, and that in its govern-ment the deliberative forces should prevail over the arbitrary.").

9. *See, e.g.,* Mark Berman, *What Do We Really Know about the Shooting of Michael Brown, and of Brown Himself?,* WASH. POST, Aug. 12, 2014 at A12, http://www.washingtonpost.com/news/post-nation /wp/2014/08/11/what-you-need-to-know-about-the-death-of-an-unarmed-black-teenager-in-missouri; *Tracking the Events in the Wake of Michael Brown's Shooting,* N.Y. TIMES (Nov. 24, 2014), http://www .nytimes.com/interactive/2014/11/09/us/10ferguson-michael-brown-shooting-grand-jury-darren-wilson .html?_r=0.

10. DOJ REPORT, *supra* note 1; DOJ INVESTIGATION, *supra* note 1.

11. DOJ REPORT, *supra* note 1 at 12, 44.

12. *E.g.,* Petition, *Abdullah, supra* note 4, at 3–4.

13. *Id.* at 1–2.

14. *Id.*

15. See more generally the use of "manner of walking" violations by police in Ferguson. DOJ INVES-TIGATION, *supra* note 1, at 27–28.

16. *Abdullah,* 52 F. Supp. 3d at 942:

> The evidence from plaintiff's witnesses shows that the police, including those from St. Louis County, told many people who were either peacefully assembling or simply stand-ing on their own that they would be arrested if they did not keep moving. Some law enforcement officers told people that they could stand still for no more than five sec-onds. Others gave instructions that people were walking too slowly, or that they could

not walk back and forth in a small area. Some law enforcement officers did not make people keep moving, others did. Some officers applied the strategy to reporters, others did not. Many officers told people who were standing in small groups on the sidewalks during the daytime hours that they would be arrested if they did not keep moving.

17. McCullen v. Coakley, 134 S. Ct. 2518, 2529 (2014) ("These places—which we have labeled 'traditional public fora'—have immemorially been held in trust for the use of the public and, time out of mind, have been used for purposes of assembly, communicating thoughts between citizens, and discussing public questions." (internal quotes and citations removed)). Ironically, perhaps, the protesters chanting, "Whose streets? Our streets!" gave a more accurate view of the law than the officials who devised and tried to enforce the five-second rule. (Thanks to Joe Welling for this point.)

18. F.C.C. v. Fox Television Stations, Inc., 132 S. Ct. 2307, 2317 (2012):

> Even when speech is not at issue, the void for vagueness doctrine addresses at least two connected but discrete due process concerns: first, that regulated parties should know what is required of them so they may act accordingly; second, precision and guidance are necessary so that those enforcing the law do not act in an arbitrary or discriminatory way. When speech is involved, rigorous adherence to those requirements is necessary to ensure that ambiguity does not chill protected speech. (citation deleted)

19. *ACLU Fights Ferguson's "Don't Stand Still" Order*, Courthouse News Serv. (Aug. 18, 2014), http://www.courthousenews.com/2014/08/18/70523.htm.

20. *Abdullah*, 52 F. Supp. 3d at 939–40.

21. *Id.* at 941 ("At the hearing the defendants provided evidence that earlier that afternoon they had established an alternate place where protesters and others could gather and express themselves without being required to keep moving. I denied the request for a temporary restraining order.").

22. *Id.* at 942–42:

> After the [initial] hearing one of the ACLU lawyers went to Ferguson and tried to find the alternative protest area. Highway Patrol officers told him that they did not know anything about an approved protest zone. He was twice told to keep moving while he attempted to ask other people whether they knew of an alternative site. He returned to the area the next morning, on August 19, again to try to locate the alternate protest zone. The place that seemed to correspond to the testimony was either an open field, or a parking lot by a furniture store. The owner of the furniture store told him that the parking lot was his private property and that he had not agreed it could be used as a protest zone. The witness asked several police officers the location of the area designated for protesters to stand still and they either told him there was no such thing or that they had no idea what he was talking about. He also observed police telling people they must keep walking, even though there was no unrest or violent behavior at that time.

See Cory Doctorow, *Ferguson's "Free Speech Zone" Is a Padlocked No-Man's-Land*, BoingBoing (Aug. 21, 2014, 6:00 AM), http://boingboing.net/2014/08/21/fergusons-free-speech-zone.html ("The ACLU was denied an emergency injunction against Ferguson's cops' illegal 'no standing on the sidewalk' rule because Ferguson promised to erect a 'free speech zone,' but the only thing on that site is a fenced-off, locked-up pen that no one is allowed to use.").

23. The judge seemed to acknowledge this in her subsequent order granting the injunction. *See Abdullah*, 52 F. Supp. 3d at 947 (noting protest zone was "belatedly established" and was not an "adequate alternative forum").

24. *Id.* at 946 ("the keep-moving policy cannot meet constitutional standards for definiteness and clarity").

25. *Id.*

26. *Id.* at 946–47.

27. Also, as noted earlier, the judge found the alternative protest area to be inadequate. *Id.* at 947.

28. Consent Judgment, *Abdullah*, 52 F. Supp. 3d 936 (E.D. Mo. Nov. 5, 2014), https://cbsstlouis.files.wordpress.com/2014/11/ferguson_consent_judgment_11-5-14.pdf.

29. DOJ REPORT, *supra* note 1, at 13–14, 27, 29, and passim.

30. On the history of "unlawful assembly" laws in Missouri, see John Inazu, *Unlawful Assembly as Social Control* (July 27, 2015) (unpublished manuscript) (on file with author).

31. The violence continued well after the death of Michael Brown, for example, when two police officers were hit by bullets—although it is unclear whether the person who did the shooting was involved in the protests. Krishnadev Calamur, *Arrest Made in Shooting of Two Officers in Ferguson, Police Say*, NAT'L PUB. RADIO (Mar. 15, 2015), http://www.npr.org/blogs/thetwo-way/2015/03/15/393177470/arrest-made-in-shooting-of-two-officers-in-ferguson-police-say.

32. The judge continued, "The police must be able to perform their jobs. . . ." *Abdullah*, 52 F. Supp. 3d at 949.

33. *E.g.*, *Armed w/ Military-Grade Weapons, Missouri Police Crack Down on Protests over Michael Brown Shooting*, DEMOCRACY NOW (Aug. 14, 2014), http://www.democracynow.org/2014/8/14/armed_w_military_grade_weapons_missouri.

34. "The Unified Command includes the St. Louis County Police Department and the Missouri State Highway Patrol, among others." Joanie Vasiliadis, *Unified Command Speaks on Ferguson Aftermath*, KSDK.COM (Nov. 25, 2014), http://www.ksdk.com/story/news/local/ferguson/2014/11/25/unified-command-speaks-on-ferguson-aftermath/70111216/.

35. Petition, *Templeton*, *supra* note 4, at 1–2.

36. *Id.* at 2.

37. *Id.* at 23–24.

38. *Id.* at 1.

39. *Id.* at 11.

40. Temporary Restraining Order, Templeton v. Dotson, No. 4:14-cv-2019 (CEJ) (E.D. Mo. Jan. 5, 2015), http://www.stltoday.com/temporary-restraining-order-issued-by-u-s-district-judge-carol/pdf_3dc9af8b-07f7-5d8c-a7f1-7dbb7be08df3.html.

41. *Id.* at 2.

42. *Id.*

43. *Id.* at 3.

44. "The evidence establishes that the defendants created policies and procedures for the law enforcement response to the protests, including authorizing the use of tear gas and other chemical agents for the purpose of dispersing crowds of protesters." *Id.*

45. Jason Parham, *Ferguson Police Release Name of Officer Who Killed Michael Brown*, GAWKER (Aug. 15, 2014), http://gawker.com/ferguson-police-release-name-of-officer-who-killed-mich-1622033925.

46. *E.g.*, *Socket Error*, SNOPES, http://www.snopes.com/info/news/wilson.asp (last updated Nov. 25, 2014).

47. *See, e.g.*, Holly Yan, *Attorney: New Audio Reveals Pause in Gunfire When Michael Brown Was Shot*, CNN (Aug. 27, 2014, 12:42 PM ET), http://www.cnn.com/2014/08/26/us/michael-brown-ferguson-shooting/.

48. Koran Addo et al., *Release of Information—Some Demanded, Some Unexpected—Changes Dynamics in Ferguson Shooting*, ST. LOUIS POST-DISPATCH (Aug. 15, 2014 11:45 PM), http://www.stltoday.com/news/local/crime-and-courts/release-of-information-some-demanded-some-unexpected-changes-dynamics-in/article_0aa34e2b-bd3e-5fb1-81d6-736f98cccfcb.html.

49. Ferguson Police Chief Thomas Jackson—hours after documents came out labeling the 18-year-old Brown as the "primary suspect" in the store theft—told reporters the "robbery does not relate to the initial contact between the officer and Michael Brown." Greg Botelho & Don Lemmon, *Ferguson Police Chief: Officer Didn't Stop Brown as Robbery Suspect*, CNN (Aug. 15, 2014, 10:29 AM), http://www.cnn.com/2014/08/15/us/missouri-teen-shooting/. Wilson's story on this point seems to have changed, however. He later claimed that he did know that Brown was a suspect in the robbery. Laura Collins, *Exclusive: Darren Wilson Changed Crucial Elements of His Story in Aftermath of Michael Brown Shooting—Including Whether He Knew Teenager Was "Wanted Thief,"* DAILY MAIL (Dec. 2, 2014, 11:24 AM), http://www.dailymail.co.uk/news/article-2857630/EXCLUSIVE-Darren-Wilson-changed-crucial-elements-story-aftermath-shooting-Michael-Brown-dead-including-knew-teenager-wanted-thief.html.

50. *See* Addo, *supra* note 48.

51. First Nat'l Bank of Bos. v. Bellotti, 435 U.S. 765, 801 (1978). Indeed, the expansiveness (and emptiness) of the very idea of the "press" was evident in the protests in Ferguson—where news was conveyed by ordinary people via posts on Twitter, Vine, blogs, and Facebook. For a contrary view, and a defense of the institutional press's constitutional specialness, see Sonja R. West, *Awakening the Press Clause*, 58 UCLA L. Rev. 1025 (2011).

52. *In re* Roche, 411 N.E.2d 466, 472 n.9 (Mass. 1980) ("[T]he powerful rostrum of a newsroom or a broadcast studio may confer status of a type that is both real and laden with responsibility, but not, in [the Court's] view, status of constitutional dimension.").

53. *See generally* Pen Am., Press Freedom under Fire in Ferguson (Oct. 27, 2014), http://www.pen.org /sites/default/files/PEN_Press-Freedom-Under-Fire-In-Ferguson.pdf (describing the many instances of press suppression in the wake of the Brown shooting and subsequent protests).

54. Wesley Lowery, *First Person: A Reporter's Arrest*, Wash. Post, Aug. 14, 2014, at A14, http://www .washingtonpost.com/politics/in-ferguson-washington-post-reporter-wesley-lowery-gives-account-of-his -arrest/2014/08/13/0fe25c0e-2359-11e4-86ca-6f03cbd15c1a_story.html.

55. *Id.*

56. *Id.*

57. *Id.*

58. Brian Stelter, *6 More Journalists Arrested in Ferguson Protests*, CNN (Aug. 19, 2014, 8:31 PM ET), http://www.cnn.com/2014/08/19/us/ferguson-journalists-arrested.

59. Petition at 4, Hussein v. Cnty. of St. Louis, Mo., No. 4:14-cv-1410 (E.D. Mo Aug. 14, 2014), http://www aclu mo.org/files/3414/0804/0291/08-14-14_Videotaping_Complaint.pdf.

60. *Id.*

61. Order, Hussein v. Cnty. of St. Louis, Mo., No. 4:14-cv-1410-JAR (E.D. Mo. Aug. 14, 2014), http:// www.clearinghouse.net/chDocs/public/PN-MO-0001-0005.pdf.

62. DOJ Investigation, *supra* note 1, at 26–28.

63. *Id.* at 26.

64. David Klinger, Assoc. Professor of Criminology and Crim. Justice at Univ. of Mo. St. Louis, Remarks in Panel 1: Reflections on Policing Protest, at the Saint Louis University Public Law Review Symposium: The Thin Blue Line: Policing Post Ferguson (Feb. 20, 2015), http://law.slu.edu/event/thin -blue-line-policing-post-ferguson (video).

65. *See generally* Radley Balko, *After Ferguson, How Should Police Respond to Protests?*, Wash. Post (Aug. 14, 2014), http://www.washingtonpost.com/news/the-watch/wp/2014/08/14/after-ferguson -how-should-police-respond-to-protests.

66. Eli Yokely, *Officials Defend Handling of Ferguson Case*, N.Y. Times, Feb. 20, 2015, at A11, http:// www.nytimes.com/2015/02/21/us/officials-defend-handling-of-ferguson-case.html.

67. *See* Elahe Izadi & Wesley Lowery, *Meet the Missouri Highway State Patrol Captain Who Has Taken Over in Ferguson*, Wash. Post (Aug. 15, 2014), http://www.washingtonpost.com/news/post-nation /wp/2014/08/14/meet-the-missouri-highway-state-patrol-captain-who-is-taking-over-in-ferguson.

68. *Id.*

69. Klinger, *supra* note 64.

70. *Id.*

71. Arguably there was more than enough time to do this between the shooting of Michael Brown and the release of the grand jury verdict.

72. Alana Horowitz, *Ferguson Prosecutor Robert McCulloch Gives Bizarre Press Conference*, Huffington Post (Nov. 24, 2014), http://www.huffingtonpost.com/2014/11/24/bob-mcculloch-ferguson_n_6215986 .html.

73. David Hammer, *Ferguson Grand Jury Documents Withheld*, KSDK.com (Dec. 13, 2014, 4:56PM CST), http://www.ksdk.com/story/news/local/ferguson/2014/12/08/ferguson-grand-jury-documents-withheld /20077183/.

74. *E.g.*, *Ferguson Grand Jury Documents*, KSDK.com (Dec. 14, 2014, 6:53 PM), http://www.ksdk .com/story/news/local/ferguson/2014/11/25/ferguson-grand-jury-documents/70100296/.

75. Aamer Madhani, *Ferguson Grand Juror Sues to Remove Gag Order*, USA Today, Jan. 5, 2015, http://www.usatoday.com/story/news/nation/2015/01/05/ferguson-michael-brown-grand-juror-sues-gag-order/21284797/.

76. Mo. Rev. Stat. § 540.080 (2000).

77. Petition, *supra* note 5, at 6; *see* Eugene Volokh, *Ferguson Grand Juror Sues, Seeking Right to Speak about His Reactions to the Evidence*, Wash. Post (Jan. 5, 2015), http://www.washingtonpost.com/news/volokh-conspiracy/wp/2015/01/05/ferguson-grand-juror-sues-seeking-right-to-speak-about-his-reactions-to-the-evidence/ ("But the plaintiff's lawyer told me—in response to an e-mail from me—that the plaintiff seeks only to disclose his or her own thoughts and reactions to the evidence, not the other grand jurors' reactions.").

78. Butterworth v. Smith, 494 U.S. 624, 625 (1990).

79. Petition, *supra* note 5, at 7–8.

80. *Doe*, 2015 WL 2092492, at *1, *7.

81. *Id.* at *1 ("I find that Missouri courts should be given the opportunity to resolve this issue before Juror pursues a federal constitutional challenge.").

82. *Grand Juror Doe v. Robert McCulloch*, Am. Civil Liberties Union of Mo., http://www.aclu-mo.org/legal-docket/grand-juror-doe-v-robert-mcculloch/ (last updated May 29, 2015).

83. DOJ Investigation, *supra* note 1, at 2.

84. DOJ Report, *supra* note 1, at 86.

85. DOJ Investigation, *supra* note 1, at 1–6.

86. *Id.*

87. *Id.* at 7, 25, 26.

88. *Id.* at 27.

89. *Id.* at 35.

90. DOJ *Id.* at Investigation, *supra* note 1, at 26.

91. As this chapter was being prepared for publication, rumors surfaced of a new report to be released by the Department of Justice chastising the police response to the Ferguson protesters for increasing tensions, rather than reducing them. *See* Pete Williams, *DOJ Report Faults Police Response to Ferguson Protests*, NBCNews.com, June 30, 2015, http://www.nbcnews.com/news/us-news/doj-report-faults-police-response-ferguson-protest-n384561.

92. Ronald K.L. Collins & Sam Chaltain, We Must Not Be Afraid to Be Free: Stories of Free Expression in America 55 (2011) (describing the "safety valve" theory); C. Edwin Baker, Human Liberty & Freedom of Speech (1992) (analyzing the "marketplace of ideas" metaphor).

Chapter 12

The Uncertain Hope of Body Cameras

Howard M. Wasserman

There is little agreement about Ferguson.

A Pew Research Center poll in early December 2014 showed sharp racial, demographic, and political divisions about the Michael Brown shooting and everything surrounding it. While 80 percent of Black and 62 percent of Hispanic responders disagreed with the grand jury's decision not to indict Officer Darren Wilson in Brown's death, 64 percent of White respondents agreed with the decision. Fifty percent of people aged 18–29 disagreed, while all other age groups agreed, the number increasing with age. Sixty percent of Democrats disagreed, while 76 percent of Republicans agreed.[1]

The only point of cross-group agreement has been the appropriate policy response—equip police officers with body cameras. And that agreement is widespread. A whitehouse.gov petition in August 2014 calling for a federal law requiring all state, county, and local police to wear cameras garnered more than 150,000 signatures.[2] The White House responded by touting the benefits of police cameras, including their inclusion in a consent decree the Department of Justice (DOJ) reached with the City of New Orleans.[3] A proposed consent decree between the United States and Ferguson gave the City 180 days to equip all appropriate officers and all marked police vehicles with cameras and microphones and to establish comprehensive policies for their use.[4] Police rank and file previously had embraced cameras, although that support has cooled as the idea has gained wider popular currency.[5] Law enforcement executives and the American Civil

---

This chapter elaborates and updates arguments previously published in *Moral Panics and Body Cameras*, 92 Wash. U. L. Rev. 831 (2015), and *Epilogue: Moral Panics and Body Cameras*, 92 Wash. U. L. Rev. 845 (2015).

Liberties Union are behind cameras.[6] Members of Congress have called for federal legislation on the subject.[7] Democratic presidential candidate Hillary Clinton stated her support for cameras in the wake of riots and protests in Baltimore following the death of an African American man in police custody.[8] One week after the nonindictment of Wilson, President Obama announced a community-policing initiative that included $75 million in matching funds to help local police departments establish programs and purchase 50,000 cameras; DOJ announced the first phase, a $20 million pilot partnership aiming to provide cameras to 50 agencies, in May 2015.[9] And that same December 2014 study showed overwhelming bipartisan and cross-racial public support for body cameras.[10]

Body camera proponents reflexively cite three broad benefits, although those benefits may be contradictory. First, everyone—police and members of the public—will behave better in police encounters, knowing they are being recorded and that the recording may be used as evidence or information in subsequent investigations, litigation, disciplinary proceedings, public conversations, and other processes. Second, if anyone does misbehave, cameras offer unambiguous, neutral, objective, and certain evidence in all future police-citizen encounters. Third, there will be fewer citizen complaints about police abuse, less constitutional litigation, and the results of any proceedings that do occur will be more accurate thanks to this new evidence. The result is both transparency in policing and accountability of both police and members of the public for their misconduct. Indeed, police body cameras represent the next piece of an ever-expanding network of recording devices ready to capture every police-citizen encounter gone wrong, from smartphones to tablets to dashboard cameras to miniscule video or audio recorders.[11]

Cameras may well produce some or all of these expected benefits. Perhaps if Wilson had been wearing a camera, we could have seen the encounter and might agree on whether the Brown shooting was justified. Perhaps if Ferguson police had body cameras in August 2014, we would know whether officers overreacted to peaceful, constitutionally protected demonstrations or whether members of the public engaged in violent and unlawful rioting that warranted forceful police response.

The problem instead is one of rhetoric. Body cameras are perceived, and discussed, as a panacea—as a single, comprehensive, unambiguous, and infallible solution to police misconduct and police-public conflict. As always, the issue is more complicated and the solution less certain than public discussion and debate recognizes or acknowledges. Even if everyone agrees that widespread adoption of body cameras is a good idea, the surrounding rhetoric and expectations must remain realistic about the technology, its true benefits, and its very real limitations.

The Brown shooting kicked-off more than a year of incidents that demonstrate the competing perspectives on what video might contribute.

Less than two weeks after the Wilson grand jury decision, a grand jury in New York declined to indict New York City Police Officer Daniel Pantaleo in the choking death of Eric Garner.[12] Unlike in Ferguson, that encounter had been captured on a bystander's cell-phone video, in which Garner can be heard saying he could not breathe.[13] That this grand jury nevertheless reached the same conclusion as the one in Missouri demonstrates that video and cameras do not simply, automatically, or necessarily ensure accountability or prevent "the next Ferguson."

At the opposite end of the spectrum are multiple cases in which police officers were charged with crimes, including homicide, at least partly on the strength of video evidence. In each case, prosecutors defended the charging decision by pointing to body-cam, dashcam, and other video that appeared to show wrongdoing and, more importantly, appeared to contradict officers' written reports and statements about the incidents.[14]

This chapter considers the benefits and limitations of body cameras and video evidence and how the policy debate should account for them going forward. Body cameras and video are a good idea, they may achieve the hoped-for benefits, and their use should be encouraged and enabled. But expectations and demands must remain grounded in the realities of litigation and public policy, the limitations of video technology, and the function of video evidence. And so must the public conversation.

Unknown Effects and Unintended Consequences

We can only speculate whether recording deters bad behavior and incentivizes good behavior by police and the public in these encounters. The technology and its use by real police in real-world situations is too new to fully understand its true effect and effectiveness.

Two studies offer some preliminary answers. The first examined a pilot program in Mesa, Arizona, which equipped 50 officers with body cameras and left 50 without cameras. The study made three key findings: (1) Camera-equipped officers conducted "significantly" fewer stop-and-frisks and made significantly fewer arrests than their non-camera-equipped colleagues; (2) camera-equipped officers wrote more tickets and citations; and (3) camera-equipped officers were more likely to initiate contact with citizens they encountered on the street but less likely than non-camera-equipped colleagues to respond to dispatch calls.[15] In fact, the percentage difference in stop-and-frisks performed by each group was larger than the actual percentage of stop-and-frisks performed by camera-equipped officers.[16] Mesa also saw fewer total complaints against officers with cameras and nearly three times as many complaints against officers without cameras.[17]

A second study examined camera use in the police department in Rialto, California. When wearing cameras, officers were less likely to use weapons and less likely to initiate physical contact with suspects, doing so only when physically threatened; when not wearing cameras, officers were more likely to initiate physical contact and more likely to use force even when not physically threatened. The study similarly found a dramatic reduction in citizen complaints and use-of-force incidents compared with the previous 12 months.[18]

The question is what to conclude from such studies. Perhaps they confirm what supporters hope: when wearing body cameras, officers are more proactive, more risk-averse, and more willing to avoid invasive or forceful policing strategies except when necessary. Officers think more carefully about whether they have sufficient cause to stop and frisk or to arrest before confronting people.[19] They are more cautious about using force, although less cautious about noninvasive actions, such as issuing citations. Meanwhile, these effects carry to citizens, who are less likely to proceed with questionable or nonmeritorious complaints, knowing that video evidence undermines their version of events.

On the other hand, it is risky to generalize from these studies. Rialto and Mesa are not New York City or Chicago or even St. Louis; the number of officers to be equipped, the raw number of encounters to be recorded, and the amount of video to be stored and processed in those two communities are not comparable to what we see in larger urban centers. Nor can we overlook the relative absence in these communities of demographic trends and characteristics that trigger controversial police practices with potentially racially disparate impact—such as stop-and-frisk in New York City or arrests on outstanding warrants for high-fee nonviolent offenses, the pervasive practice in Ferguson that created some of the distrust between the public and police.

We also might question how much cameras genuinely deter. The presence of cameras (from media members and from phone- and camera-toting observers) during the Ferguson demonstrations in August and December 2014 seem to not have deterred demonstrators from destroying property or police from overreacting to peaceful protests. The deterrence argument is thrown into further doubt by the seemingly regular flow of new videos showing apparent police misconduct—typically excessive force or attempts to skirt constitutional limitations on their authority to stop, search, and seize members of the public—in incidents from Texas[20] to South Carolina[21] to California,[22] to New York,[23] to Minnesota,[24] to Indiana.[25] And this includes situations in which members of the public attempted to record law-enforcement officers performing those very functions.[26] The immediate public reaction to videos depicting police violence against unarmed individuals is often that the police overstepped, thereby directing the public discussion in a particular direction. Whether the video justifies that reaction—whether it shows genuine misconduct or constitutionally appropriate force—often gets lost in the conversational noise.

Moreover, an unintended consequence of deterrence is overdeterrence. As organizational-behavior scholar Ethan Bernstein explains, knowing that they are being recorded and evaluated based on the recording, "workers are likely to do *only* what is expected of them, slavishly adhering to even the most picayune protocols."[27] Bernstein found that assembly-line workers avoided creative timesaving devices or training methods, instead adhering rigidly to precise written policies, fearing having to explain themselves to anyone watching the video.[28]

Carried to the policing context, overdeterrence might mean "sacrificing the kind of educated risk-taking and problem solving that's often needed to save lives."[29] Police officers may steer well clear of the constitutional line out of fear of having to explain or justify behavior that, while not necessarily unconstitutional, looks questionable on video, especially to members of the public untrained in the nuances of police practices and the Fourth Amendment. As a practical matter, the prospect of being recorded, and fear of the public reaction to that recording, might cause an officer in a potentially dangerous situation to hesitate in using force, perhaps endangering his life or safety or the life and safety of the public.

As a legal matter, overdeterrence underpins the defense of qualified immunity in constitutional litigation, which protects executive officials from suit so long as their conduct does not violate clearly established constitutional rights of which a reasonable officer would have been aware.[30] Immunity provides officers with breathing space; it ensures that they are not unnecessarily risk-averse, that they do not perform their official functions less vigorously or with "unwarranted timidity," and that they do not forgo potentially beneficial policing strategies out of fear of personal liability.[31] Given the expansion of qualified immunity in recent years,[32] it would be ironic if police departments were to widely adopt a practice that creates the very overdeterrence that qualified immunity is designed to avoid.

On the other hand, whatever timesaving creativity might be lost from overdeterrence will hopefully be outweighed by officers not violating individuals' constitutional rights. We might welcome video if the effect is that officers hew more closely to formal, written department policies, procedures, and training, rather than going "off-script" in a way that might produce constitutional deprivations. The doctrine of municipal liability is premised on the idea that departments create policies and procedures for their officers, train them in those policies, and hold them to account for failing to follow them.[33] To the extent pervasive video recording enforces that idea, it benefits the overall constitutional system. In fact, in firing a South Carolina deputy sheriff for throwing a female high-school student to the ground—a seizure captured on multiple student cellphones—the Sheriff emphasized that the deputy failed to follow proper training and procedures.[34]

Limits of Video Evidence

More problematic is the insistence that body cameras will provide video evidence that is always an objective, neutral, certain, unambiguous, and accurate representation of what happened in an encounter, leaving no doubts and no he-said/he-said disputes. The assumption, in the Supreme Court's words, is that video can "speak for itself."[35] In fact, this bromide is false.

First, as any undergraduate film student knows, what video actually "says" depends on various qualities of the video—who and what is depicted, who created the images, and details of the images themselves (length, clarity, lighting, distance, angle, scope, speed, steadiness, manner of shooting, and others).[36] Second, as Dan Kahan and his co-authors showed, what any viewer "sees" in a video—and the inferences and conclusions she draws from what she sees—is influenced by the viewer's cultural, demographic, social, political, and ideological characteristics.[37] Video speaks "only against the background of preexisting understandings of social reality that invest those facts with meaning."[38] All of this affects the inferences drawn from video, as viewers identify many different possible meanings, interpretations, and conclusions about an event, depending on the particular video and the particular viewer.[39]

Two of Kahan's studies are especially pertinent in understanding the efficacy of body cameras and video in the context of Ferguson. One study tested whether viewers saw a particular use of force (an officer intentionally ramming his car into a fleeing car to end a high-speed chase, resulting in the fleeing car rolling into a ravine[40]) as constitutionally excessive, finding division along political and ideological attitudes.[41] A second study found that viewers' opinions about reproductive freedom tracked whether they saw events outside a reproductive health clinic as peaceful assembly and protest or as unlawful and violent attempts to blockade the clinic.[42]

Both questions—whether some force was excessive and whether a gathering was peaceful protest or lawless riot—are precisely at issue in deciding what happened in Ferguson, with respect to both the Brown shooting and the protests and demonstrations that followed. And there is no reason to believe that Kahan's findings would not be replicated there. Had Officer Wilson been wearing a body camera when he encountered and shot Michael Brown, opinions about what the video "showed" almost certainly would have split along political divisions about race, racial justice, police practices, and concepts of law and order. For comparison, while a majority of viewers believed the video of Eric Garner's death showed constitutionally excessive force, that belief was far stronger among Blacks and Hispanics, younger people, and Democrats.[43] Similarly, viewer opinions about whether Ferguson demonstrators were peacefully assembling or unlawfully rioting likely would track opinions about the First Amendment, public protest, and the permissible use of the streets for expressive activity, not to mention opinions about the underlying events being protested—the Brown shooting and the grand jury decision not to indict.

Of course, the Supreme Court shows no sign of moving from its view that video can be (and often is) so conclusive and unambiguous that a court in a civil rights action can determine its meaning without the need for jury consideration.[44] Paradoxically, then, body cameras may prove worse for civil rights plaintiffs—more constitutional cases will feature video, offering courts more opportunities to misuse video evidence on summary judgment and more opportunities to keep cases and videos away from civil juries.

The limits of body cameras and video arguably became clear from the nonindictment of Officer Pantaleo in Garner's death less than two weeks after the nonindictment of Wilson. One might conclude from that contemporaneous decision that body cameras would not have made a difference in Ferguson, in turn casting doubt on their efficacy as a response to police misconduct and police-public conflict. Video or not, the outcome was the same in both cases—no criminal punishment, no police accountability, and no justice for a seemingly unarmed African American man killed at the hands of police. If the Garner video was not sufficient to secure an indictment (much less a conviction) in what most viewers saw as a clear case of unreasonable force against an unarmed, nonresisting suspect with whom police initiated physical contact in response to a "broken windows" violation, accountability is unattainable. And body cameras and video do not change or improve anything.

At worst, the Garner case confirms Kahan's point that video never speaks for itself, but depends on who is watching and what is being watched. No matter the broad public and popular perception of the story told in the Garner video, most or all of the grand jurors—likely reflecting a different political, social, and demographic makeup than the broader national public watching the video—saw a different story and decided accordingly. The case also highlights the need to view video in conjunction with witness testimony, not as a substitute or as a singular video narrative that justifies ignoring testimony.[45] Finally, video's indeterminacy remains a constant—in criminal and civil proceedings and even when a fact-finder[46] is given an opportunity to see the video and resolve the case.[47] Any judge, grand jury, or petit jury may view any video differently than does the public, prompting the same disagreements, the same popular outrage, and the same concerns about police nonaccountability when an officer goes unsanctioned.

But just as we should not be overly optimistic about the potential of body cameras, neither should video's acknowledged limitations warrant entirely rejecting them as a useful tool. First, the conversation about body cameras must focus not only on how video affects judicial proceedings, but also how it influences the public and political conversation.[48] And the Garner case highlights video's significant extra-judicial effects and benefits. While opinion about the Brown nonindictment split sharply along racial and political lines, a cross-racial majority—no doubt under the video's influence—believed the Garner grand jury got it wrong.[49] Public preferences and perceptions of that video, and thus perceptions of the case, might prompt some responses to Garner's death that we did not see in response to Brown's death. The DOJ declined, following an investigation, to pursue federal civil rights charges against Officer Wilson.[50] But as of November 2015, it continued to investigate charges against Officer Pantaleo, a strategy that may have appeared more promising given the potential for a different grand or petit jury (drawn from a broader pool of an entire federal district) to view and interpret that video differently.[51] The New York City Police Department's internal affairs division also was investigating Pantaleo's actions,[52] whereas Wilson simply (although not quietly) resigned from the Ferguson Police Department.[53] And New York City settled a threatened civil action with Garner's family for almost $6 million.[54]

Moreover, sometimes video will prompt prosecutors to pursue charges against law-enforcement officers, with video validating that decision both internally and publically. This is especially likely when the video appears to contradict officers' written reports, initial statements, or testimony about incidents, thereby overcoming fact-finders' tendency to credit officer testimony. Consider examples from 2015 alone. University of Cincinnati police officer Ray Tensing was indicted for murder in the shooting death of Sam DuBose during a traffic stop on the strength of videos from multiple body cameras.[55] Chicago police officer Jason Van Dyke was indicted for first-degree murder in the shooting death of Laquan McDonald. Van Dyke shot McDonald sixteen times and defended his actions by reporting that McDonald had charged towards him with a knife; dashcam video (released only after an open-records lawsuit) showed McDonald walking away from the officers.[56] In North Charleston, South Carolina, an officer was indicted on murder charges in the shooting death of Walter Scott, an African American man; a bystander recorded the officer firing eight rounds, shooting Scott in the back as Scott ran at slow speed from a routine traffic stop, and handcuffing the prone body immediately afterwards.[57] And in November, Louisiana indicted two state police officers for second-degree murder and attempted second-degree murder arising from a recorded post-chase shooting that left a father hospitalized and his six-year-old son dead.[58]

Video may even affect cases of non-lethal police misconduct. In December, New York City Police Officer Jonathan Munoz was indicted for official misconduct and lying on a criminal complaint. In March 2014, Munoz had arrested Jason Disisto for obstructing government administration, disorderly conduct, and resisting arrest; Disisto had attempted to record Munoz frisking and arresting a friend of Disisto's, and Munoz stated in the incident report that Disisto had lunged at him and tried to punch him. But footage from a security camera was later found, seeming to show that Munoz had initiated the physical confrontation, apparently to stop Disisto from recording the underlying incident.[59]

Again, however, charges or an indictment do not mean a conviction; a jury may ultimately acquit in each of those cases if it sees a different story or finds different meaning in that same video than the one carried by prosecutors, grand jurors, or the public. And the same public outrage and public frustration may follow.

Implementation: The Devil in the Details

Ultimately, the effectiveness of body cameras depends not on the effectiveness of cameras and video in the abstract, but on the hard details of implementation. Law enforcement agencies must enact policies addressing everything about how cameras should be deployed and used. It is not enough to call for body cameras; public discussion must consider the difficult endeavor of making them work.

In 2014, the Police Executive Research Forum (PERF) and the DOJ's Community Oriented Police Services Program published the results of a yearlong study that included a survey of police departments, interviews with executives in departments that have implemented body camera programs, and a one-day conference of law enforcement officials and other policy experts. The report offered more than 30 recommendations of protocols for equipping officers with cameras, recording events, and storing, reviewing, using, and releasing recordings. At its heart was recognition that agency policies and training materials must provide clear, specific, and detailed guidelines.[60] And the first round of federal funding for local body camera programs explicitly targeted law enforcement agencies that already had considered and established camera policies, requiring that any funding applicant "must establish a strong plan for implementation of body-worn cameras and a robust training policy before purchasing cameras."[61]

Consider, for example, the debate over when officers must turn cameras on and record a particular public encounter. ACLU representatives argued that officers should record all encounters with the public, because continuous recording eliminates "any possibility that an officer could evade the recording of abuses committed on duty"; law enforcement officials wanted a more limited approach vesting officers with discretion to keep cameras off during certain encounters and events, particularly where privacy concerns are implicated or when recording would be "unsafe" or "impossible."[62] The PERF report ultimately recommended that officers record "all calls for service and during all law enforcement-related encounters and activities that occur while the officer is on duty," subject to officers obtaining consent to record from crime victims and retaining discretion to keep cameras off when entering people's homes and when talking with victims, witnesses, or other people reporting crimes, particularly in sexual assault and child abuse cases.[63] While siding with the discretionary approach, the report also recommended that officers explain and justify any decision not to record a particular encounter.[64]

Of course, vesting officers with discretion may create a different unintended consequence—more opportunities for dispute, complaint, and litigation. As police cameras become more pervasive, it becomes impossible to avoid expectations and demands—from courts, litigants, juries, citizens, the media, and civilian police-review boards—that cameras always will be used, that video always will be available, and that the absence of video evidence will itself be evidence of misconduct.[65] There also will be inevitable disappointment among those same groups when the video does not offer a single, unambiguous, commonly agreed-upon, and satisfying story about what happened in an encounter. The absence or ambiguity of video will itself become a subject of dispute and controversy in the media, in police departments and local governments, in the public discourse, and in the courts. The proposed consent decree with the City of Ferguson provided that "in order to continue to promote transparency, foster accountability, and enhance public trust in FPD, the City agrees to make body-worn and in-car camera recordings publicly available to the maximum extent allowable under Missouri law."[66]

Unfortunately, the maximum extent may not be that great, as Missouri officials at least initially appeared unwilling to strike the balance recommended by PERF and suggested in the consent decree. Indeed, the ACLU, perhaps the strongest voice in favor of broad disclosure, acknowledged the significance of those countervailing privacy concerns.[67] While most state open records and Freedom of Information laws contain exemptions for evidence, ongoing investigations, and privacy, the PERF report urged departments to use "these exceptions judiciously to avoid any suspicion by community members that police are withholding video footage to hide officer misconduct or mistakes."[68] PERF insisted that a "broad public disclosure policy" demonstrates commitment to transparency and accountability; it called on departments to make clear the processes for responding to disclosure requests, for determining what videos will be disclosed to the public, and for explaining to the public why some video was or was not released.[69]

Unfortunately, Missouri officials at least initially appeared unwilling to strike a similar balance. In February 2015, a panel convened by Missouri Attorney General Chris Koster recommended that the General Assembly amend the state's Sunshine Law to define data from any "mobile video recorder" (including police vehicle and body cameras) as "closed records," not subject to public request and accessible only to those involved in the incident for purposes of civil litigation or by court order. Koster warned of technology "lead[ing] to a new era of voyeurism and entertainment television at the expense of Missourians' privacy."[70]

Missouri legislators initially appeared ready to follow that recommendation. A February 2015 proposal in the state senate would have categorically exempted all official video from any public disclosure or open records request. Proponents of the measure cited privacy concerns; the problem, it was argued, was that video could end up on YouTube, where an officer's single "mistake" would remain forever.[71] Interestingly, state legislators seemed more concerned with the privacy of their police officers than the privacy of victims, witnesses, and others in the video, to say nothing of the public and its interest in identifying and checking abuse of government power. This one-sided sympathy stood in marked contrast to the PERF study's balanced approach recognizing the countervailing weight of transparency and accountability.

The Missouri proposal would functionally eliminate police-created video from meaningful public discussion and debate over incidents of police conduct. The public would only see video that law enforcement chooses to release, which likely would be only video supporting and exonerating the officers involved in a confrontation—it rarely will be in the government's interest to voluntarily disclose video depicting officer misconduct. The Laquan McDonald case illustrates the point. It took more than a year and an order from a state trial court before the City of Chicago released dashcam video of a fatal shooting for which the officer was charged with first degree murder.[72]

This places significant weight on citizen video—from smartphones, small recorders, and other devices—to capture and publicize police-public encounters and misconduct. In other words, we end up exactly where we have been before police donned body cameras, relying on the public to record events.

Unfortunately, the public records police subject to an ongoing threat of officers actively interfering with those recording efforts[73] and to conflicting judicial signals about the public's First Amendment right to record police activity in public. During the August 2014 Ferguson demonstrations, the ACLU filed a lawsuit specifically challenging police interference with citizen recordings, resulting in a settlement in which St. Louis County officials publically and formally acknowledged the public's right to record.[74] The proposed consent decree with the United States required Ferguson to continue acting in accordance with that agreement, including training and supervising officers to not interfere with non-disruptive public recording of police activities and providing that recording may not in and of itself constitute a threat to officer safety.[75] And one of the plaintiffs in a § 1983 damages action arising from the August protests specifically alleged that officers had seized and destroyed the memory card from his camera.[76]

But federal courts are divided on the First Amendment question.[77] And one Texas legislator proposed prohibiting all non-media personnel from coming within twenty-five feet of police officers while filming them performing their functions in public, although his bill was met with sharp criticism, was likely unconstitutional, and was quickly withdrawn.[78] The point is that if body camera videos are not released as a matter of state policy and citizen video becomes difficult to obtain, video ceases to form any meaningful part of the public conversation about law enforcement behavior.

One unexpected obstacle to implementing body cameras is the new opposition, or at least hesitancy, of police unions and rank-and-file officers. As recently as 2012, a study of 785 law enforcement professionals found overwhelming support for cameras, with 85 percent saying they would be effective in reducing litigation and false claims of officer misconduct.[79] But as more people in and out of government have seized on body cameras and video as the solution and as agencies have begun establishing programs, the rank and file has resisted. Unions and officers in several cities have cited everything from officer privacy to citizen privacy to lack of evidence that cameras work to the breaking of trust between police and the communities they serve.[80] The last of these points seems especially ironic, given that the loss of trust between police and their communities has produced the very police-citizen conflicts that body cameras are designed to record, reveal, and deter.

In any event, this new opposition implicitly acknowledges two things: interpretations of video will vary and some portion of the public will—for demographic, political, sociological, or attitudinal reasons—virtually always see police misconduct in any video depicting police using force, especially against unarmed individuals. The way to avoid making the police look bad, the officers seem to suggest, is to eliminate video evidence from debates and discussions about their behavior.

One case, appropriately enough from St. Louis, illustrates the consequences of officer uncertainty about implementation. An April 2014 traffic stop over an illegal turn escalated to the driver being pulled from the car, kicked, and tased. Part of the encounter was captured by the dash cam of one squad car, until a later-arriving officer can be heard saying, "We're red right now, so if you guys are worried about cameras, just wait," at which point the audio and then the video were shut off. Charges against the driver were dropped, either because the truncated video contradicted the officers' written reports (the driver's version) or because the "the action of turning off the dash cam video diminished the evidentiary merits of the case" (the government version). The officer who called for the video to be shut off was suspended for violating department regulations requiring that dashboard cameras remain on until an incident is over. While defending that suspension, the chief of the St. Louis Police also insisted that the video did not depict any wrongdoing by the officers involved, making it all the more inexplicable to him why the officer turned off the video.[81]

While the driver's civil rights action remains pending as of this writing, the case captures many of the problems of implementation and incentives that come with body cameras. The simplistic presumption is that the officer turned the camera off because she saw her colleagues engaging in misconduct, which might explain why the chief felt the need to simultaneously defend the officers shown using force and suspend the officer who shut off the camera. On the other hand, the officer who shut off the camera likely did so assuming that any force against a seemingly unarmed man during a routine traffic stop would be viewed by the public as unconstitutionally excessive, even if the force was legally justified. In turning off the video, however, she created the very public-perception problem she was trying to avoid. Body cameras make this calculus ever more common.

The perverse incentives on display here disappear if Missouri succeeds in exempting all police-created video from public disclosure. That officer no longer worries about how the public will perceive the video, and thus no longer feels the need to turn the camera off, because the public never sees (or gets to consider and discuss) the video unless and until litigation.

Unfortunately, this creates further perverse incentives for officers to impede citizen-created video of public encounters—to confiscate iPhones or to order citizens to stop recording, thereby eliminating the only source of video that might still make it onto YouTube for public consumption or that might affect public attitudes toward the officers' conduct. And this brings us back to the new wariness over body cameras among police rank and file. Officers could reasonably conclude that the best course is to not even engage with the web of confusion, uncertainty, competing incentives, and criticism that cameras create.

Conclusion

Police body cameras offer numerous benefits and are likely a net positive, especially with members of the public increasingly concerned about police misconduct and excessive force and increasingly armed with their own recording technology. But the public debate about body cameras must reflect the nuance and complexity of camera policy, grounded in the limitations of video evidence and the hard questions of implementation. The current discussion—in which cameras are erroneously touted as magic solutions that resolve all problems—highlights the failure to recognize that complexity. And it should prompt government officials and all other stakeholders in the public debate to take a more cautious, realistic, and, hopefully, more effective approach to body cameras and to video evidence. If there is a common lesson from Ferguson, that should be it.

Notes

1. *Sharp Racial Divisions in Reactions to Brown, Garner Decisions*, Pew Res. Ctr. (Dec. 8, 2014), http://www.people-press.org/2014/12/08/sharp-racial-divisions-in-reactions-to-brown-garner-decisions/ [hereinafter *Sharp Racial Divisions*].

2. Mike Brown Law. Require All State, County, and Local Police to Wear a Camera, White House (Aug. 13, 2014), https://petitions.whitehouse.gov/petition/mike-brown-law-requires-all-state-county -and-local-police-wear-camera/8tlS5czf (online White House petition garnered more than 154,000 signatures).

3. Roy L. Austin, Jr., *Response to Your Petition on the Use of Body-Worn Cameras*, White House (Sept. 12, 2014), https://petitions.whitehouse.gov/response/response-your-petition-use-body-worn -cameras (official White House response to petition).

4. Consent Decree ¶¶ 228–229, *United States v. City of Ferguson* (E.D. Mo.), http://www.ferguson city.com/DocumentCenter/View/1920 [hereinafter *Consent Decree*]; Ben Mathis-Lilly, *City of Ferguson Agrees to Policing Reforms in Proposed Deal with Department of Justice*, Slate (Jan. 27, 2016), http://www .slate.com/blogs/the_slatest/2016/01/27/ferguson_police_agree_to_department_of_justice_reforms .html.

5. Compare Doug Wyllie, *Survey: Police Officers Want Body-Worn Cameras*, PoliceOne (Oct. 23, 2012), http://www.policeone.com/police-products/body-cameras/articles/6017774-Survey-Police-officers -want-body-worn-cameras/, with O'Ryan Johnson & Erin Smith, *Boston Brass, Police Union Fear Body Cams on Cops*, PoliceOne (Dec. 3, 2014), http://www.policeone.com/police-products/body-cameras /articles/7921491-Boston-brass-police-union-fear-body-cams-on-cops/, and Douglas Hanks, *Police Union Tries to Block Camera Plan for Miami-Dade Officers*, Miami Herald (Aug. 22, 2014), http://www .miamiherald.com/news/local/community/miami-dade/article1981217.html.

6. Jay Stanley, Police Body-Mounted Cameras: With Right Policies in Place, a Win for All, ACLU (2013), https://www.aclu.org/files/assets/police_body-mounted_cameras.pdf.

7. Arthur Delaney, *Adam Schiff Pushes Body Cameras for Cops*, Huffington Post (Aug. 27, 2014), http://www.huffingtonpost.com/2014/08/27/body-worn-cameras_n_5722762.html.

8. Zeke J. Miller, *Clinton to Call for Body Cameras, End to "Era of Mass Incarceration,"* Time (Apr. 29, 2015), http://time.com/3839637/clinton-to-call-for-body-cameras-end-to-era-of-mass-incarceration/.

9. Press Release, U.S. Dep't of Justice, Justice Department Announces $20 Million in Funding to Support Body-Worn Camera Pilot Program (May 1, 2015), http://www.justice.gov/opa/pr/justice -department-announces-20-million-funding-support-body-worn-camera-pilot-program [hereinafter $20 Million in Funding].

10. *Sharp Racial Divisions*, *supra* note 1.

11. Howard M. Wasserman, *Orwell's Vision: Video and the Future of Civil Rights Enforcement*, 68 Md. L. Rev. 600, 600 (2009).

12. J. David Goodman & Al Baker, *Wave of Protests after Grand Jury Doesn't Indict Officer in Eric Garner Chokehold Case*, N.Y. Times (Dec. 3, 2014), http://www.nytimes.com/2014/12/04/nyregion/grand -jury-said-to-bring-no-charges-in-staten-island-chokehold-death-of-eric-garner.html?_r=0.

13. *Id.*

14. *See* discussion *infra* notes 54-58.

15. Justin T. Ready & Jacob T.N. Young, The Impact of on-Officer Video Cameras on Police-Citizen Contacts: Findings from the Mesa Field Experiment 21–22, 24–25 (2014) (unpublished manuscript) [hereinafter Ready & Young, *Impact*] (on file with author); Justin T. Ready & Jacob T.N. Young, *Three Myths about Police Body Cams*, Slate (Sept. 2, 2014), http://www.slate.com/articles/technology/future _tense/2014/09/ferguson_body_cams_myths_about_police_body_worn_recorders.html [hereinafter Ready & Young, *Three Myths*].

16. Ready & Young, *Impact*, *supra* note 15, at 22.

17. Police Exec. Res. Forum, Implementing a Body-Worn Camera Program: Recommendations and Lessons Learned 6 (2014), http://www.policeforum.org/assets/docs/Free_Online_Documents/Technology/imple menting%20a%20body-worn%20camera%20program.pdf.

18. *Self-Awareness to Being Watched and Socially-Desirable Behavior: A Field Experiment on the Effect of Body-Worn Cameras on Police Use-of-Force* 8–9, POLICE FOUND. (Mar. 2013), http://www.police foundation.org/content/body-worn-camera; POLICE EXEC. RES. FORUM, *supra* note 17, at 5.

19. Ready & Young, *Impact, supra* note 15, at 24.

20. Meghan Keneally, *McKinney Police Office Eric Casebolt Resigns in Wake of Pool Video*, CNN .COM (June 9, 2015), http://abcnews.go.com/US/mckinney-police-officer-eric-casebolt-resigns-wake-pool /story?id=31649084.

21. Mark Berman, *South Carolina Police Officer in Walter Scott Shooting Indicted on Murder Charge*, WASH. POST (June 8, 2015), http://www.washingtonpost.com/news/post-nation/wp/2015/06/08 /police-officer-who-shot-walter-scott-indicted-for-murder/; Eyder Peralta, *South Carolina Police Officer Charged with Murder after Shooting Man in Back*, NPR (Apr. 7, 2015), http://www.npr.org/blogs/thetwo -way/2015/04/07/398140336/south-carolina-police-offcer-charged-with-murder-after-shooting-man-in -back; Emma Brown, T. Rees Shapiro & Elahe Izadi, *S.C. Sheriff Fires Officer Who Threw Student across the Classroom*, WASH. POST (Oct. 28, 2015), https://www.washingtonpost.com/news/education /wp/2015/10/28/s-c-sheriff-to-announce-results-of-invetigation-into-officer-who-threw-student/; Howard Wasserman, *Determining the Effect of Video*, PRAWFSBLAWG (July 8, 2014), http://prawfsblawg.blogs.com /prawfsblawg/2014/07/determining-the-effect-of-video.html.

22. Daniel Politi, *L.A. Police Caught on Video Shooting Homeless Man to Death*, SLATE (Mar. 2, 2015), http://www.slate.com/blogs/the_slatest/2015/03/01/video_shows_lapd_shooting_and_killing_homeless _man.html; Wasserman, *supra* note 21.

23. Andres Jauregui, *NYPD Appears to Slam Pregnant Woman Sandra Amezquita to Ground*, HUFFINGTON POST (Sept. 24, 2014), http://www.huffingtonpost.com/2014/09/24/nypd-pregnant-woman -video-sandra-amezquita_n_5872286.html; Daniel Politi, *Video: New York State Officer Appears to Slap Man Who Didn't Want Car Searched*, SLATE (Nov. 9, 2014), http://www.slate.com/blogs/the_slatest /2014/11/09/saratoga_country_officer_appears_to_slap_man_who_didn_t_want_car_searched.html.

24. Ben Mathis-Lilley, *"I'm Not Your Brother," Says Officer Tasering Black Minnesota Man in Front of His Children*, SLATE (Aug. 29, 2014), http://www.slate.com/blogs/the_slatest/2014/08/29/minnesota _taser_video_christopher_lollie_of_st_paul_tased_in_front_of_children.html.

25. Wasserman, *supra* note 21.

26. Joseph Serna, *With Smartphones Everywhere, Police on Notice They May Be Caught on Camera*, L.A. TIMES (Apr. 21, 2015), http://www.latimes.com/local/lanow/la-me-ln-feds-probe-video -phone-in-south-gate-20150421-story.html; Ronald K.L. Collins, *Citizen Recording of Police in Public Place—First Amendment Protection?*, CONCURRING OPINIONS (Apr. 29, 2015), http://concurringopinions .com/archives/2015/04/fan-58-first-amendment-news-citizen-recordings-of-police-in-public-places-first -amendment-protection.html.

27. Ethan Bernstein, *How Being Filmed Changes Employee Behavior*, HARVARD BUS. REV. BLOG NET- WORK (Sept. 12, 2014), http://blogs.hbr.org/2014/09/how-being-filmed-changes-employee-behavior/.

28. *Id., see also* Ethan Bernstein, *The Transparency Trap*, HARV. BUS. REV. (Oct. 2014), http://hbr .org/2014/10/the-transparency-trap/ar/4.

29. Bernstein, *supra* note 27.

30. Pearson v. Callahan, 555 U.S. 223, 231 (2009).

31. Filarsky v. Delia, 132 S. Ct. 1657, 1665 (2012); Ashcroft v. Iqbal, 556 U.S. 662, 686 (2009).

32. Ashcroft v. al-Kidd, 131 S. Ct. 2074, 2085 (2011) (stating that qualified immunity protects "all but the plainly incompetent or those who knowingly violate the law") (citation and internal quotation marks omitted).

33. Connick v. Thompson, 131 S. Ct. 1350, 1359–60 (2011).

34. Brown et al., *supra* note 21.

35. *Compare* Scott v. Harris, 550 U.S. 372, 378 n.5 (2007), *with* Wasserman, *supra* note 11, at 624–25.

36. Wasserman, *supra* note 11, at 619–20.

37. Dan M. Kahan et al., *Whose Eyes Are You Going to Believe?* Scott v. Harris *and the Perils of Cognitive Illiberalism*, 122 HARV. L. REV. 837, 879 (2009); *see also* Wasserman, *supra* note 11, at 627.

38. Kahan et al., *supra* note 37, at 883.

39. *Id.* at 841–42; Wasserman, *supra* note 10, at 618–21, 624–27; Howard M. Wasserman, *Video Evidence and Summary Judgment: The Procedure of* Scott v. Harris, 91 Judicature 180, 182–83 (2008).

40. Scott v. Harris, 550 U.S. 372, 374–75 (2007).

41. Kahan et al., *supra* note 37, at 841.

42. Dan M. Kahan et al., *"They Saw a Protest": Cognitive Illiberalism and the Speech-Conduct Distinction*, 64 Stan. L. Rev. 851, 884 (2012).

43. *Sharp Racial Divisions, supra* note 1.

44. *See, e.g.*, Plumhoff v. Rickard, 134 S. Ct. 2012, 2021 (2014) (approving summary judgment in favor of defendant based on video of alleged excessive force); Scott v. Harris, 550 U.S. 372, 378–80 (2007) (insisting that video of high-speed chase told the complete story of what happened during the chase and did not merit jury consideration); *see also* Howard M. Wasserman, *Mixed Signals on Summary Judgment*, 2014 Mich. St. L. Rev. 1331.

45. *Compare* Wasserman, *supra* note 11, at 633, *with Scott*, 550 U.S. at 380–81.

46. One can debate whether the Garner or Brown grand juries were used in ordinary or appropriate ways, in which the grand jury follows the prosecutor's lead based on the state's strongest evidence, or whether they were used in an atypical manner as fact-finders outside an open and adversarial trial process. *See* Dahlia Lithwick & Sonja West, *Shadow Trial*, Slate (Nov. 26, 2014), http://www.slate.com/articles/news_and_politics/jurisprudence/2014/11/ferguson_grand_jury_investigation_a_shadow_trial_violates_the_public_s_right.html.

47. Wasserman, *supra* note 11, at 643–44.

48. *Id.* at 644–48.

49. *Sharp Racial Divisions, supra* note 1.

50. *See* Matt Apuzzo & Michael S. Schmidt, *U.S. Not Expected to Fault Officer in Ferguson Case*, N.Y. Times (Jan. 21, 2015), http://www.nytimes.com/2015/01/22/us/justice-department-ferguson-civil-rights-darren-wilson.html?hp&action=click&pgtype=Homepage&module=first-column-region&region=top-news&WT.nav=top-news&_r=0.

51. Att'y Gen. Eric Holder, Statement by Attorney General Holder on Federal Investigation into the Death of Eric Garner, (Dec. 3, 2014), http://www.justice.gov/opa/speech/statement-attorney-general-holder-federal-investigation-death-eric-garner; Howard Wasserman, *Video and Public Opinion*, PrawfsBlawg (Dec. 11, 2014), http://prawfsblawg.blogs.com/prawfsblawg/2014/12/video-and-public-opinion.html; Howard Wasserman, *Prosecuting Police—the Role of the Grand Jury Pool*, PrawfsBlawg (Dec. 4, 2014), http://prawfsblawg.blogs.com/prawfsblawg/2014/12/prosecuting-police-the-role-of-the-grand-jury-pool.html.

52. Hilary Hanson, *NYPD Investigators Question Chokehold Officer for More than 2 Hours*, Huffington Post (Dec. 10, 2014), http://www.huffingtonpost.com/2014/12/10/nypd-investigation-eric-garner-daniel-pantaleo_n_6304874.html.

53. *Darren Wilson Resigns from Ferguson Police Force*, Huffington Post (Nov. 29, 2014), http://www.huffingtonpost.com/2014/11/29/darren-wilson-resigns_n_6241834.html.

54. J. David Goodman, *Eric Garner Case Is Settled by New York City for $5.9 Million*, N.Y. Times (July 14, 2015), http://www.nytimes.com/2015/07/14/nyregion/eric-garner-case-is-settled-by-new-york-city-for-5-9-million.html.

55. Ben Mathis-Lilley, *Cincinnati Prosecutor Announces Indictment of Officer for "Senseless" Murder of Black Driver,* Slate (July 29, 2015), http://www.slate.com/blogs/the_slatest/2015/07/29/sam_dubose_murder_ray_tensing_university_of_cincinnati_police_officer_charged.html; Jeremy Stahl, The Sam DuBose Police Report Is Full of Falsehoods from Ray Tensing's Fellow Officers, Slate (July 29, 2015), http://www.slate.com/blogs/the_slatest/2015/07/29thesamdubosepolice_report_is_full_of_falsehoods_from_ray_tensing_s_colleagues.html.

56. Leon Neyfakh, *Chicago Cop Charged With First-Degree Murder,* Slate (Nov. 24, 2015), http://www.slate.com/articles/news_and_politics/crime/2015/11/laquan_mcdonald_chicago_police_shooting_involving_officer_who_fired_16_shots.html; Leon Neyfakh, The Graphic Footage of Laquan McDonald Being Killed by a Police Officer is Horrifying, Slate (Nov. 24, 2015), http://www.slate.com/blogs/the

_slatest/2015/11/24/laquan_mcdonald_video_watch_graphic_footage_of_black_teen_in_chicago_being
.html.

57. Berman, *supra* note 21; Peralta, *supra* note 21.

58. Marina Koren, Body Cameras and the Death of a 6-Year-Old Boy, The Atlantic (Nov. 7, 2015), http://www.theatlantic.com/national/archive/2015/11/jeremy-mardis-police-shooting/414789/.

59. Leon Neyfakh, *Another Police Officer Indicted After Video Proves He Lied,* Slate (Dec. 23, 2015), http://www.slate.com/blogs/the_slatest/2015/12/23/nypd_cop_jonathan_munoz_indicted_based_on
_jason_disisto_arrest_video.html.

60. Police Exec. Res. Forum, *supra* note 17, at 38; Stanley, *supra* note 6, at 1–2.

61. *$20 Million in Funding, supra* note 9.

62. *Compare* Stanley, *supra* note 6, at 2, *with* Police Exec. Res. Forum, *supra* note 17, at 12–13.

63. Police Exec. Res. Forum, *supra* note 17, at 40–41.

64. *Id.* at 13.

65. *Id.* at 28–29.

66. *Consent Decree* ¶ 249, *supra* note 4.

67. *Id.* at 15; Stanley, *supra* note 6, at 1.

68. Police Exec. Res. Forum, *supra* note 16, at 18.

69. *Id.* at 64 (recommendation 25).

70. Office of the Mo. Att'y Gen., Attorney General Chris Koster's Roundtable on Representative Policing: Report and Recommendations (2014), https://ago.mo.gov/docs/default-source/press-releases/2015/agkoster-roundtablerepresentativepolicingreport.pdf?sfvrsn=1.

71. Alex Stuckey, *Missouri Senate Measure Would Keep Police Recordings from the Public*, St. Louis Post-Dispatch (Feb. 19, 2015), http://www.stltoday.com/news/local/crime-and-courts/article_fc30bc64-16f7-562b-bdcf-51807cd01f62.html.

72. Serna, *supra* note 26.

73. *See* sources cited *supra* note 56.

74. Agreement at 1, *Hussein v. County of St. Louis,* No. 14-CV-1410 (E.D. Mo. Aug. 15, 2014), http://www.clearinghouse.net/chDocs/public/PN-MO-0001-0002.pdf; Byron Tau, *Missouri ACLU, Authorities Reach Agreement on Recording of Police*, Politico (Aug. 15, 2014), http://www.politico.com/blogs/under-the-radar/2014/08/missouri-aclu-authorities-reach-agreement-on-recording-194043.html.

75. *Consent Decree* ¶¶ 112–117, *supra* note 4.

76. Complaint, White v. Jackson, No. 4:14-cv-01490 (E.D. Mo. Aug. 28, 2014), https://ia601400.us.archive.org/14/items/gov.uscourts.moed.135403/gov.uscourts.moed.135403.1.0.pdf.

77. *Compare* Am. Civil Liberties Union of Ill. v. Alvarez, 679 F.3d 583 (7th Cir. 2012), *and* Glik v. Cunniffe, 665 F.3d 78 (1st Cir. 2011), *with* Kelly v. Borough of Carlisle, 662 F.3d 248 (3d Cir. 2010), *and ACLU of Ill.*, 679 F.3d at 611–12, 614 (Posner, J., dissenting); *see also* Collins, *supra* note 26.

78. Allison Wisk, *Bill to limit filming of police activity is dropped,* The Dallas Morning News (Apr. 10, 2015), http://www.dallasnews.com/news/politics/state-politics/20150410-bill-to-limit-filming-of-police-activity-is-dropped.ece; Howard Wasserman, *A Texas bill that is both stupid and unconstitutional,* PrawfsBlawg (Mar. 23, 2015), http://prawfsblawg.blogs.com/prawfsblawg/2015/03/restricting-recording-of-police.html.]

79. Wyllie, *supra* note 5.

80. *See* sources cited *supra* note 5.

81. Christine Byers, *Though Officer Turned off Dash Cam, Cops Weren't Doing Anything Wrong, St. Louis Chief Says*, St. Louis Post-Dispatch (Feb. 18, 2015), http://www.stltoday.com/news/local/crime-and-courts/article_f46c9c9b-f61f-5b9b-a79b-ccaecbbc7466.html; Robert Patrick, *Police Dash Cam Shows Part of Contested Arrest—Until St. Louis Officer Turns Camera Off*, St. Louis Post-Dispatch (Feb. 16, 2015), http://www.stltoday.com/news/local/crime-and-courts/article_f4c65142-f3be-57f1-a957-9f256fb02459.html.

Chapter 13

Policing in the 21st Century

Tracey L. Meares

Introduction

In the months since August 9, 2014, the nation has trained its attention on fatalities resulting from incidents of police use of force occurring all over this country. Since that date, which is the day that unarmed African American teenager Michael Brown was killed by a white police officer in Ferguson, Missouri, the country has learned about and even watched on video several more African American males be killed by (mostly) white, male police officers. These incidents are visceral and palpable, and they are often highlighted in the news media and on social media over and over again. The seemingly regular occurrence of these incidents, along with the protests in response to them in many cities—but especially in the St. Louis metropolitan area, New York City, and, most recently, in Baltimore—has raised questions about the scale and depth of the problem of police violence in the United States today.

Despite the fact that policing is inherently a local enterprise,[1] President Obama believed that a federal response was necessary. To that end, the president signed on December 18, 2014, an executive order establishing the Task Force on the 21st Century Policing. This Task Force, composed of 11 members representing various perspectives including those of police executives, civil rights lawyers, community activists, union representatives, and academics, came together to hear testimony about, deliberate on, and then report to the president regarding a number of recommendations aimed at promoting collaborative relationships built on trust between the police and the communities they serve, while maintaining and enhancing public safety.[2] In establishing this Task Force, President Obama noted:

> When any part of the American family does not feel like it is being treated fairly, that's a problem for all of us . . . it is not just a problem for some. It's not just a problem for a particular community or a particular demographic. It means we are not as strong as a country as we can be. And when applied to the criminal justice system, it means we're not as effective in fighting crime as we could be.[3]

Central to the president's observation is the role of public trust in government. Public trust importantly flows from perceptions of fairness, and the research reviewed below in this essay indicates that people care about fairness a great deal. This may seem surprising today when there is so much discussion of police effectiveness at crime reduction in media and policy circles. Interestingly, the notion that police effectiveness at crime reduction is a metric that should matter with respect to evaluation of police is of relatively recent vintage. For decades many, including police, believed that law enforcement had little impact on crime rates.[4] David Bayley, in his 1994 book, *Police for the Future*, summed up this view nicely:

> The police do not prevent crime. That is one of the best-kept secrets of modern life. Experts know it. The police know it, but the public does not know it. Yet, the police pretend that they are society's best defense against crime and continually argue that if they are given more resources, especially personnel, they will be able to protect communities against crime. This is myth.[5]

This is no longer true. Police executives are expected—and expect themselves—to reduce crime rates in their jurisdictions. Scholars of policing devote themselves to finding causal connections between various police practices and crime statistics, typically by relying on a theoretical model that assumes offenders are rational actors who are persuaded to desist from criminal behavior when the prospect of formal punishment outweighs the benefits of that behavior. Interestingly, however, while police seemingly have become better and better over time at reducing and addressing crime, surveys indicating levels of public support for and confidence in police have remained relatively *flat* over the period of time in which crime rates have fallen precipitously.[6] This finding is consistent with research suggesting that people's perceptions of fairness of legal authorities is not motivated primarily by their assessments of police effectiveness at crime reduction.[7]

One might ask then, if police effectiveness does not drive public trust, then what does? One answer might be police *lawfulness*. Again, in light of the repeated incidents of quite shocking police brutality—consider here the tragic death of Walter Scott in North Charleston, South Carolina, who was shot in the back by a white police officer as he fled—we might think that commitment to the rule of law and especially constitutional constraints that shape engagements between the public and the police would support public trust. Police compliance with the law is a foundational component of a legitimate state. The very existence of the rules of law designed to shape and constrain the power the police officers exert in public contexts justifies the claim that police are a rule-bound institution that consequently should be empowered to make discretionary decisions as they engage in the pursuit of justice, the protection of individual liberties, and, the battle against crime.[8]

There are at least two issues with a potential relationship between levels of public trust and police commitment to lawfulness. The first is an objective measure of the extent to which police obey the relevant law over time. While likely unlawful incidents repeatedly shown in the media might cause people to question the extent to which police obey the law with respect to police use of deadly force, there is wide scholarly consensus that *over time* the level of unlawful police killings has decreased significantly.[9] The second issue is the public's perception of the extent to which police actually obey the law. Research suggests that the public is not, unsurprisingly, very good at making such assessments. In short, public judgments of police legitimacy connected to public trust and confidence are not very sensitive to whether or not police behavior is consistent with constitutional law. The public does not understand lawfulness or determine sanctioning in the same way that police and other legal authorities do.[10]

This chapter explains a framework for understanding the path to be taken to promote public trust in policing. To make good on the effort to promote trust it is necessary to see how the two dominant ways of evaluating police leave little room for considering how ordinary people assess their treatment by state authorities. Experts, whether they are police officials or scholars, assess the justifiability of police action according to its lawfulness. Effectiveness at crime fighting has become the other primary police evaluation metric.

There is, however, a third way, in addition to lawfulness and effectiveness, to evaluate policing—"rightful policing." Rightful policing attempts to account for what people say that they care about when they assess individual officer behavior as well as agency conduct generally. It differs from lawful policing and effective policing in at least two ways. First, rightful policing does not depend on the lawfulness of police conduct. Rather, it depends primarily on the procedural justice—or fairness—of that conduct. Second, rightful policing does not depend on an assessment of police as effective crime fighters (although it turns out that rightful policing often leads to more compliance with the law and therefore lower crime rates). This third way rests on decades of research that was critical to the president's Task Force recommendations concerning promotion of public trust and may well help us move toward police governance that is substantively, as opposed to rhetorically, democratic. Finally, rightful policing is better for officers on the street. Its precepts not only encourage the people whom police deal with on a daily basis to comply with the law and police directives, they also encourage behaviors in encounters that tend to keep police safe.

Two Views: More Law? Or Less Crime?

To understand what "rightful policing" is, it is useful to understand what rightful policing is not. Rightful policing is not confined simply to constitutional policing, nor is it subsumed entirely by policing aimed at crime reduction. Rather, it is about how to achieve both by promoting fairness and engendering trust in police among the public.

One useful context to examine is the recent controversy in New York City regarding hundreds of thousands of stops and frisks of nameless, primarily young, African American men. The criticism of "stop and frisk" leveled against the police in New York was not limited to that city or this country. Philadelphia, for example, has been embroiled in a similar controversy, and London police have come under fire for implementing what critics believe to be a too aggressive "stop and search" strategy. In each of these cities, there have been vocal complaints about what critics claim is the overbroad exercise of state power in the form of searches and seizures. These criticisms usually are asserted in legal terms and framed around precepts of constitutional law. The critics' preferred remedies in turn are usually described with the same set of tools—the architecture of law and rights.

Thinking about police lawfulness in terms of a tradeoff between the risk of arbitrary or oppressive enforcement and an individual's right to privacy and autonomy is a dominant approach in the literature.[11] Those who measure good policing with reference to its lawfulness do not usually focus on police effectiveness at reducing crime. Rather, the lawfulness metric almost always casts police power as a necessary evil as opposed to a welcome utility or a potentially critical mechanism for empowering communities to pursue their own democratically chosen goals and projects. According to the "more lawfulness" view, police adherence to strict dictates that constrain their discretion generally results in less policing and more liberty for individuals. The higher level of crime that might result from less policing is simply a price citizens pay for more freedom in society.[12]

Police executives who are committed to lowering crime rates in their communities do not agree that less policing is an ideal they should seek to achieve. In pursuit of accountability, one of the four cornerstones of the new professionalism advocated by Stone and Travis[13]— the primary components of which include reducing crime and making communities safer, controlling costs, and conducting themselves with respect toward the public whom they serve[14]—police have become much more concerned with effectiveness, considering commitment to crime reduction a prime aspect of accountability.[15] The question is no longer whether or not police can make a difference. Police executives instead ask, "How much of a difference in crime rates can police make?" The new literature on the relationship between crime rates and policing is voluminous. Criminological research over the last couple of decades has shown that deploying police forces in geographically focused ways—"hot spot policing"—can significantly reduce crime without displacing it to other areas.[16] Other scholars have demonstrated that strategies such as problem-oriented policing and community policing can be useful to address crime and/or the fear of crime.[17] The advances in statistical approaches are striking and useful, but a weakness of the scholarship on police effectiveness is that lawfulness is largely irrelevant to it.

Those who promote success at crime fighting as the best way to assess police effectiveness fail to understand that police failure to adhere to law is a proper lens through which to view public perception of overbroad policing—in the form of too-prevalent stop and frisk, widespread public surveillance, more-regularly publicized incidents of use of force, or other everyday policies and practices. Comments by both former Mayor Bloomberg and former Police Commissioner Ray Kelly in reaction to the federal court order striking down New York

City's prominent stop, question, and frisk practice illustrate this attitude on the part of police agencies and public officials. Following District Judge Shira Sheindlin's order declaring the practice in violation
of both the Fourth and Fourteenth Amendments as it operated at the
time the order was issued, Bloomberg and Kelly claimed that the judge
had imperiled the city's safety by limiting liberal use of the practice.[18]
On the other hand, those who promote lawfulness as the best metric
too often ignore the fact that crime and predation among individuals
results in significantly less freedom for residents of high-crime communities even though private actors impose that constraint on freedom.
Residents of high-crime communities often see higher levels of policing
as a way to achieve freedom as opposed to its constraint.[19]

Rightful policing is attentive to both lawfulness and effectiveness,
and it captures important dimensions that neither of the prevalent
modes of evaluation does. The notion of rightful policing importantly
includes a critique of a "get-tough" approach to law enforcement,
which uses as its principal touchstone instrumental theories of deterrence. Deterrence, without the balance of a focus on legitimacy, can
result in crime reduction, but its effects often are short-lived and
expensive to implement, and predictably will backfire in communities that need crime reduction most.[20] There is also strong reason to
believe that many heavy deterrence strategies are not particularly
effective in encouraging offenders to desist from crime.[21]

Legitimacy as an Element of Rightful Policing

Police actions such as stop and frisk can be costly even when they are
lawful, constitutional, and short. Most people would not automatically
approve of a stop just because an officer is legally entitled to make one.
This reality crystallizes a basic problem with focusing on lawfulness as
the single yardstick for rightful police conduct. Indeed, research I have
conducted with Tom Tyler suggests that the public does not seem to
recognize lawful police conduct when they see it.[22]

If people do not focus on the lawfulness of police conduct, what
do they care about? Although it seems counterintuitive, decades of
research show that people typically care much more about *how they
are treated* by law enforcement agents than about the *outcome of the
contact*. Even when people receive a negative outcome in an encounter,
such as a speeding ticket, they tend to feel better about that incident

than they feel about an experience in which they do not receive a ticket but are treated poorly.[23] In addition to being treated with dignity and respect, research shows that people look for behavioral signals that allow them to assess whether or not a police officer's decision to stop or arrest them was made fairly—that is, accurately and without bias. These two factors—quality of treatment and indications of high-quality decision-making—matter much more to people than the outcome of the encounter.

Two additional factors matter as well. People report higher levels of satisfaction in encounters with authorities if they feel that they have an opportunity to explain their situation and their perspective on it—i.e., to tell their story.[24] Finally, in their interactions with police, people want to believe that authorities are acting out of a sense of benevolence toward them. They want to believe that the authorities' motives are sincere and well-intentioned, and that the authorities are trying to respond to people's concerns.[25] All four of these factors—quality of treatment, decision-making fairness, voice, and expectation of benevolent treatment—make up what psychologists call "procedural justice."

Procedural justice is a fundamental concern in civil society. One important consequence of people's perceptions of procedural fairness according to these terms is that they lead to popular beliefs of legitimacy. When social psychologists use the term "legitimacy," they are referring to a "property that a rule or an authority has when others feel obligated to voluntarily defer to that rule or authority. A legitimate authority is one that is regarded by people as entitled to have its rules and decisions accepted and followed by others."[26] This conception of legitimacy is not normative. When psychologists discuss legitimacy they are not exploring in some philosophical sense whether people ought to defer to legal authorities; rather, they are seeking to determine whether in fact people do defer. Their approach is positive and empirical. Thus, when researchers have sought to determine why people obey the law, the legitimacy-based explanation is distinct from an explanation grounded in fearing the consequences of failing to do so and from one grounded in morality. When people voluntarily comply with rules and laws because they believe authorities have the right to dictate roper behavior, their compliance is legitimacy-based. Rightful policing leverages these ideas.

A robust body of social-science evidence from around the world shows that people are more likely to obey the law when they believe that authorities have the right to tell them what to do.[27] Research shows that people are motivated more to comply with the law by the belief that they are being treated with dignity and fairness than by fear of punishment. Being treated fairly is a more important determinant of compliance than formal deterrence.[28] When police generate good feelings in their everyday contacts, people are motivated to help them fight crime. All of this encourages desistance from offending, law abiding, and assistance to the police, contributing to lower crime rates.

The research supports more complex findings as well. One might be concerned that the argument laid out here is in service of creating a mindless public composed of compliant automatons. In a well-functioning democracy we value citizens who respect the law, to be sure; but equally if not more important is a public that is active and willing to engage and cooperate with authorities in a co-productive effort to address crime and to complete other community projects. Recent research indicates that legitimacy is supportive of these goals as well.[29]

Police are conceived and constituted by and through law, but focusing only or primarily on the lawfulness of police conduct can obscure one's ability to identify and remedy policing behavior that the public may well view as problematic. It is important to see that although procedural justice can be related to the lawfulness or legality of police conduct, these two valences do not proceed in lockstep. One way of thinking how these valences relate to one another is to imagine points on a compass (see Figure 13.1). If we array lawfulness from west to east, with lawfulness to the east and unlawfulness to the west, then we would expect police to be as far east as possible. Now, imagine procedural justice or legitimacy as running north and south on the compass. When police are respectful and procedurally just, they are headed north. When they are not, that behavior is categorized as "running south." Putting the two parts together, one sees that the best place for law enforcement to be is in the northeast.[30] That is where one finds rightful policing.

But, this image does something else. It also reveals the southeast and the northwest. A primary problem with street policing in urban cities such as New York and Chicago, and in many communities across the globe as well, is that too often such policing comprises behavior I would locate in the southeast: police conduct that is very likely lawful, but that citizens in many encounters perceive as deeply illegitimate, using the term as defined here. For example, if one asks a lawyer what constitutes racial profiling, that person typically will answer, police behavior that is solely or even partially motivated by race, but many

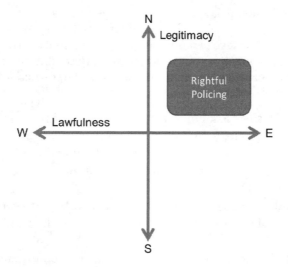

Figure 13.1. Rightful Policing as the Convergence of Lawfulness and Legitimacy

Source: Tracey L. Meares, *The Good Cop: Knowing the Difference between Lawful or Effective Policing and Rightful Policing—And Why It Matters*, 54 Wм. & Mary L. Rev. 1865, 1879 (2012).

who believe themselves to have been profiled care little about the legal determinants of their encounters with police.

The bottom line is clear: regardless of the lawfulness of police behavior, lack of procedural justice in encounters can change public perceptions of policing agencies, leading to lack of trust, ill-will, and ultimately less law abiding.[31] Considering both the lawfulness and the legitimacy of police conduct allows both the police officer and the citizen stopped to be right in a way that is not possible when one operates solely in the dimension of lawfulness. The possibility of both sides being right can lead to fruitful conversation about the rightfulness of policing.

Recommendations of the Task Force

This review of research should make clear why the president's Task Force built its recommendations around building trust and legitimacy, which was our first and foundational pillar. The first page of the executive summary notes:

> Building trust and legitimacy on both sides of the police/citizen divide is the foundational principle underlying the nature of

> relations between law enforcement agencies and the communities they serve ... The public confers legitimacy only on those whom they believe are acting in procedurally just ways. ... [L]aw enforcement cannot build community trust if it is seen as an occupying force coming in from outside to impose control on the community.[32]

To this end, the Task Force made a number of recommendations in support of Pillar One, which in turn provides a bedrock for the pillars that follow: Policy and Oversight, Technology and Social Media, Community Policing and Crime Reduction, Training and Education, and Officer Safety and Wellness.

In the end, the Task Force made many substantive recommendations. In light of the topic of this book, I would like to highlight three of them.

First, the Task Force recommended that law enforcement agencies embrace a guardian mindset in order to build public trust and legitimacy.[33] This recommendation encapsulates the thinking of another Task Force member, former sheriff Sue Rahr, who has written that officers must shift from a warrior mindset to a guardian mindset in order to adopt behaviors consistent with procedural justice. Importantly, this cultural change has both internal and external aspects in that officers must be treated with procedural justice within their organizations in order to foster this guardian mindset, which in turn will support their ability to treat the public with procedural justice.

Second, the Task Force recommended that agencies acknowledge the role of policing in past and present injustice and discrimination and how it is a hurdle to the promotion of community trust. This recommendation cannot be emphasized enough. There have been powerful and poignant examples of practices whereby police officials have come together with representatives of affected communities and neighborhoods for conversations about dueling narratives that, if left unresolved, undermine trust. One story in particular makes the point quite succinctly. Fifty-two years after Rep. John Lewis and his fellow Freedom Riders crossed the Edmund Pettus Bridge on their way from Selma to Montgomery, Alabama, Montgomery Police Chief Kevin Murphy offered Rep. Lewis his badge and an apology as a gesture of reconciliation, saying,

> When you got off the bus in 1961, you didn't have a friend in the police department. ... I want you to know that you have friends in the Montgomery Police Department—that we're for you, we're

with you, we want to respect the law and adhere to the law, which is what you were trying to do all along. This symbol of authority, which used to be a symbol of oppression, needs to be a symbol of reconciliation.[34]

Third, it is imperative that policing agencies recognize that crime reduction is not self-justifying. Police action taken for the purpose of making communities safer, especially aggressive police action, can have the counterproductive result of destroying the very reservoir of trust on which communities and policing agencies depend for a properly functioning system. Critical to understand here is that promotion of public trust is actually associated with compliance. This means that policing agencies can achieve their goal of enhancing public safety while at the same time pursuing the mandate ideal of increasing public trust through a greater commitment to procedural justice.

Conclusions and Implications for Policing

If legitimacy is as important as I have argued, then it raises the questions of how the police should incorporate this approach and what the obstacles are to implementation. I think we can make progress on answering these questions by considering three issues: training, strategies and tactics, and democracy and community participation.

Training

Much police training outside the initial recruitment phase, despite improvements over the last 20 years, retains a strong bias in favor of learning the rules, particularly legislation, procedure, and departmental policies. This does not apply only at the initial recruitment phase. In the United Kingdom, for example, the key gateway for promotion for all first-line managers is to pass a set of examinations in the law and procedures for crime, roads policing, general duties, and evidence and procedure.[35] Such reliance on law and procedure as the qualification for recruits and managers is typical across most jurisdictions. As Chan and colleagues showed, this is now frequently supported by programs to address behaviors and practical skills, but almost never by an educational approach that provides officers with the means and material to understand the social-science evidence for what works in policing or how approaches such as legitimacy make their practice more effective.[36] Furthermore, Chan and colleagues demonstrated how the legal valence of frontline culture undermined even the attempts to inject some "social context." Neyroud has recommended a much more fundamental shift in the framework of training for recruits, specialists, and managers so that police training in the United Kingdom would be governed by a new professional body and start with a prequalification that incorporates a new emphasis on learning about evidence-based practice.[37] Without such a radical shift, it seems likely from studies such as that of Chan and colleagues that police training will continue to be dominated by a legalistic way of thinking about problems and their solutions. There are promising signs of change, however. Chicago Police Superintendent Garry McCarthy has instituted a day-long training in police legitimacy and racial reconciliation for the entire force. To date, more than 8,000 officers and leaders have been trained.[38] Early assessments of the program are extremely positive.[39] In the United Kingdom, extensive practical training on procedural justice in particular situations is also becoming the norm.[40]

Strategies and Tactics

Too often, compelled by the always present demand to bring crime statistics down (especially in big cities), police executives focus on strategies and tactics designed to reduce violence in too cramped ways. If this is right, then police executives should consider problem solving in more holistic ways that will yield approaches that are designed not only to quell violence but also to enhance safety by changing the attitudes and dispositions of those alienated from them in ways that sustain voluntary compliance. I have in mind here hot-spot policing that is not only deterrence based but also legitimacy based. Braga and Garrett recently found in a review of broken-windows policing strategies a distinct contrast between the effectiveness of aggressive, deterrence-focused broken-windows approaches, such as stop and frisk in New York City, and other more legitimacy-based approaches. Only the latter group produced large and statistically significant impacts on crime.[41] Moreover, commitment to legitimacy can also help police increase safety and, by implication, quell violence at the incident level by encouraging officers to engage in tactics that defuse violent incidents.[42]

Democracy and Community Participation

I agree with Loader when he notes, "The police, in short, are both minders and reminders of community—a producer of significant messages about the kind of place that community is or aspires to be."[43] Policing makes community. It is no accident that an iconic symbol of Britain itself is the bobby's hat.[44] In the United States, policing's symbolic connotations are not so positive. At least one scholar has located the genesis of American policing not in the benevolent image of a kindly community protector but in the more sinister form of the slave patroller.[45] The procedural justice literature reviewed above makes clear the ways in which this dark history can and likely does undermine trust in police in the modern era. And yet this same literature provides a roadmap for a more positive relationship that not only benefits those who need help from the police but also potentially supports their participation in democratically led government. It is important for people to feel that if they call on the police (and other legal actors and institutions), not only will their security be protected, but they will also be treated with respect, their rights will be recognized, and they will be subject to fair decision-making. The fact that most people in a community rarely call on the police for services does not change the desire for procedural justice, because police and other legal actors are in the background in every community and shape what people think, feel, and do. People want to feel comfort, not fear, when the police are present and to anticipate that they will receive help and professional treatment when they need it. When they do, they become invested in the communities in which they live. Research on popular legitimacy, to which police contribute, suggests that when people evaluate their police and court systems as procedurally fair, they identify more with their communities and engage in them socially by trusting neighbors, politically by voting, and economically by shopping and going to entertainment venues within that community.[46]

Police play a critical role in teaching the people with whom they interact (and those who observe those interactions) what it means to be a citizen.[47] Recently in the *Annals*, Justice and Meares argue that the criminal justice system offers a curriculum of lessons on what it means to be a citizen much as public schools do. The overt curriculum of policing is designed to convey concern for rights. People's interests in autonomy, privacy, and bodily integrity ought not to be subject to the whim of an individual police officer. We are a government of laws designed to restrain state power against the individual. But education theorists explain that a hidden curriculum is often taught alongside the overt. In schools, the hidden curriculum may be found in adult-student and student-student interactions, in the enforcement of school discipline policies and behavior codes, in the deeply buried assumptions and narratives of history textbooks, in a school's choice of mascot, in who gets to sit where in the cafeteria, or in the musical selections at the prom. The hidden curriculum of policing, similarly, is a function of how people are treated in interactions and the ways in which groups derive meaning regarding their status in the eyes of legal authority resulting from that treatment. Too often, the hidden curriculum of policing strategies sends certain citizens clear signals that they are members of a special, dangerous, and undesirable class—the mirror image of the positive overt curriculum. People do not necessarily learn these lessons. What is learned depends in part on the degree and frequency of exposure and on individual and community resilience. As Justice and Meares note:

> The hidden curriculum flourishes in those contexts where democracy is dislocated. In high-performing public and private schools, teachers and students work together toward common goals that honor the social contract between the school, the student, the family, and the community; punishment is appropriate and merciful, and offers forgiveness; interpersonal interactions encourage success and reaffirm belonging; trust is endemic. Remove the confluence of interests, the accountability of those with authority to those under it, the fundamental sense of legitimacy, and the hidden curriculum eats away at the overt.[48]

Commitment to rightful policing can help, but executives cannot be sanguine about its potential impact absent further measures. The approach requires broadly conceived and coordinated efforts among a variety of contexts: crime reduction, community relations and, importantly, internal discipline, to effect real change.[49]

Notes

1. I want to emphasize that by making this point I do not mean to suggest that local police agencies are unconstrained by federal mandates. Obviously, at a bare minimum, police agencies must not violate individual civil rights when carrying out daily tasks.

2. I was appointed by the president to be a member of his Task Force. While this chapter will summarize some of the Task Force's recommendations, I want to make clear that the opinions expressed here are my own.

3. Rebecca Kaplan, *Obama on Ferguson Follow-Up: "This Time Will Be Different,"* CBS News (Dec. 1, 2014, 6:34 PM), http://www.cbsnews.com/news/obama-on-ferguson-follow-up-this-time-will -be-different/.

4. Christopher Stone & Jeremy Travis, Toward a New Professionalism in Policing (2011), http://www.nij .gov/pubs-sum/232359.htm.

5. David H. Bayley, Police for the Future 3 (1994).

6. President's Task Force on 21st Century Policing, Final Report of the President's Task Force on 21st Century Policing 9 (2015), http://www.cops.usdoj.gov/pdf/taskforce/TaskForce_FinalReport.pdf.

7. Tom R. Tyler & Jonathan Jackson, *Popular Legitimacy and the Exercise of Legal Authority: Motivating Compliance, Cooperation, and Engagement*, 20 Psychol. Pub. Pol'y & Law 88 tbl. 7 (2014) (showing the relative importance of effectiveness on legitimacy as compared to procedural justice factors).

8. The alternative is, of course, a despotic state; the reason why the concept of legality is a foundational principle of criminal law and why control of discretion, particularly police discretion, is one the central problems of constitutional criminal procedure. For one of the best discussions of the role of legality, see John Jeffries, *Legality, Vagueness, and the Construction of Penal Statutes*, 71 Va. L. Rev. 189 (1985) (discussing the justifications for the legality principle including separation of powers concerns, notice arguments, and discretion control).

9. Nat'l Res. Council (U.S.), Fairness and Effectiveness in Policing: The Evidence 260–61 (Wesley Skogan & Kathleen Frydl eds., Nat'l Acads. Press 2004).

10. Tracey L. Meares et al., *Lawful or Fair? How Cops and Laypeople View Good Policing*, 105 J. Crim. L. & Criminology 297 (2016).

11. For one example criticizing the police lawfulness tradeoff, consider the discussion by Meares and Kahan of the legal struggle regarding searches for guns in Chicago public housing. *See* Tracey L. Meares & Dan M. Kahan, Urgent Times: Policing and Rights in Inner-City Communities (1999).

12. *See id.* at 18–22.

13. Stone & Travis, *supra* note 4, at 1 (noting that accountability is a critical aspect of what they call the "new professionalism," along with legitimacy, innovation, and national coherence).

14. *See id.* at 12 ("The best chiefs speak confidently about 'the three C's': crime, cost and conduct. Police departments today are accountable for all three.").

15. *Id.* at 12–15.

16. *See* Anthony A. Braga & David L. Weisburd, Policing Problem Places: Crime Hot Spots and Effective Prevention (2010).

17. *See* Nat'l Res. Council, supra note 9, at 297; Anthony A. Braga, Brandon C. Welsh & Cory Schnell, *Can Policing Disorder Reduce Crime? A Systematic Review and Meta-Analysis*, 52 J. Res. Crime & Delinquency 447–63 (July 1, 2015); Anthony A. Braga, Problem-Oriented Policing and Crime Prevention (2d ed. 2008).

18. *See* Transcript, *Bloomberg Vows to Appeal Federal Judge's Ruling That Stop-and-Frisk Policy Violated Civil Rights in Press Conference*, N.Y. Daily News, Aug. 12, 2003, http://www.nydaily news.com/news/politics/bloomberg-vows-appeal-federal-judge-ruling-stop-stop-and-frisk-policy-article-1. 1424630; *See also* John Eterno & Eli Silverman, *Mike Bloomberg's Fact-Free Defence of Stop-and-Frisk*, Guardian, Sept. 11, 2003, http://www.theguardian.com/commentisfree/2013/sep/11/stop-and-frisk -michael-bloomberg.

19. *See* Tracey L. Meares & Dan M. Kahan, *Law and (Norms of) Order in the Inner City*, 32 Law & Soc'y Rev. 805, 830–32 (1998) (discussing community empowerment through law enforcement).

20. Lawrence W. Sherman, *Defiance, Deterrence, and Irrelevance: A Theory of the Criminal Sanction*, 30 J. Res. Crime & Delinquency 445–73 (1993).

21. Todd R. Clear, Imprisoning Communities: How Mass Incarceration Makes Disadvantaged Neighborhoods Worse (2007).

22. Tracey L. Meares et al., Lawful or Fair? How Cops and Laypeople View Good Policing (Yale Law School, Working Paper No. 255, 2012), http://papers.ssrn.com/abstract=2116645.

23. *See* Tom R. Tyler & Jeffrey Fagan, *Legitimacy and Cooperation: Why Do People Help the Police Fight Crime in Their Communities?*, 6 Ohio St. J. Crim. L. 231, 262 (2008); Tom R. Tyler & Cheryl Wakslak, *Profiling and Police Legitimacy: Procedural Justice, Attributions of Motive, and Acceptance of Police Authority*, 42 Criminology 253, 255 (2004); Tom R. Tyler, Trust in the Law: Encouraging Public Cooperation with the Police and Courts (2002); Raymond Paternoster et al., *Do Fair Procedures Matter? The Effect of Procedural Justice on Spouse Assault*, 31 Law & Soc'y Rev. 163 (1997).

24. *See* Tom R. Tyler, *Enhancing Police Legitimacy*, 593 Annals Am. Acad. Pol. & Soc. Sci. 84, 94 (2004).

25. *See id.*

26. Nat'l Res. Council, supra note 9, at 297.

27. *See generally* Legitimacy and Criminal Justice: International Perspectives (Anthony Braga et al. eds., 2007) (exploring the impact of perceptions of legitimacy in criminal justice systems across the globe).

28. Tom R. Tyler, Why People Obey the Law (rev. ed. 2006).

29. Tom R. Tyler & Jonathan Jackson, *Popular Legitimacy and the Exercise of Legal Authority: Motivating Compliance, Cooperation, and Engagement*, 20 Psychol. Pub. Pol'y & L. 78–95 (2014).

30. *See* Tracey L. Meares, *The Good Cop: Knowing the Difference between Lawful or Effective Policing and Rightful Policing—And Why It Matters*, 54 Wm. & Mary L. Rev. 1865, 1879 (2012) (providing this illustrative figure).

31. *See, e.g.*, Tracey L. Meares, *The Legitimacy of Police among Young African-American Men*, 92 Marq. L. Rev. 651 (2009).

32. President's Task Force on 21st Century Policing, Final Report of the President's Task Force on 21st Century Policing 1 (2015), http://www.cops.usdoj.gov/pdf/taskforce/TaskForce_FinalReport.pdf.

33. President's Task Force on 21st Century Policing, *supra* note 6.

34. http://www.msnbc.com/rachel-maddow-show/civil-rights-leader-rep.

35. Peter W. Neyroud, Review of Police Leadership and Training (Report to Home Sec'y, 2011).

36. *See* Janet B. L. Chan et al., Fair Cop: Learning the Art of Policing (Univ. of Toronto Press 2003).

37. *See* Neyroud, *supra* note 34

38. *See* Pam Grimes & Gaynor Hall, *Respectful Policing in Chicago: Changing the Us vs Them Mentality* (WGN-TV television broadcast, Sept. 9, 2013), http://wgntv.com/2013/09/09/respectful-policing-in-chicago/.

39. Wesley G. Skogan et al., *Training Police for Procedural Justice*, J. Experimental Criminology 1–16 (2014).

40. Levin Wheller et al., The Greater Manchester Police Procedural Justice Training Experiment: Technical Report (2013), http://library.college.police.uk/docs/college-of-policing/Technical-Report .pdf.

41. *See* Anthony A. Braga et al., *Can Policing Disorder Reduce Crime? A Systematic Review and Meta-analysis*, 52 J. Res. Crime & Delinquency 567–88 (2015).

42. John D. McCluskey, Police Requests for Compliance: Coercive and Procedurally Just Tactics (2003), http://site.ebrary.com/lib/yale/Doc?id=10056589.

43. *Id.* (citing Neil Walker, *Policing and the Supranational*, 12 Policing & Soc'y 307, 315 (2002)).

44. *See* Ian Loader & Aogán Mulcahy, Policing and the Condition of England: Memory, Politics and Culture (2003). Another primary iconic symbol is the red telephone box, not to be confused with the blue police box.

45. Markus Dirk Dubber, The Police Power: Patriarchy and the Foundations of American Government (2005).

46. Tom R. Tyler & Jonathan Jackson, *Popular Legitimacy and the Exercise of Legal Authority: Motivating Compliance, Cooperation and Engagement*, 20 Psychol., Pub. Pol'y & L. 78 (2014).

47. Benjamin Justice & Tracey L. Meares, *How the Criminal Justice System Educates Citizens*, 651 Annals Am. Acad. Pol. & Soc. Sci. 159 (2014).

48. *Id.* at 175.

49. *See* Bernard K. Melekian, Values-Based Discipline: The Key to Organizational Transformation within law Enforcement Agencies (July 24, 2012) (unpublished Ph.D. dissertation, Univ. of S. Cal.) (on file with the Price School of Public Pol'y, Univ. of S. Cal.).

About the Contributors

Christopher A. Bracey is an internationally recognized expert in the fields of U.S. race relations, individual rights, and criminal procedure. He teaches and researches in the areas of the legal history of U.S. race relations, constitutional law, criminal procedure, civil procedure, and civil rights. A magna cum laude and Phi Beta Kappa graduate of the University of North Carolina, Professor Bracey received his law degree from Harvard Law School, where he served as a supervising editor on the *Harvard Law Review*, a general editor on the *Harvard Civil Rights–Civil Liberties Law Review*, and an editor on the *Harvard Blackletter Law Journal*. He clerked for the Honorable Royce C. Lamberth of the U.S. District Court for the District of Columbia, and subsequently joined the Washington, D.C. office of Jenner & Block, where he litigated a variety of civil and criminal matters. He is the author of *Saviors or Sellouts: The Promise and Peril of Black Conservatism, from Booker T. Washington to Condoleezza Rice* (Beacon Press 2008) and co-author of *The Dred Scott Case: Historical and Contemporary Perspectives* (Ohio University Press 2009). His articles and essays have appeared in a number of leading law reviews, including *Northwestern University Law Review, University of Southern California Law Review, Yale Law Journal Pocket Part, University of Pennsylvania Journal of Constitutional Law, Journal of Law and Criminology*, and *Alabama Law Review*, among others.

Chad Flanders has taught at Saint Louis University School of Law since 2009. He teaches and writes in the areas of criminal law, constitutional law, and the philosophy of law. In the 2012–2013 academic year Professor Flanders was a Fulbright Lecturer at Nanjing University, China, and during 2013–2014 Flanders was a visiting professor at DePaul University School of Law. Professor Flanders received his doctorate in philosophy from the University of Chicago in 2004 and his law degree from Yale Law School in 2007. After law school, Professor Flanders served as a law clerk to the Honorable Warren Matthews of the Alaska Supreme Court and the Honorable Michael McConnell of the Tenth

Circuit Court of Appeals. Since arriving at SLU, Professor Flanders has published more than 20 articles or essays in journals such as the *Florida Law Review*, the *California Law Review*, the *Missouri Law Review*, and the *Alaska Law Review*, and his work on *Bush v. Gore* has been cited by state and federal courts.

Phillip Goff is an Associate Professor of Social Psychology at the University of California, Los Angeles, on leave this year as a Visiting Scholar at the Harvard Kennedy School. He is the co-founder and president of the Center for Policing Equity (CPE), and an expert in contemporary forms of racial bias and discrimination, as well as the intersections of race and gender. Most recently, Dr. Goff led the CPE in becoming one of three Principal Investigators for the Department of Justice's new National Initiative for Building Community Trust and Justice. The National Initiative will contribute information to another major project by the CPE, the National Justice Database, the first national database on racial disparities in police stops and use of force. Dr. Goff's model of evidence-based approaches to fairness has been supported by the National Science Foundation, Department of Justice, Kellogg Foundation, Open Society Institute, Open Society Institute-Baltimore, Atlantic Foundation, William T. Grant Foundation, the COPS Office, and Major Cities Chiefs, the NAACP LDF, NIMH, SPSSI, the Woodrow Wilson Foundation, the Ford Foundation, and the Mellon Foundation, among many others.

Colin Gordon is Professor of History and Public Policy at the University of Iowa. He is the author of *Growing Apart: A Political History of American Inequality* (Institute for Policy Studies, 2013); *Mapping Decline: St. Louis and the Fate of the American City* (University of Pennsylvania Press, 2008); *Dead on Arrival: The Politics of Health in Twentieth Century America* (Princeton University Press, 2003), and *New Deals: Business, Labor and Politics, 1920–1935* (Cambridge University Press, 1994). He has written for the *Nation, In these Times, Z Magazine, Atlantic Cities,* and *Dissent* (where he is a regular contributor).

Katherine Goldwasser is a Professor of Law at Washington University in St. Louis. Before entering academia she served for four years as a federal prosecutor in the U.S. Attorney's Office for the Northern District of Illinois. She specializes in the areas of criminal procedure and trial practice and regularly teaches courses in those areas, including a course in which she supervises students who work with prosecutors in the U.S. Attorney's Offices for both the Eastern District of Missouri and the Southern District of Illinois. She received her BA from the University of Illinois and her JD from Temple University School of Law.

Thomas B. Harvey is an attorney and the Executive Director and co-founder of ArchCity Defenders (ACD), a nonprofit law firm providing holistic legal services to the indigent in the St. Louis region and pursuing policy advocacy and impact litigation arising from its direct legal services. His work focuses on the way the legal system disproportionately impacts poor people and communities of color to create or maintain poverty. He is the lead author of a recently released White Paper that documented systemic abuses in the St. Louis region's courts, showing that by disproportionately stopping, charging, fining, and incarcerating the poor and minorities these courts not only prey on the poor and violate the Constitution but also create and maintain poverty. Harvey has been interviewed by the *Washington Post, New York Times, Wall Street Journal, and BusinessWeek* as well as featured on MSNBC and NPR to provide valuable context in explaining the distrust between the people of the region and the authorities following the killing of Mike Brown.

Kira Hudson Banks is an Assistant Professor in the department of psychology at Saint Louis University. Her research examines the experience of discrimination, its impact on mental health, and intergroup relations. Her courses have ranged from Abnormal Psychology to the Psychology of Racism. She has published in American Psychological Association journals such as *American Psychologist, Cultural Diversity and Ethnic Minority Psychology*, and *Journal of Diversity in Higher Education*. As a consultant, she has worked with schools, communities, institutions of higher education, and corporations to improve diversity and inclusion efforts and engage people in productive dialogue and action. She received her BA from Mount Holyoke College, where she was inducted into Phi Beta Kappa, and her MA and PhD from the University of Michigan.

Tracey L. Meares is the Walton Hale Hamilton Professor of Law at Yale Law School. She has a BS in general engineering from the University of Illinois and a JD from the University of Chicago Law School. Before arriving at Yale Law School, she was Max Pam Professor of Law and Director of the Center for Studies in Criminal Justice at the University of Chicago Law School. She has held positions clerking for the Honorable Harlington Wood, Jr., of the U.S. Court of Appeals for the Seventh Circuit and as a trial attorney in the Antitrust Division of the U.S. Department of Justice. Since 2004, she has served on the Committee on Law and Justice, a National Research Council Standing Committee of the National Academy of Sciences. Additionally, she has served on two National Research Council Review Committees: one to review research on police policy and practices and another more recently to review the National Institute of Justice. In November of 2010, she was named by Attorney General Eric Holder to sit on the Department of Justice's newly-created Science Advisory Board. In 2014 she was named by President Obama to join his newly created Task Force on 21st Century Policing.

Candice Norwood is a master's student at American University studying international media, an interdisciplinary program that combines international relations and media production coursework. The majority of her academic research examines how modern news coverage and digital media shape race and gender relations. Norwood graduated from the University of Illinois at Urbana-Champaign in 2013 with a BS degree in news-editorial journalism and a minor in Spanish. Following graduation, she worked in Madrid, Spain, as an assistant English teacher during the 2013–2014 school year. She has reported stories for a variety of news organizations including NPR, Newsday, U-T San Diego, and C-SPAN. She has published several news articles and one of her stories, "Never Give Up," was featured in *Slices of Life*, edited by Walt Harrington (News Gazette 2013). She plans to continue working in news production with a focus on international human rights.

Kimberly Jade Norwood is a Professor of Law at Washington University School of Law in Saint Louis. She has a BS degree from Fordham University and a JD from the University of Missouri-Columbia. She clerked for a federal district judge after law school and practiced law as a litigator at a major law firm before joining the faculty of the Washington University School of Law in 1990. Professor Norwood teaches Torts, Products Liability, Race, Education and the Law, and Education Equality, Justice, and Reform. She has taught abroad, including in China, Ghana, Japan, and The Netherlands. In 2007 she created a high school to law school pipeline program at Washington University

School of Law, which has received both national and local acclaim and is still in operation. She has published several pieces on the meaning of being Black in America, on the academic toll Black students have suffered when confronting the stigma of acting White, and on the urban education plight of Black children in public schools in America. She is the Editor and Contributor of the book *Color Matters: Skin Tone Bias and the Myth of a Postracial America.* She is a recipient of the 2015 Washington University Distinguished Faculty Award.

Jason Q. Purnell, PhD, MPH, is Assistant Professor in the George Warren Brown School of Social Work, Faculty Director for Thriving Communities in the Center for Social Development, and Faculty Scholar in the Institute for Public Health at Washington University in St. Louis. His research examines the sociocultural and socioeconomic factors that drive disparities in health behaviors and health outcomes, with a specific focus on the health implications of education and economic status. Dr. Purnell is lead investigator on For the Sake of All, a multidisciplinary, academic-community project to improve the health and well-being of African Americans in St. Louis through the presentation of research, community mobilization, and key stakeholder engagement.

L. Song Richardson is a professor of law at the University of California, Irvine, School of Law. Her interdisciplinary research uses lessons from cognitive and social psychology to study criminal procedure, criminal law, and policing. Professor Richardson's scholarship has been published by law journals at Yale, Cornell, Northwestern, Southern California, and Minnesota, among others. Her article, "Police Efficiency and the Fourth Amendment" was selected as a "Must Read" by the National Association of Criminal Defense Attorneys. Her co-edited book, *The Future of Criminal Justice in America*, was published by Cambridge University Press in 2014. Professor Richardson's legal career has included partnership at a boutique criminal law firm, work as a state and federal public defender in Seattle, Washington, and Assistant Counsel at the NAACP Legal Defense and Educational Fund, Inc. Professor Richardson is the proud 2011 Recipient of the American Association of Law School's Derrick Bell Award, which recognizes a junior faculty member's extraordinary contribution to legal education through mentoring, teaching, and scholarship.

Brendan Roediger is a professor of law at Saint Louis University School of Law. He heads the school's Civil Advocacy Clinic, which focuses on court-reform and the representation of low-income individuals in the St. Louis region. Professor Roediger is active in litigation and advocacy directed at eliminating racial profiling, revenue-based policing, and unconstitutional court practices in Ferguson and throughout the St. Louis region. His work on these issues has been featured in national media sources such as *The New York Times*, ABC, MSNBC, and NPR. Professor Roediger has taken an important role in the legal response to the events in Ferguson, working with local and national organizations to provide legal representation to activists and to monitor and combat civil rights violations.

Terry Smith is a Distinguished Research Professor at DePaul College of Law. Prior to joining DePaul's faculty, he taught for 16 years at Fordham Law School, clerked on the U.S. Court of Appeals for the Sixth Circuit, and practiced labor and employment law at Kirkland & Ellis. A specialist in labor and employment law as well as voting rights, Professor Smith is the author of numerous law review articles and the book *Barack Obama, Post-Racialism, and the New Politics of Triangulation* (2012). **Publisher:** Palgrave Macmillan; 2012 edition (May 31, 2012)

Vetta L. Sanders Thompson, PhD, is a Professor at Washington University in St. Louis, in the George Warren Brown School of Social Work, Public Health Program and Urban Studies Program. Her research has focused on racial identity, psychosocial implications of race and culture for mental health and health communication, services utilization, and health disparities among ethnic minorities. Dr. Thompson has completed funded research examining cultural competence in the provision of mental health services, colorectal cancer screening promotion and communication, and HPV attitudes and vaccination in the African American community and experiences of discrimination among users of Consumer Operated Services Programs. She received her bachelor's degree in Psychology and Social Relations from Harvard University and her master's and doctorate in psychology from Duke University, where she also completed the Clinical Training program. Dr. Thompson is a licensed psychologist and health service provider in the state of Missouri.

Howard M. Wasserman is Professor of Law at FIU College of Law, where he has taught since 2003. He graduated magna cum laude from Northwestern University School of Law, where he was an associate articles editor of the Law Review and was named to the Order of the Coif. Following law school, he clerked for Chief Judge James T. Giles of the U.S. District Court for the Eastern District of Pennsylvania and Judge Jane R. Roth of the U.S. Court of Appeals for the Third Circuit. He also has been a visiting professor at Saint Louis University School of Law and Florida State University College of Law. Professor Wasserman's scholarship focuses on procedure in constitutional litigation and he has written extensively on the role of video evidence in civil rights enforcement. He is the author of *Understanding Civil Rights Litigation* (2013). **Publisher:** LEXISNEXIS (September 4, 2013)

Index

ABA FUND FOR JUSTICE AND EDUCATION

As a lawyer and a member of the American Bar Association, your influence on the world is that much greater. Your membership proves you believe in the ABA's commitment to serving equally the needs of our members, our profession, and the public.

The ABA and its members must serve as social engineers of justice. By charitably supporting the public service and educational programs of the Association, you are putting your ABA membership to another good use – making change possible.

For more than 50 years, the **ABA Fund for Justice and Education (FJE)** has served as the 501(c)(3) charitable arm of the American Bar Association. Today, the FJE combines and leverages your charitable support with the ABA's annual investment in its entities to provide quality programming that strengthens the legal profession and improves access to justice.

The partnership between the **ABA Section Section of State and Local Government Law** and the **ABA Coalition on Racial and Ethnic Justice (COREJ)** demonstrates the impact this Association can have on informing members of the bar and the public on laws that impact our fundamental right to life and liberty.

Your tax-deductible donation to the Section or COREJ, received through the FJE, will help the ABA undertake further life-changing programs that will make diversity and inclusion possible.

Change is a powerful thing. Believe in the power of one person who can make a difference.

DONATE TODAY!
HTTPS://DONATE.AMERICANBAR.ORG/STATELOCAL
HTTPS://DONATE.AMERICANBAR.ORG/COREJ